lonely planet

Libya

Anthony Ham

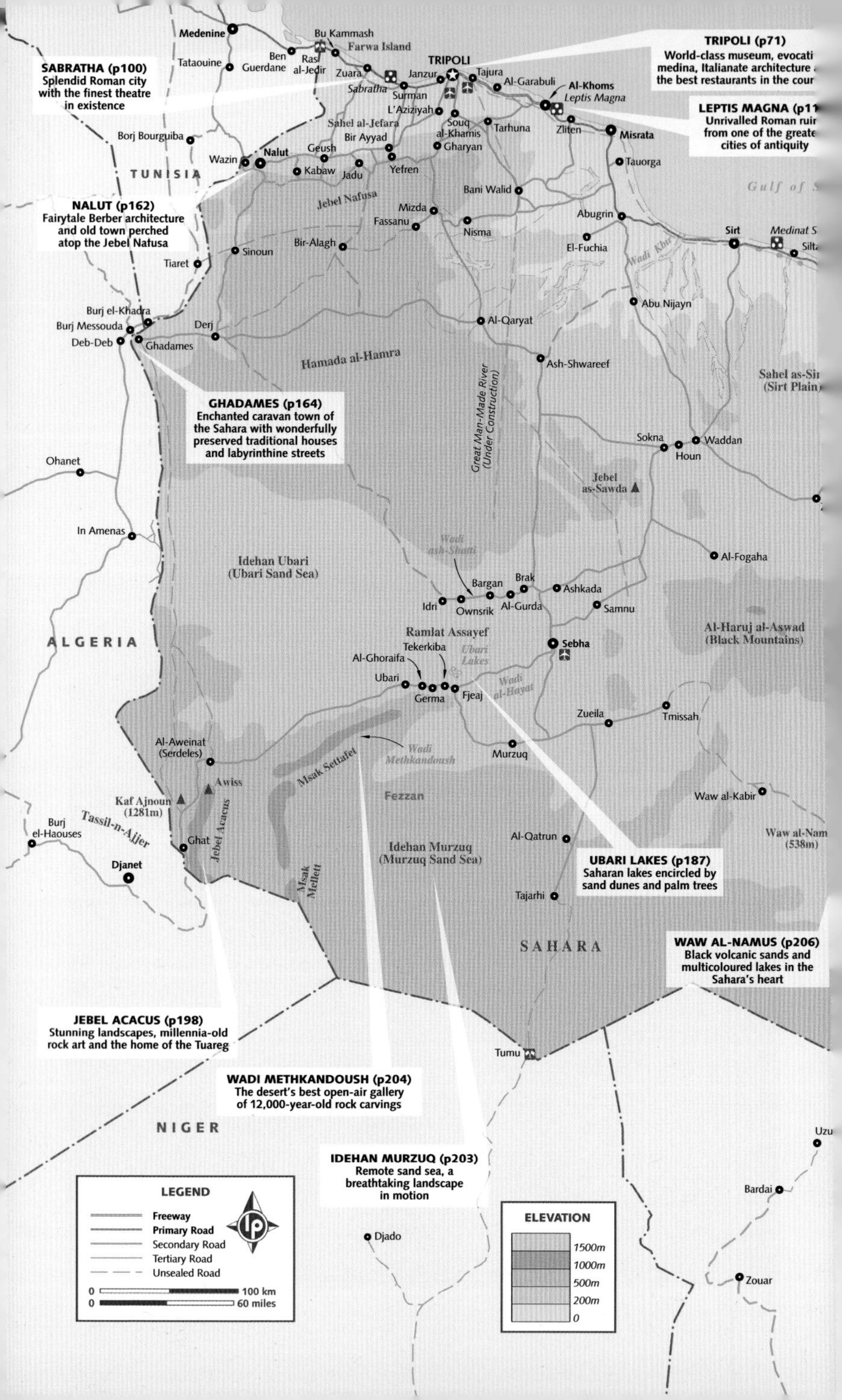

TRIPOLI (p71)
World-class museum, evocati
medina, Italianate architecture
the best restaurants in the cour
SABRATHA (p100)
Splendid Roman city
with the finest theatre
in existence
LEPTIS MAGNA (p1
Unrivalled Roman ruir
from one of the greate
cities of antiquity
NALUT (p162)
Fairytale Berber architecture
and old town perched
atop the Jebel Nafusa
GHADAMES (p164)
Enchanted caravan town of
the Sahara with wonderfully
preserved traditional houses
and labyrinthine streets
UBARI LAKES (p187)
Saharan lakes encircled by
sand dunes and palm trees
WAW AL-NAMUS (p206)
Black volcanic sands and
multicoloured lakes in the
Sahara's heart
JEBEL ACACUS (p198)
Stunning landscapes, millennia-old
rock art and the home of the Tuareg
WADI METHKANDOUSH (p204)
The desert's best open-air gallery
of 12,000-year-old rock carvings
IDEHAN MURZUQ (p203)
Remote sand sea, a
breathtaking landscape
in motion
Medenine
Bu Kammash
Farwa Island
Ben Guerdane
Ras al-Jedir
Zuara
Sabratha
Tataouine
TRIPOLI
Janzur
Tajura
Al-Garabuli
Al-Khoms
Leptis Magna
Surman
L'Aziziyah
Souq al-Khamis
Tarhuna
Zliten
Misrata
Sahel al-Jefara
Bir Ayyad
Gharyan
Borj Bourguiba
TUNISIA
Wazin
Nalut
Geush
Kabaw
Jadu
Yefren
Tauorga
Gulf of S
Jebel Nafusa
Bani Walid
Mizda
Fassanu
Nisma
Abugrin
Sirt
Medinat S
Silta
El-Fuchia
Wadi Kbir
Bir-Alagh
Sinoun
Tiaret
Abu Nijayn
Burj el-Khadra
Burj Messouda
Deb-Deb
Ghadames
Derj
Al-Qaryat
Hamada al-Hamra
Ash-Shwareef
Sahel as-Sir
(Sirt Plain)
Great Man-Made River
(Under Construction)
Sokna
Houn
Waddan
Ohanet
Jebel as-Sawda
In Amenas
Wadi ash-Shati
Al-Fogaha
Idehan Ubari
(Ubari Sand Sea)
Bargan
Brak
Ashkada
Idri
Ownsrik
Al-Gurda
Samnu
ALGERIA
Ramlat Assayef
Al-Haruj al-Aswad
(Black Mountains)
Tekerkiba
Ubari Lakes
Sebha
Al-Ghoraifa
Ubari
Germa
Fjeaj
Wadi al-Hayat
Zueila
Tmissah
Al-Aweinat
(Serdeles)
Wadi Methkandoush
Msak Settafet
Murzuq
Awiss
Fezzan
Kaf Ajnoun
(1281m)
Waw al-Kabir
Burj el-Haouses
Tassil-n-Ajjer
Jebel Acacus
Ghat
Al-Qatrun
Waw al-Nam
(538m)
Idehan Murzuq
(Murzuq Sand Sea)
Djanet
Msak Mellett
Tajarhi
SAHARA
Tumu
NIGER
Uzu
Bardai
Djado
Zouar
LEGEND
Freeway
Primary Road
Secondary Road
Tertiary Road
Unsealed Road
0
100 km
0
60 miles
ELEVATION
1500m
1000m
500m
200m
0

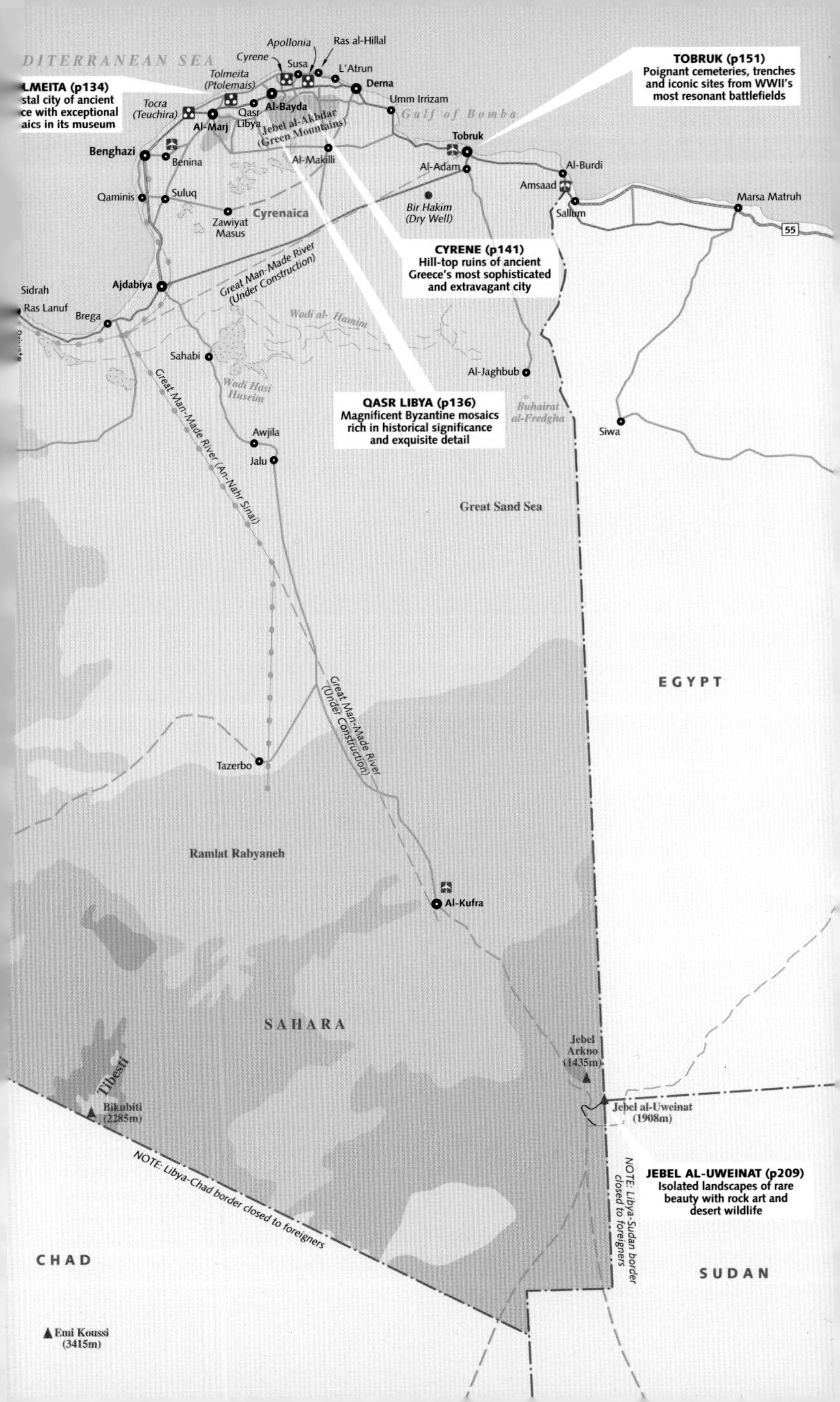

DITERRANEAN SEA
LMEITA (p134)
stal city of ancient
ce with exceptional
aics in its museum
Apollonia
Ras al-Hillal
Cyrene
Susa
L'Atrun
Tolmeita (Ptolemais)
Derna
Tocra (Teuchira)
Qasr Libya
Al-Bayda
Al-Marj
Umm Irrizam
Gulf of Bomba
Jebel al-Akhdar (Green Mountains)
TOBRUK (p151)
Poignant cemeteries, trenches and iconic sites from WWII's most resonant battlefields
Tobruk
Benghazi
Benina
Al-Makilli
Al-Adam
Al-Burdi
Amsaad
Sallum
Marsa Matruh
55
Qaminis
Suluq
Zawiyat Masus
Cyrenaica
Bir Hakim (Dry Well)
CYRENE (p141)
Hill-top ruins of ancient Greece's most sophisticated and extravagant city
Great Man-Made River (Under Construction)
Sidrah
Ras Lanuf
Ajdabiya
Brega
Wadi al-Hamim
Sahabi
Al-Jaghbub
Wadi Hasi Huseim
QASR LIBYA (p136)
Magnificent Byzantine mosaics rich in historical significance and exquisite detail
Buhairat al-Fredgha
Siwa
Awjila
Jalu
Great Man-Made River (An-Nahr Sinai)
Great Sand Sea
EGYPT
Great Man-Made River (Under Construction)
Tazerbo
Ramlat Rabyaneh
Al-Kufra
SAHARA
Jebel Arkno (1435m)
Jebel al-Uweinat (1908m)
Tibesti
Bikubiti (2285m)
NOTE: Libya-Chad border closed to foreigners
NOTE: Libya-Sudan border closed to foreigners
JEBEL AL-UWEINAT (p209)
Isolated landscapes of rare beauty with rock art and desert wildlife
CHAD
SUDAN
Emi Koussi (3415m)

On the Road

ANTHONY HAM

As this photo was taken, I was all-too-aware that I was rather too close to the edge of a 10m drop. Behind me is one of the *dammous*, the underground Berber homes that are so distinctive of **Gharyan** (p158). I love the Berber architecture of the Jebel Nafusa, which seems so perfectly attuned to the rugged environment. No, I didn't fall.

MY FAVOURITE TRIP

Tripoli (p71) is one of my favourite cities, but after a detour to **Leptis Magna** (p110) I'd dive into the Jebel Nafusa, visiting **Qasr al-Haj** (p160) and **Nalut** (p162) with an overnight in **Yefren** (p159) en route. If I had to pick one place I'd never miss, it would be **Ghadames** (p164). After crossing the **Hamada al-Hamra** (p177) and the **Idehan Ubari** (p186), I'd make for **Wadi Meggedet** (p193), **Ghat** (p194) and the **Jebel Acacus** (p198), before escaping the world amid the sand dunes of the **Idehan Murzuq** (p203). **Waw al-Namus** (p206) is always on my list, as is the remote solitude of **Jebel al-Uweinat** (p209) in the far southeast. If time permits, I'd seek out **Awjila** (p131) on my way to incomparable **Cyrene** (p141).

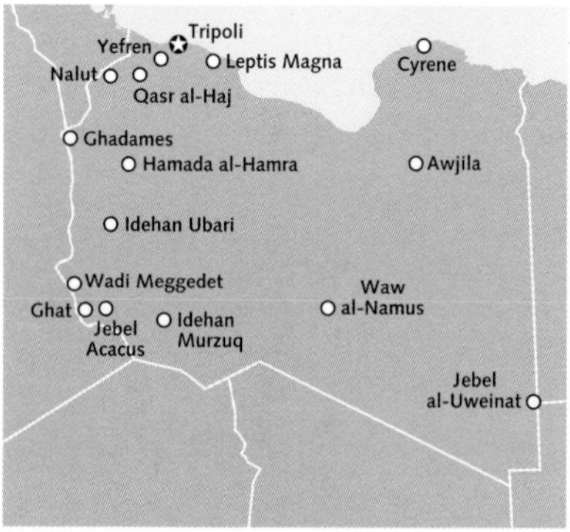

ABOUT THE AUTHOR

In another life Anthony was a refugee lawyer who represented clients from the Middle East and obtained a Masters degree in Middle Eastern politics. Now a full-time writer and photographer based in Madrid, Anthony fell in love with Libya's hospitable people and the gravitas of its Saharan landscapes on his first visit to Libya in 2001 and the love affair deepens every time he returns.
In addition to the first two editions of Lonely Planet's *Libya*, Anthony has contributed to more than 30 Lonely Planet guides and has visited every country that borders Libya. He also wrote the Libya chapter for Lonely Planet's *Middle East* guide.

Destination Libya

Libya has it all: ancient cities of rare splendour, the Sahara that you thought existed only in your imagination and the unmistakeable cachet of being ruled by one of the 20th century's most iconic figures, Colonel Muammar Qaddafi.

A great crossroads of ancient civilisations, Libya boasts two of the finest Roman cities in existence, Leptis Magna and Sabratha, while Cyrene, Apollonia and Tolmeita are exquisite monuments to the glories of ancient Greece. Elsewhere, the mosaics of Qasr Libya evoke all the richness of Byzantium.

Libya has few peers when it comes to the solitude and otherworldly beauty of the world's largest desert. The Ubari Lakes surrounded by sand dunes, the eerie black sands and multicoloured lakes of Waw al-Namus; and the stunning desert massifs of the Jebel Acacus and Jebel al-Uweinat have taken on the quality of legend. Ghadames is arguably the Sahara's finest oasis town, while the Tuareg are the Sahara's most enigmatic personality. The Berber fortresses of the Jebel Nafusa, cosmopolitan Tripoli and the poignant WWII cemeteries of Tobruk will also live long in the memory.

Libyans are, however, the country's greatest gift. While other countries were selling their soul to the god of tourism, Libya held fast to its traditions of warmth and hospitality and this is one of the most hassle-free destinations on earth.

Libyans have a saying that you should enter the country with its people. Yes, it's true that the only way to visit is on an escorted tour. Complain if you will, but by the time you leave Libya you'll have seen the country through Libyan eyes and been initiated into its splendid secrets by its people.

AMERENS HEDWICH

Ancient Cities

PATRICK BEN LUKE SYDER

See the exquisite monuments of the ancient Greeks at the Temple of Apollo (p145), Cyrene

Examine the mosaic artistry of the Romans in the splendid seaside Villa Sileen (p107)

ANTHONY HAM

Explore the majestic ruins of the Eastern Church (p149), Apollonia

JANE S

TONY WHEELER

Be mesmerised by the Mediterranean vistas from the theatre (p115) of Leptis Magna

DOUG MCKINLAY

Seek out the last remnant of Roman Oea at the Arch of Marcus Aurelius (p84), Tripoli

Gaze at the fine collection of Byzantine mosaics of Qasr Libya (p136)

DOUG MCKINLAY

Saharan Landscapes

ANTHONY HAM

Marvel at the forbidding rock walls of the Jebel Acacus (p198)

Escape the crowds in the stone-pillared landscape of Wadi Meggedet (p193)

ANTHO

Old Saharan Cities

DOUG MCKINLAY

Explore the labyrinthine, covered passage-ways of Ghadames (p167)

JANE SWEENEY

Visit the Sultan of Fezzan's former castle (p205), Murzuq

DOUG MCKINLAY

Partake in a unique dining experience inside a traditional house (p175), Ghadames

Stroll through the mud-brick structures of Ghat's ancient medina (p195)

ANTHONY HAM

Berber Architecture

ANTHONY HAM

Delight in a bird's-eye view over dramatic pits leading into traditional *dammous* (underground Berber houses; p158), Gharyan

Ponder the well-preserved fortified granary of Qasr al-Haj (p160)

PATRICK BEN LUKE

WWII & Italian Colonial Rule

ANTHONY HAM

Survey the still-intact brick Italian-era fort of Qasr Athani (p155), Al-Jaghbub

PATRICK BEN LUKE SYDER

Contemplate Tripoli's remnants of WWII (p38)

Pause to reflect on the fallen at the Tobruk (Commonwealth) War Cemetery (p152)

PATRICK BEN LUKE SYDER

Modern Cities

PATRICK BEN LUKE SYDER

Enjoy the views across the inner harbour of Benghazi (p125)

JANE SWEENEY

Soak up the atmosphere under the Ottoman clock tower in Tripoli's medina (p82)

ANTHONY HAM

Visit the hub of cosmopolitan Tripoli at Green Sq (Martyrs' Sq; p87)

Find a teahouse to partake in the local tradition of smoking a nargileh

JANE SWEENEY

People

ANTHONY HAM

Meet the bearers of a proud desert culture, the nomadic Tuareg (p48)

Be enchanted by local Libyan faces

DOUG MCKINLAY

Spot a billboard of the iconic leading figure, Colonel Muammar Qaddafi (p39)

TONY WHEELER

Rock Art

DOUG MCKINLAY

Enjoy a guided tour of the Unesco World Heritage–listed rock-art carvings of the Jebel Acacus (p198)

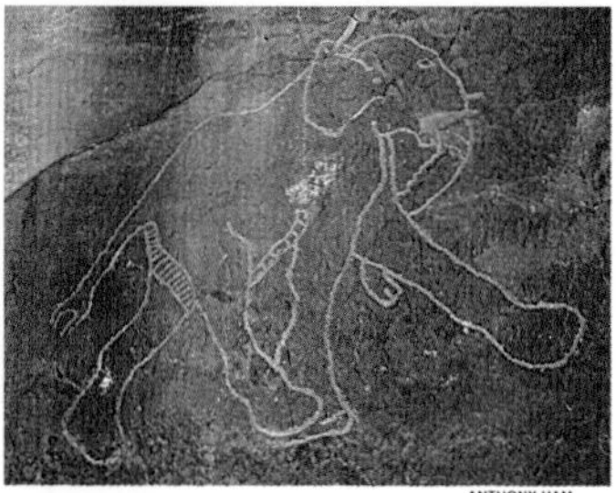

ANTHONY HAM

Marvel at the execution of a 12,000-year-old elephant carving (p201), Wadi Tashwinat

Glimpse the beautifully rendered wedding scenes (p201), Wadi Tashwinat

ANTHONY HAM

Admire the 12,000-year-old representation of two catlike figures sparring on hind legs in Wadi Methkandoush (p204)

ANT

Sand Seas

DOUG MCKINLAY

Explore the spectacular sand seas of the Sahara in a 4WD convoy (p214)

Discover the majestic oases hidden amid the dunes of the Idehan Ubari (Ubari Sand Sea; p186)

JANE SWEENEY

Soak up the solitude and silence in the incomprehensibly vast sand dunes of the Idehan Murzuq (Murzuq Sand Sea; p203)

ANTHONY HAM

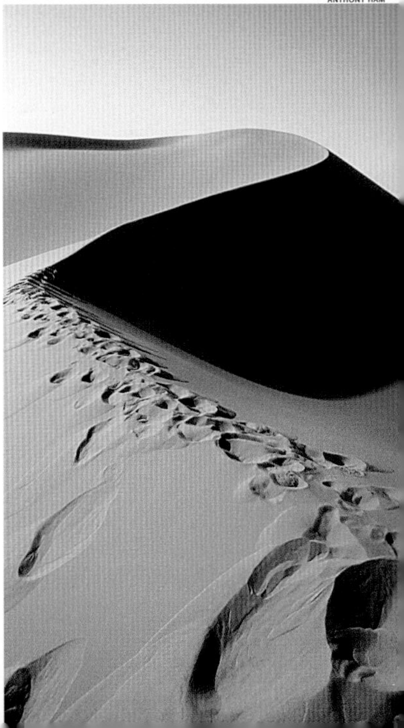

Islamic Libya

JANE SWEENEY

Visit the remains of early Islamic tombs (p206) which grace the desert near Zueila

DOUG M

View the fine Arabic façades of the Mausoleum and Mosque of Sidi Abdusalam (p118), Zliten

Look at the magnificently adorned interiors of the Gurgi Mosque (p85), Tripoli

ANTHO

Contents

Regional Map Contents

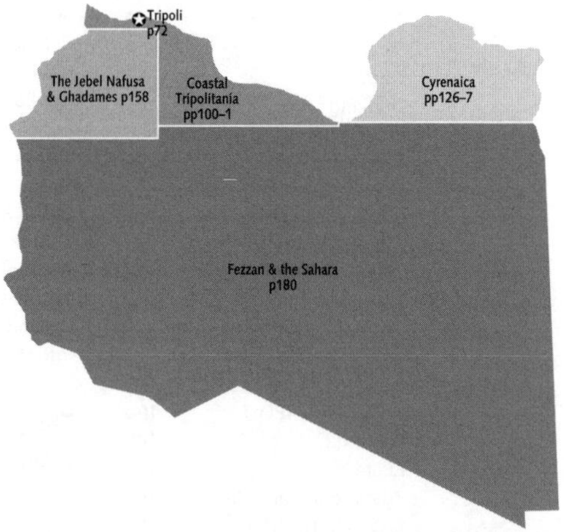

Getting Started

Obtaining a Libyan visa – an invitation from a Libyan tour company is required and travel inside Libya is only possible in the company of a Libyan guide – is what most occupies the minds of travellers before they get on the plane. The visa process is not, however, as complicated as it first appears (for a full explanation on the process, see p227) and the requirements of escorted travel in Libya do have some advantages. For a start, Libya is a vast country and having a local fixer to arrange hotels, transport and other logistics enables you to see far more of the country than would otherwise be possible. Many tour operators are quite flexible in allowing you to custom-make your own itinerary. Having a local on hand to answer questions or facilitate in meeting locals also promises a depth of insight to your travels that you simply couldn't manage on your own. Who knows, you might even make a lifelong friend, especially if you're travelling alone or in a small group.

In many ways it's a shame that the question of visas often becomes an all-consuming predeparture concern for travellers because there are so many more, infinitely more interesting preparations that you can undertake.

WHEN TO GO

Libya is at its best in October and November when the skies are clear, the temperatures are mild and, depending on end-of-summer rains, the desert may even have a greenish tinge in places. The next best alternative is from March through to early May, although there's a higher chance of sandstorms in April and, by May, temperatures are really starting to rise. December through to February is also a popular time, although temperatures can be surprisingly cool and night-time temperatures in the Sahara routinely drop below zero; we've 'slept' under the stars in -5°C and it's not something we'd recommend. In summer (mid-May to September), temperatures can be fiercely, unbearably, witheringly hot – don't even think of a desert expedition at this time.

See Climate Charts (p216) for more information.

DON'T LEAVE HOME WITHOUT...

- A Libyan visa or, if you plan to pick it up on arrival, a letter from your tour company confirming your visa number (p227)
- Travel insurance (p220) – accidents do happen
- Driving licence, car documents and appropriate car insurance (p238) if bringing your own car
- Extremely warm clothes for winter (above)
- A universal bathplug – you'll thank us when you emerge from the desert
- An MP3 player – the desert can be beautiful but there are days when epic distances and empty horizons can do your head in
- Mosquito repellent – that unmistakeable high-pitched whine in the ear is death to sleep in many Saharan oases
- Emptying your suitcase or car of alcohol (p216)
- Enough space in your suitcase for a copy of *The Green Book* (p40)
- A small size-three football (soccer ball) – a great way to meet locals

VISITING LIBYA IN RAMADAN – TRAVELLERS' DEBATE

If you go in Ramadan, as I did, resign yourself to not finding many restaurants open. Then between 6pm and 8pm people break their fasts, but the point is they do it at home, never in public. If a restaurant does open it will be after 8pm, but many don't bother, as I discovered to my cost, since after 9pm and until around 1am or even later everyone goes off walking and talking and shopping with their friends. You're supposed to have eaten by then…It should be plain by now that Ramadan is not a good time to go to Libya.

Anonymous

[In Ramadan] there's a certain charm to seeing everyone come out when the evening meal has been wolfed down and, provided you plan ahead and take account of things, it's not really a hindrance. Tripoli restaurants, particularly in the Green Square and embassy area, are open for lunch and dinner and our various taxi drivers went out of their way to tell us that they would not be offended if we wanted to eat or drink in the cab (which we didn't but could have). One thing to watch out for is that things close an hour earlier (to allow people to get home for sundown).

Sara Partington, London, UK

Apart from a sprinkling of festivals (see p219), the other main consideration is Ramadan (for dates see p220), the holy month of fasting which sneaks into October in 2007 and then edges its way into summer in subsequent years. Ramadan is universally observed by Libyans, but many restaurants open during the day for tourists.

COSTS & MONEY

At one level, Libya is expensive primarily because you're obliged to travel as part of an organised tour. At the same time, once you've paid for your tour there are very few other ways to spend your money. The fee you'll pay to your tour company will include everything – accommodation (see p211), transport and petrol, entry fees and most meals. Prices for tours vary widely. As a starting point, a rough average is around €1500 per person for a 15-day tour. All that's left to worry about is money you decide to spend while in Libya, especially shopping. Most travellers find that up to 500LD is difficult to spend during two weeks.

For details on money matters, see p222, but a few things to note before you go: Libyan dinars can only be purchased on arrival in the country and you should travel primarily with cash, although those with a Visa card, and to a far lesser extent MasterCard, can obtain cash advances in larger towns.

HOW MUCH?

Museum or archaeological site entry: 3LD (plus 5/10LD for camera/video)

Tripoli-Benghazi flight: 37.50-45.50LD

Colonel Qaddafi watch: 10-25LD

Internet connection: per hour 1LD

4WD rental per day: 80-120LD

TRAVEL LITERATURE

South from Barbary (by Justin Marozzi) is an acclaimed account of an epic modern journey by camel from Ghadames to Al-Kufra, and it contains a wealth of historical detail but reads like a boy's own adventure at times.

In the Country of Men (by Hisham Matar) is a complete change of pace – a compelling, if somewhat harrowing, novel that observes the uncertainties of Qaddafi's Libya through the eyes of a nine-year-old boy. This book was shortlisted for the 1986 Booker Prize.

Difficult & Dangerous Roads – Hugh Clapperton's Travels in Sahara & Fezzan 1822-25 (by Hugh Clapperton) returns you to the world of desert exploration and is a sometimes cranky, but highly readable account of

TOP PICKS

CITIES OF ANTIQUITY

- Leptis Magna (p110)
- Cyrene (p141)
- Sabratha (p100)
- Tolmeita (p134)
- Apollonia (p147)

SAHARAN BEAUTY

- Waw al-Namus (p206)
- Umm al-Maa (p188)
- Ghadames (p167)
- Jebel Acacus (p198)
- Wadi Meggedet (p193)
- Idehan Murzuq (p203)
- Jebel al-Uweinat (p209)
- Wadi Methkandoush (p204)
- Wan Caza (p203)
- Great Sand Sea (p155)

MAGICAL MEDINAS

- Ghadames (p167)
- Tripoli (p82)
- Ghat (p195)
- Garama (Germa; p189)
- Nalut (p162)
- Awjila (p131)

Clapperton's journeys through the Libyan Sahara. See also The Era of European Exploration, p179.

A Cure for Serpents (by Alberto Denti di Piranjo) transports you into the Italian colonial period with an engaging and unusually sympathetic account of Libya and its people as told by a charismatic Italian doctor.

Desert Encounter (by Knud Holmboe) provides a profoundly contrasting account of a journey across Libya under the Italians. One of the few first-hand accounts of the Italian occupation of Libya in the early 1930s, it reveals the devastation wrought by Italian rule on ordinary Libyan society.

On the Shores of the Mediterranean (by Eric Newby) offers a small section only on Libya, but there's no more entertaining account of modern Libya before the tourists arrived.

For more information on Libyan literary traditions, see p56.

INTERNET RESOURCES

Libya Online (www.libyaonline.com) One of the most extensive and professional directory devoted to Libyan society with a contemporary twist – everything from recipes to Libyan fashion.

Libya Our Home (www.libya-watanona.com/libya1/) An expansive range of links on Libya, with sections on history, the arts, sport, human rights and travel.

Libyana (www.libyana.org) Another excellent site devoted to Libyan arts, especially music and poetry.

Sahara el-Kebira (www.sahara.it) Italian-language site devoted to the Sahara.

Sahara Overland (www.sahara-overland.com) Companion to the excellent desert guidebook of the same name; good site for desert enthusiasts, with up-to-date travel reports and news.

Society for Libyan Studies (www.britac.ac.uk/institutes/libya/) Useful for researchers and those interested in the archaeological work being undertaken in Libya.

Tripoli Post (www.tripolipost.com) The Libyan government's English-language newspaper.

Itineraries

CLASSIC ROUTES

CITIES OF ANTIQUITY **One week / Tripoli to Tripo**

Tripoli (p71) is a terrific place to get your bearings. That's easy enoug at the **Jamahiriya Museum** (p76), the best imaginable primer to Libya' ancient past, but you'll quickly lose your bearings again in the twistin lanes of the **medina** (p82); on no account miss the **Arch of Marcus Aureliu** (p84). From your comfortable Tripoli base, take sidetrips to **Sabrath** (p100) and to the incomparable **Leptis Magna** (p110) with a stopover i mosaic-strewn **Villa Sileen** (p107). After flying to **Benghazi** (p125), spen a day exploring its understated charms, including the ancient site o **Berenice** (p126). Pause briefly at ancient **Tocra** (Teuchira; p133), then de tour to **Tolmeita** (Ptolemais; p134), one of Libya's more underrated sites The wonderful mosaics of **Qasr Libya** (p136) and the **Temple of Aesculapiu** (p138) in Al-Bayda are both must-sees. **Cyrene** (p141) could occupy th best part of a day, but allow time for a pre-sunset amble through it former port, **Apollonia** (p147). After sleeping alongside the ruins in **Sus** (p147), head for Benghazi for your flight back to Tripoli.

Covering this route in one week is only possible if you fly from Tripoli to Benghazi and back. If you do so, you'll travel around 800km by road. If you drive the whole way, you'll add 2000km and three days to your journey for no discernible reward.

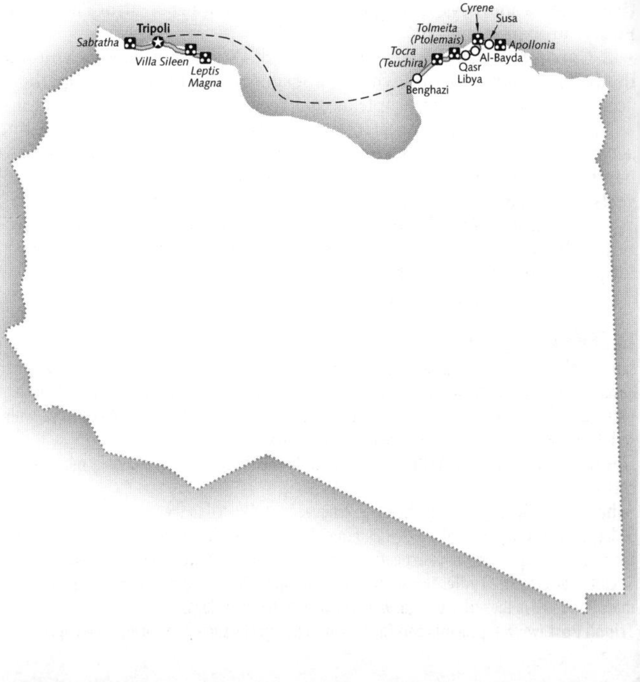

DEEP DESERT IMMERSION **Two weeks / Tripoli to Tripoli**

So many 19th-century expeditions by European explorers began at the **Old British Consulate** (p85) in Tripoli's medina and yours should be no exception. To maximise your time in the desert, speed through the Jebel Nafusa, pausing only in **Qasr al-Haj** (p160) and **Nalut** (p162) en route to **Ghadames** (p164). Now's the time to make the slower rhythm of desert life your own and linger in this most enchanted of Saharan caravan towns whose **traditional houses** (see p168) and covered laneways are the best preserved in the Sahara. Too soon, it's time to cross the void that is the **Hamada al-Hamra** (p177) bound for **Idri** (p184) from whose castle you can survey what lies ahead – the ocean of dunes that comprise the **Idehan Ubari** (Ubari Sand Sea; p186). Crossing the sands is like trespassing upon a land of solitude and rare beauty. Having briefly put the tyres on the tarmac in the Wadi al-Hayat, venture back into the dunes and the glorious **Ubari Lakes** (p187). After a night under the stars, pass through Germa to visit the ruined Garamantian capital of **Garama** (p189) and the fine **museum** (p190) before pushing on to the 12,000-year-old rock engravings of black-as-black **Wadi Methkandoush** (p204) before sleeping amid the dunes of the **Idehan Murzuq** (Murzuq Sand Sea; p203), a true landscape of the soul. As you head west, **Wan Caza** (p203) promises more exceptional dunescapes en route to the extraordinary massif of **Jebel Acacus** (p198), as beautiful as it is famed for its superb rock art. Work your way north, through **Awiss** (p199), and emerge onto the highway at **Al-Aweinat** (Serdeles; p193). A long drive back to **Sebha** (p181) should take you straight to the airport for your flight back to Tripoli.

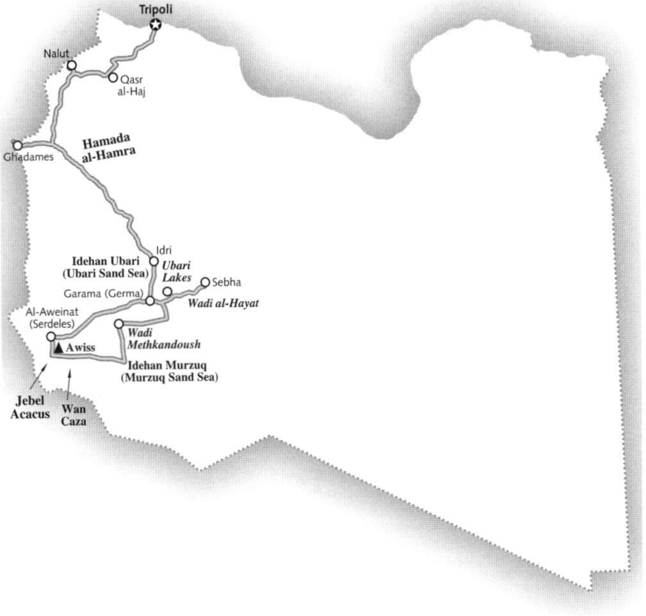

Despite covering over 3000km in two weeks, you've enough time for four days in the Jebel Acacus and three more crossing from Ghadames to the lakes. A 4WD is necessary for all but the Tripoli-Ghadames and Al-Aweinat to Sebha sections.

ROADS LESS TRAVELLED

THE REMOTE SOUTHEAST

Two weeks / Tobruk to Sebha

Most roads from **Tobruk** (p151) lead east to Egypt or west towards well-trodden Libyan trails, but one often-neglected road leads south to **Al-Jaghbub** (p154). Apart from its Italian fort and rich history, Al-Jaghbub has petrified forests, rock carvings and fine lakes. One such lake, **Buhairat al-Fredgha** (p155) marks the entry point to the **Great Sand Sea** (p155), where travellers are as scarce as water. The three-day crossing leaves you in **Al-Kufra** (p207) and the promise of a bed and much-needed shower. Suitably refreshed, you should return to the desert trails and take the empty **tracks** (p208) lined with camel carcasses southeast to **Jebel Arkno** (p208), which is spectacularly remote and the improbable home of an old army tank, reclusive desert wildlife and prehistoric rock carvings. Not far away, where Libya meets Sudan and Egypt, **Jebel al-Uweinat** (p209) is even better, with exceptional rock paintings and scenery. After retracing your steps to Al-Kufra, cross the **Ramlat Rabyaneh** (p207) to the pretty spa lake and abandoned town of **Buzeima** (p207). Stop for supplies in **Tazerbo** (p207) and then it's on to the black-sand volcano of **Waw al-Namus** (p206), arguably the single most eye-catching spot in the Libyan Sahara. When you finally reach **Tmissah** (p206), the sudden silence of a paved road is like a balm to the soul (not to mention your bottom). To delay your return to the madding crowds, pause at the tombs of **Zueila** (p205) and the castle in the old caravan town of **Murzuq** (p205) before heading for **Sebha** (p181).

A 4WD is the only way to go on this 3000km+ route. Make sure your expedition is well-equipped with at least two vehicles, plenty of food and water, a satellite phone and experienced desert guide. Two weeks allows you to not feel like you're always hurrying.

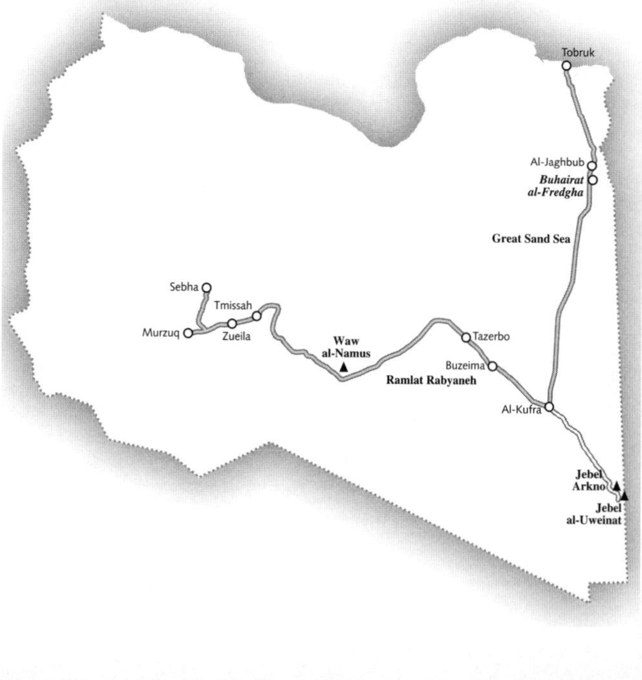

QUIET DESERT TRAILS

Ten days / Sirt to Ghat

Sirt (p121) is the soulless showpiece of Colonel Qaddafi's revolution but it does do a fine line in revolutionary murals. Otherwise use it as a starting point only. Almost as soon as you leave the town's southern outskirts, you've left the traffic behind and you're on your way to **Al-Jufra** (p184), with its quiet oasis towns of **Houn** (p184), **Sokna** (p185) and **Waddan** (p185). Here you'll enjoy exploring each of the old towns safe in the knowledge that you're almost certainly the only tourist in town. The brooding volcanic terrain of **Al-Haruj al-Aswad** (p185), which revels in the strangely compelling name of 'The Black Haruj', is similarly untrammelled by tourist feet. After detouring here and wandering through the old town of **Al-Fogaha** (p185), take the quiet road via Ashkada and into the **Wadi ash-Shatti** (p183). At the wadi's end in **Idri** (p184) – the really adventurous among you will savour the prospect of an east-west crossing of the **Idehan Ubari** (p186) and some of the most challenging dune pistes in Libya; *never* attempt this in a single vehicle and *always* take along an experienced guide who knows the route. Recharge the batteries in **Al-Aweinat** (p193) and then leave the road again to cross more sand dunes in search of **Wadi Meggedet** (p193), home to the most surprising, yet rarely visited landscapes of Libya's extreme southwest. Shadow the Algerian border as close as you dare and approach with caution the haunted desert citadel of **Kaf Ajnoun** (p193). **Ghat** (p194) is your prize at the end of this epic journey and its charming, abandoned mud-brick medina perfectly captures the Saharan isolation that Ghat wears so well.

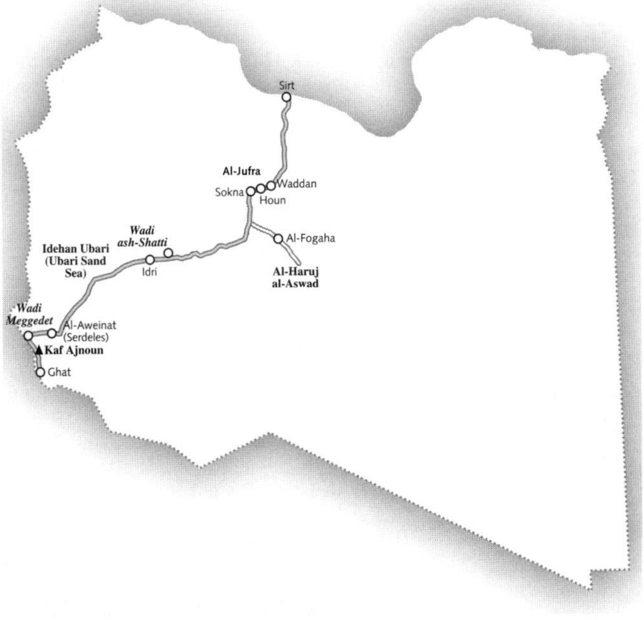

From Sirt to Ghat by road is 1144km, but you could travel double that during the 10 days once you factor in desert detours. A 4WD is essential for Al-Haruj al-Aswad and from Idri to Ghat.

TAILORED TRIPS

ARCHITECTURAL ODYSSEY

Libya has some of the most striking indigenous architecture in North Africa. Most arose from the midst of Libya's Berber population, but there have been some fine, more recent additions to the genre.

The old city of **Ghadames** (p167) is the most extensive and still-habitable medina in all the Sahara; if you don't believe us, just ask Unesco. **Nalut** (p162) is your southwestern gateway to the Jebel Nafusa, home to Berber (often called troglodyte) architecture without peer. Nalut itself has a rambling old town, some delightful old mosques and a **qasr** (fortified granary store; p163), where a backdrop to a *Star Wars* movie springs to mind. **Kabaw** (p162) is 700 years old and has the same could-be-sci-fi, could-be-primitive feel as in Nalut. **Qasr al-Haj** (p160) is more intimate and arguably the most impressive of the Jebel Nafusa *qasrs*. The underground pit-homes *(dammous)* of **Gharyan** (p158) are another world again. **Tripoli's medina** (p82) bears a pastiche of international styles but is very much a local product, while Zliten's **Mausoleum and Mosque of Sidi Abdusalam** (p118) is one of the most beautiful mosques in Libya. And if you can handle the long roads to get here, Awjila's **Al-Kabir Mosque** (p132) is the best and most curious of its kind anywhere in the Libyan Sahara.

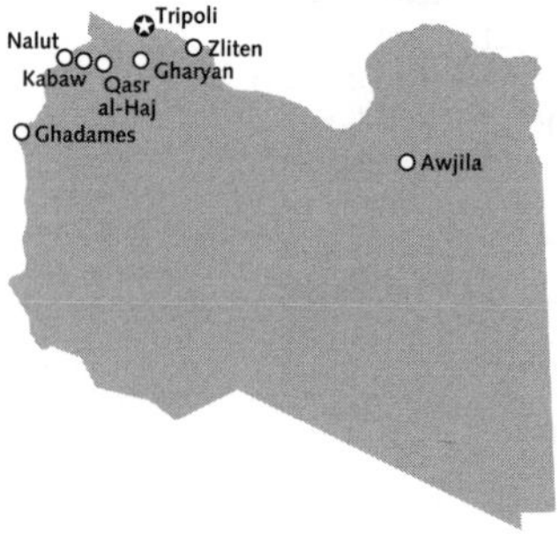

ROCK ART

Prehistoric carvings, some dating back 12,000 years, and exquisite rock paintings litter the Sahara and Libya lays claim to some of the best such galleries in North Africa.

The **Jebel Acacus** (p198), together with the Tassili-n-Ajjer just across the border in Algeria, is the Louvre of the rock-art world, with **Wadi Tashwinat** (p200) and **Awiss** (p199) home to especially fine paintings that reach astonishing levels of sophistication and skill. **Wadi Methkandoush** (p204) is just as impressive, but this time for arguably the best carvings in the Sahara: the two mythical catlike figures fighting on their hindlegs high on the wadi wall is the enigmatic *Mona Lisa* of the desert. Nearby wadis are also impressive, none more than **Wadi Tiksateen** (p204). Far away in the southeast, where Libya meets Sudan and Egypt, **Jebel Arkno** (p208) was once, impossible as it is to imagine, home to giraffe if the local artists of antiquity are anything to go by. **Jebel al-Uweinat** (p209) is even better, with possibly the richest single-wall gallery in Libya. It's not for nothing that the rock-art centrepieces of the movie *The English Patient* were based on this region. Close to remote Al-Jaghbub, many miles north across the Great Sand Sea, more engravings are found at **Buhairat al-Malfa** (p155) and **Buhairat al-Fredgha** (p155).

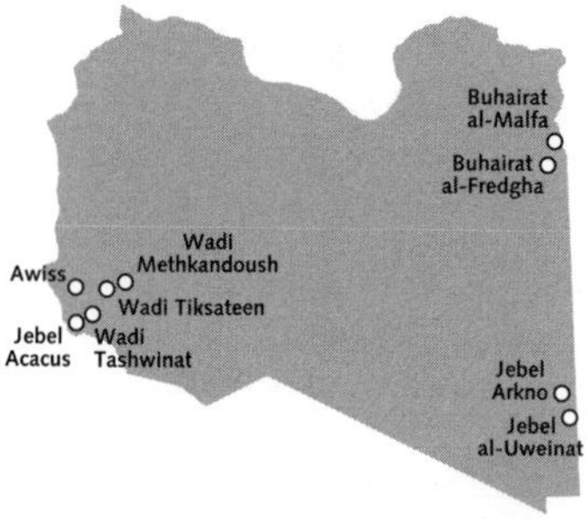

IBYAN CIVILISATIONS

ibya in ancient times was not just about Romans and Greeks. A number f Libyan civilisations thrived here, especially the Garamantes (p30) who uled the Libyan Sahara for almost 1500 years until AD 500 from their ase near Germa.

The ancient city of **Garama** (p189), located close to the modern settlement f Germa, is the most extensive signpost to the might of the Garamantes mpire, its mud-brick ruins suggesting that this was a city of size and of reat significance. The Germa **museum** (p190) contains some signifiers f the Garamantian might, while nearby **Zinchecra** (p191) and the royal yramid tombs of **Ahramat al-Hattia** (p191) are all that remain of this 00-king dynasty.

In the far northeast of the country, in the ebel al-Akhdar, the small site of **Slonta** (p140) s home to a temple with childlike yet sophisticated carved figures that pre-date the Greek arrival in Libya (making them well over 2700 years old).

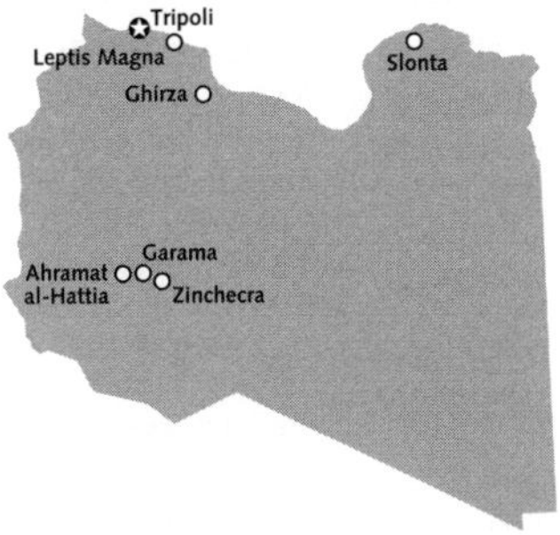

Remote and clearly influenced by the Romans, **Ghirza** (p121) has stone temples, tombs and fortified farms that date back 1700 years. Gallery 5 of Tripoli's **Jamahiriya Museum** (p78) is dedicated to ancient Libyan civilisations and contains exhibits from Garama, Zinchecra, Slonta and Ghirza. Room 18 of the **Leptis Museum** (p117) also provides a further historical context to Ghirza.

WWII

Libya was the scene of some of WWII's most bitter North African battles as Rommel's Axis forces clashed with British, Australian and other Allied soldiers. Many of these battles took place around **Tobruk** (p151). Tobruk honours its dead well, with poignant **cemeteries** (p152), the famous **Australian (Fig Tree) Hospital** (p152), **Rommel's Operations Room** (p153) and you can even see the now-somewhat-bleak hotel, **Funduq al-Jebel al-Akhdar** (p153), where Rommel slept the night.

Another important piece of WWII memorabilia is the **'Lady Be Good'** (see p156), the US plane whose story is one of the saddest of a most tragic war.

In **Al-Burdi** (p154) is John Brill's Room where the paintings of this talented but soon-to-be dead young man take pride of place.

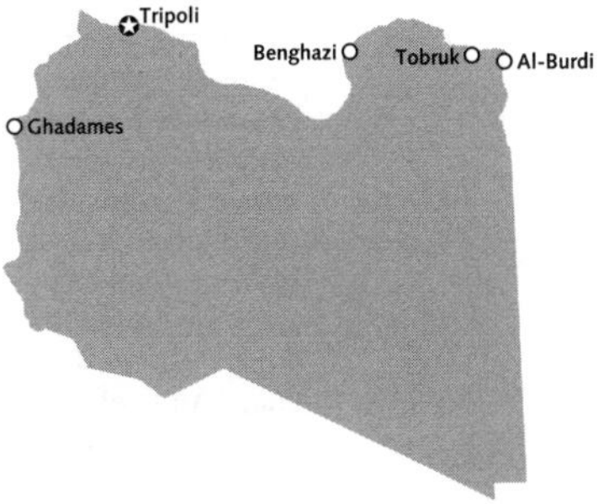

Benghazi has another **Commonwealth War Graves Cemetery** (p127), while Benghazi's lack of an old town is largely due to its near-demolition by bombing during WWII.

One major reason why Tripoli's **medina** (p82) is in danger of falling down in parts is because of heavy WWII bombardments, while the town of **Ghadames** (p172) offers a reminder that far more Libyans died as a result of the war than did Western soldiers in Libya. On 11 November 1943, the French flattened parts of the Italian-occupied old city, destroyed the Atik and Yunis Mosques (p166), Ghadames' oldest, and killed 40 of its local inhabitants.

Snapshot

Libya is a country on the upswing and most Libyans still can't quite believe that the long years of isolation are finally over. Libya awoke from its nightmare when Colonel Muammar Qaddafi announced in December 2003 that Libya would relinquish its nuclear, chemical and biological weapons programme, and when Seif al-Islam al-Qaddafi – Colonel Qaddafi's urbane, Western-educated and media-savvy son – told the Davos 2005 World Economic Forum that 'the old times are finished', you could almost hear the collective sigh of relief from Libyans (for more information see p42).

FAST FACTS

GDP per capita: US$11,800

Unemployment: 30%

Inflation: 3.4%

Life expectancy at birth: 76.69 years (men 74.46; women 79.02)

Oil production: 1.643 million barrels per day

Male/female/youth literacy rate: 91.8/70.7/97%

Population under 15/over 65: 30.8/2.9%

Doctors per 100,000 people: 129 (UK = 164)

Under-five mortality rate per 1000 live births: 16 (1970 = 160)

Libya ranked 58th out of 177 countries on the UN's Human Development Index – the highest ranking of any African country

Although the almost euphoric wave of optimism that swept the country in the aftermath of Libya's return to the international fold has given way to the harsher economic realities of rebuilding Libya's moribund economy, Libyans have been waiting for this moment for most of their lives. If Libyans seem genuinely happy to see you, that's partly because Libya was almost hermetically sealed off from the outside world for decades and your presence is confirmation that the country is back in business.

It's always dangerous to generalise but most Libyans are clamouring not for Western-style democracy but for the prosperity that they feel they deserve. 'Libya could have been Dubai' is an oft-heard refrain and, looking closely at this oil-rich country with its small population, it's hard to disagree with them. That's why Libyans are impatiently waiting for the day when they no longer need to work two jobs in order to live a comfortable life, the day when salaries rise above subsistence levels. The dire state of the Libyan economy (see p46) is the primary preoccupation of ordinary Libyans.

The majority of Libyans have known no other Libya than Colonel Qaddafi's permanent revolution (see p39) and they have become weary of being seen as pariahs in the international community through no fault of their own (see p41). And yet, there is a widespread if grudging respect for the man who has kept their lives in a permanent state of flux. Yes, they grumble about the colonel, but many of his causes – egalitarianism, fighting US imperialism, fighting Islamic fundamentalism, support for the Palestinians – are dear to the heart of the ordinary Libyan. As one such Libyan told us in a sentence that could be the catch-cry of a nation, 'if Colonel Qaddafi leaves me to live my life, I don't care if he stays for 100 years'.

Libyans are too busy making up for lost time (and working very hard to make ends meet) to spend too much time worrying about the future, and Colonel Qaddafi shows no sign of disappearing from the scene despite having mellowed considerably in recent years. But the great unspoken question in Libya is what will happen after the colonel dies. No-one knows the answer, perhaps not even the all-knowing colonel who once said that all Libyans will be president after he dies. For his part, Seif al-Islam al-Qaddafi has denied that he will one day succeed his father (see p43). If the Qaddafis don't know, then the chances are that no-one else does. A battle for control of the country between the revolutionary old guard and reform-minded democrats? The spectre of an Islamic fundamentalism so alien to the mind-set of ordinary Libyans? No-one knows the answer, and Libyans are hoping that they can enjoy their moment in the sun a little before they have to find out.

History

The Libya story is one of history's grand epics. Ancient civilisations, the empires of the Middle Ages and great powers of our age have all fought over Libya. But it's a story that goes on, a work-in-progress that remains in the hands of Colonel Muammar Qaddafi, one of the most recognisable and enigmatic figures of modern times.

THE SAHARA ONCE WAS GREEN

Hundreds of millions of years ago, the Sahara was covered by expansive inland seas. Tens of millions of years ago, the Sahara was a desert larger than it is today. Tens of thousands of years ago, the Sahara again turned green. As Europe shivered under the Ice Age, the Sahara was home to lakes and forests and a pleasant Mediterranean climate.

African Rock Art (by David Coulson & Alec Campbell) is wonderfully illustrated and the text brings to life rock art and every aspect of its historical context.

Perhaps drawn by this idyllic climate, two distinct races appeared in North Africa between about 15,000 and 10,000 BC, the Oranian and then the Capsian. Their integration with indigenous peoples resulted in the spread of Neolithic (New Stone Age) culture and the introduction of farming techniques. The earliest evidence of lasting or semipermanent settlements in Libya dates from this period (8000 BC).

Rock paintings and carvings in the Jebel Acacus (p198) and at Wadi Methkandoush (p204), as well as in the Tassilin-Ajjer in Algeria) are the greatest source of knowledge about this time of abundant rainfall and vegetation, when rivers ran through grassy plateaus across which ranged a rich abundance of wildlife. The Sahara was the earth's idyll, its land of plenty, a fertile territory capable of sustaining all the life of the land for generations.

Libyan Studies is a yearly journal published by the Society for Libyan Studies (www.britac.ac.uk/institutes/libya/) and there's no finer barometer of current research into Libya's ancient history.

It is from these Neolithic peoples that the Berbers (the indigenous peoples of North Africa; see p47) are thought to be descended. Taking into consideration regional variations and the lack of hard evidence, they appear to have been predominantly nomadic pastoralists, although they continued to hunt and occasionally farm. By the time of contact with the first of the outside civilisations to arrive from the east, the Phoenicians, these local tribes were already well established.

PUNIC TRIPOLITANIA (1000–201 BC)

The Phoenician empire, with its origins and base in the Levantine ports of Tyre, Sidon and Byblos (all in modern-day Lebanon), were a seafaring people renowned for their trading activities, and they were the first of the great civilisations of antiquity to turn their sights on Libya. By the 12th century BC, Phoenician traders were active throughout the Mediterranean, arriving regularly on the Libyan coast by 1000 BC.

Historical Dictionary of Libya (by Ronald Bruce St John) is a comprehensive A-Z look at Libyan history from the Abbasid to the Zirid dynasties with detours into the ancient world en route.

After around 700 BC, their need for permanent settlements to facilitate their trade in gold, silver, raw metals, ivory and even apes and peacocks saw them establish the colonies of Lebdah (Leptis Magna; p110), Oea (Tripoli; p73) and Sabratha (p100). Other ports were later built at Macomades-Euphranta (near modern Sirt) and Charax (Medinat Sultan). Each was a small but essential link in a chain of safe ports stretching from the Levant to Spain.

The strategic importance of the Libyan coast was not the only reason for Phoenician interest in Libya – the ports also provided a base for Phoenician merchants to trade with the Berber tribes of the interior, with whom they signed treaties of cooperation.

Phoenician civilisation in North Africa came to be called 'Punic', a derivation of both the Latin Punicus and Greek Phoinix. The colonies were governed from the city of Carthage (in modern Tunisia), a city whose dominance of North Africa represented the pinnacle of Punic civilisation.

Carthage was founded in 814 BC. Long politically dependent on the mother culture in Tyre, Carthage eventually emerged as an independent, commercial empire. By 517 BC, the powerful city-state was the leading city of North Africa and by the 4th century BC, Carthage controlled the North African coast from Tripolitania to the Atlantic.

Ultimately, ongoing tension with the nascent Roman Empire weakened Carthage and spelled the death-knell for Carthaginian rule. In what was to become a recurring theme in Libyan history, the Carthaginian empire governed Tripolitania from afar. There were few material benefits for Libya's indigenous inhabitants, yet the province was not spared the devastation caused by the Punic Wars with Rome (264–241 BC, 218–201 BC and 149–146 BC). The wars reduced Carthage to a small, vulnerable African state. It was razed by the Romans in 146 BC, the site symbolically sprinkled with salt and damned forever. Tripolitania was left to fend for itself.

The Garamantes of Southern Libya (by Charles Daniels) dates from 1970 and is hard to find, but it's one of very few studies of the Garamantes empire.

MAKING THE DESERT BLOOM (900 BC–AD 500)

While the Phoenicians were establishing themselves along Libya's Mediterranean Coast, the Garamantes were emerging as Libya's first indigenous empire. They ruled southern Libya from their base in the Wadi al-Hayat from 900 BC, first from Zinchecra (p191) and later from Garama (p189) at the location of what is now modern Germa. At once warlike and a sophisticated, urban community that made the desert bloom, the Garamantes are thought to have partly descended from Neolithic peoples or migrated from the oases to the east, carrying with them a knowledge of cultivation.

Garamantes sent dates, precious stones, ostrich feathers, ivory and slaves to Leptis Magna in exchange for pottery, glass, clothes and other Mediterranean produce.

Archaeologists have found evidence to suggest that Garamantian cities were more than mere desert outposts. Rather, they were thriving urban centres with markets and forums for public entertainment and the Garamantes were one of the most advanced peoples of their time; many believe that the Garamantes and their forerunners may have been responsible for the rock art of southern Libya. The Garamantes' stock-in-trade was, however, control over the ancient trans-Saharan caravan routes, and the lucrative commodities of salt, slaves and gold all converged on Garama from Egypt and sub-Saharan Africa.

With their connections to a wider world, the Garamantes were responsible for introducing writing, horses, wheeled transport and, finally, camels to the Sahara.

Most remarkably of all, the Garamantes empire thrived because of its agricultural prowess, even though the Garamantes lived far from recognised water sources. Herodotus spoke of the Garamantes as 'a very numerous tribe of people who spread soil over the salt to sow their seed in'. Archaeologists have discovered the remains of hundreds of underground channels, known as *foggara*, which enabled a boom in farming activity in the oases of the wadi. Ultimately, however, this tapping of underground water reserves, an approach adopted nearly 2500 years later by the modern Libyan state (see The Eighth Wonder of the World, p64), sowed the seeds of the Garamantian decline. As underground water supplies dried up as a result of overexploitation, by AD 500 the last of the Garamantes people had either died or abandoned Garama. Apart from Garama, the only lasting remnants of Garamantian civilisation in the Wadi al-Hayat are the royal tombs of Ahramat al-Hattia (p191) near Germa.

GREEK CYRENAICA (631–96 BC)

Legend has it that the inhabitants of the Greek island of Thera (modern Santorini) were told by the oracle of Apollo at Delphi to migrate to North Africa. In 631 BC, they established the city of Cyrene (p141). Within 200 years, during the period of great Hellenic colonisation, the Greeks had established four more cities – Teuchira (Tocra; p133), Ptolemais (Tolmeita; p134), Eusperides (at Benghazi; p125) and Apollonia (the port for Cyrene; p147). These semi-autonomous city-states came to be known as the Pentapolis (Five Cities) that became so significant that by around 500 BC the Greeks divided the world into three parts – Asia, Europe and Libya.

The Histories (by Herodotus) provides evidence why the writer has become known as the 'Father of History' with engaging and highly readable 5th-century BC text laced with references to Libya.

In 331 BC, the armies of Alexander the Great made a triumphant entrance into Cyrenaica from Egypt, although the great man himself stopped at the border after the Cyrenaicans greeted him with promises of loyalty. Upon his death in 323 BC, Alexander's empire was divided among his Macedonian generals. Egypt, along with Cyrene, went to Ptolemy. Again, the cities of the Pentapolis retained a significant degree of autonomy, although Greek influence was limited to the coastal areas, with minimal penetration of the Berber hinterland.

Libya – The Lost Cities of the Roman Empire (by Robert Polidori et al) is the peerless (and magnificently photographed) resource on the history of the Roman and Greek occupation of Libya.

Despite political turmoil throughout the years of the Pentapolis, Cyrene, in particular, flourished. In the economic sphere, the fertile slopes of the Jebel al-Akhdar provided Greece with valuable grain, wine, wool, livestock and a herb from the silphium plant (see p144), which was unique to Cyrenaica. Cyrene also became one of the Greek world's premier intellectual and artistic centres, producing and exporting some of the finest scholars of the age. The city was famed for its medical school, its learned academics and for being home to some of the finest examples of Hellenistic architecture anywhere in the world. The Cyrenians also developed a school of philosophy with a doctrine of moral cheerfulness that defined happiness as the sum of human pleasures. (Such a philosophy was undoubtedly made easier by the temperate and altogether pleasant climate.) For more details on Cyrene's history, turn to p141.

The halcyon days of Greek rule could not last forever. With Greek influence on the wane, the last Greek ruler, Ptolemy Apion, finally bequeathed Cyrenaica to Rome which formally annexed the territory in 96 BC.

ROMAN LIBYA (46 BC–AD 431)

After the final defeat of Carthage in the Punic Wars (see p29), the Romans assigned Tripolitania to their ally, the Berber king of Numidia. In 46 BC, Julius Caesar deposed the final Numidian king, Juba I, who had sided with Pompey, a general in the Roman army and rival of Caesar in the Civil Wars of Rome. Tripolitania was thereafter incorporated into the new province of Africa Nova (later called Africa Proconsularis).

Defeating the Numidians was one thing but the Garamantes (opposite) of southern Libya proved more resilient. Roman expeditions against the Garamantian cities in 20–19 BC and again in AD 69–70 were sent packing. Thereafter, the Romans and Garamantes signed a military and commercial treaty and became firm trading partners.

In AD 68–69, the territories belonging to Leptis Magna were devastated by Garamantian raiders who united with Oea (Tripoli) in its war with Leptis; the elites of Leptis Magna cowered behind the city walls.

Elsewhere, Rome had completed the pacification of Sirtica (along the southern coast of the Gulf of Sirt) by the end of the 1st century AD, and Tripolitania and Cyrenaica were united under one administration for the first time.

The era that followed was one of Libya's finest. The Pax Romana saw Tripolitania and Cyrenaica become prosperous Roman provinces, part of a cosmopolitan state with a common language, legal system and identity. Many of the towns along the coast enjoyed the full range of urban amenities for which Roman cities were famous – a forum, markets, amphitheatres and baths – and traders flocked to the Libyan coast from throughout the empire. Tripolitania was a major source of olive oil for Roman merchants and also operated as an entrepôt for gold and slaves brought to the coast by Berbers and the Garamantians. Cyrenaica was equally prized, as it had been under Greek rule, as a source of wine, silphium and horses.

The Lost Cities of the Roman Empire (Robert Polidori et al) is a magnificent, comprehensive and beautifully photographed coffee-table book covering Libya's Greek and Roman sites. Currently out of print, but worth tracking down.

A Libyan even became emperor of the Roman Empire – it was under the tutelage of Septimius Severus (r AD 193–211), who was known as 'the grim African' (see p112), that Leptis Magna was transformed into an important cultural and commercial centre second only to Rome.

Despite the relative peace that accompanied Roman rule, the region was not immune to the political instability beyond its borders. In AD 115, a Jewish revolt among settlers from Palestine began and was not quelled until AD 118, after Jewish insurgents had laid waste to Cyrene and destroyed much of Cyrenaica.

The thinly populated territory of Libya enabled the Romans to maintain control with little more than a locally recruited legion of 5500 men.

In 300 the Roman emperor Diocletian separated Cyrenaica from the province of Crete, dividing the region into Upper and Lower Libya – the first time the name 'Libya' was used as an administrative designation. (The name 'Libya' was first used by the ancient Greeks to refer to all of North Africa, except Egypt, and comes from the ancient Egyptians who referred to all Berbers living west of the Nile as 'Lebu'.) By the 4th century AD, however, Rome was in decline and the fate of the Libyan colonies was sealed by a massive earthquake in 365 (see p143). Sabratha, Leptis Magna, Cyrene and many other Roman cities were destroyed and Roman Africa never recovered.

VANDALS & BYZANTINES

In 429 a rebellious Roman official invited the Vandals, a Germanic tribe, to Libya in an attempt to gain leverage with the authorities in Rome. The Vandals, with as many as 80,000 settlers in tow, quickly set about conquering Tripolitania, a feat they achieved in 431 under their leader Genseric (Gaeseric). Faced with little choice, the Romans recognised the Vandal ascendancy as long as Libya's civil administration remained, nominally at least, in Roman hands. In 455 the Vandals sacked Rome. The last vestiges of Roman prosperity in Libya quickly evaporated and the Vandals, more adept at pillage and overseas conquests than in administering their colonies, fortified themselves in armed camps. The outlying areas fell once again under the rule of tribal chieftains.

A Travellers' History of North Africa (by Barnaby Rogerson) is history made accessible with a region-wide focus and an ideal companion to your Libyan visit.

In 533 the Byzantine army general Flavius Belisarius captured Libya for the emperor Justinian. With Byzantine control limited to coastal cities such as Sabratha, Cyrene and Apollonia, Berber rebellions in the hinterland reduced the remainder of Libya to anarchy and the potential prosperity of the provinces was squandered. Byzantine rule was deeply unpopular, not least because taxes were increased dramatically in order to pay for the colony's military upkeep while the cities were left to decay.

ISLAMIC LIBYA

With tenuous Byzantine control over Libya restricted to a few poorly defended coastal strongholds, the Arab horsemen under the command of Amr ibn al-As first crossed into Cyrenaica in 642 and encountered little resistance. By 643 Tripoli had also succumbed. It was not until 663, when Uqba bin Nafi invaded the Fezzan, however, that Berber resistance in Libya was overcome. By 712 the entire region from Andalucía to the Levant came under the purview of the Umayyad caliph of Damascus.

Despite the rapid success enjoyed by the forces of Islam, the social character of Libya remained overwhelmingly Berber. While largely accepting the arrival of the new religion, the Berber tribes resisted the Arabisation of the region. Although Arab rule flourished in coastal areas, the enmity between the Berbers (who saw their rulers as arrogant and brutal) and the Arabs (who scorned the Berbers as barbarians) ensured that rebellions plagued much of Libya's hinterland.

In 750 the Abbasid dynasty overthrew the Umayyad caliph and shifted the capital to Baghdad, with emirs retaining nominal control over the Libyan coast on behalf of the far-distant caliph. In 800 Caliph Harun ar-Rashid appointed Ibrahim ibn al-Aghlabid as his governor. The Aghlabid dynasty effectively became independent of the Baghdad caliphs, who nevertheless retained ultimate spiritual authority.

The Aghlabid emirs are considered some of the most enlightened Islamic rulers of Libya. They took their custodianship of Libya seriously: repairing Roman irrigation systems, restoring order and bringing a measure of prosperity to the region.

In the last decade of the 9th century, the Ismailis (a branch of Shiism) launched an assault on the strongholds of the Sunni Aghlabids. The movement's spiritual leader, Grandmaster Ubaidalla Said of Syria, was installed as the imam of much of North Africa, including Tripolitania. The Berbers of Libya, always happy to thumb their noses at the orthodox Sunni aristocracy, accepted the imam as the Mahdi (Promised One).

The Shiite Fatimid dynasty conquered Egypt in 972 and set up the caliphate in Cairo. The difficulty of maintaining control over Libya plagued the Fatimids, as it had almost every authority before them. At the beginning of the 11th century, Bulukkin ibn Ziri was installed as the Fatimid governor but he quickly returned Libya to orthodox Sunnism and swore allegiance to the Abbasid caliphs of Baghdad.

The Fatimid anger at what they considered an act of gross betrayal would profoundly alter the fabric of Libyan society. Two tribes from the Arabian Peninsula – the Bani Hilal and the Bani Salim (or Bani Sulaim) – were co-opted into migrating to the Maghreb. The Bani Salim settled in Libya, particularly in Cyrenaica, while the Bani Hilal (who numbered as many as 200,000 families) spread across North Africa (see also Tribes in Libya, p45). The destruction of Cyrene and Tripoli by this unstoppable mass migration was symptomatic of arguably the most effective conquest Libya had seen. The Berber tribespeople were displaced from their traditional lands, their farmland converted to pasture and the new settlers finally cemented the cultural and linguistic Arabisation of the region.

In 1158 the supporters of the Almohad dynasty arrived in Tripolitania from Morocco and established its authority. An Almohad viceroy, Muhammad bin Abu Hafs, ruled Libya from 1207 to 1221 and established the Hafsid dynasty, which outlived the Almohads. The Hafsids ruled Tripolitania for nearly 300 years. There was significant trade with the city-states of Europe and the Hafsid rulers encouraged art, literature and architecture.

Meanwhile, in the Fezzan in the 13th century, King Danama of Kanem (near Lake Chad) annexed territories as far north as the Al-Jufra oases. His Toubou viceroy founded the autonomous Bani Nasr dynasty, which ruled the Fezzan until the 14th century. They were followed by the theocratic kingdoms of Kharijite sectarians, including the Bani Khattab in the Fezzan. In the early 16th century the Libyan Sahara fell under the sway of Muhammad al-Fazi from Morocco who, late in the 15th century, founded the Awlad Muhammad dynasty in Murzuq.

OTTOMAN RULE

By the start of the 15th century, the Libyan coast had little central authority and its harbours were havens for unchecked bands of pirates. Hapsburg Spain and the Knights of St John of Malta occupied Tripoli briefly in the early 16th century, before yielding to Khair ad-Din, a pirate king known more evocatively as Barbarossa, or Red Beard. It was then that the coast became renowned as the Barbary Coast.

When the Ottomans arrived to occupy Tripoli in 1551, they saw little reason to reign in the pirates, preferring instead to profit from the booty. The French, Dutch and British navies all bombarded Tripoli to warn off further robbery on the high seas, but the Turks saw the pirates as a second column in their battle for naval supremacy and turned a blind eye to the anarchy beyond the port.

Under the Ottomans the Maghreb was divided into three provinces, or regencies: Algiers, Tripoli and Tunis. After 1565 administrative authority in Tripoli was vested in a pasha appointed by the sultan in Constantinople. The sultan provided the pasha with a corps of janissaries (professional soldiers committed to a life of military service). This corps was in turn divided into a number of companies under the command of a junior officer with the title of bey. The janissaries quickly became the dominant force in Ottoman Libya. As self-governing military guilds answerable only to their own laws and protected by a divan (a council of senior officers who advised the pasha), the janissaries soon reduced the pasha to a largely ceremonial role. The sultan, whose forces were stretched to the limits in this vast empire, was in no position to argue.

In 1711 Ahmed Karamanli, an Ottoman cavalry officer and son of a Turkish officer and Libyan woman, seized power and founded a dynasty that would last 124 years. Again, while the Ottomans wielded ultimate authority from afar, power was vested in a local leader acting well beyond his original brief.

One of the primary preoccupations of the Karamanli dynasty was to bring Fezzan (and hence trans-Saharan trade routes) under its control. The sultans of the Awlad Muhammad based in Murzuq resisted

The Barbary Corsairs (by S Lane-Poole) is filled with the skulduggery and picaresque adventures of the pirates that raided with impunity from Tripoli.

Fazzan Under the Rule of the Awlad Muhammad (by Habib Wada'a El-Hesnawi) recounts the ebbs, flows and ultimate fall of the Awlad Muhammad and is especially good on the last days of the dynasty.

Journal of Frederick Hornemann's Travels from Cairo to Mourzouk 1797-8 (by Frederick Hornemann) is one of the earliest accounts of Fezzan through European eyes in the dying days of the Awlad Muhammad dynasty.

A STORY OF BETRAYAL

For 350 years, from the last decades of the 15th century until 1813, Fezzan was ruled by the sultans of the Awlad Muhammad tribe, but their rule was almost cut short by the Machiavellian machinations-gone-wrong of one of the sultans' wives.

In 1577 Khudah, the wife of Sultan al-Muntasir, became outraged at her husband over his perceived favouritism of his other wife. She sent a delegation to Tripoli and promised the Ottoman rulers – who had long-coveted the Fezzan – riches, and Al-Muntasir's kingdom, if they helped depose her husband. With an Ottoman detachment on its way to Sebha, Al-Muntasir arrived at Sebha's Qasr Lahmar (Red Palace) to find that Khudah had closed the gates. He besieged the palace, but the sultan died after three days, reportedly 'of chagrin'.

Faced with this sudden turn of good fortune, Khudah decided to rule Fezzan on her own. In order to deter the advancing Ottomans, Khudah dressed the stones surrounding Sebha in military uniforms. Stopped in their tracks by this seemingly formidable army, they demanded that Khudah honour her promise. She refused and when the Turks realised that the only army confronting them was an army of stones they stormed the palace, tortured Khudah and burned her alive as she was handing over her treasures. As they marched on Murzuq, Al-Muntasir's son and heir-apparent fled south. He was not to return until a decade later when a revolt swept through Fezzan and massacred the isolated Ottoman garrisons.

ROUND ONE TO LIBYA

In 1801 Yusuf Karamanli tried to coerce the newly independent United States of America into paying an annual tribute (glorified protection money) of US$250,000, just as it demanded of other, longer-established seafaring powers. When the USA offered just US$18,000 in return, the insulted Karamanli ordered the sacking of the US consulate in Tripoli. The Americans interpreted this as an act of war and, not for the last time, dispatched a warship, the USS *Philadelphia,* to the Libyan coast. The ship was overrun and the crew taken prisoner in Derna (p150). Only when US forces – assisted by Arab horsemen, Greek mercenaries and dissident members of Yusuf's own family – captured the town was the confrontation (1801–05) resolved. The Americans paid US$68,000 and Karamanli emerged as something of a local hero.

the Ottoman army, while in 1810 the Ottomans dispatched troops to Ghadames to regain control. Soon after, in 1813, the Ottomans seized on a refusal by the sultans to pay tribute to Tripoli and overthrew the last sultan of the Awlad Muhammad's 350-year rule. They thereafter re-annexed the Fezzan.

The Karamanli dynasty was, however, entering troubled times, with England and France calling in the considerable debts incurred by the Karamanli regime. Tripoli's economy collapsed and Yusuf Karamanli – who had fought and won a civil war against his father and brother in 1795 and always made a point of defying his Ottoman overlords – tried to make up the financial shortfall by increasing taxes.

Rebellions broke out across Libya and the countryside soon descended into civil war. Yusuf finally succumbed to the pressure and abdicated in 1835 in favour of his son Ali. When Ali asked the Ottoman sultan Mohammed II for assistance in repelling a European takeover of Tripoli, the Ottomans took the opportunity to rein in their troublesome offspring and brought the rule of the Karamanli dynasty to a close. With full Ottoman authority restored, the Turks once again relegated Libya to the status of a neglected outpost of the empire.

Narrative of a Ten-Years Residence at Tripoli in Africa (by Richard Tully) is filled with sharp detail and engaging commentary on the pleasures and intrigues of 1780s Tripoli during the Karamanli dynasty.

THE RISE OF THE SANUSIS

Less than a decade after the hated Ottoman authority was resumed, the indigenous Sanusi Movement, led by Islamic cleric Sayyid Mohammed Ali al-Sanusi, called on the tribes of the Cyrenaican countryside to resist Ottoman rule. The Grand Sanusi (see p36) established his headquarters in the oasis town of Al-Jaghbub (p154) while his *ikhwan* (followers) set up *zawiyas* (religious colleges or monasteries) across North Africa and brought some stability to regions not known for their submission to central authority. In line with the express instruction of the Grand Sanusi, their gains were made largely without coercion.

The highpoint of the Sanusi influence was to come in the 1880s under the Grand Sanusi's son, Mohammed al-Mahdi, who was a skilled administrator and a charismatic orator. With 146 lodges spanning the length and breadth of the Sahara, Mohammed al-Mahdi moved the Sanusi capital to Al-Kufra (p132). Harsh Ottoman rule only fuelled the appeal of the Sanusi Movement's call to repel foreign occupation. Mohammed al-Mahdi succeeded where so many had failed before him: securing the enduring loyalty of the Berber tribes of Cyrenaica.

While the Sanusis were winning hearts and minds, the last 75 years of Ottoman rule in Libya saw 33 Ottoman governors pass through Tripoli – not one of them distinguished themselves enough to be remembered by history.

London-based Darf Publishers (www.darfpublishers.co.uk) should be your first stop when trying to track down hard-to-find travellers' accounts of Libya and other studies of Libyan history that other publishers won't touch.

THE GRAND SANUSI

Sayyid Mohammed Ali al-Sanusi was born in 1787 in what is now Algeria. A descendant of the Prophet Mohammed and a Sufi, he studied in Morocco and then at Cairo's prestigious Al-Azhar University. This pious scholar was forceful in his criticism of the Egyptian ulema (religious authorities) for what he saw as their timid compliance with the Ottoman authorities and their spiritual conservatism. He also argued that all learned Muslims had the right to disregard the four classical schools of Islamic law and Quranic interpretation, and themselves engage in *ijtihad* (individual interpretation of sacred texts and traditions). Not surprisingly, this upstart from a North African backwater was denounced by the religious scholars of Cairo as a heretic and they issued a fatwa against him.

Al-Sanusi removed himself to Mecca, where he found greater support for his radical ideas. There he was influenced by the Wahhabi movement, which called for a return to the purity of Islam. In Mecca he founded his first *zawiya* (a religious college or monastery), before returning to North Africa. He settled in Cyrenaica (near Al-Bayda) in 1843 where he found fertile ground among a people known for their dislike of authority.

ITALY'S FOURTH SHORE

With Ottoman control tenuous at best, the Italian government saw an opportunity to join, albeit belatedly, the Europe-wide scramble for African colonies. On 3 October 1911 the Italians attacked Tripoli, claiming somewhat disingenuously to be liberating Libya from Ottoman rule. The Libyan population was unimpressed and refused to accept yet another occupying force. A major revolt against the Italians followed, with battles near Tripoli, Misrata, Benghazi and Derna.

The Ottoman sultan had more-important concerns and ceded Libya to the Italians by signing the 1912 Treaty of Lausanne. Tripolitania was largely under Italian control by 1914, but both Cyrenaica and the Fezzan were home to rebellions led by the Sanusis. As one historian observed, 'All Cyrenaica was hard hostile rock beneath the shallowest covering of local collaboration. The Italians found themselves not fighting an army but a people.'

Omar al-Mukhtar – The Italian Reconquest of Libya (by Enzo Santarelli) is a nuanced portrait of Libya's most famous rebel leader, casting searing light on the brutality of Italian colonial rule.

The Italian government failed to heed the unrest of a people tired of foreign occupation. In 1921 the government appointed Governor Giuseppe Volpi. The following year Mussolini announced the Riconquista of 'Libya' (a name not used as an administrative entity since Roman times). Marshal Pietro Badoglio, who commanded the Italian army under Volpi, waged a punitive 'pacification' campaign. Badoglio was succeeded in the field by Marshal Rodolfo Graziani after Mussolini became impatient with the frequent setbacks opposing the rebels. Graziani only accepted the commission from Mussolini on the condition that he was allowed to crush Libyan resistance unencumbered by the inconvenient restraints imposed by Italian and international law. Mussolini agreed immediately and Graziani intensified the oppression. It was around this time that Omar al-Mukhtar, a Sanusi sheikh, became the leader of the uprising.

After a short-lived truce collapsed in 1929, Italy's Libya policy plumbed new depths of brutality. A barbed-wire fence, still visible today on the road from Tobruk to Al-Jaghbub (see Graziani's Fence, p155) was built from the Mediterranean to the oasis of Al-Jaghbub to sever supply lines critical to the resistance's survival. Soon afterwards the colonial administration began the wholesale deportation of the people of the Jebel al-Akhdar to deny the rebels the succour of the local population. The forced migration of more than 100,000 people ended in concentration

THE LION OF THE DESERT

Omar al-Mukhtar was born in Cyrenaica in 1858. His education through the Sanusi school system invested him with a passionate faith in Islam and a belief that it was the obligation of every Libyan to resist all forms of foreign domination. He distinguished himself in the first campaign against the Italians (1911–17) and with Italian rule being increasingly marked by terror, he again took up arms. In addition to a number of unlikely successes against the better-resourced Italian army from his stronghold of Wadi al-Kuf (p137), Al-Mukhtar's greatest achievement was to unite Libya's disparate tribes into an effective fighting force. For almost 10 years, he and his fighters held out, frustrating the Italians at every turn. In 1931 Al-Mukhtar was still fighting at the age of 73, which earned him the sobriquet of 'Lion of the Desert'. When supplies for the resistance movement ran out later that year, Al-Mukhtar was captured by the Italian army and on 16 September 1931 he was hanged in Suluq in front of his followers; for more information see The Capture, Trial & Execution of Omar al-Mukhtar, p138. A likeness of Al-Mukhtar appears on the 10LD banknote.

camps in Suluq (south of Benghazi; p131) and Al-'Aghela (west of Ajdabiya; p123) where tens of thousands died in squalid conditions. It's estimated that at least 80,000 Libyans died either directly in military campaigns or through starvation and disease, including a staggering half of the Cyrenaican population. Thousands more were exiled to remote Italian islands and never returned. Up to 95% of the local livestock was also killed. It was all part of the Italian policy to win 'even if the entire population of Cyrenaica has to perish'. After Omar al-Mukhtar's capture, the rebellion petered out. The wholesale massacring of civilians fleeing Al-Kufra was the final outrage of a ruthless occupation.

Lion of the Desert (1981), starring Anthony Quinn and John Gielgud, brings the legend of Omar al-Mukhtar to life and is notable for being one of few famous movies actually filmed in Libya.

By 1934 Italian control extended into the Fezzan, and in 1937 Mussolini cynically declared himself the 'Protector of Islam', in the process filling the mosques with compliant Sunni clerics. In 1938–39 Mussolini sought to fully colonise Libya, introducing 30,000 Italian settlers, which brought their numbers to more than 100,000 (proportionally more than French settlers in neighbouring Algeria). These settlers were shipped primarily to Sahel al-Jefara (Jefara Plain) in Tripolitania (40,000) and the Jebel al-Akhdar in Cyrenaica (the remaining 60,000). In order to accommodate the new arrivals, the Fascist government appropriated 225,000 hectares of prime agricultural land from locals without compensation. For a sobering overview of the devastation wrought on Libya during the colonial period, visit the Libyan Studies Centre (p87) in Tripoli.

Desert Encounter (by Knud Holmboe) is one of the few firsthand accounts of the Italian occupation of Libya in the early 1930s and is wonderfully told. For an excerpt from this book, see p54.

Although the policy of resettling Italians in Libya was portrayed as essential to Italy's population crisis – many of the settlers were landless peasants from the desperately poor Mezzogiorno of Italy's south – the sheer cost of the exercise suggested that the colonisation was primarily driven by ideology. Indeed, Mussolini is reported to have said that resettling Italy's rural poor in Libya cost more than it would have to put them up in Rome's exclusive Grand Hotel.

By the time that Italian three decades of colonial rule in Libya ended during WWII, one quarter of Libya's population had died as a result of the occupation. Libya was one of the poorest countries on earth and, in the words of the historian Mansour O El-Kikhia, 'What the Italians left behind was a country with a decimated population; a below-subsistence level, stagnating economy; and a political vacuum almost impossible to fill. That the country's population survived was indeed a miracle.'

In July 1999 the Italian government offered a formal apology to Libya.

THINGS THEY SAID ABOUT...NEWLY INDEPENDENT LIBYA

Libya combines within the borders of one country virtually all the obstacles of development that can be found anywhere: geographic, economic, political, sociological, technological. If Libya can be brought to a stage of sustained growth, there is hope for every country in the world.

Benjamin Higgins, UN economist sent to Libya in 1952

WWII & THE ROAD TO INDEPENDENCE

Just when the Italians had beaten the Libyan resistance into submission, WWII again turned Libya into a theatre for somebody else's war. From 1940 until late 1942 the Italians and Germans, led by Lieutenant-General Erwin Rommel, waged a devastating war for the territory between Benghazi and El-Alamein (Egypt), with much of the fighting centred on Tobruk (p151); for more information on the defence of Tobruk by Allied forces, see The Rats of Tobruk, p153). In October 1942 General Montgomery's army broke through the German defences at El-Alamein. In November the Allied forces retook Cyrenaica; by January 1943 Tripoli was in British hands and by February the last German and Italian soldiers were driven from Libya.

Tobruk (by Peter Fitzsimmons) is the definitive account of the battles for the northeastern Libyan city with harrowing details and characters that bring to life the legend of the Rats of Tobruk.

The British administered Tripolitania and Cyrenaica from 1943. The initial military presence became a caretaker administration while the victorious powers decided what to do with Libya. In the meantime the French were, with British acquiescence, occupying the Fezzan, with their headquarters at Sebha. Ghat was attached to the French military region of Algeria, while Ghadames was subject to French control in southern Tunisia.

The country was hardly a lucrative prospect for potential occupiers: Libya was impoverished and had become renowned for its fierce resistance to colonial rule. The Libyan countryside and infrastructure had been devastated – it was estimated that at the end of WWII there were 11 million unexploded mines on or under Libyan soil – and prevailing infrastructure and education levels presented a damning indictment of Italy's colonial neglect.

A Yank in Libya (1942) is a classic movie about the intrigues of the European powers in Libya as they vie for the loyalty of the local Berber tribes.

The Four Powers Commission, comprising France, the UK, USSR and USA, was set up to decide Libya's fate. After the customary squabbling and distrust among the Great Powers, it emerged that Sayyid Idris al-Sanusi (the grandson of the Grand Sanusi) had received promises of independence from the British in return for Sanusi support during WWII. Among Libyans (who found themselves finally being listened to) the notion of independence quickly gathered momentum. Libyan nationalists raced against the clock to prevent France from detaching the Fezzan (with less than 60,000 people) from the provinces of Cyrenaica (300,000) and Tripolitania (750,000). The UN General Assembly approved the formation of an independent state in November 1949. On 24 December 1951 the independent United Kingdom of Libya, with the Sanusi King Idris as its monarch, was finally, and unanimously, proclaimed by the National Assembly.

THE DISCOVERY OF OIL

Libya in the 1950s seemed overwhelmed by the task at hand of building state institutions and rebuilding its shattered economy. For a time its only export was scrap-metal leftover from WWII. The monarchy quickly outlawed political parties and turned to Britain and the USA for assistance. In 1953 the Libyan government signed a treaty allowing Britain to maintain military bases on Libyan soil in return for annual aid, while a similar agreement was signed with the Americans the following year. In return, by the end of 1959, Libya had by some estimates become the largest per capita recipient of US aid in the world.

In June 1959 an oilfield was discovered at Zelten in Cyrenaica. By early 1960, 35 wells had been sunk nationwide, international oil companies clamoured to obtain exploration rights in Libya and the country had begun its transformation from economic backwater into one of the world's fastest-growing economies. In the decade that followed, average annual incomes rose from US$25 to US$2000 and major infrastructure projects – 2000km of roads, universities, hospitals, schools and housing – finally began to take shape. Libya's cities grew, often alarmingly as Libya's rural poor migrated to the cities. Tripoli's population doubled to 300,000 in just seven years.

From independence until the mid-1960s, Libya was one of the only countries in the world to have two capitals (Tripoli and Benghazi).

For all of Libya's growing prosperity, the increasingly incompetent monarchical government began to show signs that it was becoming isolated from its people. Most importantly for many Libyans, the presence of British troops and the US Wheelus Air Base in Tripoli (then the largest in the world outside the USA, now Metiga Airport), at a time when the charismatic and anti-imperialist Egyptian president Gamal Abdel Nasser was at the height of his popularity across the Arab world, was a growing cause for concern.

After the crushing defeat suffered by Arab armies in the Six Day War in June 1967 against Israel, there was widespread unrest in Libya, especially in Tripoli and Benghazi. After attacks on Western embassies and Libya's Jewish population, Libyans soon turned their anger towards their own government, which was accused of being half-hearted in its commitment to the Arab cause. The government and monarchy were caught unawares by this paradigmatic shift in the political landscape and their inability to respond effectively saw their popularity spiral downwards. Their days were numbered.

HERE COMES THE COLONEL

On 1 September 1969 an obscure group of military officers seized power in Libya. Their planning was exemplary; they waited until all senior military figures were in the country and King Idris was in Turkey receiving medical treatment, thereby denying the government a figurehead around which to rally. They reportedly even postponed their coup by a day to avoid a clash with a concert by the popular Egyptian singer Umm Kolthum. There was little opposition to the coup and very few deaths. It was not until almost a week later that a 27-year-old colonel by the name of Muammar Qaddafi emerged at the head of the Revolutionary Command Council (RCC) and as the country's charismatic new leader.

Libya – A Modern History (by John Wright; 1982) is too dated to cover much of Qaddafi's rule, but his coverage of the Libyan rise to power is excellent.

The revolutionary ripples of the coup soon began to transform almost every corner of Libyan society. Riding on a wave of anti-imperialist anger, the new leader made his first priorities the closing of British and American military bases, the expansion of the Libyan armed forces, the exile or arrest of senior officers with connections to the monarchy and the closure of all newspapers, churches and political parties. In the mosques, Sanusi clerics were replaced by compliant religious scholars. Banks were nationalised and foreign oil companies were threatened with nationalisation. All assets in Libya belonging to Italians and non-resident Jews were expropriated and close to 30,000 Italian settlers were deported. The rounding-up of political opponents saw Libya gain the unenviable prize of having the highest prison population in the world per capita.

THE GREEN BOOK

Not content with leading the revolution, Colonel Muammar Qaddafi decided to become its philosopher king. In the mid-1970s he retreated into the desert for a period of reflection and writing, only to emerge clutching what he called the 'Third Universal Theory', spelled out in *The Green Book*. Between its covers was the blueprint for Qaddafi's vision of 'peoples' power', or what would later be called a Jamahiriya (see below for more details). Neither capitalist nor communist, the colonel's radical homespun philosophy modestly claimed that 'the problem of democracy in the world is finally solved.'

The Green Book, with its strong underpinning of nationalism and religion, dismantled at a stroke the Libyan state and replaced it with a system of popular democracy based on committees open to every adult Libyan. This 21,000-word tome offers guidance not only in the economic and political spheres, but also in the areas of sport, men and women, and the home and family. Sayings from *The Green Book* can be seen everywhere in Libya, such as: 'Partners not wage-workers', 'Committees everywhere' and the one that we've never quite worked out, 'In need freedom is latent'.

The Green Book has been translated into 84 languages (including Hebrew). Reports in the 1980s from London told of bookshops giving the books away after mass deliveries by the Libyan People's Bureau and you can still pick up your copy (5LD) in Fergiani's Bookshop (p74) in Tripoli.

For many young Libyans, however, Nasser's words upon visiting Benghazi in June 1970 were music to their ears: 'In leaving you, I say to you: My brother Muammar Qaddafi is the representative of Arab nationalism, of the Arab revolution, and of Arab unity.'

Also on the plus side, the RCC injected massive new funds into agriculture and long-overdue development programmes – the RCC spent 20 times more on development than its predecessor – and there was an accompanying rise in the standard of living of ordinary Libyans. Indeed, for all the faults and eccentricities of Libya's leader, spending on social programmes – and a commitment to gender equality (see p55) – would become enduring hallmarks of Colonel Qaddafi's Libya.

REVOLUTIONARY LIBYA

Many of the economic pronouncements contained in Colonel Qaddafi's *The Green Book* may later have fallen by the wayside – the 1977 self-sufficiency drive where every Libyan was ordered to raise chickens at home was not Libya's finest hour – but his political reforms endure. In 1976 the General People's Congress was created with the express aim of political participation by all Libyans rather than a representative system (which *The Green Book* called a 'falsification of democracy'). His dream of 'committees everywhere' quickly became a reality. A year later he renamed the country the Socialist People's Libyan Arab Jamahiriya (SPLAJ); formalised on 2 March 1977. 'Jamahiriya' has no direct translation but is generally taken to mean 'a state of the masses'.

A History of Modern Libya (by Dirk Vandewalle) is the most up-to-date history of 20th-century Libya and beyond; it's also authoritative, readable and filled with fascinating detail.

The revolution's secular reforms also involved walking a fine line between its revolutionary programme and placating conservative Islamic critics of the regime's liberal social policies, and assassination and coup attempts have been regular features of the Libyan political landscape from the mid-1970s. Colonel Qaddafi declared war on the militant Islamic opposition long before it became fashionable – Qaddafi would later become in the 1990s the first leader to issue an arrest warrant for Osama bin Laden.

As the *jamahiriya's* political and social revolution began to take hold, Revolutionary Committees fanned out across the country targeting real and imagined opponents. Officially set up as conduits for raising political consciousness, they quickly evolved into the sometimes self-appointed, always zealous guardians of the revolution and enforcers of revolutionary orthodoxy. Despite occupying no formal position within the Libyan government they wielded considerable power. By 1979, 100,000 Libyans had fled the country. Some were pursued by the revolutionary committees who carried out at least a dozen assassinations against Libyan exiles in Europe. Even Colonel Qaddafi would later criticise the excesses of the revolutionary committees and, in May 1988, acknowledged that 'they deviated, harmed, tortured' and 'the true revolutionary does not practise repression.'

Libyans now refer to the period from 1978 to 1988 as the dark decade. Political repression and sudden, unpredictable shifts in government policy became a daily fact of life for many Libyans, as did critical shortages arising from experimental economic policies (all private businesses were closed down). In a country where salaries had not risen in decades, Libya soon became the most expensive country to live in the world (for further details, see Economy, p46).

Libya's Qaddafi – The Politics of Contradiction (by Mansour O El-Kikhia; 1997) was written before Libya's recent rehabilitation, but remains one of the better measured but strongly voiced critiques of the Libyan leader.

AT WAR WITH THE WORLD

Libya's descent into international isolation began in 1981 when the USA severed diplomatic relations with Tripoli over Libya's alleged support for international terrorism. In 1984 revolutionary committees took over the Libyan People's Bureau in London. In April, with Libyan exiles protesting outside, a shot was fired from inside the embassy killing WPC Yvonne Fletcher. After a 10-day siege by the British authorities, the diplomats were allowed to return to Libya, but the British government followed the US lead and broke off diplomatic ties with Libya. Libya's status as a pariah state was confirmed.

In 1986 the USA blamed Libya for terrorist attacks on Rome and Vienna airports in December 1985, in which 20 people were killed; the assailants were reportedly travelling on Libyan passports and were praised by Colonel Qaddafi. The US Sixth Fleet began conducting military exercises off the Libyan coast with a number of skirmishes resulting and then-US President Ronald Reagan labelled the Libyan leader 'the most dangerous man in the world'. The spiral into conflict became inevitable.

Asked about democracy in 2004, Colonel Qaddafi replied 'Elections? What for? We have surpassed that stage you are presently in. All the people are in power now. Do you want them to regress and let somebody replace them?'

On 5 April a bomb went off in a Berlin nightclub frequented by US soldiers, killing two and injuring more than 200. Convinced of Libyan involvement, the USA, using aircraft based in the UK and aircraft carriers in the Mediterranean, fired missiles into Tripoli and Benghazi on 15 April. The targets were officially the Aziziyah barracks (Colonel Qaddafi's residence in Tripoli) and military installations, but residential areas were also hit. Up to 100 people were killed in Tripoli and around 30 in Benghazi. Two of Qaddafi's sons were injured and his adopted daughter, Hanna, was killed. The defiant Libyan leader renamed his country the Great SPLAJ.

Libya was also under siege on other fronts, with a debilitating war with neighbouring Chad. A 1935 protocol between France and Italy granted 111,370 sq km of modern Chadian territory, including the uranium-rich Aouzou Strip, to the Libyans, although all other treaties granted the area to Chad. Libya's support for armed opposition movements inside Chad also didn't help. The conflict saw in 1980 the Libyan army briefly occupy the Chadian capital, N'Djaména, before French intervention drove it north again. It was not until 1987 that the Libyan army was finally driven back across the border. At the end of the 1980s the Libyan government was under considerable pressure and took steps towards greater openness by releasing the majority of its political prisoners.

LOCKERBIE – CONSPIRACY OR JUSTICE?

The 2001 verdict in the Lockerbie trial – which was held in The Hague before Scottish judges who acquitted Ali Amin Khalifa Fhimah but found Abdel Basset Ali Ahmed al-Megrahi guilty – should have been the end of the matter. And in some ways it was – Al-Megrahi remains in a Scottish jail serving a 27-year sentence and Libya has paid compensation to the victims. But questions remain.

Professor Robert Black, the Scottish legal expert who devised the unusual trial, confessed to being 'absolutely astounded' at the outcome, which he claimed was based on a 'very weak, circumstantial case', which couldn't convict anyone, 'even a Libyan'. Even some of the grieving families of the victims expressed doubts over the verdict.

Syria was the original suspect. But when Syria supported the Allies in the Gulf War against Iraq, suspicion suddenly shifted to Libya. One of the most credible theories was that the bombing had been ordered by Iran in retaliation for the shooting down of an Iran Air airbus by a US warship in the Persian Gulf on 3 July 1988. The story goes that the bombing was carried out by members of the Palestinian Front for the Liberation of Palestine-General Command (PFLP-GC) who have sheltered in Syria since the bombing. Immediately after the crash US investigators also secreted away an unidentified body, which crash investigators were never allowed to see.

At the time of writing, the Scottish Criminal Cases Review Commission was considering new evidence in the case in order to decide whether an appeal can be lodged.

For the full text of the Lockerbie verdict and the unsuccessful 2002 appeal, go to www.scotcourts.gov.uk/library/lockerbie/index.asp.

But in November 1991 the US and UK governments accused two Libyans – Abdel Basset Ali Ahmed al-Megrahi and Ali Amin Khalifa Fhimah – of having carried out the 1988 bombing of Pan Am flight 103 over the Scottish town of Lockerbie that killed 270 people. Libya was also suspected of involvement in the 1989 bombing of a French UTA airliner over the Sahara in which 171 people were killed.

In January 1992 the UN Security Council ordered that the two men be extradited and the International Court of Justice rebuffed Libyan attempts to stop the move. The USA and UK rejected a Libyan offer to hand over the suspects for trial in a neutral country. UN sanctions came into effect on 15 April 1992, six years to the day after the US air strikes on Tripoli and Benghazi. Libya disappeared from view.

The seven years of economic sanctions are reported to have cost Libya US$30 billion in lost revenues and production, while the Libyan government claims that 21,000 Libyans died after the air embargo prevented them from leaving the country for medical treatment. Internal opposition to the colonel's rule simmered beneath the surface throughout the mid-1990s, especially in Cyrenaica. All the while, ordinary Libyans suffered and the world rebuffed repeated Libyan offers to hand over the Lockerbie suspects for trial in The Hague, an offer the UN would later accept.

A History of Modern Libya (by Dirk Vandewalle) is the most detailed, dispassionate and up-to-date history of modern Libya; it can be a little dry at times but it's unrivalled for its coverage of Libya's last 100 years.

THE NEW LIBYA

In 1997, with international support for the embargo waning, cracks began to appear in the façade of international unity. South African President Nelson Mandela flew into Libya in defiance of the ban and a number of African leaders followed suit. In early 1999 a deal was brokered, with the international community accepting the procedural proposals that Libya had effectively been making since 1992. The bombing suspects were then handed over and UN sanctions were immediately suspended, although unilateral US sanctions remained in place.

Western businessmen and European leaders made a beeline for Tripoli, keen to re-establish diplomatic and economic ties. In March

THE FATHER OF AFRICAN UNITY

A recurring theme throughout Colonel Qaddafi's rule has been his desire for unity with other states, all to no avail. Among those who have rebuffed his advances are Egypt and Syria (1969 and 1971), Egypt (1972), Tunisia (1974), Syria (1980), Chad (1981), Morocco (1984), Algeria (1986) and Sudan (1991).

By the late 1990s, the colonel, angered by the Arab states' unwillingness to support Libya during the seven years of UN sanctions, turned his attention to Africa. It worked. In 1999 the Libyan leader hosted the Conference of African Heads of State at a cost of some US$30 million. At the summit, Qaddafi unveiled his plans for a United States of Africa. In February 2001, 41 nations signed the Constitutive Act of African Union and 13 ratified it, thereby replacing the ineffectual Organisation of African Unity (OAU) and paving the way for a future Africa-wide federation similar to the European Union. Not surprisingly, Colonel Qaddafi has been revelling in the accolades ever since. It is the acclaim for which he has been searching for much of his life.

2001 a French court finally shelved all attempts to pursue Libya over the 1989 UTA bombing. Libya, for its part, expelled Abu Nidal, one of the most shadowy figures in the terrorist world from Libya.

Keen to build on Libya's renewed ties with the West, and himself no friend of Islamic fundamentalism, Colonel Qaddafi was quick to condemn the attacks on New York and Washington on 11 September 2001. He later described the American invasion of Afghanistan as a justified act of self-defence and the Taliban as 'godless promoters of political Islam'. He even began to quietly support a two-state solution between Israel and the Palestinian Territories. But it was behind the scenes that the most dramatic change was being quietly negotiated between Libya, the USA and UK.

On 19 December 2003 Colonel Qaddafi stunned the world by announcing that Libya would give up its nuclear, chemical and biological weapons programmes and open its sites to international inspections. When asked why, Colonel Qaddafi replied that 'the programme started at the very beginning of the revolution. The world was different then.' Sounding very much the international statesman, Colonel Qaddafi also said, 'there is never permanent animosity or permanent friendship. We all made mistakes, both sides. The most important thing is to rectify the mistakes.'

Accusations of Libyan involvement in an alleged plot to assassinate then-Crown Prince Abdullah of Saudi Arabia, and the international outcry over the trial of five Bulgarian nurses and a Palestinian doctor accused of deliberately infecting children with HIV in a Benghazi hospital (see p221 for more information), have ensured that Libya's road to rehabilitation remains a rocky one. In February 2005 Colonel Qaddafi warned that Libya had been disappointed by the response to its bridge-building: 'Libya and the whole world expected a positive response – not just words although they were nice words – from America and Europe. They promised but we haven't seen anything yet.'

But plans to overhaul Libya's creaking economy are underway, if progressing slowly and Shukri Ghanem's brief stint as prime minister (he was later moved to run the oil ministry) served as confirmation that a new generation of reform-minded technocrats was starting to seize the reins from the revolutionary old guard. Libya's ranking among international oil executives as the most exciting investment opportunity of the moment also bodes well for Libya's economic health.

When the US government in 2006 quietly removed Libya from its list of states sponsoring terrorism, Libya's rehabilitation was, it seems, complete.

The key Libyan negotiator with the UK when Libya gave up its WMDs was Musa Kousa who was expelled from Libya in the 1980s for threatening to kill Libyan dissidents in the UK.

Colonel Qaddafi told Italian TV in 2004,'It was Mr Bush who promised to reward Libya if we got rid of this programme. We know that with this withdrawal, we contributed by 50% to his electoral campaign.'

When asked in 2004 if he would one day succeed his father as leader of Libya, Seif al-Islam al-Qaddafi replied: 'This is not a permanent job, the leader, and when it disappears, it disappears. It is not inherited.'

The Culture

THE NATIONAL PSYCHE

In some ways, Libyans are everything that Colonel Qaddafi isn't – reserved, famed for their tolerance, and discreet. They are self-sufficient and wonderful improvisers, characteristics forged during the long years of sanctions. They are open to outsiders, as devoid of hostility to the West as they are hospitable. This latter trait is summed up by the Libyan saying: 'if you have a good heart, one spoon can feed 100 people.' Libyans are also deeply attached to their land, proud of it and even loathe to leave it – Libya is unlike other countries in North Africa where most people dream of a better life in Europe – especially at such an exciting time in their history. Libyans never forget where they came from, whether it be their home village or the dark years of isolation. Family is everything for the ordinary Libyan and they love nothing better to take to the road for a barbecue by the beach with extended family or to spend days celebrating the latest family event. Surprisingly knowledgeable about the world, they remain refreshingly untouched by it. You'll often hear Libyans say, 'we are a simple people', which is true only to the extent that the old ways of

RESPONSIBLE TRAVEL

As one traveller wrote to us, 'We found the people the most friendly we have yet encountered in North Africa! Totally untouched by the cynicism that mass tourism brings.' This is indeed true, but how long it remains that way depends a lot on how travellers behave while in Libya.

Just because Libyans live their life through an intricate web of social codes and taboos doesn't mean that they'll expect you to do the same. But if you hear a Libyan saying *'kull bilaad wa azaaha'* (every country has its own customs), chances are that they're not celebrating the world's diversity, but very politely suggesting that you're in danger of offending local sensibilities. Listen to them. Take their advice. Ask your guide if you're not sure. And remember a few simple rules:

- Dress for both men and women should be modest, particularly when swimming, when you should avoid ostentatious displays of flesh (see p229 for more information on how to dress). Remember that this is not Saudi Arabia, but nor is it Tunisia.
- Public displays of affection are usually tolerated, but can cause discomfort.
- Libya's human-rights situation has improved in recent decades, but many Libyans are still understandably reticent about participating in political discussions; so only initiate such conversations with people you know well and never do so in public.
- Always try to remember not to receive or pass items (especially food) with your left hand (although the taboos are less strict in Libya than other Arab countries).
- Bargaining or haggling is also not the done thing in most places and trying to do so with any aggression will earn you few friends (see p225 for more details).
- Where possible, don't refuse offers of food or drink (see also Dos & Don'ts, p70).
- Male travellers should never ask a Libyan man about female members of his family, unless you have already established a friendship.
- If you're invited to someone's home, taking a small gift from your country to present to the hosts will win you friends for life.

For advice on travelling in an environmentally responsible manner in desert regions, see Environmentally Piste-off, p214 and Responsible Desert Travel, p213.

TRIBES IN LIBYA

In traditional Libyan culture in prerevolutionary times, the tribes of Libya operated both as communities of support and de facto ministates. Each tribe's existence was inextricably tied to a homeland of farms, grazing land and wells over which the tribe exercised effective ownership. These strong ties to the land were the cause of intertribal disputes, with the identity of each tribe defined on the basis of both lineage and geography.

In Tripolitania and Cyrenaica, most tribes trace their origins to the Bani Hilal and Bani Salim (or Bani Sulaim). Tribes which trace their lineage to the Bani Salim are known as *saadi* (dominant tribes). In Cyrenaica, where tribal loyalties remain the strongest, the two main *saadi* are the Gerbana and the Harabi. Other tribes that fall outside this designation are known as Marabatin – most of these claim mixed Arab and Berber descent.

When the revolutionary government took power in September 1969, pan-Arab nationalism became the ruling ideology, and, officially at least, tribal loyalties came under suspicion, being seen as obstacles to modernisation and the forging of national identity.

decency and generosity survive. But above all, for the first time in decades, Libyans are optimistic, convinced that the future is theirs.

LIFESTYLE

Libya is one of the few countries in the region to have held fast to its traditions and although Libyans are a thoroughly modern people, their allegiances and primary sources of succour remain as they have for centuries.

In precolonial times, Libyan social organisation was layered with concentric circles of loyalty and community solidarity. The primary units of allegiance and belonging were the extended family, clan or tribe. These family-based units were the centre of most people's lives, including their social and economic activity, education and, in times of trouble, protection.

The typical traditional Libyan household consisted of a husband and wife, their single sons, married sons and unmarried daughters. Upon the death of the father, each son was expected to establish his own household.

Life for the ordinary Libyan still revolves around the family, a bond that took on added significance during the years of international isolation when Libyan society turned inwards in search of company and support. Grafted onto the immediate family are the same multiple layers of identity, among them extended family, tribe and village, with an overarching national component of which every Libyan is proud. The nuclear family was traditionally large with numerous children, although some, mainly urban, Libyans now opt for a more manageable Western-style number of offspring.

Libyan schoolchildren attend six years of primary school (starting at age six), followed by six years of secondary school, which includes some instruction in English. University education is free for all Libyan citizens.

Perhaps more than any other Arab country, the role of women also has many layers, with far-reaching laws safeguarding equality in this deeply traditional society. Libyan women nominally have equal status with men, from marriage and divorce laws to rights of equal pay in the workplace (for more information, see Women in Libya, p55). Social safety nets, such as free medical care and education, are also provided by the state to all Libyans. The reality is somewhat different from the theory, with men still the predominant players of public life and few women reaching the summit of any industry. Traditional elements also remain – when guests arrive at someone's home, the men and women eat separately and the majority of women wear traditional headscarves.

Although Italian culture never really penetrated Libyan social life to the extent of other European colonies in Africa, the arrival of the Italians did prompt some moves among the elites of Tripoli and Benghazi to mimic European-style dress and customs. This tendency remains in public life to a certain extent, but Libyans have proved adept at holding

A WEDDING IN TOUNEEN *Anthony Ham*

One of the singular advantages of travelling on your own in Libya is that your entry into Libyan society is so much easier. I've lost count of the number of meals I've eaten in private Libyan homes and, in November 2006, after watching a performance of traditional Ghadames dancing laid on for tourists, I was fortunate enough to be invited to a wedding celebration in the nearby village of Touneen (p176).

Although the lights in the distance illuminating the night suggested that the women of the village were themselves enjoying a celebration (the ceremony was not to take place until the following day), ours was an all-male affair. First we wove our way through the crowds in a large tent or marquee and greeted the groom with *'mabrouk'* (congratulations or happy wishes) while he sat looking somewhat overwhelmed by all the attention. We then joined the rest of the assembled gathering lounging on cushions, while tea and sweets were served amid the agreeable hum of voices and passing well-wishers.

After a time we adjourned to one of Touneen's covered squares where even more people sat and watched (or talked loudly) while children dressed in traditional costume danced to the accompaniment of local musicians. The children yielded to men dressed as women with their faces covered – tradition dictates that the veils of these dancing men can only be removed once the elders of the village have left the scene – swayed to the sound of the *gheeta* (an instrument similar to the clarinet; see p56) and drums. Through it all, a wild-eyed man, the life of this delightfully chaste and alcohol-free party, acted as a spur whenever energy levels flagged. Soon enough, the groom, looking decidedly more happy than he had an hour or so before, entered and took his seat at the centre of proceedings flanked by his two *wazir* (attendants). He, too, would soon be dancing and the party would last long into the night.

on to traditional ways at home while adopting foreign customs as the dictates of modern public life demand.

Men generally marry later than women (often not until they are 30 years old, which is attributable in part to the high cost of staging weddings), and arranged marriages still frequently take place between the children of male cousins, although an increasing number of Libyans are choosing their partners from beyond traditional kinship circles.

In addition to the compulsory two years of military service (university students receive exemptions), all Libyan men aged 18 to 55 must, in theory, complete one month's military service every year.

ECONOMY

From one of the poorest countries in the world at independence to the richest country in Africa in just 50 years, Libya's economic journey as an independent state has been remarkable. But Libya's potential is such that these figures are seen as a disappointment. The Libyan economy was, until recently, effectively stagnant for almost three decades, a fact as attributable to decades of idiosyncratic (and, it must be said, disastrous) economic policies as to the sanctions that crippled the Libyan economy. To give a sense of what might have been, Libyans remember how the Crown Prince of Dubai visited Libya in the early 1970s and marvelled at what he saw, openly hoping that Dubai may one day reach Libya's level. The rest, as they say, is history.

To help understand the depths to which Libya sank, the statistics speak for themselves. From 1983 to 1988 real GDP fell by over 40%. At the height of the UN sanctions the economy shrank by 7% in 1993, and then by the same figure the following year. The seven years of UN sanctions are estimated to have cost the Libyan economy US$30 billion.

With such an appalling legacy of economic mismanagement and misfortune, it's a testament to the resilience and ingenuity of the Libyan people that the UN should in 2005 place Libya above Brazil, Turkey and Russia across a range of quality-of-life indicators. And that there is much to look forward to is patently clear. Since 2004, the Libyan government has embraced, publicly at least, the need for economic reform, even giving it a revolutionary semantic twist – the new rush towards private ownership is, it seems, really an 'extension of popular ownership'. A team of eminent international economists has been drafted in to help facilitate the massive task of restructuring the economy. International oil and natural gas executives consistently rank Libya as the most exciting exploration opportunity in the world, especially given that Libya's high-quality light crude oil is much sought-after and just 25% of the country has been prospected.

But it's just as well that more oil is being found. Back in 1984, one analyst said 'Libya is more likely to collapse economically after the cessation of oil reserves than any other oil-endowed state in the Arab world.' The same remains true today and with oil accounting for 95% of Libyan exports, the task of diversifying is an urgent one. Libya's unemployment rate stands (by what is a conservative estimate) at 30% and 50% of Libyan workers (almost 900,000) are still employed by the government. In other words, the possibilities for economic success are almost as great as the work that needs to be done.

Libya's per capita income grew from US$25 a year at independence in 1951 to US$2216 in 1969 and US$10,000 a decade later. The figure now stands at approximately US$11,800.

POPULATION

With its vast territory inhabited by less than three people per square kilometre, Libya's population density is one of the lowest in the world. Over 86% of people live in urban centres (some put the figure closer to 90%), in stark contrast to Libya's pre-oil days, when less than 25% lived in cities. Libya also has an overwhelmingly youthful population, with almost one third under 15 years of age.

Libya's demographic mix is remarkably homogenous – 97% are of Arab or Berber origin (below), with many claiming mixed Arab and Berber ancestry due to intermarrying between the two communities. Some figures list the Berber community at 5% of the total population. Such uniformity dates back to the 11th century when the large-scale migration of the Bani Hilal and Bani Salim (see p32) ensured that the country became linguistically and culturally 'Arabised'. For this reason, the inhabitants of Cyrenaica have a reputation for being the most purely Arab society outside the Arabian Peninsula.

Other small but significant groups include the Tuareg (p48) and Toubou (p49), the seminomadic inhabitants of the Sahara.

Libya and the XXI Century, by none other than Seif al-Islam al-Qaddafi, is the man-of-the-moment's one-time university thesis and is fascinating for its insights into a post-Muammar world. It's available from Fergiani's Bookshop (p74) in Tripoli.

Berbers

Many Berbers claim to be the descendants of Libya's original inhabitants (descended from the Neolithic peoples who arrived in the area up to 17,000 years ago) and some historians believe this to be true. Other historians claim that the Berbers are descended from the remnants of the great Garamantian empire, which flourished in the Fezzan from around 900 BC to AD 500 (see p30). Otherwise, little is known about their origins. When Arab tribes swept across Libya in the 7th and 11th centuries, many Berbers retreated into the mountain and desert redoubts that they continue to occupy.

The name 'Berber' has been attributed to a collection of communities by outsiders, although, rarely until recently, by the Berbers themselves. The name is thought to derive from the Latin word 'barbari', the word used in Roman times to classify non-Latin speakers along the North African coast. The related name of Barbary was used to describe the region.

These days the key touchstones of Berber identity are language and culture. 'Berber' is used as a loose term for native speakers of the various

Historical Dictionary of the Berbers (by Hsain Ilahiane; 2006) is the most comprehensive study of the history and culture of the Berber people of North Africa, with a range of alphabetical entries and maps.

Berber dialects, most of which go by the name of Tamazight. In fact, many Berbers do not even use a word that unites them as a community, preferring instead to define themselves according to their tribe. These days, apart from some centres in Cyrenaica (especially Awjila; see p131), most Berbers are bilingual, speaking their native language and Arabic.

Imazighen in Libya (www.libyamazigh.org) is one of few resources on the Berber people of Libya and includes a history of the Berber people and an explanation of the Tamazight language.

Within the Berber community, loyalty is primarily to the family or tribe. Households are organised into nuclear family groups, while dwellings within a village or town are usually clustered in groups of related families. The majority are located in Tripolitania (primarily in the Jebel Nafusa, the Sahel al-Jefara and a few enclaves such as Zuara along the coast).

In keeping with their centuries-long resistance to foreign domination and to the imposition of religious orthodoxy, the majority of Berbers belong to the Kharijite sect (see p51). True to their religious beliefs, Berber communities have long prided themselves on their egalitarianism. The traditional Berber economy consists of farming and pastoralism, meaning that most people live sedentary lifestyles, while a small minority follow seminomadic patterns, taking flocks to seasonal pasturelands.

It is also worth noting that Berber leaders played a significant role in the battle for Libyan independence.

Tuareg

The Tuareg are a nomadic, camel-owning people who traditionally roamed across the Sahara from Mauritania to western Sudan. They are the bearers of a proud desert culture whose members stretch across international boundaries into Algeria, Niger, Mali, Burkina Faso and Mauritania. In Libya, this once-nomadic people are concentrated in the southwestern desert, particularly the oases around Ghadames, and Ghat and in the Jebel Acacus.

Art of Being Tuareg – Sahara Nomads in a Modern World (2006) is a stunning pictorial study of Tuareg life, with informative essays on Tuareg culture, including poetry, music and the role of women.

Their origins are not fully understood, although it is widely believed that the Tuareg were once Berbers. There is also some evidence to suggest that many of those who would become Tuareg began as Berbers in the oasis of Awjila (p131), in Cyrenaica, although Tuareg stories of their origin also suggest that many came from the region around Ghadames (p164). Such theories are supported by the marked similarities between many words in the Tuareg Tamashek and Berber Tamazight languages.

When the Arab armies of Islam forced many Berbers to retreat into the desert in the 7th century, and again when waves of Arab migration swept across the region in the 11th century (see p32), those who would become Tuareg fled deep into the desert where they have remained ever since. Until the early 20th century the Tuareg made a fiercely independent living by raiding sedentary settlements, participating in long-distance trade and exacting protection money from traders passing across their lands.

The Tuareg traditionally followed a rigid status system with nobles, blacksmiths and slaves all occupying strictly delineated hierarchical positions, although the importance of caste identity has diminished in recent years.

The veils *(taguelmoust)* that are the symbols of a Tuareg's identity – the use of indigo fabric, which stained the skin, has led them to be called the 'Blue People of the Sahara' – are both a source of protection against desert winds and sand, and a social requirement; it is considered improper for a Tuareg man to show his face to a man of higher status. Tuareg men traditionally rarely removed their shawl to expose the lower half of their faces in company and, when drinking tea, passed the glass under their *taguelmoust* so as not to reveal the mouth. Traditionally, Tuareg women were not veiled and enjoyed a considerable degree of independence.

ENCOUNTERS WITH THE TUAREG

Although many travellers will find Tuareg guides or drivers to be their entry point into the Tuareg world, there are a handful of Tuareg families who still live a traditional life across southwestern Libya. Apart from the Tuareg who continue to play an important role in the life of Ghadames, there were, at last count, 13 Tuareg families still living in the Jebel Acacus. Most live in semi-permanent shelters, although it's not uncommon to find young Tuareg girls or boys herding their goats in remote wadis or old Tuareg men similarly far from home.

If you do encounter the Tuareg in this manner, there are a few things to remember. The most important is that these families live in the Acacus because they choose to pursue a traditional lifestyle, not for the benefit of tourists. An increasingly exploitative relationship threatens that choice and Tuareg families are in danger of becoming a tourist sideshow as foreigners seek to meet an 'authentic' Tuareg family. It's a difficulty faced by indigenous peoples the world over and the most important things to remember are to treat them with the utmost respect and discretion. If you meet an elderly Tuareg man, address him as 'Sheikh' or 'Haj' as a mark of respect. The Tuareg are also a mine of information about the region and its history and spending time talking with them is far more important than sneaking a photo.

Although one old Tuareg man told us that he had never left the Acacus, there are already signs that the Tuareg have learned the ways of the world. Many Tuareg will only allow their photos to be taken if you pay money or buy something from them, while one old Tuareg man said that he allowed photos to be taken by those with a digital camera so that he could then see himself! To avoid it becoming a one-way encounter, consider making a small contribution to fuel or firewood stocks, or purchasing one of the small items they offer for sale.

Some Tuareg openly wonder whether this will be the last generation of their people who live a traditional life. As one old man told us, there were, until quite recently, many more families living in the region, but they moved to the cities after the patriarch of the family died. He suspected that his children were waiting for him to die before they, too, would abandon their ancestral home.

The name 'Tuareg' is a designation given to the community by outsiders and it's only recently that the Tuareg have called themselves by this name. The name is thought to be an adaptation of the Arabic word *tawarek*, which means 'abandoned by God'. The Tuareg themselves have always, until recently, preferred to be known as *Kel Tamashek* (speakers of the Tamashek language), *Kel Taguelmoust* (People of the Veil) or *Imashaghen* (the 'noble and the free').

The majority of Tuareg in Libya (said to number up to 50,000) have close relationships with their fellow Tuareg across the border in Algeria and Niger. In recent times, however, most have had to abandon their traditional way of life, primarily because of drought, and many have moved southwards to settle near cities.

The Tuareg (by Jeremy Keenan) is considered one of the best and most readable anthropological studies of the Algerian Tuareg with whom Libya's Tuareg people share many characteristics.

Toubou

Southeast Libya is home to another nomadic community – the Toubou, a Muslim people who were strongly influenced by the Sanusi Movement during the 19th century. Numbering as few as 2600 in Libya, this community has links with a larger population of Toubou across the border in Chad. Although they display considerable cultural and linguistic similarities, many Toubou speak related but mutually incomprehensible dialects of Tebu, which fosters a high level of independence for each community. Their basic social unit is the nuclear family, with each community divided into patrilineal clans.

Hugh Clapperton described the Toubou as 'few in number but extraordinarily diffuse, lacking political or social coherence – the principle of freedom raised almost to the level of anarchy.' If the Toubous have a definable home, it is the Tibesti (p206), which Clapperton again described as 'less a homeland than a centre of attraction'. They are viewed by other Libyans as a tough and solitary people and are concentrated around Murzuq. Their economy is a blend of pastoralism, farming and date cultivation.

SPORT

The Green Book describes sport as 'like praying, eating and the feeling of warmth and coolness'. Elsewhere, the colonel denounces spectator sports in which people watch rather than participate and instead prefers 'mass games', such as communal tug-of-war.

Football (soccer) is the number-one (and only significant) sport in Libya and although Italian football is followed with great passion here, Libyan football itself has distinguished itself more with grand gestures than any great success. The most obvious case of this is Colonel Qaddafi's son, Al-Sa'adi al-Qaddafi, who signed for Italian Serie A club Perugia amid much fanfare in 2003 and later largely disappeared from view.

Libya has also been a regular bidder for the right to host the African Nations Cup and even the World Cup with little success to date. Such bids did, however, lead to the highpoint of Libya's football history in 1982 when it hosted the African Nations Cup and made it through to the final stages, finally losing to Ghana on penalties.

Games (admission 3LD) take place in winter and you should check local newspapers or ask your tour company to find out the exact times and locations of matches. The country's two major stadiums are in: Tripoli, at the Sports City (Al-Medina ar-Riyaddiyat), about 5km southwest of the parliament building; and Benghazi, on the eastern side of the harbours.

MULTICULTURALISM

After decades of turning a blind eye to widespread illegal immigration from sub-Saharan Africa, Libya claimed in 2004 to have deported 40,000 illegal migrants in a single year.

Despite the apparent Arab-Berber homogeneity of Libyan society, the presence of large numbers (possibly hundreds of thousands) of undocumented migrants from sub-Saharan Africa adds a certain multicultural face to modern Libya. Although their presence sits uneasily with many Libyans, an Africa without borders has, until recently, been a cornerstone of Colonel Qaddafi's policy of a United States of Africa (see p43 for more information). Many immigrants see Libya as a staging post en route to Europe and end up working in menial jobs, marking time until they find the means to board a boat to Italy or Malta (a seat in such a boat can cost as much as €1000).

Libya's open-door policy has, however, been complicated in recent years by Libya's warming relationship with Europe and growing resentment among Libyans who point to their own high rates of unemployment. Since 2004 Libya has stepped up cooperation with European navy patrols. If you travel along the coastal highway close to Zuara after dark, expect more checkpoints than usual as police search for illegal immigrants.

Not all Black Africans in Libya are recent immigrants. The *harathin* (ploughers and cultivators) have lived in the oases of the Sahara for centuries and are thought to once have been the servants of Tuareg nobles.

MEDIA

As *The Green Book* says, 'Democracy means popular rule not popular expression' and Libya's authorities keep a strict hold over locally produced media. All newspapers, radio stations and TV channels are government-owned and most content either serves as an official mouthpiece or otherwise acquiesces the government line.

The government's power to control the flow of information to Libyans has, however, been compromised by the near-universal availability of satellite TV channels beamed into Libya from across the world. The Libyan government did attempt, for a time, to make satellite dishes illegal, but the sea-change was irreversible as the forest of satellite dishes atop the rooftops of every Libyan town attests. Libyans do keep an eye on local media as it's the medium of choice for many government announcements, but most Libyans keep their televisions permanently tuned to 24-hour Gulf-based news or Lebanese music channels.

RELIGION

More than 95% of Libya's population is Sunni Muslim. The country has small communities of Kharijites (an offshoot of orthodox Islam) and Christians (Roman Catholics, Coptic Orthodox and Anglicans), who number around 50,000.

The Last Jews of Libya (http://geoimages.berkeley.edu/libyajew/) is devoted to the history of Libya's Jewish community and has an online museum covering food and other cultural traditions.

Foundations of Islam

Islam shares its roots with the great monotheistic faiths that sprang from the unforgiving and harsh soil of the Middle East – Judaism and Christianity – but is considerably younger than both. Muslims believe in the angels who brought God's messages to humans, in the prophets who received these messages, in the books in which the prophets expressed these revelations and in the last day of judgement. The Quran (the holy book of Islam) mentions 28 prophets, 21 of whom are also mentioned in the Bible; Adam, Noah, Abraham, David, Jacob, Joseph, Job, Moses and Jesus are given particular honour, although the divinity of Jesus is strictly denied.

For Muslims, Islam is the apogee of the monotheistic faiths, from which it derives so much. Muslims traditionally attribute a place of great respect to Christians and Jews as Ahl al-Kitab (People of the Book), and it is usually considered to be preferable to be a Christian or Jew than an atheist. However, the more strident will claim Christianity was a new and improved version of the teachings of the Torah and that Islam was the next logical step and therefore 'superior'.

THE JEWS OF LIBYA

Libya was home to a thriving Jewish community from the 3rd century BC until the early 1970s, although from the beginning their position was frequently uncertain. Under the Romans their prosperity was dependent upon their continued submission to Roman rule. After Jewish revolts in AD 73 and AD 115 in Cyrenaica, the Roman response was brutal, with the leaders murdered and many wealthy Jews put to the sword (see p31).

Because of their status as Ahl al-Kitab (People of the Book; see above), the Jews of Libya coexisted peacefully with Muslims after the arrival of Islam in the 7th century. The community lived in relative security under successive Islamic dynasties until the 20th century when the rise of fascism in Europe and the creation of the State of Israel threatened their continued presence.

When the Italians first arrived in Libya in 1911, there were about 21,000 Jews in Libya, with the overwhelming majority living in Tripoli. Despite persecution by the Italian authorities, Jews made up more than one-quarter of Tripoli's population, according to some reports. When the Germans occupied the Jewish quarter of Benghazi in 1942, Jewish businesses were destroyed and many Jews were forcibly marched across the desert with great loss of life.

When the State of Israel was declared in 1948, as many as 30,000 of Libya's 35,000 Jews fled the country as recriminations rippled across the region, with more following after the 1967 Six Day War. Keen to showcase his pan-Arab credentials and his empathy for the Palestinians, Colonel Qaddafi cancelled all debts owed to Jews and sequestered Jewish property rights. In 1974 it was estimated that there were less than 100 Jews left in Libya and officially there are no Jews left in Libya today.

Monuments to the heritage of Libyan Jews are few and those that remain are in a derelict state. Two examples worth seeking out are former synagogues in Tripoli (p89) and Yefren (p159).

Mohammed, born into one of the trading families of the Arabian city of Mecca (in present-day Saudi Arabia) in 570, began to receive the revelations in 610 from the Archangel Gabriel and after a time began imparting the content of Allah's message to the Meccans. The revelations continued for the rest of Mohammed's life and they were written down in the Quran (from the Arabic word for 'recitation') in a series of suras (verses or chapters). To this day, not one dot of the Quran has been changed, making it, Muslims claim, the direct word of Allah. The essence of it was a call to submit to God's will ('islam' means submission).

Covering Islam (by Edward Said; 1981) is a searing study of how stereotypes have shaped Western views of Islam, Muslims and the Middle East. Although the examples used are dated, the book remains as relevant today as when it was written.

By Mohammed's time, religions such as Christianity and Judaism had become complicated by factions, sects and bureaucracies, to which Islam offered a simpler alternative. The new religion did away with hierarchical orders and complex rituals, and instead offered believers a direct relationship with God based only on their submission to God. (See also The Five Pillars of Islam, opposite, for more information.)

Not all Meccans were terribly taken with the idea. Mohammed gathered quite a following in his campaign against Meccan idolaters and his movement especially appealed to the poorer levels of society. The powerful families became increasingly outraged and, by 622, had made life sufficiently unpleasant for Mohammed and his followers to convince them of the need to flee to Medina, an oasis town some 300km to the north and now Islam's second-most holy city. This migration – the Hejira – marks the beginning of the Islamic calendar, year 1 AH (AD 622).

In Medina, Mohammed continued to preach and increase his supporter base. Soon he and his followers began to clash with the Meccans, possibly over trade routes. By 630 they had gained a sufficient following to return and take Mecca. In the two years until Mohammed's death, many of the surrounding tribes swore allegiance to him and the new faith.

Upon Mohammed's death in 632, the Arab tribes spread quickly across the Middle East with missionary zeal, quickly conquering what makes up modern-day Jordan, Syria, Iraq, Lebanon, Israel and the Palestinian Territories and, by 710, Andalucía in Spain was under Muslim rule.

Islam in Libya

Libya was conquered for Islam in 643. The initial conquests, which included the taking of Libya, were carried out under the caliphs, or Companions of Mohammed, of whom there were four. They in turn were followed by the Umayyad dynasty (661–750) in Damascus and then the Abbasid line (750–1258) in the newly built city of Baghdad (in modern Iraq). Given that these centres of Islamic power were so geographically removed from Libya, the religion of Islam may have taken a hold, but the political and administrative control which accompanied Islamic rule elsewhere was much more tenuous in Libya.

The Cambridge Illustrated History of the Islamic World (by Ira M Lapidus and Francis Robinson) is comprehensive, beautifully illustrated and contains references to Libya and the Kharijites.

The leading strands of Islamic thought nonetheless brought transformations to Libyan life, many of which survive to this day. The orthodox Sunnis divided into four schools *(madhab)* of Islamic law, each lending more or less importance to various aspects of religious doctrine. In Libya, the Maliki rite of Sunni Islam came to predominate and still does. Founded by Malik ibn As, an Islamic judge who lived in Medina from 715 to 795, it is based on the practice that prevailed in Medina in the 8th century. The generally tolerant Maliki school of Islamic thought preaches the primacy of the Quran (as opposed to later teachings). In

THE FIVE PILLARS OF ISLAM

To live a devout life and as an expression of their submission to Allah, a Muslim is expected to adhere to the Five Pillars of Islam.

Profession of Faith (Shahada)

This is the basic tenet of Islam: 'There is no God but Allah and Mohammed is his prophet' *(La illaha illa Allah Mohammed rasul Allah).* It is commonly heard as part of the call to prayer and at other events such as births and deaths.

Prayer (Sala)

Ideally, devout Muslims will pray five times a day when the muezzins call upon the faithful, usually at sunrise, noon, mid-afternoon, sunset and night. Although Muslims can pray anywhere (only the noon prayer on Friday should be conducted in the mosque), a strong sense of community makes joining together in a mosque preferable to elsewhere. The act of praying consists of a series of predefined ablutions and then movements of the body and recitals of prayers and passages of the Quran, all designed to express the believer's absolute humility and God's sovereignty.

Alms-giving (Zakat)

Alms-giving to the poor was, from the start, an essential part of Islamic social teaching and was later developed in some parts of the Muslim world into various forms of tax to redistribute funds to the needy. The moral obligation towards one's poorer neighbours continues to be emphasised at a personal level, and it is not unusual to find exhortations to give alms posted-up outside some mosques. Traditionally Muslims are expected to give one-fortieth of their annual income as alms to the poor.

Fasting (Sawm)

Ramadan, the ninth month of the Muslim calendar, commemorates the revelation of the Quran to Mohammed. In a demonstration of a renewal of faith, Muslims are asked to abstain from sex and from letting anything pass their lips from sunrise to sunset every day of the month (this includes smoking). For the dates when Ramadan commences over the coming years, see Islamic Holidays, p220.

Pilgrimage (Haj)

The pinnacle of a devout Muslim's life is the pilgrimage to the holy sites in and around Mecca. Every Muslim capable of affording it should perform the Haj to Mecca at least once in their lifetime. The reward is considerable – the forgiving of all past sins. Ideally, the pilgrim should go to Mecca in the last month of the lunar year and the returned pilgrim can be addressed as Haji, a term of great respect. In simpler villages at least, it is not uncommon to see the word Al-Haj and simple scenes painted on the walls of houses showing that its inhabitants have made the pilgrimage, while in Ghadames, the doors of homes are adorned with colourful leather studs to signify that the owner has made the pilgrimage (see p171).

this sense, orthodox Islam in modern Libya bears strong similarities to the teachings of the Sanusi sect, which ruled Libya for a number of centuries (see p35).

Libya also has a small population of Kharijites, a sect whose name literally means 'seceders' or 'those who emerge from impropriety'. Their doctrine that any Muslim could become caliph (they believed that only the first two caliphs were legitimate), which questioned the Arab monopoly over Muslim legitimacy, naturally appealed to the Berbers when Islam arrived in Libya.

THE MOSQUE

Embodying the Islamic faith, and representing its most predominant architectural feature, is the mosque (masjed or *jama'a*). The building was developed in the very early days of Islam and takes its form from the simple, private houses where believers would customarily gather for worship.

The house belonging to the Prophet Mohammed is said to have provided the prototype for the plan of the mosque. The original setting was an enclosed, oblong courtyard with huts (housing Mohammed's wives) along one wall and a rough portico providing shade. This plan developed with the courtyard becoming the *sahn*, the portico the arcaded *riwaqs* and the *haram* the prayer hall. The prayer hall is typically divided into a series of aisles; the centre aisle is wider than the rest and leads to a vaulted niche (mihrab) in the wall – the mihrab indicates the direction of Mecca, which Muslims must face when they pray.

Islam does not have priests as such. The closest equivalent is the mosque's imam, a man schooled in Islam and Islamic law. He often doubles as the muezzin, who calls the faithful to prayer from the tower of the minaret – except these days recorded cassettes and loudspeakers do away with the need for him to climb up there. At the main Friday noon prayers, the imam gives a *khutba* (sermon) from the *minbar* (a wooden pulpit that stands beside the often-beautiful mihrab); the Gurgi Mosque (p85) in Tripoli is a particularly fine example. (In older, grander mosques, these *minbars* are often beautifully decorated.)

Before entering the prayer hall and participating in the communal worship, Muslims must perform a ritual washing of their hands, forearms, face and neck. For this purpose, mosques have traditionally had a large ablutions fountain at the centre of the courtyard, often carved from marble and worn by centuries of use. These days, modern mosques just have rows of taps.

The mosque also serves as a kind of community centre, and often you'll find groups of children or adults receiving lessons (usually in the Quran), people in quiet prayer and others simply dozing – mosques provide wonderfully tranquil havens from the chaos of the street.

Visiting Mosques

With few exceptions, non-Muslims are welcome to visit Libyan mosques at any time other than during noon prayers on Friday. You must dress modestly. For men that means no shorts; for women that means no shorts, tight pants, shirts that aren't done up, or anything else that might be considered immodest. Shoes have to be removed. In Libya, women visitors are generally as free to enter mosques as men and often no headscarf is required. For information on visiting mosques in Tripoli's medina, see p85.

Islam: A Short History (by Karen Armstrong; 2006) is an accessible and sympathetic biography of the world's fastest-growing religion without the sensationalism.

Most Libyans today have an unshakeable belief in Islam, which they keep largely to themselves. Friday prayers at mosques are well-attended and your drivers or guides will often pull over to the side of the road to pray, but there's a discretion about the way most practise their faith that leaves the sense that it's a private matter between them and Allah. (See also The Mosque, above.)

The holy fasting month of Ramadan (see The Five Pillars of Islam, p53) is an exception as it is (and always has been) universally and very publicly observed. The occasion of breaking the fast at the conclusion of Ramadan (when the moon is sighted) is a time of great celebration. In the 1930s the Danish traveller Knud Holmboe described the scene in Tripoli:

> 'It ought to be tonight,' said a young Arab who stood next to me, as he scanned the sky eagerly. Hour after hour passed, and it was beginning to look as if Ramadan would have to be continued over the next day when suddenly the cry went up: 'El Ahmar, el Ahmar!' (The moon, the moon!) The festival began. The long month of fasting was over. All night they danced and ate to their heart's content in the Medina.
>
> *Knud Holmboe,* Desert Encounter

WOMEN IN LIBYA

Libya remains a deeply traditional society where public life remains dominated by men and the private realm is the domain of women. It is also true, however, that Libya has made more advances in women's rights than perhaps any other Arab country.

One of the more radical social changes introduced after the coup was in the role of Libyan women in society. In spite of the reforms of the 1960s, which gave women the vote, the role of women remained restricted to the private domain in what was still a deeply patriarchal society. As in many traditional societies, the honour of the family or tribe was vested in women – any perceived public dishonour, whether real or imagined, was avenged, with women having to pay the price for restoring honour.

Three months after coming to power, the revolutionary government granted women equal status with men under the law. In practice, one of the most significant reforms was in the laws governing marriage. The minimum age for marriage was set at 16 for women and 18 for men. Marriage by proxy was outlawed. In 1972 a law was passed decreeing that a woman could not be married against her will. Were a father to prohibit the wedding of a woman under 21 to a man of her choice, she had the right to petition the court. Divorce rights for women were also strengthened and women have since been granted the right to own and dispose of property independently of any male relatives. The principle of equal pay for equal work and qualifications has also been sanctioned under the law.

In addition to the legal changes, government policies since the early 1970s have encouraged women to seek employment or membership in what were long considered bastions of exclusively male activity. In the early 1980s Qaddafi founded what became known as the 'Nuns of the Revolution', a special police force attached to revolutionary committees and whose membership was drawn from female conscripts who attended military academies (see also Colonel Qaddafi's Female Bodyguards, below). Other fields of employment were also opened up to women and an increasing number of girls attended secondary schools.

In spite of these changes, restrictions upon women remained, with the government often unwilling to jeopardise the support of powerful traditional constituencies by granting women more rights. Despite an early plan by Colonel Qaddafi to outlaw polygamy, the practise of marrying more than one wife remains legal, although rare, in Libya.

Laws promoting gender equality have also not translated into the workforce with very few women rising to senior positions in business or government. In 2006 one Libyan woman interviewed by the BBC said that if Libyan women don't wear a headscarf 'people look at you as if you're doing something horribly wrong.' Libyan women also talk of having to choose between working outside the home and getting married as the two are not seen as compatible by many Libyan men.

Women at Arms – Is Ghadafi a Feminist? (by Maria Graeff-Wassink) answers the question you never thought to ask with a look at the Libyan government's policies towards women. It's available from Fergiani's Bookshop (p74) in Tripoli.

The Shadows of Ghadames (by Joelle Stolz; 2006) is a coming-of-age novel for young teenagers about a 12-year-old Ghadamsi girl confronting her path into adulthood in the sometimes intimate, sometimes claustrophobic Ghadames world.

Araboo (www.araboo.com/dir/libyan-women) has a range of links to Libyan women's issues, including everything from online chat forums to recipes and fashion.

COLONEL QADDAFI'S FEMALE BODYGUARDS

One of the most enduring images of Colonel Muammar Qaddafi's rule has been his phalanx of formidable female bodyguards dressed, not surprisingly, all in green (although recently they have switched to blue). Western reporters, keen for any opportunity to trivialise the eccentricities of Libya under Qaddafi, referred to them as the 'Amazon Women'. Libyans know them as the 'Revolutionary Nuns'. Whether or not they were intended for show, they represented a bold step for the Libyan leader, placing his personal security in the hands of women in a region where a combination of machismo and Islamic conservatism would normally preclude such a step.

ARTS
Literature

Libya has a strong literary tradition that has always been highly politicised, which may explain why very little has been translated into English or other languages. At first it was associated with resistance against the Italian occupation (Suleiman al-Baruni, Al-Usta Omar, Ahmed Qunaba and Alfagi Hassan) and later with the 1960s preoccupation with imperialism and the massive social change that Libya was experiencing (Khalifa Takbali and Yusuf al-Sharif).

Libyan Stories – Twelve Short Stories from Libya (edited by Ahmed Ibrahim al-Fagih) is outstanding, and is one of very few such collections available in English, with an excellent introduction to some of Libya's best-known writers.

The 1969 revolution brought about a sea change in Libyan writing. After literature had spent decades on the margins, the government-sponsored Union of Libyan Writers was founded by Ahmed Ibrahim al-Fagih and new publishing houses were established. A new relationship with the state transpired, moving writers from a position of rebellion to the chief advocates of the revolution, and the work of those who succeeded typically blurs the line between fiction and propaganda. With government sanction, writers became seen as among the primary intellectuals of Libyan society, with Mohammed az-Zawi of particular significance.

Libya's best-known writer throughout the Arab world is Ibrahim al-Kouni who was born in Ghadames and later served as chief of the Libyan People's Bureau in Warsaw. His works reveal a fascination with the desert and his evocation of the allure and fear of the Sahara will resonate with many travellers. Perhaps his most famous short story is *The Drumming Sands*, a tale of death in the desert near Ubari that is filled with a strong element of creeping menace. Of his novels, the only ones currently available in English are *The Bleeding of the Stone* (2002), a stirring ecological desert fable, and *Anubis: A Desert Novel,* a magical realist tale of the last days of Tuareg isolation in Wadi Methkandoush. Both novels are available in Fergiani's Bookshop (p73) in Tripoli.

Ismailia Eclipse: Poems (by Khaled Mattawa) is an important contribution to the Libyan literary landscape by the Benghazi-born poet, who left Libya at age 15 and now writes from exile.

A younger generation of Libyan writers has emerged in recent years, although none has yet made an appearance in English translation. Of the novelists, Khalifa Hussein Mustapha has come to prominence, while poetry is increasingly the preserve of voices such as Gillani Trebshan and Idris at-Tayeb. Libya's literary heritage is clearly dominated by men, but the voice of women is slowly coming to the fore in the short stories of Lutfiah Gabayli and the poetry of Mariam Salama and Khadija Bsikri. Bsikri's published collections of poetry include *Woman for all Possibilities* and *I Put My Hand on My Heart*. One of her poems, *Ghat*, transforms the faces of past invaders of Libya into those of Amazonian Libyan women.

Music
TRADITIONAL MUSIC

Traditional Libyan music is often performed in conjunction with ritualistic dances (p60) and has always played an important role in traditional celebrations, such as weddings and local festivals. Important musical instruments include the clarinet-like *gheeta* (in the northwest, especially Ghadames, and the south), the *nay* (a soft, emotion-laden flute) and the *zukra* (similar to bagpipes), in the south and west. In the east, the *zukra* is smaller and without the attached bag.

Musiques du Sahara (by Touareg de Fewet) is one of the few internationally available Libyan CDs and its mesmerising drums and repetition are as pure and raw as the Sahara itself.

One of the most famous music forms in Libya is the *mriskaawi,* which came from Murzuq and forms the basis for the lyrics of many Libyan songs. It has since been modernised and is played on the accordion at a party on the Wednesday night before a wedding, especially in northern Libya. During celebrations on the wedding night (Thursday), music known as *malouf* is played. Carried to Libya from Moors fleeing Anda-

MUAMMAR MIA

Confirmation that Colonel Muammar Qaddafi had become one of the cultural icons of the 20th century came in 2006 when a London theatre staged 'Gaddafi – The Opera'.

Set to the tune of the Asian Dub Foundation and staged by the English National Opera, this part-musical, part-operatic spectacular was perhaps the most unlikely performance ever staged by a leading European opera house. The performance included a rather raffish-looking colonel singing a duet with former US president Ronald Reagan at the UN General Assembly, or singing the praises of women's liberation while his legendary female bodyguards danced around him in fishnets and feather boas. The opera was an ambitious attempt to trace the story of 20th-century Libya and its most charismatic figure. At one point a reflective colonel says with his customary love of catch-phrases, 'Only in the desert is there true union between me and myself'.

Traditionalists in the audience were reportedly not amused at the colonel's storming of the barricades of high culture. The reaction of the man himself is not on record. A spokesperson for the producers told reporters on the eve of the show that 'He's aware of it, and interested, but he hasn't asked to see the text'.

lucía in the 15th century, *malouf* involves a large group of seated revellers singing, reciting poetry of a religious nature or about love; groups capable of performing *malouf* are highly sought-after.

Another form of traditional music is *'alaam,* which is often performed by two people. The first person makes a short heartfelt statement to which the other makes a similarly meaningful reply, and so it continues.

The Rough Guide to World Music – Africa & the Middle East (2006) is one of very few sources to discuss Libyan music at length with an overview of Libya's musical history and major performers.

TUAREG MUSIC

Although Libya's Tuareg have made few contributions to the phenomenon of desert blues music that has become a cause célèbre for world-music fans in 2005 and beyond, Libya does have a claim to fame in this regard. The celebrated Tuareg group Tinariwen hail from the remote Kidal region of northeastern Mali, but they spent much of the 1980s and 1990s in exile as famine and then rebellion raged in their homeland. Part of that exile was spent in military training camps funded by the Libyan government. It was there that the band members learned to play the guitar and much international success has followed.

MODERN MUSIC

The Libyan pop-music industry is generally drowned out by the noise of its Egyptian cousin across the border. You are far more likely to hear Libyans listening to music from elsewhere in the Maghreb (Tunisia,

LIBYA'S POP IDOL

Big Brother may not have taken off in the Arab world, but *Superstar* – think *Pop Idol* or the *Eurovision Song Contest* beamed out of Beirut – certainly has. This 21-week epic culminates with the final in August and is shown on the Lebanese satellite TV channel Future TV. Voted for by a region-wide TV audience, *Superstar* has rapidly become compulsory viewing across the region and especially in Libya. Undaunted by Muslim clerics' condemnation of the show as an un-Islamic pandering to Western culture, contestants quickly become national celebrities in their home countries – it's safe to say that when Ayman al-Aathar of Libya surprisingly won the 2004 competition, Tripoli had never seen anything like it with rock-star-like adulation showered upon the winner upon his return to the country. He was even granted an audience with Colonel Muammar Qaddafi who was not, incidentally, a fan of such frivolities. The flipside was, of course, that someone had to lose and when the Palestinian finalist failed to defeat Al-Aathar, there were street demonstrations in the Palestinian Territories.

Algeria or Morocco) or the late Egyptian diva Umm Kolthum than you are to come across home-grown talent. In fact, so popular is the music of Umm Kolthum that some reports suggest that the coup in 1969 was delayed by a day so as not to interrupt an Umm Kolthum concert in Benghazi.

Libyana (www.libyana.org) is an accessible site with a small range of links to the works of Libyan painters, poets (with English translations) and an online Libyan musical jukebox (in Arabic).

Libya's best-known singer of long standing is Mohammed Hassan, who has become something of a Libyan institution and is a native of Al-Khoms. His music carries all the heartfelt passion of Arab music elsewhere, but it's the subject matter, rather than the style, which marks him out as distinctively Libyan. His better-known songs include the love song *Laysh buta marsolik anni* (literally, 'Why is your messenger late?'), *Salaam aleik* (a cry of lament for a distant love) and *Adi meshan* (a rousing song lauding Colonel Qaddafi). Another male singer of note is Mohammed Sanini. Libya's best-loved female singer is Salmin al-Zarouq.

Architecture

Most of Libya's architecture has been shaped by the dictates of climate and geography. The ancient Berbers built structures that utilised the natural fortifications of the mountains they inhabited, while the peoples of the Sahara used building materials that protected them from the harsh desert climate. Libya also inherited a rich array of architectural gems left by the invading armies who occupied Libyan soil. The superb examples of Roman, Greek and Byzantine architecture are discussed at length throughout this book.

The most common building materials in Saharan architecture are animal dung, sun-dried clay and mud brick that contains straw and a high concentration of salt. Reinforcements (and doors) were usually made from the wood of palm trunks.

BERBER ARCHITECTURE

Stunning representations of indigenous Libyan architecture are the Berber *qasrs* (literally castles, but actually fortified granaries) of the Jebel Nafusa, see p160. There are other fine examples in Qasr al-Haj (p160), Kabaw (p162) and Nalut (p162), dating back as far as the 12th century.

The other highlights of Berber architecture are the underground houses *(dammous)* in Gharyan (p158), Yefren (p159), Zintan (p160) and elsewhere. Built to protect against fierce summers, cold winters and invading armies, a circular pit (up to three storeys deep and around 10m in diameter) was dug into the earth. The rooms were cut into the base of the walls around the sunken courtyard and they were reached via a tunnel that ran from the upper level (ie normal ground level) down through the earth to the base of the pit. The surprisingly spacious living quarters included living rooms, a kitchen, bedrooms and storage areas.

LIBYA'S TOP ARCHITECTURAL HIGHLIGHTS

Al-Kabir Mosque (Awjila; p132) An enchanted mud-brick world of beehive domes and innovative adaptations to the dictates of desert life.
Galleria De Bono (Tripoli; p87) The best of the dazzling white Italianate façades in downtown Tripoli.
Gurgi Mosque (Tripoli; p85) The pick of a very fine bunch in Tripoli's medina.
Masjed Jamal Abdel Nasser (Tripoli; p87) A towering temple of light and airy sandstone symmetry.
Mausoleum and Mosque of Sidi Abdusalam (Zliten; p118) Libya's most dazzling example of modern Islamic architecture.
Old City (Ghadames; p167) The best-preserved caravan town in the entire Sahara Desert.
Qasr al-Haj (p160) Fairytale Berber troglodyte *qasr* (fortified granary) with cave-like doors.
Medina (Ghat; p195) A crumbling mud-brick medina deep in the heart of the central Sahara.
Medina (Tripoli; p82) The Ottoman heart of Libya's cosmopolitan capital, with richly decorated mosques and whitewashed homes.
Underground houses (Gharyan; p158) A perfect Berber marriage of invention and necessity.

OUT WITH THE OLD

Soon after coming to power, Libya's revolutionary government decided that Libya was to be transformed into a modern nation. As part of this goal, entire communities were moved from Saharan oases into often custom-built accommodation, encouraged by free, modern housing with electricity, air-conditioning and integrated sewage systems. The most obvious examples are in Ghadames, Ghat, Murzuq and Gebraoun. Some of the aims of the programme were laudable and few could resist the lure of modern amenities. Officially the moves were to be voluntary, but reports of discontent among the communities of the Ubari Lakes suggest that not all went freely. Many would argue that the benefits of such a move outweigh the loss of traditional ways of life and that a romantic attachment to vernacular architecture is something only outsiders can benefit from. Yet, the characterless, modern houses to which the inhabitants moved and the subsequent rapid deterioration of the old towns suggest that a rich desert heritage is being lost.

SAHARAN ARCHITECTURE

The mud-brick dwellings of the Fezzan were well suited to the harsh demands of desert life. In Ghadames the ancient building methods are still sufficiently intact for some of the inhabitants to move from their new air-conditioned houses into the Old City (p167) during summer. Most of the medinas of the Sahara have been abandoned for modern housing (see Out With the Old, above) and are rapidly deteriorating. The decaying mud-brick structures can be quite evocative of the ancient caravan towns; the medina at Ghat (p195) is arguably the finest example.

In smaller settlements, many traditional flat-roofed Fezzani houses have been neglected to the point of dereliction as a result of the relocation of their residents. Part of the problem lies in the fact that many are roofed with palm beams and fronds, which in the absence of regular maintenance are liable to collapse on the rare occasions when it rains.

Architecture and Tourism in Italian Colonial Libya (by Brian McLaren; 2006) may read at times like an academic dissertation but it's a fascinating insight into the way that Libya's colonial rulers tried to shape Libya's architectural history.

ITALIAN ARCHITECTURE

One of the few legacies of Italian colonial occupation for which Libyans are grateful is the Italian Modernist architecture of the northern coast, especially in Tripoli. With a decidedly Mediterranean feel, many of the elegant whitewashed façades east of Tripoli's Green Sq (p87) and the Old Town Hall (p127) in Benghazi are splendid. Along the coast, particularly between Tripoli and Misrata and around Gharyan, you may also come across abandoned Italian churches and farmhouses.

ISLAMIC & OTTOMAN ARCHITECTURE

Most of Libya's mosques and madrassas date from the Ottoman era. They have typically narrow, pencil-thin minarets, sometimes octagonal in shape. The Ottoman mosques of the Tripoli medina, especially those of Ahmed Pasha Karamanli Mosque (p84), Draghut Mosque (p85) and Gurgi Mosque (p85), showcase Libya's finest collection of tile mosaics and woodcarvings. These mosques, built in the North African (Maghrebi) style, have superbly decorated small domes surrounding a larger dome above the prayer hall, which is often surrounded by closely packed pillars. There is also a strong Andalucían influence in many mosques evidenced by the use of elegant arches. (For more information on mosques see p54.)

Islam: Art & Architecture (edited by Markus Hattstein and Peter Delius) is a stunning reference work on the history of Islamic architecture with detailed sections on North Africa.

Modern Islamic architecture in Libya is not that much different from elsewhere in the Arab world, with extensive use of marble, sandstone, lavish tile work and cavernous prayer halls rising several stories high. The finest examples include the Mausoleum and Mosque of Sidi Abdusalam (p118) in Zliten, the New Mosque (p169) in Ghadames and the Masjed Jamal Abdel Nasser (p87) in Tripoli.

The oldest surviving examples of Islamic architecture in Libya are generally to be found in its desert regions. The unusual Al-Kabir Mosque and tombs of the followers of the Prophet Mohammed in Awjila (p132) sport conical, pyramidal domes not found elsewhere. The vernacular-style mosques of the Fezzan usually do not have a courtyard, and above the prayer hall rises a squat, almost triangular minaret built in the Sudanic style, sometimes with protruding wooden struts. The best examples are in Murzuq (p205) and Ghat (p195).

Libya Net (www.libyanet.com) has wide-ranging links (many in Arabic) to Libyan musicians, writers, poets and painters music, painting and literature.

See also p82 for extensive descriptions of the Ottoman residential architecture of Tripoli's medina.

Painting & Sculpture

Libyan painters are little-known outside Libya. Some of the more famous painters working at the moment include Ali al-Abani (from Tarhuna), who specialises in landscapes; Ali Zwaik (from Az-Zawiya), whose paintings are more abstract; and Ramadan Abu Ras (from Sabratha), who moves between abstracts and landscapes. Other fine artists, whose work can be seen on the internet, include Mohammed Zwawi (cartoons), Afaf al-Somali (a female painter specialising in watercolours), Taher al-Maghrabi, Ali Gana (oil paintings) and Bashir Hammoda (abstracts).

ROCK ART

The rock art that adorns the walls of desert massifs in the south of Libya is one of the undoubted highlights of any visit to Libya. Some of it dates back 12,000 years.

African Rock Art (by David Coulson & Alec Campbell) represents the definitive guide (in coffee-table format) to Saharan rock art with extensive sections on Libya and marvellous photography.

The two main types of rock art in the Libyan Sahara are paintings and carvings (also known as petroglyphs). The paintings were usually made by a brush made of feathers or animal hair, a spatula made of stick or bone, or the fingers of the artist. To ensure accurate proportions, the artists are believed to have painted the images in outline and then coloured them in. Most of the paintings in the Jebel Acacus are red, which was achieved through the use of a wet pigment thought to have been derived from ground-and-burned stone; the colour came from soft rock containing oxidised iron (hematite or ochre). A liquid binder was then applied, most often egg-white or milk, although urine, animal fat and blood were also used. It is to these binding agents that we owe the remarkable longevity of the paintings.

Trust for African Rock Art (www.africanrockart.org) has a links section that takes you to groups around the world dedicated to studying and preserving Africa's and Libya's prehistoric rock art.

The carvings or petroglyphs are concentrated in the Msak Settafet, especially Wadi Methkandoush (p204), although there are some examples in the Acacus (p198). The engravings were achieved through a method known as 'pecking', which involved the use of a heavy, sharp stone. A second stone was sometimes used to bang the sharp stone like a pick. Like the paintings, the outline was usually completed first, often by scratching. Upon completion, some of the lines were ground smooth and, on occasion, the rock face was smoothed first as a form of preparation. After metal was introduced to the Sahara around 3200 years ago (1200 BC), a metal spike may have been used.

For more information on the various historical periods of rock art, see p200.

Dance

Libya has a diversity of traditional dance, all of which is strongly influenced by Berber and Tuareg folklore. There are no organised dance troupes other than those which perform at private Libyan parties or weddings, or at festivals. You're most likely to come across these performances at the festivals in Ghadames, Ghat, Kabaw or Zuara (see p219 for dates), but the most enjoyable are when a traveller is invited to a local wedding celebration. For more information about the music at Tripolitanian weddings, see p56.

Ghadames is the best place to see re-enactments of traditional dances – see p173 for details.

If you do get invited to a wedding, dances to watch out for:

Az-Zlabin (Tripolitania) The groom circles a group of men and when one of them gives him money, the groom returns to the centre of the circle and publicly lauds the giver. Accompaniment is on the *zukra* (see p56).

Cuzca (Tripolitania) Dancers parade in circles of two lines, with each dancer holding a small piece of wood, which is tapped against those of other dancers in time to the music.

Kishk (Cyrenaica) This involves rhythmical, repetitive chants, which a group of men standing in a circle repeats after a designated leader. A woman, adorned with henna and a brocaded dress, dances around the circle in a series of increasingly small and mesmeric steps while the men, also in traditional costume, vie for her attention with large, open handclaps. She then chooses one to dance with her, a decision which is always greeted by great acclaim. Don't tell anyone, but we were there in Tobruk when Michael Palin was drawn into the circle and danced a mean *kishk* in 2001.

Majruda (Cyrenaica) Similar to the *kishk*, the *majruda* involves very small, fast, alternating handclaps.

In the oases of the south, most of the dances are either oasis or nomadic Tuareg in origin. One Tuareg dance that you may see in Ghat during its New Year festival (p197) involves seated women playing the *tende* (a drum made of skin stretched over a mortar) and singing ballads glorifying Tuareg figures, while men on their finest camels circle round the women.

In 1798 the German explorer Frederick Hornemann wrote, 'The women of Fezzan generally have a great fondness for dancing and every amusement...They dance publicly in the open places of the town, not only in the day time, but even after sunset.'

Environment

> Libya is full of wild beasts; while beyond the wild beast region there is a tract which is wholly sand, very scant of water, and utterly and entirely a desert.
>
> *Herodotus,* The Histories

THE LAND

Imagine Italy, Germany, France and Spain combined or two Egypts, but with the population of Denmark. Now imagine that territory as an ocean of sand and rock with small islands of fertility and towns. If you take these cognitive leaps, you have a pretty accurate picture of Libya.

Geographically speaking, Libya occupies one of the most extreme territories on earth. You like deserts? A mere 95% of Libya is covered by the Sahara of which 20% rises as sand dunes. You're a fan of the Mediterranean? Libya has an enviable 1770km of Mediterranean coastal frontage. Longing for a river or great stands of trees? Bad luck, because Libya has not a single permanent river and just 1% of Libya is forested. And if you were dreaming of that farm in Africa, look elsewhere because a pitiful 1% of Libyan territory can support any form of agriculture.

The highest temperature ever recorded on earth was at L'Aziziyah, 43km south of Tripoli, on 13 September 1922: 57.8°C.

Much of the country, which is the fourth-largest country in Africa (after Sudan, Algeria and the Democratic Republic of Congo), forms part of the great North African Plateau whose unrelenting plains stretch from the Atlantic Coast of Morocco and Mauritania to Egypt's Red Sea. Atop this plateau, Libya shares borders with six countries: Egypt, Sudan, Chad, Niger, Algeria and Tunisia.

Tripolitania (approximately 285,000 sq km) in the northwest of the country contains one of Libya's few pockets of fertility, the Sahel al-Jefara (Jefara Plain) along Tripoli's narrow strip of Mediterranean coast. The plain rises to the formerly volcanic hills of the Jebel Nafusa with an average elevation of 600m to 900m.

Geomorphology in Deserts (by Robert Cooke and Andrew Warren) may have been written in 1973, but it remains the definitive work on the Sahara's geography.

The hills give way to a series of east-west depressions that lead into the Fezzan (approximately 570,000 sq km) and into the Sahara. The most dominant features of the Libyan Sahara include *hamada* (plateaus of rock scoured by wind erosion), *sarir* (basins, formed by wadis, in which salt is deposited after evaporation), *idehan* (sand seas) and, in the south, basalt mountain ranges. Libya's highest point is Bikubiti (2285m), situated in the extreme south of the country, hard up against the border of Chad.

In Cyrenaica (about 905,000 sq km), the low-lying terrain of the Sahara is separated from Libya's northeastern coastline by the fertile Jebel al-Akhdar (Green Mountains), which drop steeply into the Mediterra-

CURIOSITIES OF THE LIBYAN DESERT

Al-Haruj al-Aswad (p185) An extinct volcano covering 45,000 sq km; its massive size derives from the fact that lava is believed to have flowed from the volcano like water, rather than shooting into the air.

Hamada al-Hamra (p177) An unrelenting void where people from the Jebel Nafusa go to search for truffles (really!).

Idehan Ubari (Ubari Sand Sea; p186) Every year six million tons of sand are added to this sand sea by the wind.

Waw al-Namus (p206) Another extinct volcano where the extent of the eruption is apparent in the black sand that extends from the crater's rim into the desert for miles around.

nean from a height of around 600m. In the far east, the terrain descends more gradually towards the Egyptian border.

Note that in the foregoing description we have used Libyan administrative boundaries, whereas the chapters in this book annexe large swathes of Cyrenaica (p124) and we've attached to it a chapter called Fezzan & the Sahara (for more information, see p178) – it just made more sense that way.

WILDLIFE

Animals

The prehistoric rock-paintings of the southern Sahara suggest that elephants, giraffes and rhinoceros once roamed the region. Even 2500 years ago elephants, lions, horned asses and bears were reported in Cyrenaica. Not surprisingly, none remains and Libya has few surviving mammal species.

Species which survive include gazelle and the painfully shy waddan, which is a large goatlike deer whose agility is perfectly suited to its steep mountain domain. The fennec fox is a gloriously adapted, largely nocturnal species with fur-soled feet to protect against scorching sands, comically large ears and it spends most of the hot daylight hours underground. The largest rodent in the Libyan Sahara is the gundi, which can stop breathing for up to a minute to hide itself from prey.

Libyan Mammals (by Ernst Hufnagle) can be exceptionally hard to track down and is in need of an update, but it has the only comprehensive coverage of Libya's wildlife in English.

Although there are numerous species of snake – a photo of a python that gorged itself on a baby goat near Gharyan was doing the rounds when we were there, while cobras have been sighted at Leptis Magna – and wolves in the Jebel Nafusa, and foxes in the Jebel al-Akhdar, most of Libya's remaining mammals call the desert home.

Your best chances of seeing desert species are in areas where there are few tourists and a long way from human settlements. The signature species of the Libyan Sahara – the waddan, gazelle and fennec fox – are all present in Jebel Arkno (p208) and Jebel al-Uweinat (p209) in the far southeast of the country, Wadi Meggedet (p193) in the far southwest, as well as Al-Haruj al-Aswad (p185) and the wadis of the Msak Settafet behind Wadi Methkandoush (p204). Gazelle, waddan and fennec fox are also present in the Jebel Acacus (p198), but they keep well-hidden during the peak tourist months, emerging into the open during daylight hours only in summer.

If you're not likely to see such creatures in the Libyan wild, Tripoli Zoo (p90) has some species, while the small private zoo at Fezzan Park (p181) has quite a comprehensive collection of desert species.

Sahara: A Natural History (by Marq de Villiers and Sheila Hirtle) is a lively biography of the desert with sections on the Sahara's climate, wildlife and human inhabitants and much more.

Lizards, snakes (the striped sand snake, the horned viper and the Saharan sand snake) and scorpions are also quite common; you are extremely unlikely to encounter snakes in winter.

Libya is on the migratory route of many species of bird, although most sightings are restricted to the coast. Birds that you may come across include the Lanner falcon, desert sparrow, Egyptian vultures (in Cyrenaica), shrikes, larks, crows, turtle doves and bulbul. The Houbara bustard is a particular favourite of Libyan and foreign hunters and is now considered highly endangered. We've seen it in both the Hamada al-Hamra (see p177) and Al-Haruj al-Aswad (p185).

Further south you may come across the occasional migratory bird species blown into the desert, while the sociable moula moula bird, with a black body and striking white face and tail, is a constant companion in the south; the Tuareg call it the messenger bird or the deliverer of happiness.

Plants

Along the coast of Libya, the usual array of Mediterranean flora thrives, with large areas given over to the cultivation of olives and citrus fruit. You may also come across eucalyptus, bougainvillea and oleander. Inland, the only vegetation is largely confined to the oases, where the date palm reigns supreme, along with figs, tamarisk and oleander trees. Outside the oases, Acacia arabica (acacia) provides the only shade in the middle of the desert wilderness. Alfalfa grass and salt bushes often appear as if by miracle after rains.

Recent radiocarbon dating suggests that the water currently stored beneath the Sahara has been there for between 14,000 and 38,000 years, with smaller deposits from 7000 years ago.

ENVIRONMENTAL ISSUES

With 95% of Libyan territory covered by desert, water is not surprisingly the major environmental issue. Some say that the last regular rainfalls in Libya ceased 8000 years ago and underground water reserves have been Libya's only reliable water sources ever since. By the 1970s Libya was facing an unprecedented crisis and some analysts believe that Libya, which relied solely on wells and a few token desalination plants, may have become the first country in the world to run out of water. Colonel Qaddafi's solution was to tap the vast underground basins with sandstone shelves that lie beneath the Sahara, which have been filled with water since the time when the Sahara was a green and fertile land of abundant rains, and pipe it to Libya's thirsty coastal cities. For more information, including the controversies raging about the project, see The Eighth Wonder of the World, below.

By the time the Great Man-Made River is completed, over 4000km of prestressed concrete pipes, each up to 4m in diameter, will criss-cross the country with a daily capacity of 6 million cu metres.

Libya also depends completely on fossil fuels for its power needs, although it is estimated to be responsible for just 0.2% of world carbon emissions.

There's always talk of new tourist developments being powered by solar energy, something that already happens with some military checkpoints. Wind farms, built in conjunction with a German engineering company,

THE EIGHTH WONDER OF THE WORLD

The Great Man-Made River (GMR; Al-Nahr Sinai), is one of the most ambitious development projects attempted anywhere in the world. Never one to hide his light under a bushel, Colonel Muammar Qaddafi described his pet project as the 'Eighth Wonder of the World'.

The project is breathtaking, both in its conception and the scale of its ambition. The early stages extracted water from the Tazerbo and Sarir Basins (which have a storage capacity of 10,000 cu km) and piped it to Benghazi and Sirt, while the Murzuq Basin (over 450,000 sq km in size, with a storage capacity of 4800 cu km) now supplies the Sahel al-Jefara of Tripolitania and Tripoli with 2.5 million cu metres a day. Tripoli received its first supplies of GMR water in September 1996amid much fanfare. Later stages bring the massive Al-Kufra Basin (capacity of 20,000 cu km) into play, extending coverage to Tobruk, while other underground basins near Ghadames and Al-Jaghbub are also slated for exploitation.

Depending on your perspective, the GMR is either visionary or grossly irresponsible. No-one yet knows the environmental side-effects on water tables in agricultural areas or the oases of the Sahara. There are also concerns that the amount of money spent on the first stage of the project alone could have been used to fund five desalination plants. Neighbouring Sudan and Egypt have weighed in, concerned over the threat to their own underground water supplies. And it's possible that the underground water supplies may be exhausted in 50 years, an event eerily reminiscent of the time when the Garamantes empire, having exhausted their water supplies, came to an end (p30).

For all the criticism, Libyans are almost universally supportive of the GMR; as one told us, 'We had no other choice'.

TRAVEL WIDELY, TREAD LIGHTLY, GIVE SUSTAINABLY – THE LONELY PLANET FOUNDATION

The Lonely Planet Foundation proudly supports nimble nonprofit institutions working for change in the world. Each year the foundation donates 5% of Lonely Planet company profits to projects selected by staff and authors. Our partners range from Kabissa, which provides small nonprofits across Africa with access to technology, to the Foundation for Developing Cambodian Orphans, which supports girls at risk of falling victim to sex traffickers.

Our nonprofit partners are linked by a grass-roots approach to the areas of health, education or sustainable tourism. Many – such as Louis Sarno who works with BaAka (Pygmy) children in the forested areas of Central African Republic – choose to focus on women and children as one of the most effective ways to support the whole community. Louis is determined to give options to children who are discriminated against by the majority Bantu population.

Sometimes foundation assistance is as simple as restoring a local ruin, such as the Minaret of Jam in Afghanistan; this incredible monument now draws intrepid tourists to the area and its restoration has greatly improved options for local people.

Just as travel is often about learning to see with new eyes, so many of the groups we work with aim to change the way people see themselves and the future for their children and communities.

are also planned in northeastern Libya. However, such fledgling measures don't yet even come close to redressing Libya's energy imbalance.

Another major environmental problem for Libya is rubbish – lots of it. The fields littered with black plastic bags on the outskirts of most towns can somewhat diminish Libya's aesthetic appeal for many visitors. Our vote for the worst outskirts of any Libyan town is for those surrounding Ajdabiya (p131).

For advice on minimising your impact upon the environment when travelling in the Libyan Sahara, see Camel Safaris & 4WD Expeditions (p214) and Responsible Desert Travel (p213).

Food & Drink

As you contemplate your thirteenth plate of chicken *(djeaj)* with couscous or rice with chicken, contemplate this: Libya has some of the best food you'll never eat.

In Libya you'll eat well and you'll rarely leave a restaurant hungry. Libyan restaurants are getting better all the time and most are excellent, sometimes filled with character and with friendly service guaranteed to make you feel at home. Servings are also generous. It's just that there's little on offer that will live long in the memory, as Libyan restaurant food bears only a passing resemblance to what Libyans themselves eat. Libyan home-cooking is varied, tasty and deserves international recognition as one of the more interesting cuisines of North Africa. But such recognition will never come until more than a handful of people in the Libyan restaurant business understand that sampling creative local cuisine is one of the joys of travel.

Libyan Cuisine and Recipes (http://ourworld.compuserve.com/homepages/dr_ibrahim_ighneiwa/food.htm) has little commentary but its 59 recipes (in English) are easy to follow and range from couscous or rice to pastries.

STAPLES & SPECIALITIES

Eating Libyan-style usually involves a banquet that begins with soup (the standard Libyan soup is a spiced minestrone broth with lamb and pasta) and then moves on to a simple salad of tomato, onion and lettuce. Bread *(khobz)* is often somewhere in the vicinity as an accompaniment, although it's more often Western-style, rather than flat, Arab-style bread. Up until this point, Libyan restaurants are true to their Libyan roots.

Libyan restaurants catering to tourists, however, usually skip the enticing range of entrées that accompany the salad – dips such as hummus (chickpea) or *baba ghanooj* (eggplant), stuffed peppers, rice-filled vine leaves, deep-fried cauliflower, to name just a few – and head straight for the main dish.

The main course usually revolves around rice (in Cyrenaica) or couscous (in Tripolitania and Fezzan), served with a sauce containing chicken, meat or fish and a few token vegetables. For a little variety, there may be macaroni-based dishes inspired by the Italians; the subtly different Libyan version goes by a number of names, including *mbakbaké*. *Tajeen,* a lightly spiced lamb dish with a tomato and paprika-based sauce, would be an unimaginable treat. Throw in a soft drink and tea or coffee and you've had yourself a fine, if unexciting meal…again.

Al-Bab (www.al-bab.com/arab/food.htm) has extensive links to the food of the Arab world with three recipe-dominated sites for Libya.

While it's true that Libyans do eat a lot of rice or couscous, they eat so much more. A small handful of restaurants do serve local specialities (see Libya's Top Five, p69), but few of them seem to be on most tourists' itineraries – something to definitely talk to your tour company about. The best local specialities, in addition to *osban* (see Travel Your Tastebuds, opposite) that can be tracked down:

algarra Lamb or seafood cooked in a high-temperature oven in a pottery amphora with mint, basil, tomato and green peppers; the amphora is brought to your table and then broken open with a hammer. You can find it at Athar Restaurant (p93) in Tripoli's medina.

bourdim Meat slow-cooked in a sand pit; try this at Mat'am al-Najar (p109) or Mat'am al-Khayma (p109), both near Al-Khoms.

fitaat Lentils, mutton and buckwheat pancakes cooked together in a tasty sauce in a low oven and eaten with the hands from a communal bowl. *Fittat* is served in some of the old houses of Ghadames (see p174).

rishda This delicately spiced vermicelli-style noodles with chickpeas, tomatoes and caramelised onions can be tried at Mat'am al-Bourai (p93) in Tripoli.

TRAVEL YOUR TASTEBUDS

as-sida – flour, boiled with salt, and eaten with olive oil and date juice or jam; it's often reserved for special occasions (see p68)

bseesa – bread made from seeds crushed to a flour-like consistency and mixed with oil and eaten for breakfast or with tea (western Libya)

osban – a sheep's stomach cleaned out and filled with rice, herbs, liver, kidney and other meats, and steamed or boiled in a sauce; eat this at Mat'am al-Bourai (p93) in Tripoli's medina

zumeita – dish of heated barley in water and oil

We dare you...

Libyan's eat most parts of the sheep as should be clear if you've eaten *osban*, but that extends even to the sheep's head. You'll find *osban* on a few restaurant menus, such as at Haj Hmad Restaurant (p94) in Tripoli, and in some roadside stalls, especially in Cyrenaica. Please note, the piles of food wrapped in aluminium foil aren't baked potatoes.

Two dishes among the many that you might eat if you're lucky enough to eat at home with a Libyan family, but which you're unlikely to ever find on a restaurant menu:

bazin Unleavened bread made from barley and flour but without sugar and cooked into a dough-like consistency. A staple of Tripolitanian families, it's eaten with the hands from a communal bowl with plenty of sauce. It's often followed by fish – a speciality of Zuara. Libyans dream of this dish and having eaten it twice, we're already dreaming of our next one.

matruda Thick, oven-baked bread chopped into small pieces and then, while still warm, added to milk, dates and finally honey and a home-made butter called *samel*. A delicacy of the Jebel al-Akhdar, we ate this around a campfire on a beach near Al-Bayda and can guarantee that it's a delicious way to warm the heart in winter.

Libya has used the water from the Great Man-Made River (see p64) to irrigate vast agricultural projects in desert areas, such as Al-Kufra. Many of these projects are now viable, but at the beginning this extremely expensive undertaking meant Libyan wheat cost 20 times the world market price.

One final food worthy of special mention is Tuareg bread, *taajeelah* (also known as sand or desert bread in English or *khobzet al-milla* in Arabic), which is a travellers' favourite during desert expeditions. The bread is prepared from flour, water and a little salt. After the fire has been burning for some time, it's cleared away; the dough is laid on the hot sand, covered, then cooked beneath the sand for 15 minutes, uncovered, turned over, covered again and cooked for a further 15 minutes. It makes a meal on its own but is at its best when still warm, accompanied by a stew or sauce and then eaten in the middle of nowhere under a canopy of stars. *Don't,* under any circumstances, let the cook wash it 'for the tourists' – soggy Tuareg bread is as unappealing as it sounds and a little bit of sand ('desert spice' as the Tuareg like to say) never hurt anyone.

And any discussion of Libyan cuisine wouldn't be complete without paying homage to the Libyan love of sweets *(helawiyat)*. Patisseries line the main streets of most towns and while there's not much that's discernibly local in inspiration, pastries dripping with sugar, almonds and/or honey are enough to make most Libyan eyes light up.

In 390 BC Cyrene saved Greece from famine with a massive export of grain. The Roman cities of Sabratha and Leptis Magna once supplied Rome with olive oil and in the 1st century AD Leptis paid an annual tax of up to three million litres of olive oil.

DRINKS

There's not a lot of choice when it comes to beverages. Soft drink and, to a lesser extent, bottled water are available in even the smallest towns. One drink that breaks the monotony in some Tripoli restaurants is the *masabiyah jamaica,* a cocktail of 7-Up, Mirinda and Coke. Libyan tea is very strong and is sometimes served with mint *(shay na'ana)* or peanuts. Coffee-drinkers can choose between instant *(nescafé)* or the thick Arab coffee *(qahwa)*, in which you could stand your spoon without fear of it falling.

Alcohol is illegal in Libya, although in trusted company you may be offered *bokha,* a potent home-brew that could start your car; it's also known as 'Libyan tequila'. The most widely available nonalcoholic beer is Becks (1LD to 2LD), but you'll also find Crown, a malty brew from Morocco.

CELEBRATIONS

Weddings usually take place in summer because guest lists often run into the hundreds (and last for days) and outdoor areas are often the only spaces capable of accommodating the crowds. Some Libyans lament the fact that weddings these days last only for three days, rather than the original seven! Food, music (p56) and traditional dances (p60) are the centrepieces of any Libyan wedding celebration with vast quantities of food consumed. The contents of such a wedding banquet depend on where the wedding is being held with almost as many varieties as there are regions of Libya. Grilled meats, sweet pastries and gallons of tea are among the regular features. For a first-hand account of wedding celebrations, see A Wedding in Touneen, p46.

Weddings in Tripolitania (by Abdelkafi) provides an interesting overview of how wedding traditions differ throughout Tripolitania, from the coast to the Jebel Nafusa; it's available from Fergiani's Bookshop (p74) in Tripoli or at www.darfpublishers.co.uk.

Other celebrations revolve around important dates in the Islamic calendar (see p220). In addition to music, large public gatherings and often fireworks, at such times many Libyans hold a special meal of *as-sida* (p67) to commemorate the Prophet Mohammed's Birthday. This dish is also eaten in Tripolitania to celebrate the birth of a child.

Libyans also regard the weekly Friday holiday as a reason to celebrate. Roads and roadsides are crammed with large family groups heading out into the countryside or to the beach for a picnic. They're usually well-equipped expeditions, and end up with a barbecue of grilled meats, fish or seafood.

WHERE TO EAT & DRINK

In Tripoli and Benghazi, the range of restaurants is seemingly endless. Tripoli in particular has everything from small, cheap restaurants offering hamburgers, pizza slices or *shwarma* (meat sliced off a spit and stuffed in a pocket of pita-type bread with chopped tomatoes) to higher-quality sit-down restaurants where you'll be served three-course banquet-style meals. The latter is where you'll spend most of your time while in Libya. One thing you won't find a lot of is restaurants serving international flavours, which is why you'll be thankful for the Turkish restaurants of Benghazi where the cheese bread is divine. Apart from anything else, these Turkish restaurants just add a little variety to your standard Libyan tourist meal.

Libya is the 9th-largest producer of dates in the world, and Tripoli hosted the first-ever International Date Conference in 1959. Some of the most popular Libyan varieties come from Houn in the Al-Jufra oasis, including *halima* and *magmagat ayoub,* or from Zliten *(tarbuni).*

Once you get beyond Tripoli and Benghazi, you'll be lucky to find a tourist-standard restaurant or good hotel restaurant. Sebha, Ghadames, Leptis Magna, Sirt, Tobruk, Derna and Nalut all have at least one good restaurant, while elsewhere Germa and Yefren each promise a hotel that serves good food. Otherwise, it will be chicken and rice or couscous all the way, in whatever cheap roadside restaurant you can find.

All hotels include breakfast as part of the room price. Breakfast here generally consists of a buffet with various types of bread or pastry, olives, orange juice, coffee or tea and sometimes cereal.

Coffeehouses are a Libyan institution that serve an important (if predominantly male) social purpose as well as providing a substitute for any other form of evening entertainment. Most Libyan villages, towns and cities have at least one coffeehouse, usually with outdoor tables, where men or, on Friday nights, families gather to drink tea or coffee, smoke the nargileh, catch up on the latest news and otherwise pass the time.

LIBYA'S TOP FIVE

Traditional Houses (Ghadames; p175) Sit amid the splendour of a traditional Ghadames house and eat *fitaat* (p66) from the communal bowl.
Mat'am Obaya (Tripoli; p93) Delicious home-cooking with stuffed calamari, octopus salad and fish couscous like none you've ever eaten.
Fish market (Tripoli; p95) Choose the freshest fish and seafood and wait while they cook it for you; it's always packed with locals at night.
Mat'am al-Bourai (Tripoli; p93) One of the few Tripoli restaurants catering primarily to locals; the décor's basic but the *rishda* (p66) and *osban* (p67) are just like Mama used to make.
Al-Khoms region (Mat'am al-Najar, p109, or Mat'am al-Khayma, p109) Enjoy as much *bourdim* (p66) as you can handle at these roadside restaurants, which are favourites of Libyan travellers.

Quick Eats

In addition to the sit-down meals that are the traveller's staple, there are also cheap restaurants in every town that can make chicken *shwarma*, pizza, hamburger or sandwiches; if you don't like liver, ask for *bidoon kibdeh* (without liver). Often you'll be asked if you want *harisa* – it's a spicy tomato paste. In Cyrenaica, *ta'amiyya* (the Egyptian variety of felafel) is also possible. One 'Libyan' variation of fast food is 'Kentucky' (spelled in as many ways as there are restaurants) – fried chicken, often served with French fries – which is found in almost every town in Libya. Generally hygiene standards are reasonable and street food such as this is perfectly safe to eat. That said, the situation seems to be more patchy in the east, especially in Ajdabiya and Al-Kufra.

Food in the Ancient World (by Shaun Hill and John Wilkins) is for those who always wondered what the ancient Romans or Greeks ate atop the mosaics in the pleasure domes of Leptis Magna or Cyrene.

VEGETARIANS & VEGANS

Like in most Middle Eastern and North African countries, vegetarianism is something of an alien concept for Libyans. Vegetarians should always specify their requirements as soon as they arrive in the restaurant (ask for *bidoon laham,* without meat) and tour companies should also be told in advance (to help with planning). Although most restaurants are obliging and keen to make sure you don't leave hungry, many won't be able to offer more than bread, salad, French fries, plain rice and perhaps an omelette. Many soups are precooked and include meat as a matter of course; often no substitute is available.

EATING WITH KIDS

When Libyans eat out they usually do so as a family; as such waiters are uniformly accepting of children and will usually go out of their way to make them feel welcome (offerings of fried potato chips being a tried-and-true method), although don't expect high chairs. A handful of restaurants in Tripoli and elsewhere have a special children's menu (eg main meals and a drink cost usually 6LD to 8LD). Otherwise Libyan food is rarely spicy and is generally child-friendly.

For general advice on travelling with children, see p215.

Major crops grown in Libya include olives, dates, wheat, barley, citrus fruits, vegetables, peanuts and soybeans. The major agricultural areas are the Sahel al-Jefara (Jefara Plain; Tripolitania) and the Jebel al-Akhdar (Cyrenaica). Libya imports 75% of its food needs.

HABITS & CUSTOMS

In most restaurants, etiquette is identical to what you'd find back home. Eating a meal in a private home or with Libyan friends is, apart from being a great way to cement new-found friendships, quite different.

When at home, Libyans usually spread out a plastic tablecloth atop a carpet on the floor and eat together with their hands from a communal bowl. Prior to eating, the host will usually bring a jug of water, soap and

DOS & DON'TS

- Never take or pass food using your left hand, which is traditionally used for ablutions. In practice, Libyans are forgiving of tourists who forget this rule, but you should always try to use the right hand.
- If you arrive at a private gathering while people are eating, it is customary to sit apart and wait until everyone has finished before shaking hands.
- If drinking tea with the Tuareg, it is traditionally considered polite to accept the first three rounds of tea which are offered.

a small plastic receptacle and will then proceed to pour so that each guest can wash their hands. At home, Libyan families eat together, but when guests arrive, men and women usually eat separately; Western women are generally considered honorary men and in such circumstances the traditional rules of segregation probably don't apply. As the meal commences, many say *'bismillah'* (a form of asking Allah to bless the meal). During the meal, the best morsels of meat will be gently pushed in the direction of an honoured guest. When sated, Libyans will say *'al-hamdu lillah'* (thanks be to God) whereupon other diners will encourage the person to eat more; if the person truly has finished, someone will say *'Saha, Saha'*, meaning 'good health'.

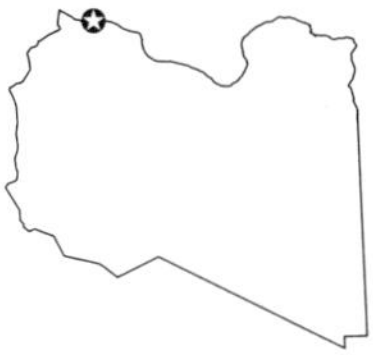

Tripoli طرابلس

Sophisticated and strongly traditional, Libya's capital (Tarablus in Arabic) is its most alluring city. Tripoli – which once went by the historical sobriquet of the 'White Bride of the Mediterranean' and has more recently been called 'the Havana of North Africa' – is rich in historical influences and brilliantly captures that irresistible fusion of languid Mediterranean charm and clamorous Arab medina. More than anything else, this friendly city is the ideal place to catch the buzz of optimism that characterises the new Libya.

The disparate civilisations that have occupied this stretch of coast all left their mark. The Roman Arch of Marcus Aurelius tells just how many centuries the world's powers have coveted one of North Africa's best natural harbours. The Turkish mosques of the medina speak of Tripoli's historically deep connections to the wider Islamic world; the medina itself is a labyrinth of meandering souqs (markets) and stunning public buildings. The decaying Italianate façades of the city centre offer a reminder of an outside world that's never quite been able to leave Libya alone.

The Tripoli that you now see is a boom town, revelling in its oil wealth and Libya's burgeoning friendship with the West. Yet, with its face to the sea and its back to the Sahara Desert, Tripoli has always been a meeting place of travellers and a crossroads city whose fortunes ebbed and flowed with the political and economic currents of the day. The overall effect is a cosmopolitan, modern city overlaid with the fascinating signposts of history.

HIGHLIGHTS

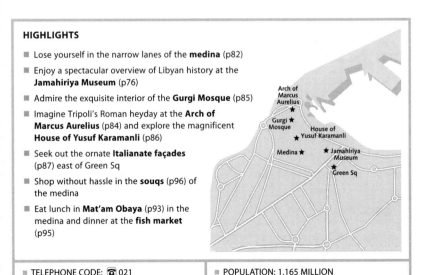

- Lose yourself in the narrow lanes of the **medina** (p82)
- Enjoy a spectacular overview of Libyan history at the **Jamahiriya Museum** (p76)
- Admire the exquisite interior of the **Gurgi Mosque** (p85)
- Imagine Tripoli's Roman heyday at the **Arch of Marcus Aurelius** (p84) and explore the magnificent **House of Yusuf Karamanli** (p86)
- Seek out the ornate **Italianate façades** (p87) east of Green Sq
- Shop without hassle in the **souqs** (p96) of the medina
- Eat lunch in **Mat'am Obaya** (p93) in the medina and dinner at the **fish market** (p95)

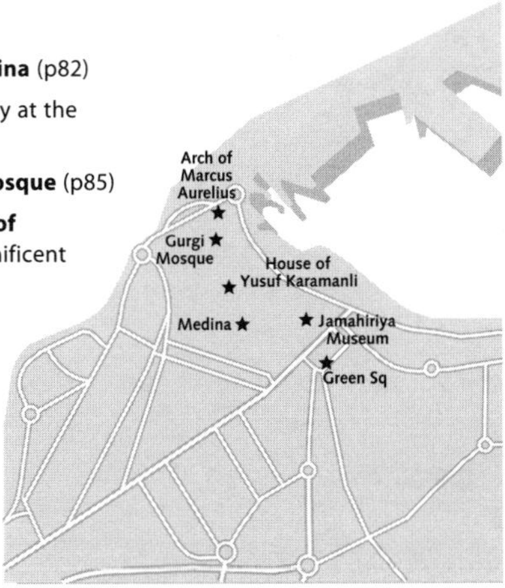

- TELEPHONE CODE: ☎ 021
- POPULATION: 1.165 MILLION

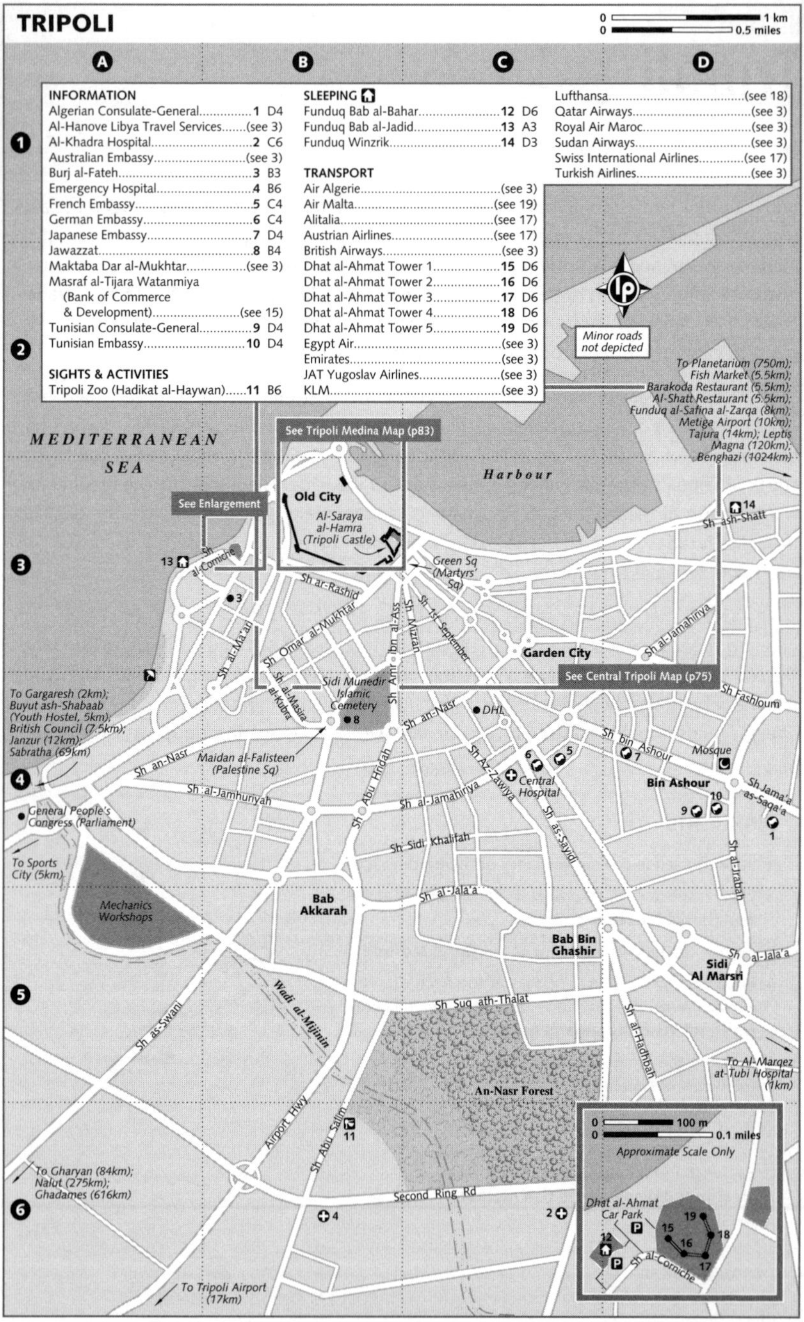
TRIPOLI
0 1 km
0 0.5 miles
A B C D
1 2 3 4 5 6
INFORMATION
Algerian Consulate-General...............1 D4
Al-Hanove Libya Travel Services.......(see 3)
Al-Khadra Hospital...........................2 C6
Australian Embassy.........................(see 3)
Burj al-Fateh.......................................3 B3
Emergency Hospital...........................4 B6
French Embassy..................................5 C4
German Embassy................................6 C4
Japanese Embassy..............................7 D4
Jawazzat..8 B4
Maktaba Dar al-Mukhtar.................(see 3)
Masraf al-Tijara Watanmiya (Bank of Commerce & Development)........................(see 15)
Tunisian Consulate-General...............9 D4
Tunisian Embassy.............................10 D4
SIGHTS & ACTIVITIES
Tripoli Zoo (Hadikat al-Haywan)......11 B6
SLEEPING
Funduq Bab al-Bahar.......................12 D6
Funduq Bab al-Jadid........................13 A3
Funduq Winzrik................................14 D3
TRANSPORT
Air Algerie...(see 3)
Air Malta..(see 19)
Alitalia..(see 17)
Austrian Airlines..............................(see 17)
British Airways.................................(see 3)
Dhat al-Ahmat Tower 1....................15 D6
Dhat al-Ahmat Tower 2....................16 D6
Dhat al-Ahmat Tower 3....................17 D6
Dhat al-Ahmat Tower 4....................18 D6
Dhat al-Ahmat Tower 5....................19 D6
Egypt Air...(see 3)
Emirates...(see 3)
JAT Yugoslav Airlines.......................(see 3)
KLM...(see 3)
Lufthansa...(see 18)
Qatar Airways.....................................(see 3)
Royal Air Maroc..................................(see 3)
Sudan Airways.....................................(see 3)
Swiss International Airlines............(see 17)
Turkish Airlines...................................(see 3)
Minor roads not depicted
To Planetarium (750m); Fish Market (5.5km); Barakoda Restaurant (5.5km); Al-Shatt Restaurant (5.5km); Funduq al-Safina al-Zarqa (8km); Metiga Airport (10km); Tajura (14km); Leptis Magna (120km); Benghazi (1024km)
MEDITERRANEAN SEA
Harbour
See Tripoli Medina Map (p83)
See Enlargement
Old City
Al-Saraya al-Hamra (Tripoli Castle)
Green Sq (Martyrs' Sq)
Sh ash-Shatt
Sh al-Corniche
Sh ar-Rashid
Sh Omar al-Mukhtar
Sh al-Ma'ari
Sh Amr ibn al-Ass
Sh Mizran
Sh 1st September
Garden City
Sh al-Jamahiriya
See Central Tripoli Map (p75)
Sidi Munedir Islamic Cemetery
Sh al-Masira al-Kubra
Sh an-Nasr
DHL
Sh Fashloum
Sh bin Ashour
Mosque
Bin Ashour
Sh Jama'a as-Saqa'a
To Gargaresh (2km); Buyut ash-Shabaab (Youth Hostel, 5km); British Council (7.5km); Janzur (12km); Sabratha (69km)
Maidan al-Falisteen (Palestine Sq)
Sh al-Jamhuriyah
Sh Abu Hridah
Sh Az-Zawiya
Central Hospital
Sh as-Sayidi
General People's Congress (Parliament)
To Sports City (5km)
Sh Sidi Khalifah
Sh al-Irabah
Mechanics Workshops
Bab Akkarah
Sh al-Jala'a
Bab Bin Ghashir
Sidi Al Marsri
Sh Suq ath-Thalat
Wadi al-Mijinin
Sh as-Swani
Sh al-Hadhbah
To Al-Marqez at-Tubi Hospital (1km)
An-Nasr Forest
Airport Hwy
Sh Abu Salim
To Gharyan (84km); Nalut (275km); Ghadames (616km)
Second Ring Rd
To Tripoli Airport (17km)
0 100 m
0 0.1 miles
Approximate Scale Only
Dhat al-Ahmat Car Park
Sh al-Corniche

HISTORY

Tripoli was founded by the Phoenicians in around 500 BC. It became one of the four Punic settlements of significance (the others being Carthage, Sabratha and Leptis Magna). Tripoli is Libya's only ancient city to have been continuously occupied since that time.

Following the fall of Carthage in 146 BC, the city came briefly under the jurisdiction of the Nubian kingdom, before becoming a Roman protectorate. Under the Romans, who named the city Oea, Tripoli grew prosperous and, together with Sabratha and Leptis Magna (the other cities of the 'tripolis' that gave Tripoli its name), provided the Roman Empire with grain, wild animals and slaves.

After the golden age of the 2nd century AD Oea fell into decline. When the Vandals overran North Africa in the 5th century, the damage to the city was devastating. The conquest by the Byzantines in AD 533 arrested the decline, but Tripoli nonetheless spent the following centuries in a much reduced state.

The Arab invasion in the 7th century saw a new town, named Tarablus, built among the ruins of the old. The city grew and, by the 10th century, the Arab geographer Ibn Hawkal described Tripoli as a wealthy and powerful city with a vast market and a busy port. By 1000, Tripoli had become an important centre of intercontinental trade between sub-Saharan Africa, southern Europe, Egypt and the Middle East. It was after the second Arab invasion in 1046 that the old city walls (p82) were rebuilt, using Roman remains as foundations. Roman pillars are still in evidence in parts of the medina, most notably at the Roman Column Crossroads (p89).

The Arab town flourished in the 14th and 15th centuries. In 1460 Tripoli declared itself an independent city-state. During the 16th century the city was occupied in quick succession by the Spanish and by the Knights of St John of Malta. The most visible result of their occupation is the work they carried out on Al-Saraya al-Hamra (Tripoli Castle; p81).

The Ottoman Turks occupied Tripoli from 1551. In the centuries that followed, they constructed most of the mosques, hammams (bathhouses) and souqs visible today, defined the boundaries of the old city and laid out the city's winding lanes. They called the city Tarablus al-Gharb (Tripoli of the West) to distinguish it from the Lebanese city of the same name. By the end of the 17th century, Tripoli was Libya's only city of size and had over 30,000 inhabitants.

After the Italians invaded in 1911 and conquered Libya, the city burst beyond the confines of the city walls. The Italians built colonnaded streets and numerous public buildings. After WWII many families left the old city to live in the recently vacated Italian apartments and houses. The newly empty old city, damaged by bombing during the war, fell into disrepair.

Since the 1950s, when the population was just over 100,000, Tripoli has grown tenfold.

> **THINGS THEY SAID ABOUT...TRIPOLI**
>
> And now again the story of Tripoli changes. But whatever the outcome, she will still have her limpid skies, her air like wine, and a climate where it is a sin to acknowledge an ache or a pain, old age or unhappiness.
>
> *Mabel Loomis Todd,* Tripoli the Mysterious *(1912)*

ORIENTATION

Tripoli's most recognisable landmark is the castle, Al-Saraya al-Hamra, which sits on the eastern corner of the medina alongside the central Green Sq (Al-Sada al-Khadra or Martyrs' Sq). The medina stretches out west of Green Sq, while the towers rising beyond the medina's walls and close to the waterfront are home to hotels, airline offices, travel agencies, banks and a number of embassies. Southeast of Green Sq is one of Tripoli's main shopping districts with plenty of restaurants and a number of hotels.

INFORMATION

Bookshops

Fergiani 2 Bookshop (Map p75; ☎ 3330192; fergiani_b2@hotmail.com; Sharia Mizran; ⌚ 10am-2pm & 5-9pm Sat-Thu, 5-9pm Fri) Fergiani's is such an institution in Libya that it's opened a second branch with a similar selection to its sister shop around the corner and plenty of language-learning materials. The knowledgeable staff can point you in the right direction.

TRIPOLI IN...

Two Days

Spend a day exploring the **medina** (p82); see p88 for more advice. The medina has many faces. To catch a glimpse of ancient Tripoli, seek out the last remnant of Roman Tripoli, the **Arch of Marcus Aurelius** (p84). To get a sense of the medina as a Muslim city, visit the **Ahmed Pasha Karamanli Mosque** (p84), **Draghut Mosque** (p85) and **Gurgi Mosque** (p85). Tripoli's role as a centre of domestic and international intrigue is evident at the elegant and tranquil **Old British Consulate** (p85), the **Old French Consulate** (p86) and the **House of Yusuf Karamanli** (p86). Don't neglect to also spend some time smoking a nargileh at the **Magha as-Sa'a** (p95), while the medina also offers some of the best **shopping** (p96) in Libya. Punctuate your medina day with lunch at **Mat'am Obaya** (p93) or **Mat'am al-Bourai** (p93) and dinner at one of the medina's other excellent restaurants (p93).

On your second day, spend as long as you can at the outstanding **Jamahiriya Museum** (p76), and wandering amid the **Italianate façades** (p87) and **Masjed Jamal Abdel Nasser** (p87). For dinner, head for the **fish market** (p95).

Four Days

If you have four days, you could do everything in the two-day itinerary and spend a day each at the outstanding Roman ruins of **Sabratha** (p100), with a stop at **Janzur Museum** (p98) on the way, and **Leptis Magna** (p110). All are an easy day trip from the capital.

Fergiani's Bookshop (Map p75; ☎ 4444873; Sharia 1st September; 🕑 10am-2pm & 5-9pm Sat-Thu, 5-9pm Fri) This terrific bookshop has an excellent selection of Arabic- and English-language books, coffee-table books, fascinating travel literature, modern studies of Libya, a smaller number of books in French and Italian and excellent postcards. This is a good place to pick up your copy of *The Green Book* (5LD; see p40).

Maktaba Dar al-Mukhtar (Map p72; Ground fl, Burj al-Fateh; 🕑 9am-2pm & 5-9pm Sat-Thu) This stationery and bookstore is one of the few places in Libya to stock a few international newspapers and magazines (including the *International Herald Tribune, Financial Times* and *Newsweek*).

Tripolitania Bookshop (Map p83; Sciara G Mahmud) The friendly Mukhtar runs this eclectic shop of bric-a-brac and second-hand books, but he juggles it with other projects and hence it can be a challenge to find the shop open. When you find him, Mukhtar has an encyclopaedic knowledge of the medina and is a loquacious host.

Cultural Centres

British Council (☎ 4843164; www.britishcouncil.org/libya; Sharia Casablanca, Hay el-Wihda el-Arabia, Siyahia; 🕑 9am-4pm Sun-Thu) Newly opened in Libya, it's around 8km west of the city centre, signposted north off the road to Janzur. It organises language courses and a small range of cultural events.

Emergency

Emergency Hospital (Map p72; ☎ 121; Second Ring Rd)

Internet Access

Cybercafés are springing up all over Tripoli and connections are reasonably fast. As usual in Libya, look for the Internet Explorer icon on the window to find them. Most also allow internet-connected phone calls (for more information see p226).

Bakka Net (Map p75; cnr Sharias Mizran & Haity; per hr 1LD; 🕑 8.30am-midnight Sat-Thu, 6pm-midnight Fri) One of Libya's better and longer-standing internet cafés.

Internet café (Map p75; per hr 1LD; 🕑 9am-midnight Sat-Thu, 5pm-midnight Fri) At Funduq al-Soraya, off Sharia Omar al-Mukhtar.

Internet café (Map p75; per hr 1LD; 🕑 9am-midnight Sat-Thu, 5pm-midnight Fri) Off Sharia 1st September.

Jawazzat

You're unlikely to need to visit the **jawazzat** (passport office; Map p72; ☎ 3334657; Maidan Falisteen or Palestine Sq) in person as visa registrations and extensions should be handled by your tour company. In case you do, it's the five-storey concrete block behind the Sidi Munedir Islamic Cemetery.

Laundry

There are dry-cleaning laundries throughout Tripoli, although most are in the residential districts away from the centre of town; ask your tour company for the nearest one or get your clothes cleaned in the hotel. Hotels generally charge 2LD for a

CENTRAL TRIPOLI

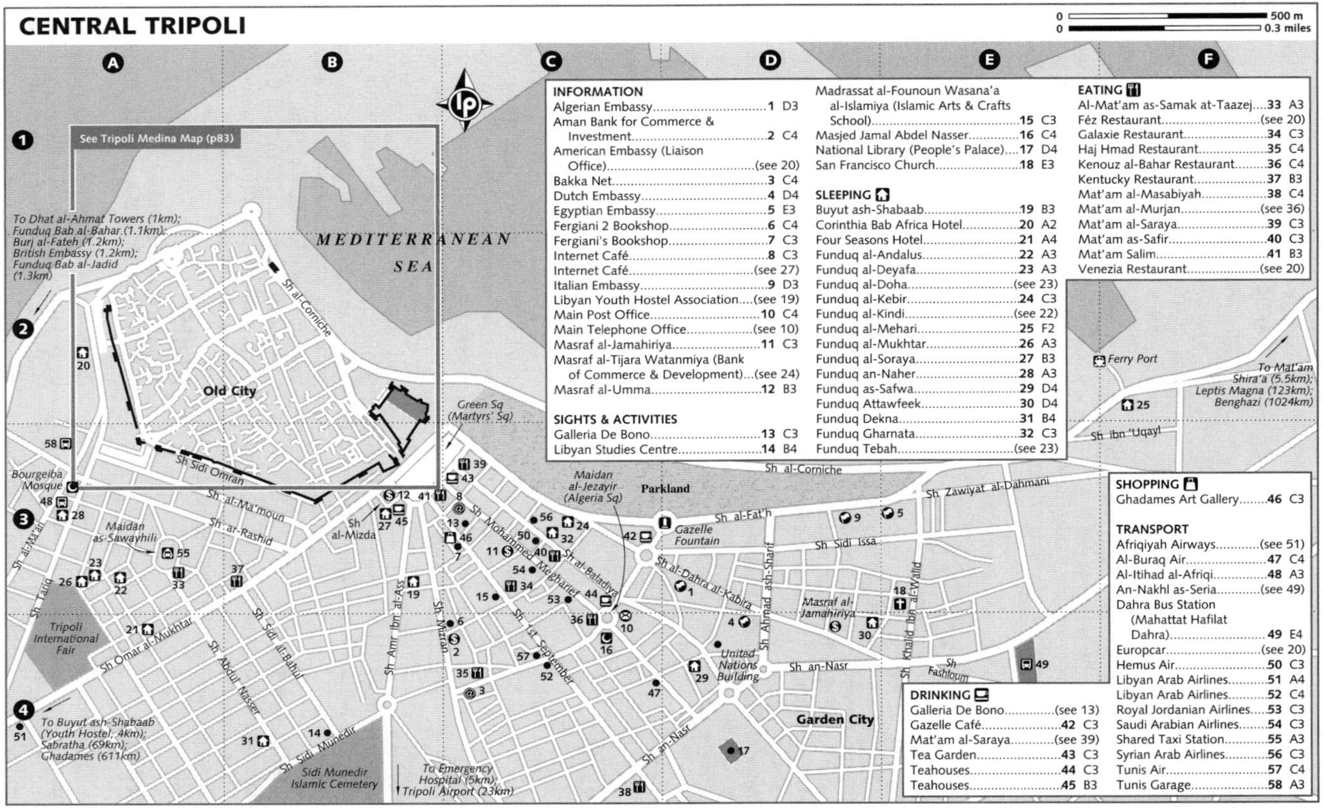

INFORMATION
Algerian Embassy....1 D3
Aman Bank for Commerce & Investment....2 C4
American Embassy (Liaison Office)....(see 20)
Bakka Net....3 C4
Dutch Embassy....4 D4
Egyptian Embassy....5 E3
Fergiani 2 Bookshop....6 C4
Fergiani's Bookshop....7 C3
Internet Café....8 C3
Internet Café....(see 27)
Italian Embassy....9 D3
Libyan Youth Hostel Association....(see 19)
Main Post Office....10 C4
Main Telephone Office....(see 10)
Masraf al-Jamahiriya....11 C3
Masraf al-Tijara Watanmiya (Bank of Commerce & Development)....(see 24)
Masraf al-Umma....12 B3

SIGHTS & ACTIVITIES
Galleria De Bono....13 C3
Libyan Studies Centre....14 B4
Madrassat al-Founoun Wasana'a al-Islamiya (Islamic Arts & Crafts School)....15 C3
Masjed Jamal Abdel Nasser....16 C4
National Library (People's Palace)....17 D4
San Francisco Church....18 E3

SLEEPING
Buyut ash-Shabaab....19 B3
Corinthia Bab Africa Hotel....20 A2
Four Seasons Hotel....21 A4
Funduq al-Andalus....22 A3
Funduq al-Deyafa....23 A3
Funduq al-Doha....(see 23)
Funduq al-Kebir....24 C3
Funduq al-Kindi....(see 22)
Funduq al-Mehari....25 F2
Funduq al-Mukhtar....26 A3
Funduq al-Soraya....27 B3
Funduq an-Naher....28 A3
Funduq as-Safwa....29 D4
Funduq Attawfeek....30 D4
Funduq Dekna....31 B4
Funduq Gharnata....32 C3
Funduq Tebah....(see 23)

EATING
Al-Mat'am as-Samak at-Taazej....33 A3
Féz Restaurant....(see 20)
Galaxie Restaurant....34 C3
Haj Hmad Restaurant....35 C4
Kenouz al-Bahar Restaurant....36 C4
Kentucky Restaurant....37 B3
Mat'am al-Masabiyah....38 C4
Mat'am al-Murjan....(see 36)
Mat'am al-Saraya....39 C3
Mat'am as-Safir....40 C3
Mat'am Salim....41 B3
Venezia Restaurant....(see 20)

DRINKING
Galleria De Bono....(see 13)
Gazelle Café....42 C3
Mat'am al-Saraya....(see 39)
Tea Garden....43 C3
Teahouses....44 C3
Teahouses....45 B3

SHOPPING
Ghadames Art Gallery....46 C3

TRANSPORT
Afriqiyah Airways....(see 51)
Al-Buraq Air....47 C4
Al-Itihad al-Afriqi....48 A3
An-Nakhl as-Seria....(see 49)
Dahra Bus Station (Mahattat Hafilat Dahra)....49 E4
Europcar....(see 20)
Hemus Air....50 C3
Libyan Arab Airlines....51 A4
Libyan Arab Airlines....52 C4
Royal Jordanian Airlines....53 C3
Saudi Arabian Airlines....54 C3
Shared Taxi Station....55 A3
Syrian Arab Airlines....56 C3
Tunis Air....57 C4
Tunis Garage....58 A3

shirt, while other laundries charge around 1LD per item.

Medical Services

The best idea is to get a recommendation from your tour company or embassy.

Al-Khadra Hospital (Map p72; ☎ 4900752; Sharia al-Hadba)

Al-Marqez at-Tubi (Medical Centre; ☎ 4263701/15; Sharia Jamia) This is the best hospital, near Al-Fatah University. Rebuilt in the late 1990s, it's relatively new.

Emergency Hospital (Map p72; ☎ 121; Second Ring Rd)

Money

The most easily accessible *masraf* (banks) are in the streets between Green Sq and Maidan al-Jezayir (Algeria Sq). Masraf al-Umma and Masraf al-Jamahiriya have the most branches around town.

Aman Bank for Commerce & Investment (Map p75; Sharia Mizran) Has a MasterCard–enabled ATM, with another at the airport.

Masraf al-Tijara Watanmiya (Bank of Commerce & Development) Sharia al-Fat'h (Map p75; lobby, Funduq al-Kebir, Sharia al-Fat'h); Dhat al-Ahmat Tower 1 (Map p72; Ground fl, Dhat al-Ahmat Tower 1) You can obtain cash advances on your Visa card at all the branches mentioned. Also has branches (and/or ATMs) in the arrivals hall of the airport, on the and the 1st floor of the Burj al-Fateh (Map p72).

A small black market operates in the medina's Souq al-Mushir and Souq al-Turk, especially in many jewellery shops, although rates are generally identical to the banks. See p222 for more details on exchanging money.

Post

Main post office (Map p75; Maidan al-Jezayir; 🕑 8am-10.30pm Sat-Thu) Has a reasonably efficient poste restante service.

Telephone & Fax

Main telephone office (Map p75; Maidan al-Jezayir; 🕑 8am-midnight) Inside the main hall there's a useful fax restante service (fax 3331199; 1LD), which is signed as 'Flash Fax'.

Toilets

There are no public toilets in Tripoli, but you're never too far from a restaurant or mosque, where they're usually happy to point you in the right direction in the event of an emergency; ask for 'al-hammam' or 'mirhad'.

> **THINGS THEY SAID ABOUT...TRIPOLI TRAFFIC**
>
> Tripolitans seem to think that traffic lights are just festive bits of colored glass strewn randomly along the road, and they rebel against their tightly regulated lives by ignoring all driving rules, blithely heading into opposing traffic on the far side of a two-way road, turning abruptly across five lanes of streaming cars.
>
> *Andrew Solomon,* New Yorker *(2006)*

Travel Agencies

There are dozens of travel agencies around Tripoli that sell domestic and international airline tickets.

Al-Hanove Libya Travel Services (Map p72; ☎ 3351099; alhanovelibya@myway.com; Ground fl, Burj al-Fateh; 🕑 10am-2pm & 5-9pm Sat-Thu) This is the most professional travel agency that we found.

DANGERS & ANNOYANCES

Tripoli is an extremely safe city with a negligible crime rate. One area where you may want to be careful of pickpockets is the Sharia al-Rashid area, southwest of Green Sq, but even here the risk is small.

The greatest danger is crossing the street as local drivers drive at high speed and will press the accelerator before they check for pedestrians. Roads where you should exercise particular caution include the one circling Green Sq, Sharia Omar al-Mukhtar and anywhere along Sharia al-Corniche. Avoid sudden and unpredictable movements and, especially around Green Sq, work your way across one lane at a time. If in doubt, ask a local to help out.

Another frustration is that all the street signs, with the exception of some in the medina, are written in Arabic.

SIGHTS

Jamahiriya Museum

Tripoli's **Jamahiriya Museum** (Map p83; ☎ 333 0292; Green Sq; admission 3LD, camera/video 5/10LD, compulsory guide 50LD; 🕑 9am-1pm & 2-5pm Tue-Sun) houses one of the finest collections of classical art in the Mediterranean. Built in consultation with Unesco at enormous cost, it's extremely well designed and the 47 galleries provide a comprehensive overview of all periods of Libyan history, from the Neolithic period right up to the present day.

If your time is limited, you may want to restrict yourself to the ground floor, which is undoubtedly the most impressive of the five levels. Also of considerable interest are the Islamic rooms (Gallery 20) on the 2nd floor as well as those devoted to Libyan resistance (31) and Libya's revolutionary rule (32–37). To take in the whole museum, you'll need a minimum of two hours.

Guides are compulsory. Most of the exhibits are labelled only in Arabic, although there are informative general descriptions in English of the relevant period of history in each room. Camera and other bags must be left in the cloak room so consider leaving any valuables at your hotel or on your tour bus.

GROUND FLOOR (GALLERIES 1–9)

Entrance Hall (Gallery 1)

This gallery provides a stunning overview of the museum's contents. On the right as you enter is an elegant statue of Venus, which was stolen during the colonial era, but finally repatriated to Libya in November 2000. On the wall behind the statue are mosaics from the 2nd century AD showing scenes of gladiatorial contests in the Leptis amphitheatre (p116). On an adjacent wall is an attractive mural of Tripoli's ancient medina (p82) and harbour – take note of how the water once came to the gates of the castle. Opposite the statue, on the left as you enter, are an imposing stone mausoleum and some tablets from Ghirza (p121), a Roman-era Libyan community that drew strongly on Roman architectural influence.

The second half of the gallery is overseen by an enormous map of Libya on which buttons (sometimes) light up prehistoric sites; areas of Punic, Greek and Roman dominance; trade and caravan routes; the Islamic conquest; and modern-day museums and archaeological sites.

Just before leaving the gallery, it's impossible to miss the funky green VW Beetle used by Colonel Qaddafi around the time of the 1969 revolution.

CITY OF CHANGE – A PERSONAL REFLECTION *Anthony Ham*

On my first visit in early 2001, Tripoli was like Damascus in the 1990s – resolutely retro, caught in a time-warp of old American cars, questionable fashion choices, patchy communications and a hint of mutual suspicion as a hangover from the not-too-distant past. My Libyan hosts were warm and friendly, but it took a while before I escaped the feeling that by watching CNN I was doing something vaguely illicit, and who's to say whether the middle-aged men slumped in the armchairs of hotel lobbies at 3am weren't there to keep an eye on me. Depressing government hotels were all the rage, not to mention the only choice in town, and there was the ever-present fear that you would return to your hotel to find your bags in the lobby because a government delegation had taken over your room without notice.

How times have changed.

Tripoli's streets are now awash with the latest-model SUVs, every second Tripolitan has a mobile phone attached to their ear, shops sell the latest fashions and a well-run new private hotel seems to open every week. What's more, Libyans, who are as warm and friendly as ever, enjoy the fact that they no longer have to explain how, contrary to the scaremongering of the 1980s, Libya is one of the safest destinations in the Middle East. Nor do they feel the same need to carry out their conversations in hushed tones lest that middle-aged man in the armchair overhear. Satellite TV channels broadcasting out of Baghdad, Beirut and Abu Dhabi have also brought Libyans up to speed, meaning that they're savvy about world events, not to mention the latest technology.

But the greatest change I have seen is that Libya – and Tripoli in particular – is now a country of optimists. No longer burdened by the depredations of the sanctions years and the uncertainties deriving from Libya's international isolation, the people of Tripoli especially sense that they are living in a time of opportunity – to make money, to join in the benefits of a sanctions-free existence and to meet on equal terms with the people of the world – that the city hasn't seen in decades.

JAMAHIRIYA MUSEUM (GROUND FLOOR)

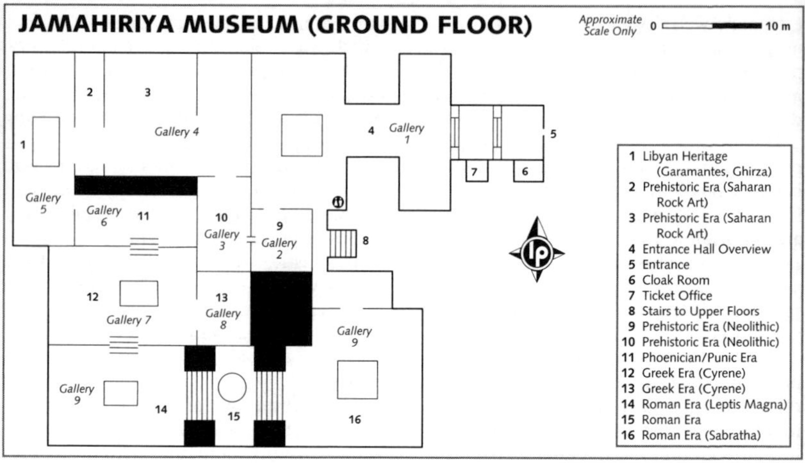

The Prehistoric Era (Galleries 2–4)

Gallery 2 contains some 300,000-year-old hand-axes and the glass cabinet in the centre of the room contains a fossilised tree found in the Libyan Sahara, while there are also examples of rock art and pottery dating from 8000 to 5000 BC.

Gallery 3 shows ceramics cast in the time before wheels were used in pottery. They date from between 6000 BC and 1750 BC.

Gallery 4 is devoted to rock art and shows you what you're missing if you don't make it to the Jebel Acacus (p198). Most of the paintings and carvings are superb reproductions of the originals, which remain on the remote mountain walls of the Sahara. Those on display span most of the known periods of Saharan rock art (see p200). In the central display cabinet is a well-preserved child's skeleton, which was 5400 years old when it was found in Wadi Tashwinat (p200) in 1958.

Libyan Heritage (Gallery 5)

This room showcases Libyan contributions to civilisation not subsumed into Roman, Greek or Punic history. The room is dominated, not surprisingly, by the relics of the Garamantes empire (p30). The centrepiece of the gallery is a royal Garamantian tomb with a stone offering tablet outside the entrance. On the right wall as you enter are displays of pottery found in the tombs, along with other objects showing the largely commercial nature of Garamantes relations with the outside world. There are also artefacts from Zinchecra, the forerunner to Garama (p189) as the Garamantian capital.

The south wall contains a number of tomb and temple reliefs from Slonta (p140). There are also more examples of the stonework of Ghirza, including a wonderful, simple relief carving of a camel and oxen ploughing the earth.

Phoenician (Gallery 6)

As the Phoenician (Punic) cities disappeared under subsequent Roman and Greek settlements, this relatively small gallery is one of the few surviving collections of Libyan-Punic artefacts; for more information see p29. Those on display include a water pitcher, a representation of a Punic priest from the 2nd century BC, two stone lions from the ancient city of Oea (Tripoli), tablets of the Punic language and the ancient symbol for Tarnit (the wife of the god, Baal).

Greek (Galleries 7 & 8)

The central display features a model of Cyrene's Temple of Zeus (p146) as well as the agora (p144), as they appeared in the 2nd century AD. On the north wall are a number of particularly fine decorative pottery pieces (3rd- to 6th-centuries BC), which were not for practical use, but rather sold as souvenirs to pilgrims and tourists outside the Temple of Zeus; tourism is clearly an ancient pursuit. Also in **Gallery 7** are imposing statues of Dionysius and Fortuna.

The tiny **Gallery 8** off the main room contains a captivating statue of the Three Graces from Cyrene; these comrades of Aphrodite were famous for their beauty and the statues reflect this superbly. On the left as you enter is a faceless Persephone. Facing her is a martial statue of Athena, the Goddess of Wisdom.

Roman (Gallery 9)

This large gallery, which consists of three parts, is the finest in the entire museum. The first room is devoted to Leptis Magna (p110). The row of statues on the right is superb, with those of Artemis and Venus at the right-hand end particularly well crafted. The large mosaic adorning the wall that faces Gallery 7 is a magnificent example of a Roman Four Seasons mosaic with its pastoral scenes. The model representation of Leptis in the central glass case gives an idea of the city's former grandeur. There is a suitably imperious Tiberius in the maroon alcove to the left as you move through the gallery. Above the low ceiling over the stairs is an inauguration tablet from the Leptis amphitheatre with inscriptions in both Latin and Punic – a reminder that Leptis was quite a multicultural city.

In the small transitional room between the two main rooms, the floor is covered with a beautiful mosaic from Roman Oea. The scenes and portrait in the centre of the mosaic are surrounded by a much larger area of geometric designs on which people sat on cushions, leaving the centre free to be admired. On the left are marble busts of the Roman emperors Hadrian, Marcus Aurelius and Lucius Verus with their wives. The display cabinets contain glassware used commonly in the 1st century AD for ash and bone after cremation.

The final (eastern) section of Gallery 9 is devoted to Sabratha (p100). There are many highlights in this room, including pillars and squat column bases with carved stone-relief scenes, breathtaking mosaics around the walls (including some comprised of exquisitely small tiles) and one marble statue (among many) of a beautiful woman washing her cascading curls. There's also a model of Sabratha in the centre of the room. This is a room in which to quietly sit and take it all in. As you leave the room, note the mosaic of Medusa heads above the exit.

1ST FLOOR (GALLERIES 10–14)

The 1st floor marks the transition from the Roman period to the Byzantine and then Islamic eras.

Gallery 10 is a continuation of exhibitions from the Roman period; most of the items date from the 1st to 3rd centuries AD. There's an excellent row of statues depicting, among others, Victoria and Apollo. Note also the particularly fine small marble statues of two children. In the glass display cabinets are a collection of delicate bronze items, miniature pottery amphorae and oil lamps. The second half of the gallery, up a few steps, contains some mildly interesting coins and oil lamps; see if you can find the small dice, which suggest that there was more to the lives of the ancients than sculpting.

Gallery 11 is dedicated to the Arch of Septimius Severus (p111) at Leptis, including some original panels and a forbidding bust (2nd century AD) of the man himself, which was found in the Leptis theatre (p115).

Galleries 12 and 13 cover the Byzantine period and contain a motley array of glass bottles, photos of mosaics, stone grave covers, an unfinished coffin and some impressive stone windows. The latter provide a good example of how a church's exterior must have looked in the 5th to 6th centuries AD.

2ND FLOOR (GALLERIES 15–30)

These galleries contain some fine examples of Islamic architecture and folklore exhibits. The best, in **Gallery 15**, is a vernacular arch, made of mortar and sun-dried brick, its palm roof and stonework highlighting a simplicity of design and construction. Note also the massive green Quran.

Gallery 16 has model displays of sandstone tombs from Ajdabiya (p131) and Medinat Sultan (p122), as well as a map of the world as it was known in 1349.

Gallery 19 is also worth visiting for its excellent model of Al-Saraya al-Hamra (p81), wonderful old map of Oea and a painting of the interior of the Ahmed Pasha Karamanli Mosque (p84) with its pleasing blue tilework and sombre dark ceiling. Other good exhibits include an evocative old wooden door, a reconstructed interior of a Ghadames house (see p168) and a Tripolitanian bedroom; this latter room, with its ornate inlaid chair, carpets, cushions and sombre wall hangings, was reserved for the bride and groom on their wedding night.

Gallery 20 is filled with a diverse range of artefacts, with lovely samovars, silver jewellery and a huge incense container being the stand-out features. Off the main room, on either side of the entrance, are two small rooms, one devoted to a Turkish-era Libyan kitchen, the other to weaving. The corridor leading to the next room is home to a glass cabinet that showcases traditional Libyan costumes. The mannequins represent, from left to right, a woman from Benghazi, a man from eastern Libya, a Tuareg woman, a Tripoli man, three people in everyday central-Libyan wear, a shepherd, the blue and black robes of Murzuq, a Tuareg, an unknown woman and another Tuareg.

Galleries 21 to 27 are mediocre. Gallery 21 is devoted to the Tuareg, with photos on the walls and glass cases containing Tuareg leather items and spears. Gallery 23 has items from southern Libya (basketwork for use in the kitchen, a thatched hut, medicines and more Tuareg leatherwork), while Gallery 26 contains an oil press used until recently in the Jebel Nafusa, other elements of olive-oil production and a stone relief from Ghirza showing a farming scene. The agricultural theme is continued in Gallery 27, which includes displays of farming implements and techniques. Beekeeping enthusiasts and devotees of the virtues of palm trees also haven't been forgotten.

The folklore exhibitions **(Galleries 28–30)** are also patchy, and some of the rooms were almost empty when we visited. Among the dusty exhibits are items used in circumcision rites, some informative posters on Libyan folklore and a few musical instruments.

3RD FLOOR

Libyan Resistance (Gallery 31)

The years of resistance to Italian rule make for sobering viewing, although the exhibits are quite understated: weaponry and the personal belongings of the prominent writer and resistance figure Suleiman al-Baruni (the photo was taken in 1912, a year before he led an ill-fated rebellion in the Jebel Nafusa) and Omar al-Mukhtar (see The Lion of the Desert, p37). There's a copy of the famous photo of Omar al-Mukhtar being led to trial, shortly before his execution, in 1931. There is also a chart documenting the massive exile of Libyan prisoners-of-war in Italy.

Revolutionary Libya (Galleries 32–37)

If you're a connoisseur of images of Colonel Muammar Qaddafi, you'll kick yourself if you miss these galleries. After refreshing your memory as to the noble aims of the English translation of the Declaration of the Establishment of the Authority of the People in 1977, you'll find photos of shouting youths, women soldiers and a child wearing a Colonel Qaddafi T-shirt **(Gallery 34)**.

Gallery 35 depicts Colonel Qaddafi the statesman, the revolutionary leader, the munificent leader of his people. The first panel of photos on your right as you enter includes a 1966 photo of the decidedly self-conscious colonel walking along a London street (second row from the top), one of the first photos taken of Qaddafi after the revolution (next row down), and photos of where he grew up (top row). Other definite highlights include the departure of some very sour-looking British troops in the early 1970s (third panel on the right) and a collection of photos of Colonel Qaddafi smiling with world leaders.

Gallery 36 lauds Libya's oil industry and the Libyan contribution to modern technology, and **Gallery 37** is given over to a long corridor containing the people's written adorations to Colonel Qaddafi – very entertaining if you can read Arabic.

Natural History (Galleries 38–47)

It's galling to find that the least interesting galleries in the museum contain some of the best English-language labels. **Gallery 38** is all rocks and geology, **Gallery 39** showcases animal fossils, while **Gallery 40** is home to stuffed desert animals, including the waddan (a large, goatlike deer; see p63). **Gallery 41** has a strong whiff of the macabre – camel embryos in glass jars and deformed animals. The stuffed animals in the central glass case include a fennec fox, small desert mice and a wolf. The remaining galleries contain insects and butterflies **(Gallery 42)**, some birds and their migratory patterns, although most of them seem to bypass Libya **(Galleries 43–44)**, fish and the huge skeleton of a sperm whale **(Galleries 45–46)** and Libyan plants **(Gallery 47)**.

Al-Saraya al-Hamra (Tripoli Castle)

Al-Saraya al-Hamra (Map p83; ☎ 3333042; Green Sq), known as Tripoli Castle or Red Castle, was closed for renovations when we visited, but it should be a fascinating window on the past when it reopens. The castle represented the seat of power in Tripolitania until the 20th century and has evolved over the centuries into a citadel containing a labyrinth of courtyards, alleyways and houses. The total area of the castle is about 13,000 sq metres, including the area surrounded by high defensive walls now given over to the museum. It will have the same entry fees and opening times as the museum when it re-opens its doors.

HISTORY

Excavations have revealed that the castle was built on the site of the Roman castrum (Roman fortified camp; a public bath from the 2nd century AD has been excavated on the site), but the fortress proper was probably not built before the Arab invasion of AD 644. Under the Spaniards and the Knights of St John of Malta in the 16th century, the defences were built up with the addition of defensive towers in the southwest and southeast of the citadel. The Turks occupied the castle in 1551. After extensive works were carried out, the governors used it as their official residence. Under the Karamanlis (1711–1835) harems and a large *salaamlik* (reception room), in which official visitors were received, was built. Much of the castle's existing interior dates to this period. The castle was also quite self-contained, with a mint, courthouse, shops, jails and mills. After the Italian conquest the governor used the castle as offices and parts were turned into a museum. Most of the buildings inside the castle are now used by the Department of Antiquities.

CASTLE OF INTRIGUE

The genteel decay of Al-Saraya al-Hamra hides the fact that it has been the scene of much intrigue and violence. When the Ottoman armies of Süleyman the Magnificent, Sultan of Turkey, launched a final assault in 1551 to drive the Christians from Tripoli, the newly reinforced bastions stood up to the fire. However, the defenders of the Knights of St John of Malta proved less resilient – an act of treachery from one of the soldiers, who provided information to the enemy pinpointing the weakest spot in the defences, meant the walls were duly breached. When the governor emerged waving a flag of truce he was unceremoniously clapped in irons, stripped and cast into slavery.

A succession of Turkish *beys* (leaders) were to meet a similar fate. Suleiman Bey withstood a punitive mission from the Ottoman sultan, only to be tricked out of the castle, taken on board one of the sultan's fleet and promptly crucified on the poop deck. The janissaries plotted to overthrow his successor, Sharif Pasha, whereupon he barricaded himself in the castle. He too was tricked out of the castle and cut to pieces by those lying in wait for him.

Ramadan Bey, who succeeded him, was persuaded to hand over power by a cunning corsair named Mohammed Saqizli. The wily Saqizli contrived to marry Miryam bint-Fawz, wife of a tribal leader, by poisoning her husband and then inviting her to come to the castle for the marriage. Bringing her wealth with her, she arrived at the castle only to be turned over to the executioner as soon as the wedding ceremony had taken place. Poetic justice prevailed: Mohammed Saqizli died at the hands of his Christian doctor who dispatched him with a poisoned apple.

From then until the Karamanlis seized power in 1711, a bewildering number of rulers came and went. One died from plague, several were killed and the rest were deposed and exiled; only one managed to die of old age.

In 1790 the three Karamanli sons of the governor, or pasha, met in the Governor's study. The youngest of the three, the ambitious Crown Prince Yusuf Karamanli, called the meeting supposedly in order to defuse simmering tensions over succession. He also asked their mother to be present as witness. The meeting progressed well, with the brothers reaching an apparent reconciliation. The Crown Prince asked them to swear their agreement on the Quran and called his servant to bring the holy book. What the servant brought, in accordance with the plan, was not the Quran but a box concealing a pistol, which he drew and shot dead his two brothers. He later succeeded his father and ruled Libya from 1795 to 1832.

EXPLORING THE CASTLE

Just after entering the castle, look for the attractive tilework on the left. A ramp leads into the heart of the castle, before which, off to the left, are the remains of a small residence with residual pillars and a well. After ascending the ramp, turn left to visit the cells of the grim prison. Up a small set of stairs, again to the left, is the old Governor's Quarters, which successive Turkish governors used as a study. It was here in 1790 that a grisly act of fratricide took place (see Castle of Intrigue, p81).

A door leads off the small courtyard of the Governor's quarters to the Spanish courtyard, which was laid out during the brief occupation by the Spanish in the 16th century. Around the courtyard, which is delightful in spring when strewn with flowers, are a number of stone lions. Stairs descend into a much larger, open courtyard with a lovely fountain as well as some pretty tilework around the perimeter. The exit leads off to the southeast and onto the eastern limb of Souq al-Mushir. The imposing arched stone gateway, which was the original entrance to the castle, but is no longer in use, is on the way back to Green Sq from the souq.

Medina

Tripoli's medina may not rival the architectural magnificence of the old cities of Morocco, but this is Tripoli at its best and most atmospheric. The medina is where the Libya of old survives – its leisurely pace of doing business, its rhythms unchanged in centuries, its soul least changed by the passage of time. In parts, the medina is ramshackle and in dire need of repair. In others, the tentative signs of rejuvenation are rising from the rubble and bringing life to the otherwise quiet lanes. It's a place of markets on show to the world, of private homes and courtyards hidden behind ornate wooden doors, of mosques where the muezzin stands at the door to call the faithful to prayer.

For a unique aerial perspective over the medina, consider riding the elevator to the 26th floor of the **Corinthia Bab Africa Hotel** (p91). One of the best guides to the old city is the delightful Dr Mustafa Turjman from the Department of Antiquities (in Al-Saraya al-Hamra; ask your tour company to track him down).

HISTORY

The first fortified wall around the medina was built in the 4th century, while further ramparts and reinforcements were added by subsequent occupiers to safeguard the city from sea-borne attack. The layout of the city follows the blueprint of the old Arab city. Although much modified, its design has changed little and it was not until the 19th century that Tripoli spread beyond the medina's walls.

Most of the mosques, public buildings and houses date from the Turkish period, although many of the exterior walls of houses within the medina also show a strong European influence, with wrought-iron balconies and wooden shutters. During the Italian occupation and the bombing of the city in WWII, the walls and some of the buildings sustained heavy damage.

The original construction materials consisted of earth and lime, covered with whitewash and decorated with colourful ceramics, although these were used sparingly. Marble was imported from Malta for use

THINGS THEY SAID ABOUT...THE MEDINA

The whole of the town appears in a semi-circle, some time before reaching the harbour's mouth. The extreme whiteness of square flat buildings covered with lime, which in this climate encounters the sun's fiercest rays, is very striking. The baths form clusters of cupolas very large, to the number of eight or ten crowded together in different parts of the town. The mosques have in general a small plantation of Indian figs and date trees growing close to them, which, at a distance, appearing to be so many rich gardens in different parts of the town, give the whole city, in the eyes of an European, an aspect truly novel and pleasing.

From the correspondence of Richard Tully, Narrative of a Ten-year Residence at Tripoli in Africa *(1783)*

in the homes of the wealthy. You'll also see the occasional Roman column at important intersections, which is typical of the gradual accretion of influences that have come to mark the medina down through the centuries.

Traditionally, the houses of the medina were built around an open internal courtyard. The most striking feature from the outside are the doors, atop most of which small arches of intricate metalwork with geometric and floral motifs radiate out from the centre, although some are in a parlous state. Although primarily ornamental they also served a practical purpose, allowing air and light into the interior without

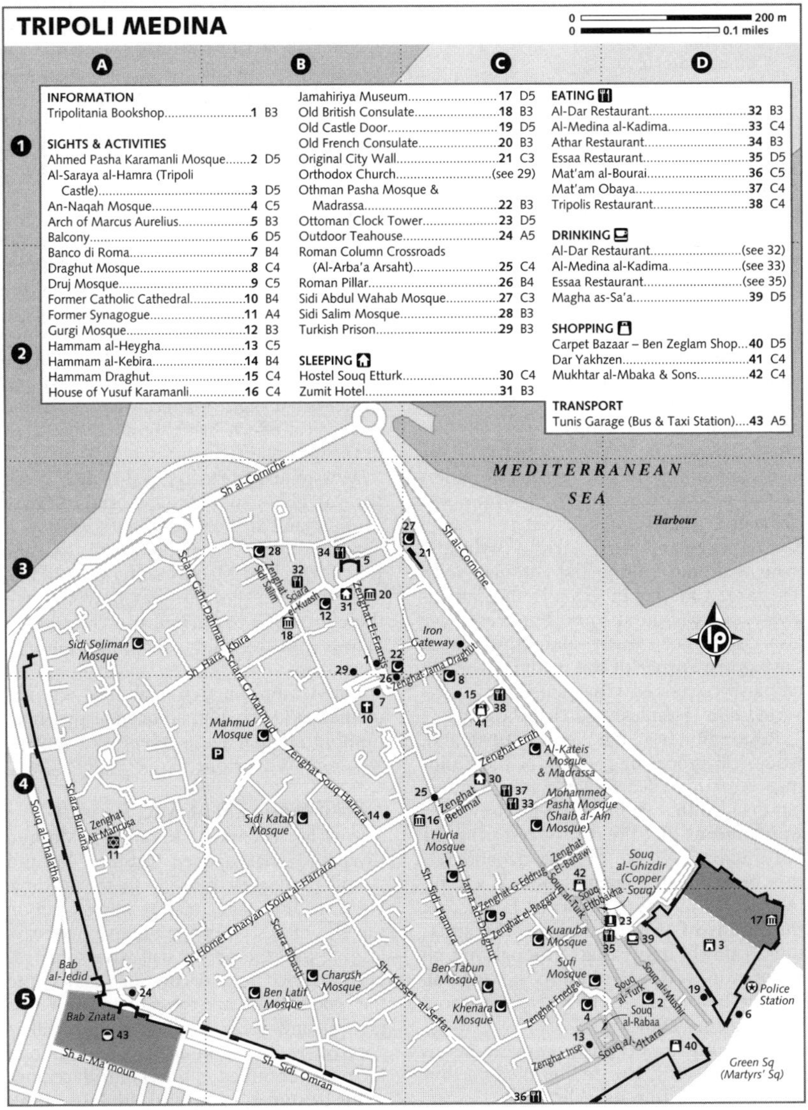

TOP FIVE RESTORED MEDINA BUILDINGS

Apart from the medina's mosques, which have long been kept in a fine state of preservations, our pick of the most beautifully preserved or restored buildings in the medina is:

- **House of Yusuf Karamanli** (p86)
- **Old British Consulate** (p85)
- **Zumit Hotel** (p90)
- **Old French Consulate** (p86)
- **Banco di Roma** (p88)

compromising the privacy of the inhabitants. There was often similar decoration on the banisters of internal staircases. In addition to providing some much-needed shade in summer, the roofs that cover some of the thoroughfares also serve to reinforce the walls of the adjoining houses.

Most of the 38 mosques in the old city, which once had adjoining hammams and madrassas (Quranic schools), have roofs with small cupolas supported by numerous pillars in the main sanctuary. Many also contain the tombs of their founders or the person to whom the mosque was dedicated. The minarets alternate between the rectangular North African style and octagonal ones built in the Ottoman style. The largest market in Tripoli's medina has always been Souq al-Turk, but there have also always been many souqs throughout the eastern corner of the medina. The old city also contained synagogues (now converted into mosques) and churches.

Restoration began in the early 1990s and, while still proceeding, many of the buildings remain under threat. Sadly, Unesco has decided that its priorities lie elsewhere, which means that the cost of restoring the old buildings of the medina depends either on the government's political will or, in the case of privately owned houses, on the means of private citizens. The situation is slowly improving, although not all restoration work is faithful to the original. For the best examples of recently restored buildings, see above.

According to the last estimate, about 3500 people still live in the medina, but 65,000 work within its walls.

ARCH OF MARCUS AURELIUS

This last remnant of the ancient Roman city of Oea was completed in AD 163–64. The Arch of Marcus Aurelius (Map p83) stood at the crossroads of the two great Roman roads of the city – the cardo maximus (running north to south) and decumanus (east to west). It therefore stood at the city's most important junction as well as providing an entrance to the city from the harbour. The fact that Oea had a triumphal arch (Leptis had five, while Sabratha had none) was a reflection of Oea's importance in the Roman Tripolis. The façades of the pillars facing to and away from the port contain niches that once hosted statues of Marcus Aurelius and Lucius Verus, above which are weather-worn portraits in relief. Look also for the carvings of Apollo and Minerva, the mythical protectors of Oea in ancient times. On the raised level to the right, behind the arch, are the remains of the pediment of the Temple of Taki (the Roman god of fortune), which dates from AD 183–85. On the tablets are the figures of Apollo, Taki and Minerva. At night, the arch is illuminated to magical effect, bringing alive the detail of the bas-reliefs.

Mussolini reportedly tried to tear down the neighbouring Sidi Abdul Wahab Mosque and section of the city walls as it appealed to his sense of grandeur that the Roman Arch of Marcus Aurelius could be seen from the port. It was only through the efforts of a brave Italian archaeologist, Salvatore Aurigemma, that the buildings were saved.

One reason the arch is all that survived of ancient Oea is that an ancient prophecy foretold terrible punishments for anyone who removed a stone.

AHMED PASHA KARAMANLI MOSQUE

The richly decorated Karamanli Mosque (Map p83) was opened in the 1730s and is still the largest mosque in the medina. Note its fine octagonal minaret built in the Ottoman style, while the five doorways leading into the prayer hall have some superbly crafted floral decorations carved into the wood; these are thought to symbolise growth and progress. The prayer hall is covered by almost 30 domes and the floral theme is continued in the colourful ceilings of the balconies, which surround the prayer hall on three sides. These are considered some of the finest examples of woodwork in Libya. Experts believe that the carvings, colours and use of arches suggest a high degree of Moroccan and Andalucían influence. The tombs of Ahmed Pasha and his family are in one of the rooms off the prayer hall.

GURGI MOSQUE

The Gurgi Mosque (Map p83), just west of the Arch of Marcus Aurelius, was built in the 19th century and was the last mosque built in Tripoli under the Turks. Although quite small, its interior is the most beautiful in the city. The main prayer hall contains imported marble pillars from Italy, ceramic tilework from Tunisia and intricate stone carvings from Morocco. The large, covered platform was reserved for VIPs. The mihrab (niche facing Mecca) and the domes above the main room are adorned with extremely beautiful stone lattice carvings, again with floral motifs; there are 16 domes but the one above the mihrab is particularly fine. The tomb of Mustapha Gurgi (a Tripoli naval captain) and his family are in an ante chamber at the back.

OTHMAN PASHA MOSQUE & MADRASSA

Immediately east of the Banco di Roma, this mosque and madrassa (Map p83) was built by Othman Pasha, who ruled Libya for 25 years, and is one of the oldest Turkish sites in Tripoli. It's set around a delightful courtyard with marble pillars from Carrara in Italy and topped with local limestone. The portico is surrounded by wooden doors underneath stone arches, and immediately left after coming in the main entrance is the stone ablutions fountain with arabesque decorations. Out the back are the tombs of the mosque's builders as well as a small garden. The Roman-era pool was used for washing the boards on which verses of the Quran were written. It's a tranquil place with unusual cupolas on the domes, and it's renowned for, unusually, having three domes, one each for the graveyard, mosque and main entrance. The school has been in use for over 350 years.

ENTERING MEDINA MOSQUES

None of the mosques in Tripoli's medina have official opening hours, but the custodians of the keys are never far away. A gentle knock on the door should elicit some response if you're prepared to be patient. If no-one appears, ask a nearby shopkeeper, who will invariably know where the *miftah* (key) is. Avoid visiting during prayer time, especially Friday prayers around noon. Entry is free, but a tip for the caretaker is appreciated.

DRAGHUT MOSQUE

This 16th-century mosque (Map p83), opposite the Othman Pasha Mosque and Madrassa, bears the name of an infamous corsair admiral and governor of Tripoli. Its elegant pillars and arches (there are 15 in the main prayer hall alone with many more in adjoining rooms) are quite stunning. Things to look out for include the green-and-white calligraphic and arabesque relief inscriptions used sparingly against a white background.

OLD BRITISH CONSULATE

The **Old British Consulate** (Map p83; Sharia Hara Kbira; admission 2LD, camera/video 2/5LD; 9am-5pm Sat-Thu) building, west of the Gurgi Mosque on Sharia Hara Kbira, was first constructed in 1744 as a residence for Ahmed Pasha (the founder of the Karamanli dynasty) during the final phase of his reign (r 1711–45). From the second half of the 18th century until 1940, it was the office of the British consul. In addition to diplomatic representation, the consul's representatives used their position to launch expeditions into the Sahara with an eye on lucrative trade routes. On a plaque outside the entrance, this history is, not without some justification, viewed with unconcealed anger. It claims that 'the so-called European geographical and exploratative scientific expeditions to Africa, which were in essence and as a matter of fact intended to be colonial ones to occupy and colonise vital and strategic parts of Africa, embarked from this same building'. The consulate also provided a place of refuge for the expatriate community during various invasions and was the unofficial centre of the diplomatic community in Tripoli.

The entrance is through a large wooden door under an archway that leads to a large courtyard paved with marble. The courtyard is surrounded on all sides by a beautiful two-storey building with elegant

A VERY BRITISH CONSUL

Tripoli in the 19th century was, according to one historian, an 'odd mixture of refinement and corruption'. On the one hand it was the home port of pirates who terrorised Mediterranean shipping with impunity. At the same time, Tripoli was seen as the gateway to the African interior by European powers jostling for position in the coming 'Scramble for Africa'. In the early part of the century, the flag of the USA and no less than eight European countries fluttered over the consulates of the old city.

This was an age when the European powers conspired, sometimes together, more often against each other as they sought to become the first to lay claim to much of Africa. It was a role ideally suited to the larger-than-life Colonel Hanmer Warrington, who served as British Consul from 1814 until 1846. No ordinary diplomat, Colonel Warrington has been described as 'in so many ways the incarnation of John Bull', a maverick who loved the intrigue of outmanoeuvring his fellow consuls and one with a decidedly chequered past. Prior to his consular career, he reportedly served time in a debtors' prison in Gibraltar, while his wife Jane was said to have been the illegitimate daughter of King George IV. On at least two occasions, Colonel Warrington broke off diplomatic relations with the Karamanli rulers without the approval of his London masters.

He was, however, tolerated by his superiors, albeit reluctantly at times, because there was no fiercer defender of British interests. In 1825 he boasted to one newly arrived traveller 'of being able to do anything and everything in Tripoli'. In particular, he was a fervent supporter of British-sponsored expeditions charged with the task of finding the riches of sub-Saharan Africa. In that sense, the plaque that you now see outside the Old British Consulate (p85) is essentially correct.

Colonel Warrington's support was so strong in the case of Major Alexander Gordon Laing (the first European to reach Timbuktu in August 1826, Laing was killed soon after he set out for home) that he engineered Laing's marriage to his daughter Emma. Such was Warrington's colourful reputation that rumours persist that he saw the marriage as a means of avoiding a calamitous union between Emma and the son of the French consul.

After Laing's death, Warrington became obsessed with suspicions that the French consul and his agents had conspired to destroy Laing's last letters (which would have confirmed that he was the first to reach Timbuktu rather than the Frenchman Rene Caillié). He even suggested that the French may have had a hand in Laing's death. The resulting bitter quarrel between Warrington and the French lasted for years, in the process paralysing Yusuf Karamanli to the extent that some historians believe Warrington's refusal to let the matter rest precipitated the end in 1832 of the 124-year Karamanli reign. Whatever the truth of such speculation, the consul's increasingly unpredictable behaviour certainly spelled the end for Warrington, who retired a broken man after having lost the support of London.

The best account of the life and career of Colonel Warrington and Tripoli in the first half of the 19th century is in *The Race for Timbuktu*, by Frank T Kryza.

Moorish archways fronting the wide verandas, behind which are the rooms that once included consular offices as well as kitchens, servants' quarters and bedrooms. It has a wonderful air of tranquillity. The building now houses a general scientific library.

OLD FRENCH CONSULATE

The **Old French Consulate** (Map p83; Zenghat el-Fransis; admission 2LD, camera/video 2/5LD; 9am-5pm Sat-Thu), not far south of the Arch of Marcus Aurelius, dates from 1630 and is arrayed around a two-storey tiled courtyard with delightful arches, coloured windows and woodwork. Note in particular the crescent and a Star of David carved into the wooden doors above the staircase. The former consular offices, also on the 1st floor, have been restored and are a study in colonial elegance. The other rooms are given over to a library and an exhibition space for the Hassan al-Fageh House of Arts. If you ask the caretaker, he may let you climb to the roof from where there are good views.

HOUSE OF YUSUF KARAMANLI

Just south of the Roman Column Crossroads, the **House of Yusuf Karamanli** (Map p83;

Hosn al-Harem or Dar al-Karamanli; Sharia Homet Gharyan; admission 2LD, camera/video 2/5LD; ⌚ 9am-5pm Sat-Thu) dates from the beginning of the 19th century and was the private residence of Tripoli's former ruler. Although this represents an extravagant example, it provides a window on the world of private houses that once hid behind the medina's high walls. The courtyard, with a fountain in the centre, is one of the loveliest in the medina and is surrounded by balconies. The house has been converted into a museum and on the ground floor is a restored traditional bedroom, displays of traditional clothing, a sitting room and the kitchen. On the 1st floor, once home to the private living quarters, there are weapons, period furniture and the beautiful 'dome's hall' – a traditional sitting room with lavish tilework, an exquisite wooden ceiling and inlaid furniture from the time of Yusuf Karamanli. Off this hall is a reconstruction of a bridegroom's room and a room given over to musical instruments from where a window looks down on Sharia Homet Gharyan. Helpfully, most of the rooms have English and Italian explanations at the door.

Green Square (Martyrs' Square)

Scour an old, pre-revolution map of Tripoli and you're likely to find yourself a little disoriented. That's because Green Sq (Al-Sada al-Khadra; Map p75) – the hub of central Tripoli where the medina meets the traffic-filled streets of modern Tripoli – was only carved out after the 1969 revolution. Until then, the square was about half of its current size and its northeastern boundary was the waterfront – in the 1970s, around 500m of land was reclaimed to ease chronic traffic congestion. In its early days, Green Sq was primarily for mass rallies in support of the revolution, and while it still serves this purpose, it more often serves as a car park or fairground during public holidays. Floodlit by night, always busy by day and just as often known as Martyrs' Sq, you're likely to pass through here time and again.

East of Green Square

The white **Italianate façades** that front onto the eastern side of Green Sq continue for many a city block and it's worth wandering these streets to admire the peeling whitewash, period balconies and finely rendered façades that are so distinctive of Tripoli. The elegant **Galleria De Bono** (Map p75), off Sharia 1st September, is a particularly fine example. Some might say that buildings like these are the only positive thing that Italy's fascist rules bequeathed to the country.

That's certainly a view shared by the scholars at the **Libyan Studies Centre** (Map p75; ☎ 4446988; libyanjihad@hotmail.com; ⌚ by appointment). Dedicated to cataloguing the repression suffered by Libyans during Italian colonial rule, the centre has an impressive collection of 10,000 tapes of oral history and over 100,000 photographs. There's also a library and reading room, including thousands of books in English. It's off Sharia Sidi Munedir.

Madrassat al-Founoun Wasana'a al-Islamiya (Map p75; Islamic Arts & Crafts School; Sharia 1st September; ⌚ 10am-6pm Sat-Thu) is worth visiting for two reasons. The first is that the beautifully arched façade conceals a delightful, expansive two-tiered courtyard, which is rich in history. Originally built as a school during the Ottoman period, it was transformed into a prison from 1911 until 1942 by the Italians, who gathered Libyan deportees here before exiling them; many never returned, as suggested by the moving sculpture near the courtyard's western end. The tree opposite the entrance dates back to 1917. The other reason for visiting is that this is once again a school, where young Libyans are taught the traditional crafts of leatherwork, woodwork and pottery among other skills. If you're discreet, teachers and students alike usually don't mind if you watch them work.

If you haven't been in Tripoli for a few years, you'll be astounded by the transformation around Maidan al-Jezayir where the austere, neo-Romanesque **former Catholic cathedral** has been transformed into the supremely elegant **Masjed Jamal Abdel Nasser** (Map p75; Jamal Abdel Nasser Mosque; Maidan al-Jezayir). The conversion from church to mosque actually took place on 29 November 1970 in the days after the revolution, but the architectural work was not completed until 2003. Much of the former structure has been retained, but the use of marble and sandstone is exquisite. Non-Muslims aren't allowed inside, but the exterior is its most impressive element, especially if viewed from the teahouse surrounded by Italianate marble across the square.

HAMMAMS

There are at least three hammams (bathhouses) in the old city. Charges are 1LD for a steam bath, 2LD for a massage and 5LD for the full-scrubbing works.

Hammam al-Heygha (Map p83; Trigh al-Heygha; ⌚ women 8am-3pm Mon, Thu, Sat & Sun, men 8am-3pm Tue, Wed & Fri)
Hammam al-Kebira (Map p83; Sharia Homet Gharyan; ⌚ women 8am-3pm Mon-Wed, men 8am-3pm Thu-Sun)
Hammam Draghut (Map p83; Souq al-Turk; ⌚ women 8am-3pm Mon-Wed, men 8am-3pm Thu-Sun)

Immediately east of the cathedral, the continuation of Sharia Mohammed Megharief leads to the domed **National Library** (Map p75), which is very photogenic just before sunset. Built in the 1930s, it was the Royal Palace under the monarchy and the People's Palace immediately after the revolution.

San Francisco Church (Map p75; ☎ 3331863; ⌚ for mass) was built in the 1930s and offers services primarily for Libya's expat community. The sanctuary is quite simple, with a towering mural behind the altar. On the walls around the 1st-floor balcony are murals of the Twelve Stations of the Cross. Mass is conducted in English, French and Italian and mass times are usually posted on the door. It's off Sharia Khalid ibn al-Walid.

Tripoli's **planetarium** (☎ 3400201; per person 2LD), east along the waterfront off Sharia al-Corniche, would be a great place to study the stars over Libya before you head south into the star-gazing paradise of the Sahara, were it not for one thing: all presentations are in Arabic only. The 40-minute showings are by reservation only so if you're part of a group, they may let your guide interpret.

WALKING TOUR

Begin outside the entrance to the Jamahiriya Museum and walk southwest along the perimeter of Green Sq, past the small **balcony (1)** high on the castle's external wall – it was from here that Mussolini addressed the crowds in 1937 not long after pronouncing himself 'Protector of Islam'. The second street off the square to your right leads beneath the stone archway, which was once the main gate into the old city, into **Souq al-Mushir (2)**, with its mix of jewellery, handicraft and luggage stores. At the far end, past the **Ahmed Pasha Karamanli Mosque** (**3**; p84) on your left, is the 19th-century **Ottoman clock tower (4)**. Behind the clock tower is **Souq al-Ghizdir** (**5**; p96) where copper artisans patiently hammer out their wares.

At the end of the copper souq, turn left into a covered lane that leads onto the main **Souq al-Turk (6)**, which runs almost the length of the medina. Built during the Ottoman period, it was once covered by a roof. Continue until the souq ends at the **Draghut Mosque** (**7**; p85). After a short detour to the right to check out the magnificent **iron gateway (8)**, return southwest, pass the **Othman Pasha Mosque and Madrassa** (**9**; p85) on your right until you reach the recently restored former **Banco di Roma (10)**. It was built in 1870 as part of an attempt by the Italians to cement their commercial links in Libya. Opposite the Banco di Roma to the east is a small **Roman pillar (11)** built into the wall. Just around the corner to the southwest is the **Turkish Prison (12)**, which was used for detaining Christian prisoners. It was built in 1664 during the reign of Othman Pasha al-Saqizli, a former janissary credited with being the first ruler to unite Tripolitania and Cyrenaica. Behind its walls is a small **Orthodox church (13)** that still services Tripoli's Orthodox community. Almost opposite the prison is the imposing **former Catholic Cathedral (14)**.

In the northern corner of the square, a narrow lane leads past the **Old French Consulate** (**15**; p86) to the **Arch of Marcus Aurelius** (**16**; p84). Closer to the waterfront, a further 150m away, is the attractive **Sidi Abdul Wahab Mosque (17)** and one of the last surviving remnants of the **original city wall (18)**. Immediately behind the arch is the **Gurgi Mosque** (**19**; p85). Running along the northwestern wall of the mosque is Sharia Hara Kbira (also signposted as Sciara El-Kuash), which follows the path of the old Roman decumanus. The first street leading up the hill to your right is Zenghat Sidi Salim, which leads to the pristine, whitewashed **Sidi Salim Mosque (20)**; there are some lovely doorways as you climb towards the mosque. Return back down the hill, and turn right. The **Old British Consulate** (**21**; p85) is a few metres away on your right.

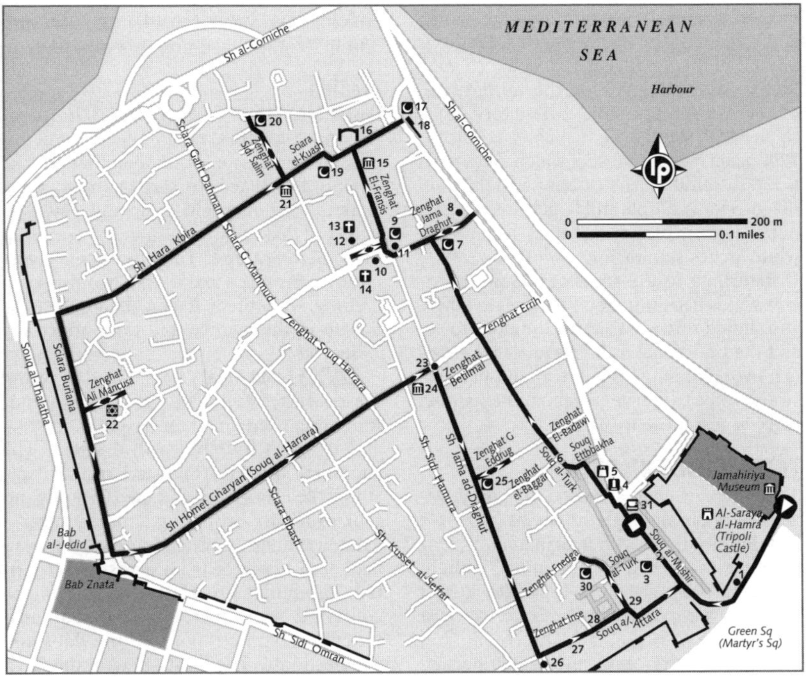

WALK FACTS

Start Jamahiriya Museum
End Magha al-Sa'a
Duration 2–3 hours
Distance about 3km

Continue southwest until the road ends at the medina wall and then turn left. After about 100m, turn left again onto the small Zenghat Ali Mancusa. The building on your right with boarded-up windows is a shell of a **former synagogue (22)**; high above the main northeastern door are some rare Hebrew inscriptions. Return to the main road and continue until it ends at Bab al-Jedid and an open area with an outdoor teahouse and (sometimes) an open-air market. Take Sharia Homet Gharyan (also signed as Souq al-Harrara) heading northeast. Along this thoroughfare, the medina begins its transition from the quiet residential streets to the busier markets and this is one of the areas in desperate need of renovation. In the lanes leading off either side are some fine doorways.

Soon enough, you'll reach the **Roman Column Crossroads** (Al-Arba'a Arsaht; **23**), where four Roman-era columns have been used to curious effect. The **House of Yusuf Karamanli** (**24**; p86) is located here. The road leading southeast passes the **Druj Mosque (25)**, which has an attractive doorway on the northern side, while the street running off to the northeast (Zenghat G Eddrug) is lined with pastel doors, shutters and occasional balconies of wrought-iron. About 150m further southeast along Sharia Jama ad-Draghut you pass under seven white arches, just before which on the right are three ornate doorways, one with a tiled arch.

Approximately 50m beyond the arches is a busy crossroads. From the crossroads, some of the old city's most attractive **Italianate façades (26)** make a rare appearance in the medina to the south. Take the walkway leading to the northeast that takes you into **Souq al-Attara (27)**. This is one of the liveliest thoroughfares of the medina with an **impromptu souq (28)** home to a crowded mix of shops and temporary stalls set up by traders without a licence; these stalls evaporate quickly as soon as a policeman is spotted. Off the northeastern side of this branch of the Souq al-Attara is the covered **Souq al-Rabaa** (**29**; p96). At the western end of the impromptu souq, a left turn leads to **An-Naqah Mosque (30)**, which is said to be 1200 years old, but most of which dates from the 17th century. The exterior and much of the interior is simple and largely unadorned, but the main prayer hall does have lovely white arches supporting the low roof.

Returning to the southwest, Souq al-Attara winds back into Souq al-Mushir, where you should turn left towards the clock tower and the traditional teahouse of **Magha as-Sa'a** (**31**; p95). Nursing a *shay* (tea) and nargileh (water pipe), you've reached the perfect place to rest those weary legs.

TRIPOLI FOR CHILDREN

There are few-child-specific sights or activities in Tripoli, although the **medina** (p82) is a labyrinth for those with imagination.

Other than that, the definite highlight is the surprisingly good **Tripoli Zoo** (Hadikat al-Haywan; Map p72; Sharia Abu Salim; adult/child 0.5/0.25LD; 9am-5pm), which you'll find south of the city centre in the 200-hectare An-Nasr Forest. Most of the enclosures are spacious and reasonably well kept and include elephants, lions, tigers, reptiles, monkeys, gazelle and waddan, among others. We're not quite sure what the Persian cats are doing there, but as our guide pointed out, they're exotic for Libyans. The landscaped grounds come alive on Fridays when you'll struggle to find picnic space amid the Libyan families – a great time for your kids to make new friends. There are a few snack stalls scattered around the grounds.

Another possibility are the ornately decorated **horse-drawn carriages** that do circuits of Tripoli from their base in Green Sq.

SLEEPING

It used to be that we listed every (usually government-owned) hotel in Tripoli for no reason other than that there weren't that many places from which to choose. But Tripoli is now a boom town and your choice of accommodation is getting better, almost literally by the day. The old government hotels often occupy the best locations, but the rooms are far better at the private places springing up all over town.

All prices include a private bathroom and breakfast unless otherwise stated.

Medina

Hostel Souq Etturk (Map p83; ☎ 3339773; Souq al-Turk; dm with shared bathroom 5LD) We mention this place for no reason other than that it's one of only two places to stay in the medina. Rooms are downright basic and you'll always feel that the staff wish they were asleep or somewhere else. Tour companies steer clear of this place and it's really only worth arguing with them if you dream of waking up in the medina and can't afford the Zumit Hotel.

our pick **Zumit Hotel** (Map p83; ☎ 3342915; www.zumithotel.com; d/ste 150/200LD;) At last a traditionally styled hotel in Tripoli's medina and it was definitely worth the wait. The rooms are arrayed around a charming, two-storey tiled courtyard and the 10 rooms and four suites are brimming with character – vaulted ceilings, elevated traditional Libyan beds and artefacts from across the country. The buffet breakfast is served in the courtyard while there's also a traditional restaurant with cushions on the floor and a coffeehouse. The location, with the Arch of Marcus Aurelius right outside the front door, is the best in all of Tripoli.

West of Green Square

Apart from the private midrange hotels south of the medina, there are two longer-standing hotels by the water (which require a taxi into town) and the Corinthia Bab Africa Hotel, the showpiece hotel of the new Libya.

BUDGET

Funduq Bab al-Jadid (Map p72; ☎ 3350670; fax 3350670; Sharia al-Corniche; s/d 25/35LD;) With a good seafront location and decent rooms, this is one of the best budget choices in town. Its problem is that it's a popular place with both tourists and local businessmen and maintenance standards aren't what they could be; some bathrooms are ageing fast. Be aware also that a basic breakfast is included in the price, but the more extensive buffet costs an additional 5LD.

MIDRANGE

The small grid of streets between Tripoli International Fair and Maidan as-Sawayhili is where Tripoli's private-hotel revolution is taking place. The hotels have high-standard rooms, reasonable prices and, although the streets are a tad ramshackle, the location is good as you're just a 10-minute walk from Green Sq and the medina.

Funduq Tebah (Map p75; ☎ 3333575; www.tebah-ly.com; Sharia al-Raza; s/d/tr/ste 40/50/70/100LD;) Slightly cheaper than Funduq al-Andalus (below), this place is a comfortable option and some rooms at the back have distant views of the Mediterranean. If we have one criticism, and now we are getting picky, the brown carpet makes the rooms look older than they are, but it is a good package overall.

Funduq al-Doha (Map p75; ☎ 4449373; fax 334-0653; Sharia al-Raza; s/d/tw/tr 40/50/60/70LD;) One of the newest (and friendliest) kids on the block, Funduq al-Doha promises a warm welcome and the whole place sparkles, although you really want a room at the front as most of those at the back have no windows. Even some at the front could do with more natural light, but that's our only problem with the place.

Funduq an-Naher (Map p75; ☎ 4446896; naherhotel@yahoo.com; Sharia Tariq; s 35-60LD, d 60-75LD;) On the fringes of the down-at-heel Sharia al-Rashid district, Funduq an-Naher has rooms that vary in size but they're all pleasant and quieter than the area suggests. The larger ones with balcony are semiluxurious and come with minibar, phone and satellite TV.

Funduq al-Deyafa (Map p75; ☎ 4448182; diafatip@hotmail.com; Sharia al-Raza; s/d/tr 40/60/70LD;) Another good choice in the area that gets good reports from travellers, Funduq al-Deyafa has decent rooms and the bathrooms have bathtubs. If you've seen every hotel room in Tripoli, like we have, you'll realise how rare that is.

Funduq al-Andalus (Map p75; ☎ 3343777; www.andalushotel.com; Sharia al-Kindi; s/d/ste 50/60/100LD;) Of the new private hotels in this area, Funduq al-Andalus is our favourite. It has all the necessary bells and whistles – satellite TV, air-conditioning, minibar – but the decoration is more stylish than most and there's plenty of natural light in most rooms. Service is also attentive and breakfasts quite good.

Funduq al-Mukhtar (Map p75; ☎ 4444536; fax 3333479; Sharia al-Raza; s/d/tr/ste 60/80/110/150LD;) We slept in this hotel on the first night it opened and have to say that we were impressed. The rooms are extremely comfortable and the bathrooms contain hairdryers and a nice basket of goodies, which probably justifies the fact that this hotel is slightly more expensive than others in the area.

Funduq al-Kindi (Map p75; ☎ 4448123; info@alkendihotel.com; Sharia al-Kindi; s/d/tr 70/85/150LD;) This place just about merits its elevated prices – the quality of the rooms and service is much the same as the others around here, but its rooms are more stylish and there's a little more space to open your suitcase.

Funduq Bab al-Bahar (Map p72; ☎ 3350676; fax 3350711; Sharia al-Corniche; s/d from 75/90LD;) Seen in the light of the Corinthia's emergence (below), the Bab al-Bahar is anything but the five stars it claims to be. The rooms are fine if a little run-down and most afford good views over the town or Mediterranean. The service is, however, woeful and prices unreasonably high for what you get. That notwithstanding, it's a favourite of tour groups and you may end up staying here whether you want to or not.

TOP END

Four Seasons Hotel (Map p75; ☎ 3332151; www.fourseasons.com.ly; Sharia Omar al-Mukhtar; s/d/ste from 90/110/140LD;) Although nothing to do with the international chain of the same name, this new hotel comes highly recommended for its large, comfortable rooms, internet connections in each room for those with laptops (the suites have PCs) and very friendly service. The decoration is over-the-top modern Libyan style but at least it has a certain kitsch character of its own.

Corinthia Bab Africa Hotel (Map p75; ☎ 3351990; www.corinthiahotels.com; Souq al-Thalatha; s/d €315/330, ste €465-1500;) A towering temple of glass and elegance, this is Libya's classiest hotel. The rooms are enormous and luxurious, the restaurants of the highest order and the service everything you'd expect for the price. The hotel has a business centre, conference facilities, two swimming pools, a gymnasium, an exclusive spa and plans for wi-fi internet connection in every room. Credit cards are also accepted. All of which adds up to Libya's premier address. Rates quoted here are the rack rates, so check the website for special offers and watch the rates fall.

East of Green Square

The streets that run southeast from Green Sq contain a number of hotels that are worth considering, although some are at least a 15-minute walk from the medina.

BUDGET

Buyut ash-Shabaab (Youth Hostel; Map p75; ☎ /fax 3330118; 69 Sharia Amr ibn al-Ass; dm with shared bathroom 5LD) Tripoli's central youth hostel is a stone's throw from Green Sq and, although it's pretty basic, these are the cheapest habitable beds in the centre of town. The shared bathrooms are fine and there's a cheap restaurant on the 2nd floor where it serves up simple spaghetti dishes for 1.5LD. Women may not feel comfortable here unless staying as part of a group. This is also the headquarters of the Libyan Youth Hostel Association (p212).

Buyut ash-Shabaab (Youth Hostel; ☎ 4776694, 4474755; dm with shared bathroom 5LD) This well-run hostel is off Sharia Gargaresh, 5km south of the town centre in the lively district of Gargaresh. It's marginally better than its more central counterpart, although it's a long way from Tripoli's sights.

Funduq al-Soraya (Map p75; ☎ 3339110; fax 3330821; s/d 20/30LD; ☒ ▣) One of the closest hotels to Green Sq, Funduq al-Soraya has simple, drab but comfortable rooms. The location, off Sharia Omar al-Mukhtar, is as central as you'll find, staff are friendly and there's an internet café next to the lobby (see p74).

MIDRANGE

Funduq Gharnata (Map p75; ☎ 3336128; fax 3336054; Sharia al-Baladiya; s with shared bathroom 25LD, s/d with private bathroom 40/45LD; ☒) This place stands out for its location, just a few blocks east of Green Sq, making it one of the most convenient places to sleep in town. The rooms are unspectacular, although they're tidy and reasonable value for money.

Funduq Attawfeek (Map p75; ☎ 4447253; attawfeek_hotel@yahoo.com; Sharia Qusban; s/d/d/ste 55/65/85LD; ☒ ▣) Although this friendly hotel is a brisk 15-minute walk from Green Sq and the medina, it's one of the best midrange hotels in town. Set in a quiet residential street across from San Francisco Church, it has spacious if simple rooms with balconies (some overlook the church), a laundry service, ADSL internet access in every room

and a good buffet breakfast. It also accepts Visa card and was adding 30 more rooms when we visited.

Funduq Dekna (Map p75; ☎ 4444403; fax 4443698; info@deknahotel.com; Sharia Abdul Nasser; s/d/ste from 65/75/175LD; ☒ ▣) Another new place that doesn't see as many tourists as it deserves, Funduq Dekna has large, bright rooms which are worth every dinar. Service is friendly once the staff warm up, internet connection in every room is free and you're a 10-minute walk from the medina.

TOP END

Funduq al-Safina al-Zarqa (☎ 3511164; fax 3511163; Sharia al-Corniche; s 75-80LD, d 100LD, ste with/without sea view 200/180LD) OK, so it's quite a long way (8km) east of town, but the Blue Boat Hotel is a popular place with large rooms and a good restaurant. We don't really see what the fuss is about when there are now plenty of high-quality places closer to the centre, but travellers we spoke to were happy with their stay here.

Funduq al-Kebir (Map p75; ☎ 3606781; fax 4445959; Sharia al-Fat'h; s/d with sea view 90/100LD, with city view 80/100LD; ☒ ▣) Once one of Tripoli's top hotels, Funduq al-Kebir is still probably the best value of the old government hotels. The rooms are very comfortable if unspectacular and the views from the top floors can be superb. Impersonal service, an airport-style X-ray machine at the door and serious-looking government types say it all about the atmosphere, but it does have a business centre, ATM machine for Visa cards and quite a few restaurants. As one reader said, don't get too excited about breakfast here.

Funduq Winzrik (Map p72; ☎ 3403570; info@wnzrikhotel.com; Sharia ash-Shatt; d 95-100LD, ste 160LD; ☒ ▣) This place is excellent if you're in town on business, although we're not sure that the addition of computers in each room (internet access costs 5LD per 24 hours) justified a doubling of its prices since we were last here. The rooms are large and very well appointed and there's also a small business centre.

Funduq al-Mehari (Map p75; ☎ 3334091/6; fax 4449502; Sharia al-Fat'h; d 150LD) Rooms at what was once Tripoli's most prestigious hotel come with most of the luxury bells and whistles and it gets good reviews from travellers. It certainly does have a touch of class that's lacking in other government hotels and there are great views from the upper floors.

Funduq as-Safwa (Map p75; ☎ 3334592; www.safwahotel.com; Sharia al-Baladiya; ste from 100LD) This suites-only hotel is in a quiet street away from the traffic noise of downtown Tripoli and its large, semiluxurious rooms are extremely comfortable. It doesn't get too many tourists here, which may be reason enough to consider it. There's a very good restaurant downstairs.

EATING

Tripoli is the best place to eat in Libya and the opening of new restaurants in the medina means that you usually get plenty of atmosphere to go with your meal. East of Green Sq, the setting is more modern but the food equally good.

There are also loads of fast-food restaurants and snack bars all over Tripoli. Apart from price, the advantage of these places is that they are invariably open in the afternoon when most other restaurants are closed. (The hours are from 11am to 11pm.) Standard fare is *shwarma* (grilled chicken kebab; 1LD to 2LD), hamburgers (1LD to 1.5LD) and pizzas (1/5LD for small/large).

To round off your meal or simply for a snack, it's hard to go past Tripoli's wonderful patisseries. There are plenty in the streets southeast of Green Sq, especially along Sharia Mizran where there's a cluster that are marked on the Central Tripoli map. Most are open 11am to 8pm Saturday to Thursday and 2pm to 8pm Friday.

Medina

our pick **Mat'am Obaya** (Map p83; ☎ mobile 0925010736; Souq al-Turk 114; mains from 5LD; lunch Sat-Thu) This is the sort of place that Lonely Planet authors hesitate to include in a book for fear that they can't get a table next time they visit. It's small with no pretensions to luxury, but there's no finer seafood in Libya and all of it is home-cooked by the amiable Mohammed Obaya, who represents all that is good about old-style Libyan warmth and hospitality. It's usually packed with tourists until around 2pm when Libyans start to muscle in for their share. The stuffed calamari (5LD) is Mohammed's own creation, not to mention the tastiest restaurant dish you'll find in Libya. The *shola* or *faruj* fish with sauce and couscous are not far behind. Expect to pay no more than 10LD for one of these main dishes, the octopus salad and a drink. Exceptional.

Mat'am al-Bourai (Map p83; ☎ mobile 0927166560; Sharia Jama ad-Draghut; meals from 10LD; lunch Sat-Thu) Above one of the liveliest thoroughfares in the medina, this bright and busy restaurant has basic décor, but excellent food. Mat'am al-Bourai's speciality is the delicious *rishda* (noodles with chickpeas and onions) and, for the more adventurous, *osban* (sheep's stomach filled with liver, kidney and other meat, rice and herbs, and steamed or boiled in a sauce), which is a Libyan favourite.

Athar Restaurant (Map p83; ☎ 4447001; starters around 3LD, mains mostly 10-15LD; lunch & dinner) Eat here at least once while you're in Tripoli. More than that, make it an evening meal so that you can sit at an outside table right next to the illuminated Roman-era Arch of Marcus Aurelius. Now that you're seated, order *algarra* (see p66) with lamb (13LD) or seafood (20LD): cooked in a high-temperature oven with mint, basil, tomato and green peppers, it's a delicious traditional dish; soon enough, they'll be bringing a ceramic amphora, and breaking it open in front of you with a hammer. Another good order is *ozhe mergaz* (Libyan sausages; 10.5LD). It also does good salads, soups, couscous, *tajeen* (a lightly spiced dish of meat or fish cooked in a ceramic pot with a tomato-and-paprika-based sauce), mixed grills and fresh fish. Both Visa and MasterCard are accepted.

Essaa Restaurant (Map p83; ☎ mobile 0912190683; meals 15-18LD; lunch & dinner Sat-Thu, dinner Fri) There's much to like about this place with its mix of traditional and modern décor, live traditional music in the evenings and the views over the Maidan al-Sa'a from some tables. The food is fairly standard Libyan restaurant fare with the usual Libyan soup, salad, fish or meat dishes and green tea. There's also a small coffeehouse downstairs.

Al-Dar Restaurant (Map p83; ☎ 3338364; meals 20LD; 11am-midnight) Another fine converted old medina building, this topnotch restaurant has loads of atmosphere from the agreeable sound of running water to cosy, individually styled rooms and good service. The roof terrace is lovely in the evening with views over the neighbouring Gurgi Mosque and Arch of Marcus Aurelius.

Tripolis Restaurant (Map p83; ☎ 0925580817; meals 15LD) Tasteful decorations, good food and uninterrupted views over Tripoli harbour make for a great dining experience on the fringes of the medina, off Souq al-Turk. Like many of the other new restaurants in the old town, the food is less inventive than enjoyable (ie you'll eat couscous or rice with soup and salad but they do it well), but we've no hesitation in recommending it for its ambience.

Al-Medina al-Kadima (Map p83; ☎ mobile 0926 889395; Souq al-Turk; meals 15LD; 🕑 8.30am-11pm Sat-Thu) Although better known as a teahouse (opposite), this nicely restored medina restaurant also serves good dishes of beans, fish couscous and seafood macaroni.

West of Green Square

The hotel boom in the area south of the medina and around Maidan as-Sawayhili is yet to be matched by a concomitant increase in the number of traveller-friendly restaurants.

Kentucky Restaurant (Map p75; Sharia Omar al-Mukhtar; meals 5LD) If you're after just a quick bite, this bright and popular place serves up dinner boxes that include three pieces of 'Kentucky' fried chicken, coleslaw, fries, two buns and a drink. It's great value, although the Colonel (Sanders, not Qaddafi) must be turning in his grave.

Al-Mat'am as-Samak at-Taazej (Map p75; ☎ 4443683; Sharia al-Kameet; meals from 8LD) This place is great value, and the huge and varied servings are presented in the squeaky-clean dining room by the ever-obliging waiters. It's something of a haven from the clamour outside, close as it is to Maidan as-Sawayhili, which is either dodgy or pleasantly seedy, depending on your perspective; we prefer the latter. It also does snacks downstairs.

Corinthia Bab Africa Hotel (Map p75; ☎ 3351990; Souq al-Thalatha) The four restaurants of Libya's top hotel are outstanding with the Venezia Restaurant (meals 20LD to 40LD) on the mezzanine floor serving Italian food and the top-floor Féz Restaurant (meals 25LD to 50LD) offering up exquisite Moroccan dishes in beautiful surroundings and with sweeping views over Tripoli. There are also two buffet restaurants in the glass atrium down the stairs from the lobby.

East of Green Square

RESTAURANTS

Haj Hmad Restaurant (Map p75; Sharia Haity; meals from 8LD; 🕑 lunch & dinner) Haj Hmad is a great place to enjoy traditional Libyan dishes heavy on internal organs, feet and heads. But there are plenty of non-offal dishes (including fish and beans) to choose from for the squeamish and it is popular with locals, which is always a good sign.

Galaxie Restaurant (Map p75; ☎ 4448764; Sharia 1st September; meals 14-18LD; 🕑 lunch & dinner) One of the best restaurants in this area, Galaxie is tastefully decorated and does the usual dishes with a touch more imagination than similar places elsewhere. The *algarra* is excellent but needs to be ordered three hours in advance. *Shwarma* and sandwiches are available downstairs.

Mat'am as-Safir (Map p75; ☎ 4447064; Sharia al-Baladiya; meals from 15LD; 🕑 lunch & dinner Sat-Thu, dinner Fri) Tucked away behind Funduq al-Kebir, this place is popular with middle-class Libyans. The dining room is a cut above most modern restaurants and is reminiscent of an ancient hammam; the atmosphere is particularly agreeable in the evenings. Service is warm and welcoming and don't neglect to try the *tajeen*.

Kenouz al-Bahar Restaurant (Map p75; ☎ 3334321; Maidan al-Jezayir; meals 15-25LD) We like this place, which is directly opposite the main post office, for its friendly service and fine cooking. The *tajeen* is especially good, but it's best known for its fish dishes, which come with some subtle Tunisian touches.

Mat'am al-Murjan (Map p75; ☎ 3336507; Maidan al-Jezayir; meals 20-25LD) Next door to Kenouz, the Mat'am al-Murjan has similarly pleasant décor, attentive service and tasty food. You can choose from up to 20 self-service salads (the salad buffet costs 7LD), a mixed plate of shrimps, fish and calamari (from 25LD) or a range of local and North African fish dishes.

Mat'am al-Masabiyah (Map p75; ☎ 3337815; Sharia al-Fateh; meals 15-25LD; 🕑 lunch & dinner Sat-Thu, dinner Fri) Particularly popular with well-to-do locals on Wednesday night, the service and food here are good and the food is tasty. The mixed grill is a highlight and for drinks you can choose from the *masabiyah jamaica* (a cocktail of 7-Up, Mirinda and Coke; see p67) or *carcedy*, a strong Sudanese drink made from leaves and served hot

(2LD). It also does pastas of varying quality and for dessert, don't miss the *mihallabia* (rice with milk).

Mat'am al-Saraya (Map p75; ☎ 3334433; Green Sq; 🕑 noon-1am) Beloved by the Corinthia set and well-to-do Libyans, this upmarket coffeehouse and restaurant serves high-quality food. The upstairs restaurant has a range of set menus (30LD to 40LD) with an emphasis on Lebanese cuisine, while you can also order lamb/seafood *mbakbaké* (lamb or seafood Libyan pasta; 35/23LD for two) off the menu. The downstairs area is for snacks, including pizza, hamburgers and sandwiches (5LD to 20LD), as well as an enticing range of desserts. The outdoor garden is a popular place to pass the evening with a nargileh.

our pick **Fish market** (5.5km east of the port along the road to Tajura) For a totally different eating experience, head to this ramshackle fish market. Choose the fish or other seafood that you want, buy it and then take it to one of the recently renovated restaurants where they'll grill it for you for a small fee (around 1.5LD). The most pleasant places to eat are **Barakoda Restaurant** (☎ 0913206971) or **Al-Shatt Restaurant** (☎ 0913771544), both of which do great salads. For a wonderfully filling and tasty meal, expect to pay 10LD to 15LD. It's wildly popular with Libyans, travellers and expats and you may have to wait for a table if you arrive late. If you're going there under your own steam, ask the taxi driver for the 'Marsa' or 'Al-Hufra' area; it's opposite the turn-off to Sharia 11 June.

QUICK EATS

The area sprawling east of Green Sq is awash with restaurants and snack bars that serve *shwarma*, hamburgers and pizzas.

Mat'am Salim (Map p75; Green Sq; hamburgers from 1.5LD, pizza 3.5-15LD; 🕑 noon-midnight Sat-Thu, 6pm-midnight Fri) Undoubtedly the pick of the snack bars that proliferate in the area, Mat'am Salim is bright, stylish and friendly with outdoor tables that are perfect for both people- and traffic-watching on Green Sq. It also has a restaurant upstairs.

DRINKING

The chaste pastime of tea-drinking is for many Tripolitans the only form of night-time entertainment and there are tea gardens and teahouses across the city that usually stay open until late. Many are men-only, but there are nonetheless plenty of places where women will feel comfortable.

Magha as-Sa'a (Clock Tower; Map p83; ☎ 0925-032510; Maydan al-Sa'a; 🕑 7am-2am) Opposite the Ottoman clock tower in the medina is Tripoli's outstanding traditional teahouse. You can sit outside, but make sure you check out the ground-floor room with its eclectic and distinctly musical themes – an old electric guitar, an archaic juke-box and gramophone. There are good views over the square from upstairs. Not surprisingly, this place has become a favourite of tour groups, but enough locals also turn up for it to feel authentic. The staff claims never to close but we didn't turn up at 4am to confirm.

Al-Medina al-Kadima (Map p83; ☎ mobile 0926889395; Souq al-Turk; meals 15LD; 🕑 8.30am-11pm Sat-Thu) In the heart of the medina, you can't miss this traditionally decorated teahouse with loads of North African knick-knacks and a mixed crowd of tourists and locals. The only drawback is that you'll need to go elsewhere if you've set your heart on smoking a nargileh. It also serves food upstairs (opposite).

Mat'am al-Saraya (Map p75; ☎ 3334433; Green Sq; 🕑 noon-1am) This upmarket restaurant (above) is classy inside, but especially popular for its outdoor tables on warm evenings where the air is thick with smoke.

Other places which are good for tea or a nargileh include Essaa Restaurant (p93) and Al-Dar Restaurant (p93); the latter's roof terrace is the place to be on a balmy Tripoli night.

Most of the above places attract a largely tourist crowd, but there are outdoor tea gardens scattered around town that are filled with families and groups of local men passing the night until midnight (or 2am on Thursday nights). At such places, a nargileh costs 1LD and tea 0.50LD. The better ones are the **Gazelle Café** (Map p75; Sharia al-Fat'h), next to a 1920s-era fountain; the open area next to where Sharia al-Baladiya meets Green Sq; the tables under the arches on Maidan al-Jezayir; and the elegant Galleria De Bono (Map p75), off Sharia 1st September. Hidden away in Sharia al-Mizda, just off Green Sq, the teahouses are like a small slice of Cairo, although women may feel uncomfortable here.

ENTERTAINMENT

You didn't come to Tripoli for the nightlife, which is just as well because there is none. Bring a good book. Linger over your evening meal. Catch up on emails in an internet café. Other than that, a night out in Tripoli consists of nursing a *shay* and nargileh in an outdoor tea garden (see p95). Even the Arabic-only cinemas (1LD) show only Egyptian, Indian or Western blockbusters interspersed with an ongoing love affair with Jackie Chan.

SHOPPING

Tripoli is the best place to shop in Libya, and just about everything that you may want to buy in the country (for advice, see p224) can be found here. The most atmospheric places to shop are in the souqs of the medina (see Tripoli's Souqs, below).

Medina

There's a reasonably good range of handicrafts (carpets, traditional clothing, jewellery) in the lanes running off to your left as you enter from Green Sq, as well as a smattering of places around the midway point of Souq al-Turk and next to the House of Yusuf Karamanli (p86). If you want a Colonel Qaddafi watch (10LD to 25LD), ask your guide, who should be able to track one down either in the medina or along Sharia al-Rashid.

Carpet Bazaar – Ben Zeglam Shop (Map p83; ☎ 0913212660; Souq al-Attara; ⏰ 10am-2pm & 5-8.30pm Sat-Thu) This is one shop that stands out in terms of quality, price and range for Libyan (mostly Berber) items, such as pottery, Tuareg jewellery, knives and boxes, flat-weave kilim cushions and larger rugs. The owner, Ahmeda Zeglam, is a delight and epitomises the old-style civility that characterises so many Libyan shopkeepers.

Mukhtar al-Mbaka & Sons (Map p83; ☎ 3331057; Souq al-Turk 12-16; ⏰ 9am-8pm) At the northwestern end of the Copper Souq, you'll find traditional Libyan silver items on offer from Mukhtar himself, who can explain the history of each piece.

Dar Yakhzen (Map p83; Souq al-Turk; ⏰ 10am-2pm & 5-8.30pm Sat-Thu) A particularly tranquil place to shop is this restored and whitewashed interior courtyard a few doors southeast of Hammam Draghut. There are handicraft stores and some traditional architectural features to contemplate while you browse.

Nearby to the carpet bazaar, behind the clock tower, the Souq al-Ghizdir (Map p83; Copper Souq) is a great place to see and hear the artisans at work in their almost medieval forges, and there are plenty of items for sale. Their specialities include *jammour* (crescents) that will one day adorn the tops of minarets; until that time many lie here against the lane's walls.

Near the southeastern end of Souq al-Turk, Souq al-Rabaa has vaulted ceilings and a range of local clothing such as *galabiyyas* (men's robes), including ones ideal for that three-year-old back home.

West of Green Square

The basic rule for the markets along Sharia al-Rashid is that if it isn't nailed down then it's probably for sale. Items on offer range from caged animals to cheap cigarettes, Ju-

TRIPOLI'S SOUQS

If you've travelled elsewhere in North Africa or the Middle East, you'll understand why the souqs of Tripoli's medina are like no others. There's no hard-sell, no expectation of payment if you get lost and ask someone for directions, no dragging you by the arm into shops to look 'just for the pleasure of your eyes'. People are genuinely helpful, like to chat and, in some places, shopkeepers almost seem embarrassed that you feel the need to pay for your purchase. We even heard stories, and have experienced ourselves, shopkeepers telling you to take your carpet or jewellery back to your hotel and bring the money later if you don't have enough cash on you.

There's one other thing about the souqs in the medina. Apart from the tourist-oriented shops in the medina's southeastern corner, most of the shops are aimed at locals. That's why, especially along the main Souq al-Turk, there's very little activity except between noon and 4pm from Saturday to Thursday. Most of the shopkeepers along this thoroughfare are gold merchants who sell by the kilo to locals as they shop for weddings or investments. You're welcome to enter the shops, but, refreshingly, you're not their main market.

ventus shirts to *galabiyyas*. Around the chaotic Tunis Garage (Map p83) at the western end are spare parts for cars, televisions, and African folk medicines sold by colourfully attired women from sub-Saharan Africa. It's worth wandering around here at least once, particularly in the evening when it can throng with people, although keep a close eye on your valuables. If you absolutely must have that Mohammed Hassan or Umm Kolthum cassette, there are shops along Sharia al-Rashid.

East of Green Square

Ghadames Art Gallery (Map p75; ☎ 3336666; 50/52 Sharia 1st September; 🕑 10am-2pm & 5-9pm Sat-Thu) Not far from Green Sq, the Ghadames Art Gallery is run by the engaging Mustafa Gayim and his friendly son, Musab. They sell old paintings and sketches of Tripoli and Libya by around 50 local artists, including some lovely acrylics, as well as old photos of Tripoli.

GETTING THERE & AWAY

Air

Tripoli airport is a 1970s-era building on a grand scale and despite minor makeovers has never really lost the feeling of a large warehouse. When you arrive, don't be put off by the bewildering slogans that proclaim 'Partners, not wage workers' and 'In need, freedom is latent'. Somewhat more helpfully, the arrivals hall has a bank where you can change money and ATMs for Masraf al-Tijara Watanmiya (Bank of Commerce & Development; for Visa) and Aman Bank for Commerce & Investment (for MasterCard).

For arriving passengers, there are usually taxis waiting outside in the event that your tour representative hasn't turned up.

Libyan Arab Airlines (Map p75; Sharia Haity ☎ 333-1143; Sharia 1st September ☎ 3616738) and **Al-Buraq Air** (Map p75; ☎ 4444811; www.buraqair.com; Sharia Mohammed Megharief) both fly from Tripoli International Airport, although Al-Buraq's international flights leave from Metiga Airport, 10km east of Tripoli.

Bus

Long-distances buses for most cities around Libya and further afield depart from Tunis Garage (Map p83) at the western end of Sharia al-Rashid.

The two main bus companies are **Al-Itihad al-Afriqi** (United Africa Bus Company; Map p75; ☎ 3342532; Sharia al-Ma'ari), which operates from the Tunis Garage perimeter, and **An-Nakhl as-Seria** (Fast Transport Company; Map p75; ☎ 3333678), which runs from the Dahra Bus Station (Mahattat Hafilat Dahra; Map p75). Sample routes include Benghazi (15LD to 23LD, twice daily, 12 hours), Sebha (15LD to 23LD, one daily, 12 hours) and Ghadames (10LD to 18LD, one daily, eight hours).

Shared Taxi & Micro

Most long-distance shared taxis and micros (minibuses) leave from Tunis Garage (Map p83) at the western end of Sharia al-Rashid. For destinations closer to Tripoli, shared taxis leave from the other stations along Sharia al-Rashid, near Maidan as-Sawayhili.

GETTING AROUND

To/From the Airport

Tripoli International Airport is around 25km south of the city. A private taxi costs 10LD, but if you're leaving after midnight, the driver will ask for more. A private taxi to Metiga Airport similarly costs 10LD.

DOMESTIC FLIGHTS FROM TRIPOLI

destination	airline	one way/return (LD)	frequency
Benghazi	Libyan Arab Airlines	37.50/75	3-4 daily
	Al-Buraq Air	45.50/91	5 daily
*Ghat	Libyan Arab Airlines	51/102	2 weekly
Lebreq (near Al-Bayda)	Libyan Arab Airlines	47/94	3 weekly
Sebha	Libyan Arab Airlines	37.50/75	1 daily
*Tobruk	Libyan Arab Airlines	51/102	

* Services to Ghat and Tobruk were suspended at the time of writing.

Car & Motorcycle

Tripoli has a difficult system of one-way streets in the area west of the medina – directions for the main streets are marked on the map.

Private Taxi

Black-and-white private taxis are everywhere in Tripoli and a trip usually costs 2LD, although it may be up to 5LD for outlying suburbs.

AROUND TRIPOLI

JANZUR جنزور

☎ 021

The small town of Janzur, 13km west of Tripoli, is in danger of being swallowed up by Tripoli's relentless sprawl. Janzur is best suited as a brief stop en route to Sabratha as there are a couple of noteworthy historical sights.

The town's main attraction is the 200-year-old **Sidi Amoura Mosque**, which has been freshly whitewashed and has a tranquil arched courtyard and, unusually for Libya, a square-sided minaret. Much of the mosque will soon be cast into shadow by a newer mosque being built alongside.

Janzur Museum (admission 3LD; 10am-6pm Tue-Sun) contains a motley collection of boneshards, pottery amphorae and oil lamps from the cemeteries that once dotted the region; most date from the 1st or 2nd centuries AD and are labelled in English. The real highlight, however, and worth the visit on its own, is the Byzantine tomb in the basement, one of 18 such underground tombs found in the area in 1958. Climb inside for some extraordinary frescoes, including one that takes the form of a river from earthly life to the afterlife.

Janzur is something of a summer resort and has a decent beach. Tastefully designed **Qaryat Janzur as-Siyahe** (Janzur Tourist Village; ☎ 4890421; s/d 25/35LD, villas 50LD) is one of Libya's better tourist complexes, but you'll have to book up to three months in advance to get a room in summer.

TAJURA تاجوراء

The small town of Tajura, 14km east of the capital, is a summer resort for Tripoli residents who don't want to stray too far from home. The settlement goes back to medieval times, and it was a refuge for the elites of Tripoli who fled during the brief Spanish occupation in the 16th century. Its main attraction is the large **Murad Agha Mosque**, which dates from the middle of the 16th century. It is very plain from the outside and features a large square minaret. Inside it has a large arcaded prayer hall with 48 columns, which were brought from Leptis Magna.

Elsewhere in Tajura is **Hammam Tajura**, a natural spring that has been turned into a health spa.

Coastal Tripolitania

Leptis Magna and Sabratha – what more do we need to say?

There is no finer ancient Roman city than Leptis Magna anywhere in the world and most travellers agree that it's Libya's most rewarding site. Leptis Magna was all about excess and extravagance, a city that embraced its moment as a centre of wealth and power. The extant ruins are so extensive, the public buildings so decadent that this is one ruined city that resonates with the spirit of those who made Leptis great.

Sabratha may always have been the relatively poor (though in reality extremely rich) cousin of Leptis, but it too is one of the most beautiful ruined Roman cities of the world. Strung out along the Mediterranean shoreline from its monumental heart, it whispers grandeur at every turn, nowhere more so than in its extraordinary theatre.

Villa Sileen is another essential element in the Leptis experience: it was to seaside villas like this that the Roman elite fled to escape from the rigours of city life. Floors composed entirely of intricate mosaics and frescoes adorning the walls provided the backdrop for the cultured art of serious Roman relaxation.

Together with Oea (which lies buried beneath Tripoli), Sabratha and Leptis Magna gave this province its Roman name: Tripolitania means 'the land of three cities'. The modern Tripolitanian coast has since sprouted many more cities such as Zliten and Misrata, but in reality these are sideshows and of interest only for their proximity to the splendour of ancient Rome.

HIGHLIGHTS

- Be spellbound by your first glimpse of the **Arch of Septimius Severus** (p111) in glorious Leptis Magna
- Survey the Mediterranean beyond the sweep of ruins from the upper levels of Leptis Magna's **theatre** (p115)
- Swim in the sea alongside the evocative ruins of **Sabratha** (p100)
- Imagine yourself a diva in Sabratha's exquisite Roman **theatre** (p105)
- Admire the Roman frescoes and mosaics in the seaside **Villa Sileen** (p107)
- Discover that there was more to ancient Libya than the Romans at **Ghirza** (p121)

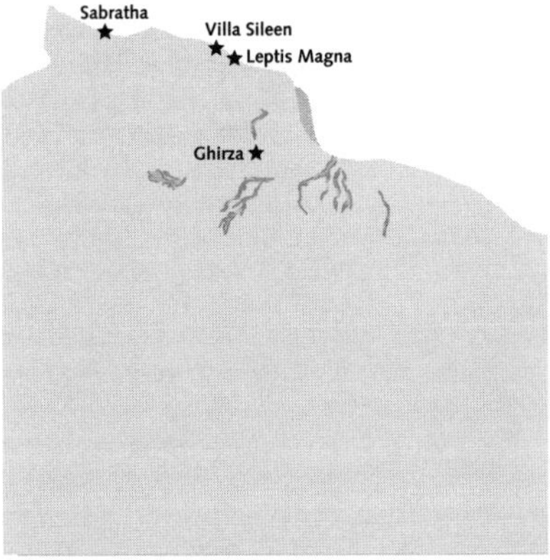

WEST OF TRIPOLI

If Libya ever develops Tunisian-style tourist resorts, chances are that most of them will be along the relatively deserted coast between Tripoli and the Tunisian border. White-sand beaches stretch to the horizon and the proximity of the ruins of splendid Sabratha, the undoubted highlight of this stretch of coast, are surely more than a glint in a developer's eye. Visit before it changes.

SABRATHA صبراتة

☎ 024 / pop 103,991

Were Sabratha anywhere other than a few hundred kilometres down the road from Leptis Magna, it would be hailed as one of the most beautiful Roman cities in the Mediterranean. In that sense, history has never been kind to Sabratha, existing as it always has in the shadow of its more famous cousin. The truth is, Sabratha is a stunning site that is a must-see, preferably before you visit Leptis. Its highlights include a theatre that was one of the most beautiful in ancient Rome, the fact that the site takes far better advantage of its seafront location than Leptis and the extant remains of Phoenician occupation that have been buried beneath the work of later civilisations elsewhere.

To catch a sense of the glories of Sabratha before you visit, Gallery 9 (p79) of Tripoli's Jamahiriya Museum has an excellent model of the ancient city in its Roman heyday.

One final piece of advance planning that will enhance your visit is to bring if not your toga then your swimmers, towel and a couple of bottles of fresh water – swimming in the Mediterranean alongside the ruins as the Romans themselves once did is one of Libya's most rarely enjoyed highlights. Other beaches to the west of the ancient city are quieter (except on Fridays) but you won't have the ruins nearby to help you dream.

History

The origins of Sabratha's name have been lost to time, although it may have been a derivation of a Libyan-Berber word meaning 'grain market'. There was a periodic (possibly nomadic) settlement here in the 5th century BC, but it wasn't until Punic settlers arrived in the 4th century BC from the neighbouring stronghold of Carthage that a permanent settlement was established. For this seafaring people, Sabratha's safe harbour was paramount and the Punic city consisted of narrow, winding streets with most houses facing the northwest to take full advantage of the seaborne winds. The arrival of Greek (Hellenistic) settlers in the 2nd century BC began to dilute the Punic character of the city as Greek architectural flourishes began to appear. One thing didn't change: Sabratha was renowned as a wealthy city and important regional centre covering at least four hectares.

COASTAL TRIPOLITANIA

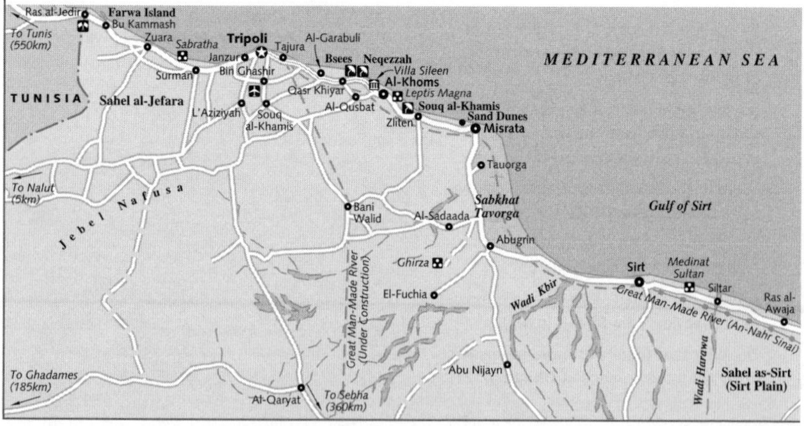

A violent earthquake destroyed much of the city in the 1st century AD and during the subsequent rebuilding phase the city's architects turned towards Rome, which at the time was the pre-eminent power in Tripolitania, for inspiration. The result was the noticeably Roman character that remains so evident today. A number of Sabratha's most important buildings – the forum (p104), the Temple of Liber Pater (p104), the Judicial Basilica (p103) and the Temple of Isis (p105) – were built during this period.

By the end of the 1st century AD, the last vestiges of Punic influence were being threatened by the inexorable weight of Romanisation. Like the other cities of the Tripolis, Sabratha's heyday was during the reigns of the four Roman emperors Antoninus Pius (r AD 138–61), Marcus Aurelius Antoninus (AD 161–80), Lucius Aelius Aurelius Commodus (AD 180–92) and Septimius Severus (AD 193–211). Although never competing for significance or grandeur with Leptis Magna, Sabratha grew in size and status, and received the coveted title of colony *(colonia)* in the 2nd century AD. The city's wealth depended on the maritime trade of animals and ivory from Africa, although the city kept a wary eye on its hinterland and on the ever-present threat of raids by Saharan tribes. Under Marcus Aurelius and Commodus, the extravagant, monumental heart of Sabratha extended ever-further south at the expense of formerly Punic structures; under Commodus, the theatre (p105) was built.

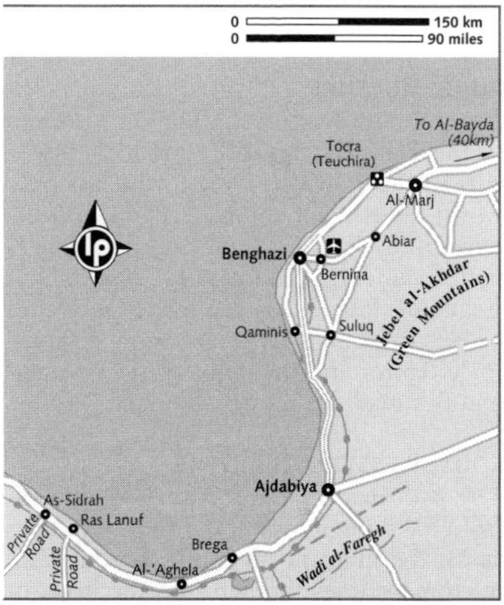

Sabratha's residents probably thought the glory days would last forever, but the terminal decline of Rome's economy in the 3rd century began Sabratha's decline and the earthquake in 365 dealt Sabratha's soft, sandstone buildings a blow from which they would never recover; for more information on the devastation wrought by the earthquake all along the coast, see p143. With the tide of Christianity sweeping the region, none of the ancient temples was rebuilt and a smaller city, a shadow of its former self, grew over the ruins.

In 533 Sabratha fell under the sway of the Byzantine general Belisarius who oversaw the rebuilding of the city walls (p102) to enclose only the western port and central area, thereby leaving the Roman parts of the city further to the east exposed and abandoned. The city survived for at least a century after the Islamic arrival in the 7th century AD, but was thereafter abandoned and left to the sands and Mediterranean winds. Sabratha was rediscovered by Italian archaeologists in the early 20th century.

Information

In order to enter the old city **site** (☎ 622214; adult/child 3/1LD, camera/video 5/10LD; 🕑 8am-6pm) you must be with a **guide** (50LD). Outside the entrance are a couple of stalls selling snacks, water and postcards. There's a public toilet inside the site, in front of the Roman Museum (the women's section is around the back).

Sights

ROMAN MUSEUM

The first site you'll reach after entering the site is the **Roman Museum** (adult/child 3/1LD, camera/video 5/10LD; 🕑 8am-6pm Tue-Sun) is excellent, although many visitors prefer to leave it until the end so as to better understand the exhibits.

The statues in the main courtyard set the tone with a winged Victoria writing on a shield while two barbarian prisoners beg for mercy. The western wing of the museum contains underground objects found in the tombs of Sabratha, while the central or southern wing contains some wonderful mosaics from the Basilica of Justinian (p104). The mosaic which once occupied the basilica's central nave shows a scene of considerable abundance, including a

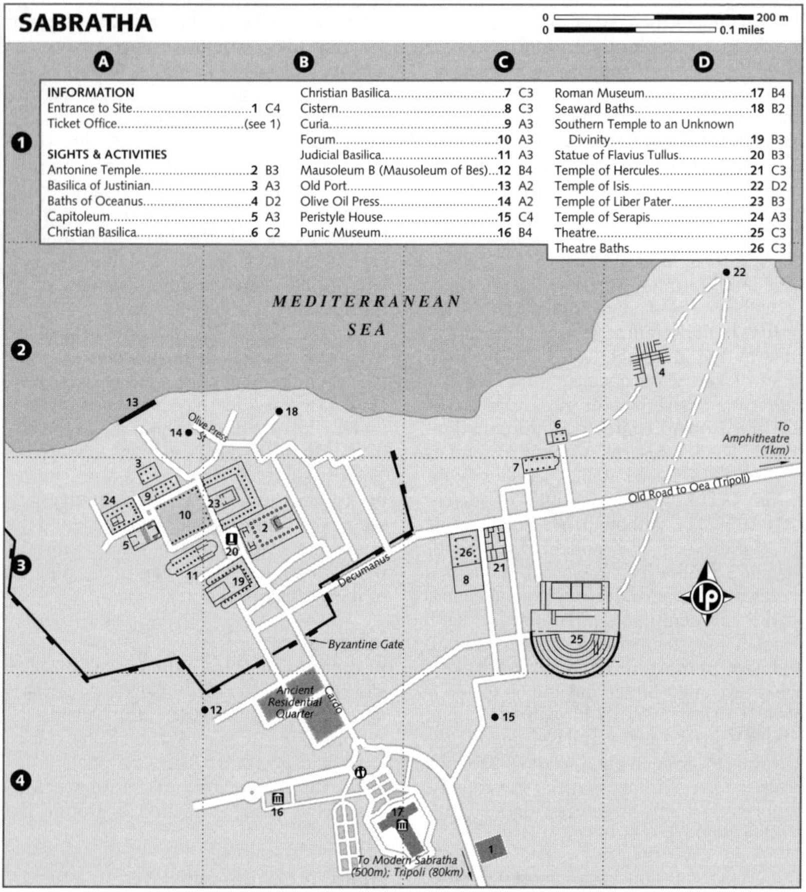

vibrantly coloured peacock. The mosaics from the basilica's two aisles are on the wall. The columns and bases are copies of the originals that remain in the basilica.

The eastern wing contains more superb mosaics and frescoes from a private house whose ornate decoration highlights the one-time wealth of Sabratha and its inhabitants. There are also some statues from the former Temple of Zeus (now the Capitoleum; p104) that was at the western end of the forum. In the fourth room is a mosaic of the Three Graces and a stunning one of Oceanus lifted from the centre of the baths that bear his name (see p105). In the final room, there is a mosaic of nymphs grooming the mythical winged horse Pegasus.

PUNIC MUSEUM

Around 50m west of the Roman Museum is the **Punic Museum** (adult/child 3/1LD, camera/video 5/10LD; 8am-6pm Tue-Sun), which is only worth the effort if you have an expert's interest in the city's earliest history. Exhibits include underground ceramic objects and fragments from Mausoleum B (Mausoleum of Bes; opposite), representations of lions, male figures and the deity of the Egyptian god Bes in all his repugnant glory.

SOUTHWESTERN QUARTERS

The path that leads north towards the sea from the Roman Museum is the old Roman **Cardo**, the main north-south thoroughfare in Roman times that led into the heart of the city. One of Sabratha's old **residential quarters** is off to the left where some houses contain cisterns and pottery shards.

Mausoleum B (Mausoleum of Bes), nearly 100m northwest of the Cardo, offers a rare insight into Punic Sabratha, although what you see is a reconstruction of the original. The mausoleum is nearly 24m tall and stands on the site of an underground funerary chamber dating from the 2nd century BC. It has a triangular base, concave façades and a small pyramidal structure on the summit. The motifs (originals of which are in the Punic Museum) show Bes and Hercules, who are thought to have been the protectors of the tomb, as well as lions. The mausoleum was dismantled by the Byzantines, who used the materials to build their wall around the city in the 6th century.

The **Byzantine wall** was designed to encircle and protect the city from restless Berber tribes from the interior. The **Byzantine Gate** was once flanked by small towers and marked an important point where access to the central commercial, administrative and religious districts could be controlled. The wall is at its most intact around the gate.

SOUTHERN TEMPLE TO AN UNKNOWN DIVINITY

The first major building on the left after you pass through the Byzantine Gate is a Roman temple built to an unknown deity; it's also known as the South Forum Temple. Much of the large rectangular courtyard still bears the original marble floor. It dates from the 2nd century AD, the great period of Roman monument building when cipolin columns and a portico once surrounded the courtyard. Apart from the marble floor, the capitals and pediment fragments are the only remaining original items.

ANTONINE TEMPLE

The elevated Antonine Temple is believed to have been dedicated to the Roman emperor Antoninus Pius, although some archaeologists believe that Marcus Aurelius was the real inspiration. It once had a small porticoed courtyard. A modern staircase allows you to climb to the top without damaging the crumbling gradations on either side. The views from the top are superb, showcasing Sabratha's prime coastal location and overlooking the adjacent public buildings that stood at the monumental heart of Roman Sabratha. Immediately outside the temple is a fine fountain and headless **Statue of Flavius Tullus** in commemoration of this fine 2nd-century citizen who commissioned an aqueduct to bring water to Sabratha.

JUDICIAL BASILICA

Also known as the Basilica of Apuleius of Madora (see also The Defence of Apuleius, below) or House of Justice, this building was originally erected in the 1st century AD. Most of what remains (marble columns and some excellent paving fragments) dates from around AD 450, during the Byzantine period. Between these dates, the building changed function as Sabratha made the transition from a Roman to a Byzantine city. Under the Romans, the basilica was broadly equivalent to a court and consisted of a large hall measuring 50m by 25m and surrounded by a portico. The Byzantines later converted it into a Byzantine church in which the main sanctuary was divided into a nave and aisles.

THE DEFENCE OF APULEIUS

In AD 158 a sensational trial rocked Sabratha from its decadent slumber with all the scandal of a modern soap opera. Apuleius was a renowned philosopher of the Plato School who travelled throughout the colonies expounding his theories to great acclaim. One of Apuleius' speaking tours took him to Sabratha, where he married Pudentilla, a rich widow many years his senior. The citizens of Sabratha were scandalised. One family, which stood to lose out on the widow's massive inheritance, formally brought a charge against Apuleius. The accusation? Using his magic powers to win over the widow (there is no record of whether she was given a say). The trial of the decade was presided over by the Roman proconsul Claudio Massimo in the Judicial Basilica (above). In a captivating oration that lasted three (some say four) days, Apuleius won his freedom. As other celebrities through the ages have discovered, the publicity only enhanced his reputation.

FORUM

Like all great Roman forums, Sabratha's forum formed the centrepiece of the ancient city and served as a market and public meeting place where the news of the city was disseminated. Most of what remains dates from restoration work in the 4th century AD; this work probably restored damage caused by the earthquake in AD 365. The original structure was built in the 1st century BC or 1st century AD. Before the Antonine Period (AD 138–61), the forum was only accessible via a single entrance. Over time, the shops and offices became more grand and more permanent, and a portico was built with grey columns of Egyptian granite. Some of these remain.

CAPITOLEUM

The Capitoleum, also known as the Temple of Jupiter or Zeus, was the principal temple of the city and dedicated to Jupiter, Juno and Minerva. The huge bust of Jupiter in the Roman Museum was found here, as were a rich storehouse of statues. The Capitoleum was first built in the 1st century AD and then reconstructed in marble the next century. Overlooking the forum as it did, its platform was the soapbox of choice for the great orators of the era. The original adornments of the platform are either gone or are now in the Roman Museum.

CURIA

On the northern side of the forum is the Curia (Senate House), marked by a restored archway at the entrance. The Curia was the meeting place of the city's magistrates and senators and consisted of a four-sided courtyard covered with a mosaic. The wide steps around the perimeter were used for portable seats upon which the great senatorial backsides could sit. It was one of very few major buildings rebuilt after the earthquake of AD 365; a portico was added during the reconstruction. Its grey-granite columns are a feature. There were three entrances to the forum from the Curia and the niches in the perimeter were adorned with statues.

TEMPLE OF LIBER PATER

East of the Curia is the Temple of Liber Pater (Temple of Dionysius), which was never rebuilt after the AD 365 earthquake. It is marked by five columns in light sandstone on a high podium overlooking the monumental heart of ancient Sabratha. It was once flanked on three sides by a double colonnade of sandstone columns. Dedicated to one of the most revered gods of Roman Africa and second only in importance to the Capitoleum in the hierarchy of temples in Roman Sabratha, this temple sat atop an elevated platform that was reached via a wide staircase. It was constructed in the 2nd century AD on the site of an earlier temple. Only the column bases and two of the columns are original.

TEMPLE OF SERAPIS

Immediately west of the Curia, this temple is dedicated to Serapis, a healer and miracle worker. The cult of Serapis, which originally came from Memphis in Egypt, was often associated in Sabratha with that of Isis. It is thought to be one of the oldest temples in the city, although its date of construction is not known. Some of the columns of the portico are still present in a combination of grey marble and limestone.

BASILICA OF JUSTINIAN

This was one of the finest churches of Byzantine Sabratha. Built in the 6th century AD, its main nave and aisles were adorned with breathtaking mosaics that now reside in the central wing of the Roman Museum (p101). Many features, including the magnificent, square-sided column on the apse with intricate acanthus motifs (2nd century AD), date from an earlier period, as construction materials were taken and reused from other parts of the city. The mosaics in the Roman Museum make it easy to imagine the grandeur of this church, which also had three naves, a pulpit and an altar (the foundations of each remain clearly visible). The pulpit originally formed a part of the cornice on the Capitoleum.

NORTHWESTERN QUARTER

The buildings overlooking the Mediterranean north and east of the Basilica of Justinian are some of the oldest in Sabratha, many dating from the 1st century AD when the city was still primarily Punic in character. This was the site of the **old port**, the launching pad of Sabratha's wealth. This was also a residential area. The ruins of an old **olive oil press** are nearby as are the public **latrines** that doubled as a meeting place (it's a pity their existence doesn't spur on the modern Libyan authorities to provide similar amenities in their cities).

Don't miss the **Seaward Baths**, which are superbly located east along the coast. One of many such complexes in Sabratha, the baths are famous for their lovely mosaics overlooking the water and for the hexagonal latrine, which is paved and lined with fine marble.

THEATRE QUARTER

About 150m southeast of the baths is the **Decumanus**, the main east-west thoroughfare of the Roman city. Flanked by parts of the old Byzantine wall, it runs past the **Temple of Hercules**, behind which is a large **cistern** used for storing water for the **Theatre Baths**, which are immediately opposite. These baths enabled the patrons of the arts to unwind before or after a performance and contain some mosaic fragments on the floors.

Northeast of these buildings are two **Christian basilicas** dating from the 4th to 5th centuries AD. They once formed part of a large religious complex under the Byzantines. A little further northeast are the **Baths of Oceanus**. The decoration of these public baths was extraordinarily lavish, with marble on every surface. You can see the *tepidarium* (warm room). The mosaic that is missing the central fragment once bore the head of the god Oceanus, but he now rests in the Roman Museum.

TEMPLE OF ISIS

The superb Temple of Isis, northeast of the Baths of Oceanus, is arguably the finest of Sabratha's temples. Built in the 1st century AD, it faces onto the Mediterranean in keeping with its dedication to the Egyptian goddess Isis, who was seen here as a protector of sailors. Every spring a great feast was held to celebrate the start of the sailing season. The colonnaded courtyard has a row of eight Corinthian columns. Look beyond the temple to the north and you can see part of the temple foundations that have been eroded by the sea; beyond that are parts of the city lost to the waves during the earthquake.

THEATRE

The outstanding theatre, south of the basilicas, is the jewel in Sabratha's crown and is visible from miles around. Construction of the theatre was begun in AD 190 under the reign of Commodus although some historians claim it was completed by Septimius Severus the following decade. It was still used into the 4th century until it was destroyed by the earthquake of AD 365. It was rebuilt by Italian archaeologists in the 1920s and is largely faithful to its original form, although the blocks used by the Italians were only half the original size. With an auditorium measuring close to 95m in diameter, it was the largest theatre in Africa.

The façade behind the stage is one of the most exceptional in the Roman world. The three tiers consist of alcoves and 108 fluted Corinthian columns that rise over 20m above the stage. There are some exquisite floral carvings atop the columns as well as carvings of divinities. The stage, 43m long and nearly 9m wide, overlooks the orchestra area that was paved with marble slabs. The front of the elevated stage is simply magnificent, and three large concave niches are the highlight. The central curved panel shows personifications of Rome and Sabratha, flanked by military figures and scenes of sacrifice. The left panel (facing the stage) depicts the nine Muses while the one on the right shows the Three Graces and the Judgement of Paris. Set back into the wall are four rectangular façades between the concave niches, which show comedy scenes as well as dancing and a few assorted divinities (including Mercury) and the Greek mythological hero Hercules.

The balustrade at either end of the orchestra area marks the seats reserved for VIPs, who were kept suitably separated from the riff-raff. The seats climb sharply skywards and once had room for 5000 people; even today it can seat 1500. Underneath the seats were three concentric semicircular passageways that were known as promenades, parts of which were lined with shops. Only two of these promenades have since been rebuilt.

PERISTYLE HOUSE

On your way back to the exit, it's worth visiting this private residence that has good views back towards the theatre. It has a number of fine mosaics, one representing a labyrinth, a few columns and underground rooms that were used in summer.

AMPHITHEATRE

A longish walk away along the old road to Oea (Tripoli) to the northeast, Sabratha's amphitheatre was built in the 2nd century on the site of a converted quarry; a century later, Christians were fed to the lions here. The amphitheatre, which is built of limestone blocks, could once seat 10,000 spectators. The arena, which measures 65m by 50m, is bisected by two deep underground tunnels that were used for storing sets and equipment as well as providing easy access to the arena for performers. The tunnels were once covered with a wooden roof. Travellers are divided over whether the walk is worth it. If you've seen the better preserved amphitheatre in Leptis (p116), you could probably give it a miss if time is short.

Sleeping & Eating

Most people visit Sabratha on a day trip or en route to the Jebel Nafusa. The sleeping options in modern Sabratha are fairly uninspiring.

Buyut ash-Shabaab (Youth Hostel; ☎ 622821; dm 5LD, camping 5LD) Around 600m east of the entrance to the old city, this hostel is basic, clean and well run; you can also pitch a tent in the grounds+.

Funduq al-Asil (☎ 620959; s/d 20/40LD) This is Sabratha's newest and best hotel, and it's located on the western side of town, around 400m south of the coastal highway to Zuara. The rooms are tidy and spacious and some at the back of the building have a distant view of the ancient theatre. There's a **restaurant** (mains 8-30LD), coffeehouse and pool table.

Mat'am al-Bawady (☎ 620224; meals 10-12LD; 🕑 lunch & dinner) Along the highway on the western side of town, Mat'am al-Bawady is the only place to consider eating while in Sabratha. The food is excellent, the prices reasonable and the service friendly. There are also some nice decorative touches, which all adds up to Sabratha's best.

Getting There & Away

Sabratha is 69km west of Tripoli. Shared taxis run regularly to Tripoli and Zuara.

ZUARA زوارة

☎ 025 / pop 184,228

Zuara, 60km east of the Libyan–Tunisian border at Ras al-Jedir and 109km west of Tripoli, is a lively Berber town with excellent white-sand beaches.

Like many towns along Libya's northwestern coast, most of Zuara is located between the shores of the Mediterranean and the highway. The banks, post office and *jawazzat* (passport office) are east of the main square (known locally as the piazza).

In August, Zuara's **Awussu Festival** takes place. If you're within striking distance, joining the locals for sailing, swimming races and folk dancing is definitely the thing to do in Libya's wilting heat. Beneath the waters off Zuara are reported to be the remains of Old Zuara, which would make for an interesting snorkel if you have your own gear.

Zuara has a **Buyut ash-shabaab** (Youth Hostel; east of main square; dm 5LD), while **Funduq Delfin** (☎ 22711; fax 22710; main highway; s/d/tr 25/50/70LD), west of the town centre on the road to the Tunisian border, is ageing but fine for a night to break up the journey.

North of the main highway around 2km west of Zuara is the **Farah Resort** (☎ 220542, mobile 0912138705; fax 021-3335819; ste 75-100LD; 5-bedroom villa 300LD), Libya's best tourist village. Opened in 2006, it has sparklingly clean and comfortable rooms, a swimming pool, medical clinic, restaurant, prime beachfront location and nice touches, such as the golf carts that take you to your suite. It also has a billiard table, quad bikes for rent, a children's playground and plans for jet skis. Beach tourism for foreign visitors hasn't yet taken off in Libya, but when it does, expect this place to be one of the most popular places. Until then, book well in advance in summer, because Libyans have already discovered this fine place.

The shared taxi station is east of the post office, with departures for Ras al-Jedir (2LD, 45 minutes), Sabratha (1LD, 30 minutes) and Tripoli (2LD, two hours). There are less-frequent departures to the Jebel Nafusa.

ZUARA TO RAS AL-JEDIR

In all likelihood, the most you'll see of this area is out of a tour-bus window as it hurtles to or from the Tunisian border. If you have the time, the beaches along this stretch of coast are some of Libya's best.

Bu Kammash, home to a petrochemical plant and a Roman-era cemetery, is the gateway to **Farwa Island**, which has a clean white-sand beach on the northern side of the island. The rest of the 471-hectare island is covered with almost 4000 palm trees, a few sand dunes and tiny villages. Farwa is separated from the mainland by a 3km-wide lagoon, although a large sand bar at the eastern end almost connects the two. Small ferries cross between Bu Kammash and Farwa (0.50LD) on an intermittent basis. At its widest point, the island is only 1.1km wide.

EAST OF TRIPOLI

East of Tripoli is all about Leptis Magna and Villa Sileen, although the coastline east of Tripoli is Libya's most densely populated region with cities, such as Al-Khoms, Zliten and Misrata making good bases for visiting the ruins.

Around 90km east from Tajura is the pleasant **Bsees beach** with white sand. The main highway in this area is dotted with makeshift stalls selling honey, olive oil and date juice.

There's another beach at **Neqezzah**, 101km east of Tajura and around 20km west of Al-Khoms. This lovely beach is popular with students from the nearby college and the place throngs with people on Thursday afternoon and Friday. Neqezzah is 4.2km off the main highway (the turn-off is a dip in the road, immediately west of three telecommunications masts). On the road down to the beach is **Funduq al-Neqezzah** (☎ 031-626691/2; tw/chalet/ste 30/40/50LD; ❄), which has spacious rooms with air-con, TV and phone; prices include breakfast.

VILLA SILEEN فيلا سيلين

The gracious Roman **Villa Sileen** (admission 3LD, camera/video 5/10LD; 🕒 9am-5pm) is all of that remains of the villas of the elite that once dominated the ocean frontage for miles around Leptis Magna. At the time of writing, it was necessary to buy your admission ticket at the site entrance to Leptis Magna (p111), although expect that to change in future.

Villa Sileen's role served a purpose akin to a country retreat from the hustle and bustle of the city and its mosaic-strewn floors and lightly frescoed baths, which together give the place its charm today, provide further confirmation that the ancient Romans really knew how to live. For more information on mosaic art, see p108.

The small garden that looks out over the Mediterranean is bounded on three sides by the compact villa. Before entering, note the mosaics depicting Nilotic scenes in the courtyard.

In the main, western wing of the villa, the floor of every room (and part of the outdoor garden area) is covered with delightful mosaic tiles, while the floor centrepieces are exquisite with tiny pieces used to extraordinarily detailed effect. These in turn are frequently encircled by repeated geometric designs of larger tiles. Our favourites in the western wing include a marvellous portrayal of the Leptis circus (p116) and a Four Seasons motif. Some of the walls are also adorned with faded frescoes of ochre-coloured human figures and pastoral scenes. There's also what was once a private church, although it was closed when we visited. The house faces onto the sea and its modern-day seclusion only adds to the beauty.

The eastern wing is topped with a number of sand-coloured domes. Inside are the former baths, complete with swimming pools and hot tubs. The small number of frescoes in these rooms are magnificent and are dominated by bath scenes. Some of the walls are made of marble. There are some mosaic pieces on the upper architraves in some rooms; imagine what these baths must have looked like when all the mosaics were intact. The main domed room also has fine stonework atop the pillars, with good mosaics of fighting scenes above some of the attractive sandstone alcoves and a wonderful mosaic showing the head of an unidentified man surrounded by sea creatures and birds (swans, crabs etc) in the centre of the floor. Throughout this section of the building are traces of pottery pipes.

Our only complaint is that, unusually for Libya's ancient sites, recent restorations have been patchy and it's sometimes necessary to walk atop the mosaics themselves in order to see them; the flimsy carpets provide scant protection. Despite having only opened to the public in 2005, there is also an air of dust and neglect.

MOSAICS – A PRIMER

The use of mosaics as adornments in important public buildings dates back to around 2000 BC when terracotta cones were embedded, point first, into a background as a means of decoration. The art form evolved slowly with different coloured pebbles used to make patterns, but it was the ancient Greeks, in the 4th century BC, who first used the pebbles to create detailed geometric motifs and depict scenes of people and animals. In the 2nd century BC, artisans began to make mosaics using the tiny made-to-measure though naturally coloured stone squares cut from larger rocks. Called *tesserae,* they were carefully laid on a thick coating of wet lime, an enduring technique that gave clarity and depth to so many of the mosaics that survive today.

In the 1st century BC, travelling Greek craftsmen introduced mosaic art to the Romans (the stunning mosaics found in Pompeii in Italy were executed by Greeks) who thereafter carried it throughout the empire and adopted it as their own. Their trademark was the use of mosaics to adorn floors in private villas and bath complexes. The larger mosaics required painstaking effort and great skill, taking months or years to complete. As a result, they were only created for wealthier citizens who could afford them and, later, for important buildings such as churches during the Byzantine period. Motifs included scenes inspired by the surrounding countryside, mythology or the more picaresque public events in Roman life, such as the superb representation of a day at the circus of Leptis on the floor of **Villa Sileen** (p107).

Unlike the mosaics found in some other countries (Italy, for example), mosaics along the Libyan coast were made primarily for the floor and were hardy enough to withstand anything, except massive earthquakes. For some reason, very few of the artists signed their names on the mosaics, possibly because so many people were involved over many years. By the time the Byzantines had taken the art form to a new level from the 4th century AD, names are sometime listed, such as the people who helped to pay for the mosaic and clergy in the church. Churches throughout Libya were adorned with floor and wall mosaics; there is no finer collection of Byzantine mosaics in Libya than those of **Qasr Libya** (p136) in Cyrenaica.

Archaeologists are still finding a rich variety of mosaics along the Libyan shore and in 2005 a German team in Wadi Lebdah (close to Leptis Magna) unveiled five extraordinary mosaics created during the 1st or 2nd century. The mosaics depict hunting and a masterfully portrayed gladiator at rest and are thought to have adorned the pool of a frigidarium in a Roman villa at Wadi Lebda in Leptis Magna. They can now be seen at the **Leptis Museum** (p117).

In addition to the spectacular mosaics of Villa Sileen, Qasr Libya and Leptis Museum, there are especially fine examples to be found in the ground-floor galleries (p77) of the Jamahiriya Museum in Tripoli, the **Roman Museum** (p101) and throughout the ancient city of **Sabratha** (p100), **Tolmeita museum** (p136) and the **House of Jason Magnus** (p144) in Cyrene.

Getting There & Away

Villa Sileen is 14km west of Al-Khoms and is almost impossible to find without a guide. There's no public transport to the site.

AL-KHOMS الخمس

☎ 031 / pop 207,248

Bustling Al-Khoms is the closest town to Leptis Magna for which it makes a reasonable base, although the hotels are better in Zliten and Misrata.

Orientation & Information

Most of the action in Al-Khoms takes place along or just off the main street, Sharia al-Khoms, which runs northeast into town from the main highway before turning east at the main roundabout, marked by a small mosque. From here Sharia al-Khoms continues east through the centre of town to Leptis Magna, around 3km away.

Internet cafés (per hr 3LD; 10am-midnight Sat-Thu) There are a number of internet cafés along Sharia al-Khoms.

Jawazzat (☎ 621375) This office is 250m west of the Mosque of Ali Pasha.

Post office (Sharia al-Jamahiriya) Next to the mosque.

Sights & Activities

There's not much to see in the town itself, although the **Mosque of Ali Pasha** in the centre of town is attractive, with a large conical dome in distinctive cream tones and a fine minaret adorned with vertical and horizontal lines.

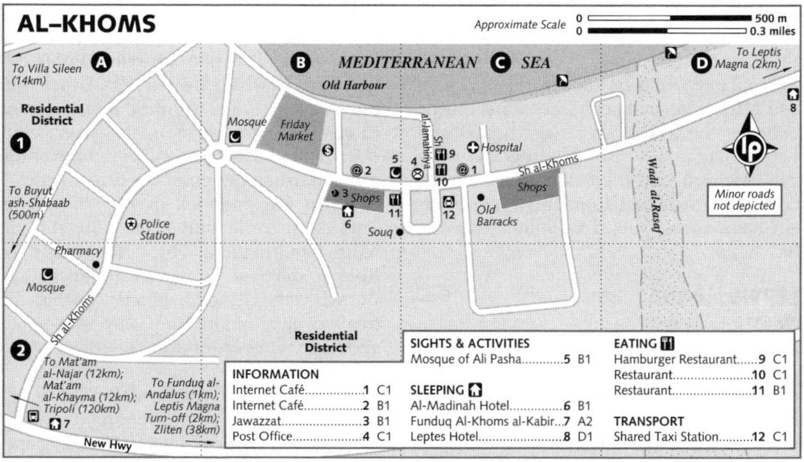

There are also some good beaches in the area so it's a great place to relax for a few days.

Sleeping & Eating

Buyut ash-Shabaab (Youth Hostel; ☎ 621880; dm 5LD) In a quiet area 2km west of the town centre, this is a basic but friendly hostel that fills up fast.

Al-Madinah Hotel (☎ 620799; al_madinahotel@yahoo.com; s/d 15/20LD;) The rooms here may be simple but they're spotless and come with TV, phone and decent bathrooms; don't expect towels in all rooms. For this price, you won't find better in Libya. Dodgy pillows are the only disappointment. It's behind the *jawazzat*.

Leptes Hotel (☎ 621252; lepdahhotel@yahoo.com; Sharia al-Khoms; s/d from 15/25LD;) Almost as good as the Al-Madinah Hotel, the Leptes is the closest hotel to Leptis Magna. The rooms (with balcony) have character, although stay here too long and you'll find them a bit dark and overdone. The bathrooms are excellent and the staff win many a vote of thanks from readers, not least the room cleaners who'll even hang your clothes in the wardrobe. Breakfasts can be something of a disappointment, as is the absence of an elevator if you're staying on the 3rd floor.

Funduq al-Khoms al-Kabir (☎ 623333; main highway; tw/ste 20/40LD;) Once Al-Khoms' finest hotel, this place near the junction of Sharia al-Khoms and the main highway is run-down, although it has been undergoing snail's pace renovations the last time we visited. The renovations clearly started with the suite, which is excellent value. The other rooms are soulless; the rooms at the back are quieter. There's a depressing restaurant, a light and airy coffeehouse, a billiard table and a teahouse next door, which goes a small way towards compensating for the distance from the centre of town.

Funduq al-Andalus (☎ 626667, fax 626199; main highway; s with shared bathroom 20LD, tw/d with bath 30/40LD;) Our love affair with this place has waned over the years. Perhaps that's because on our first visit in 2001 reasonable hotels stood out. That's no longer the case, although the rooms here are still clean and spacious if a bit drab; those at the back of the building are quieter. There's also a **restaurant** (meals 15LD).

In Al-Khoms itself, there are cheap restaurants selling hamburgers, sandwiches and pizzas along Sharia al-Khoms and another small hamburger restaurant along Sharia al-Jamahiriya.

Tell Libyans that you're passing through Al-Khoms and many will ask with envy whether you'll be eating at either **Mat'am al-Najar** (☎ 0913205398) or **Mat'am al-Khayma** (☎ 0913205169), 12km west of Al-Khoms on the road to Tripoli. That's because they're famous throughout the country for their *bourdim* (meat slow-cooked in a sand pit). Most meals go for around 8LD.

The best restaurant in the area is Mat'am Addiyafa (p118) in the grounds of Leptis.

Getting There & Away

Al-Khoms is 120km east of Tripoli along the busy coastal highway and is well-served by regular shared taxis to/from Tripoli, Zliten and Misrata. Shared taxis and micros shuttle between the town (Sharia al-Khoms) and Leptis Magna at reasonably regular intervals. Alternatively, it's a 3km walk from the centre of town to Leptis and some readers have also reported walking along the beach.

LEPTIS MAGNA لبدة

☎ 031

If Leptis Magna was the only place you saw in Libya, you wouldn't leave disappointed. Leptis (originally spelled Lepcis and often known locally in Arabic as Lebdah) was once the largest and greatest Roman city in Africa and it's a title it easily retains today. Because no modern city was later built on the site and because, unlike Sabratha, Leptis was constructed of sturdy limestone that left it more resistant to earthquakes and the ravages of time, the ruins are wonderfully well preserved and it's that rare ancient city where sufficient traces remain to imagine the city in its heyday.

But the charms of Leptis are not restricted to its state of preservation. So large is its scope that it remains a showcase of Roman town planning, with streets following an ordered pattern. Above all, it is a testament to the extravagance of ancient Rome with abundant examples of lavish decoration, grand buildings of monumental stature, indulgent bath complexes and forums for entertainment at the centre of public life. It must have been a great place to live.

After having examined the various districts of the city at close quarters, visit Room 1 of the Leptis Museum (p117) where model-map representations give a strong and evocative sense of how Leptis must once have appeared,

One final thing: if you want to make a day of your visit – Leptis deserves as much time as you can give it – bring along your swimmers and towel as a mid-afternoon dip in the Mediterranean has a certain cachet.

History

The first city on the site of what we now know as Leptis Magna is believed to date from the 7th century BC. It began as a peripheral trading port populated by Phoenicians fleeing from conflict in Tyre (present-day Lebanon) as well as Punic settlers from Carthage (in Tunisia). Other than the Old Forum (p114), little remains from this city, which lasted for up to 500 years, but it was a modest settlement with none of the ordered urban design of the Roman era.

When Carthage fell in 146 BC, Leptis nominally came under the wing of the Numidian kingdom. The shift towards the Roman sphere of influence began in 111 BC, when the city's inhabitants concluded a treaty of alliance and friendship with Rome and large numbers of Roman settlers began to arrive.

Under Emperor Augustus (r 27 BC–AD 14) Leptis' status as an important Roman city of emerging power began to take shape. The city minted its own coins, the town was laid out in the Roman style and then adorned with monuments of grandeur. It soon became one of the leading ports in Africa, an entrepôt for the trade in exotic animals that were so essential to the entertainments that so defined ancient Rome. It also fell under the spell of a wealthy Roman elite with grand visions and money to burn. One local aristocrat, Annobal Tapapius Rufus, was responsible for the construction of the market (8 BC; p115) and theatre (AD 2; p115), giving Leptis the essential touchstones of a Roman city of significance. The grand, monumental city of Leptis had begun to become a reality.

After backing the wrong side in one of Rome's internecine spats, Leptis momentarily lost its status as a friendly city and ally of Rome and was punished for good measure by an annual tax of between one and three million litres of olive oil. The city's stability was further threatened by the constant threat of invasion by the hostile tribes of the interior. In AD 69 the city was overrun by the Garamantes people of the Sahara (see p30) who had been called in to assist Oea in its dispute with Leptis.

Despite these momentary difficulties, Leptis emerged as a prosperous city that owed its wealth to agriculture (especially olives) and trade from trans-Saharan caravans and seagoing trade, particularly in exporting live animals to Rome. Successive Roman emperors continued to decorate the city with exceptionally rich public buildings. In the time of Hadrian (r AD 117–38)

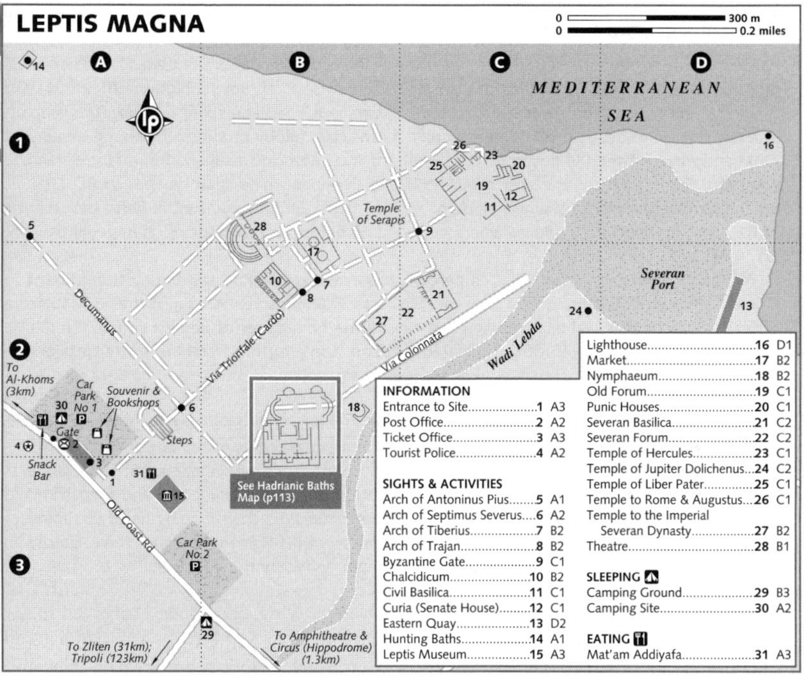

the city secured a lasting water supply via aqueducts, which in turn enabled the construction of arguably Leptis' greatest indulgence – the Hadrianic Baths (p112). In the 2nd century AD, marble began to adorn the city's buildings, embellishing the already superbly rendered limestone façades, and the city began to grow in size, extending westwards along the coast.

But it was under the reign of Leptis-born Septimius Severus (r AD 193–211) that Leptis took on the stature and grandeur for which it would be forever known. For more information, see Septimius Severus – the Grim African, p112.

Between 294 and 305, the reforms carried out by the Emperor Diocletian saw Leptis become the capital of the new autonomous province of Tripolitania. By then, though, the glory days of Leptis had passed. Earthquakes (especially in AD 365), a catastrophic flood and Rome's general decline took their toll, ushering in two centuries of neglect. By the 6th century AD, the city was in Byzantine hands and the emperor Justinian I built a wall around the city, parts of which survive to this day. There is some evidence that the city survived the Arab invasion of the 7th century AD and was occupied until the 10th century, after which it slowly disappeared under the sands.

Information

The Leptis Magna **site** (☎ 624256, 627641; adult/child 3/1LD, camera/video 5/10LD; 8am-6pm) is entered via car park No 1; the open area of the car park has book stalls, a place selling drinks and snacks and a post and telephone office. It is compulsory to visit Leptis with a **guide** (50LD).

Sights

ARCH OF SEPTIMIUS SEVERUS

This is one of Leptis' signature monuments and the grandest possible introduction to the architectural excesses of the city. It was built in AD 203 to commemorate the emperor and his family, and to mark his visit to his native city. The core of the structure was built of limestone, unusual for the time, and covered with a marble exterior. What you see today has been faithfully reconstructed

SEPTIMIUS SEVERUS – THE GRIM AFRICAN

Rarely has the identity of a city been so inextricably linked to one person, but equally rare is the fact that someone from an outpost of the empire could rise to occupy its highest office.

Lucius Septimius Severus was born in Leptis Magna in AD 145 and spent his formative years in a city that was already one of Rome's great centres. He quickly progressed through military ranks and was declared the governor of a far-off province. After the assassinations of the Roman emperors Commodus (at the end of AD 192) and Pentinax (three months later in AD 193), Septimius Severus was proclaimed emperor by his troops. Emboldened by the fierce devotion of his army, he marched on Rome where he swept all before him to assume full imperial powers in AD 193.

With its favourite son installed as emperor, Leptis came to rival Rome as the most important city in the empire. A military man first and foremost, Septimius Severus spent the early years of his reign waging a ruthless campaign to extend the boundaries of Rome's empire. By this stage known as 'the grim African', the feared emperor won a further victory over the Parthians in AD 202–3, temporarily dispelled all challenges to his power, and ushered in an era of relative peace.

Leptis celebrated both peace and its growing ascendancy with a Severan-inspired building boom that sealed the city's reputation as one of the grandest cities of the ancient world. The market (p115) was rebuilt, the Great Colonnaded St (opposite) took on its current form, while the Nymphaeum (opposite), Severan Forum (opposite), Severan Basilica (p114) and port (p115) were also constructed during this period. His fellow citizens did their part by hastily building their own monument to their emperor on the occasion of his visit to the city – the exquisite triumphal Arch of Septimius Severus (p111) to honour a visit by the emperor.

by archaeologists to stunning effect. It remains a work in progress. The friezes attached to the arch are, in fact, replicas with the originals residing in Gallery 11 (p79) of the Jamahiriya Museum in Tripoli. Other original elements of the arch are to be found in Room 4 of the Leptis Museum (p117).

The arch consists of four imposing pillars supporting a domed roof. Each of the four vertical panels on the pillars' exterior was flanked by two Corinthian columns, in between which were carved adornments in relief depicting the great virtues and successes of the Severan era. At the intersection of the dome and pillars are eagles with their wings spread – one of the key symbols of imperial Rome. Above the columns are two panels of fine detail showing triumphal processions, sacrificial scenes and Septimius Severus holding the hand of his son Caracalla. The interior of the pillars show historical scenes of military campaigns, religious ceremonies and the emperor's family.

HADRIANIC BATHS

The arrival of water and marble in Leptis Magna early in the 2nd century AD prompted the Emperor Hadrian to commission the superb baths (Map p113) bearing his name. The baths were opened in AD 137 (some archaeologists put the date at around AD 126–27) and they quickly became one of the social hubs of the city. Attention to detail was a feature of the baths and in keeping with well-established Roman tradition, the baths lay along a north-south axis and the symmetry of the buildings was a key requirement.

Entrance to the baths is from the *palaestra* (sports ground). The entrance hall *(natatio)* contains an open-air swimming pool that was surrounded by columns on three sides and paved with marble and mosaics.

Off the *natatio* was the grandest room of the baths complex and one of the most splendid in Leptis – the *frigidarium* (cold room). A total of eight massive cipolin columns nearly 9m high supported the vaulted roof and the chamber measured an impressive 30m by 15m. The floor was paved with marble and the roof adorned with brilliant blue-and-turquoise mosaics. There were pools at either end and the niches around the walls once held over 40 statues, some of which are in the museums in Leptis (p117) and Tripoli (p76).

The *tepidarium* lies immediately south of the *frigidarium*. It originally consisted

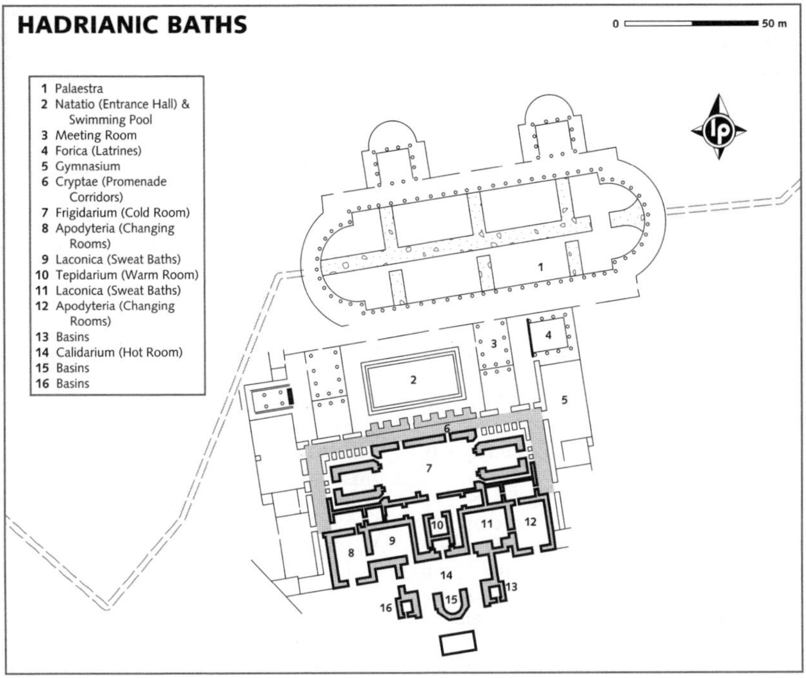

of one central pool, lined on two sides by columns; two other pools were later added. The rooms of the *calidarium* (hot room) surround the *tepidarium*. They faced south, as the theory of bath design at the time demanded, and may have had large glass windows on the southern side. The room had a barrel-vaulted roof of wonderful domes with five of the *laconica* (sweat baths) added during the time of Commodus. Outside the southern walls were furnaces used for heating the water. On the eastern and western sides of the buildings were *cryptae* (promenade corridors); many of the smaller rooms you'll see were the *apodyteria* (changing rooms). The best preserved of the *forica* (latrines) are on the northeastern side of the complex – the marble seats must have been pretty cold in winter.

NYMPHAEUM

East of the *palaestra* and Hadrianic Baths is an open square overlooked by the Nymphaeum, or Temple of Nymphs. Although half-collapsed and requiring considerable imagination, its superb façade of red-granite and cipolin columns was once reminiscent of the façade of Roman theatres and its niches were once filled with marble statues. The monumental fountain was added during the reign of Septimius Severus.

GREAT COLONNADED STREET

The square in front of the Nymphaeum represented the start of a monumental road (Via Colonnata) leading down to the port. Lined with porticoes and shops, this thoroughfare was more than 20m wide (plus an extra 20m if you include the porticoes, which were reserved for pedestrians) and around 400m long. Connecting the baths and new Severan Forum with the waterfront, it became one of the most important roads in Leptis during the Severan era.

SEVERAN FORUM

Septimius Severus' audacious transformation of Leptis involved reconfiguring the heart of the city – moving it away from the old forum to the new one that bore his name. The open-air Severan Forum measured 100m by 60m and its floor was

IMPERIAL PLUNDER

One of the reasons why Leptis is such a joy to visit is the faithful restoration work of devoted archaeologists, particularly those from Italy and Libya. Sadly, it was not always the case. From AD 1686 to 1708, the French consul to Tripoli, Claude Le Maire, used his post to plunder the wealth of ancient Leptis on behalf of his country. He excavated and exported to France an astonishing quantity of marble monuments, especially columns. With complete disregard for local heritage, many columns were laid out along the shore, only to be abandoned as too heavy. Those hundreds of items that made it to France were often dismantled and used in building the monuments of imperial France, most notably the chateau of Versailles and the church of St Germain des-Pres. The hardest-hit buildings of Leptis were the Severan Forum, the Great Colonnaded St and the Hadrianic Baths.

covered with marble. Ancient remnants of former glories are still strewn around the courtyard and it's easy to picture the forum in its heyday.

In the great tradition of Roman city squares, Septimius Severus' forum was once surrounded by colonnaded porticoes. The columns of cipolin marble rose to arches. On the façades between the arches were Gorgon heads, over 70 of which have been found. Most were symbolic representations of the Roman goddess Victory and included some superb Medusa images, as well as a few sea nymphs; look particularly for the heart-shaped eyes, necklaces of serpents and eyebrows of fish fins. Unusually, the arches were of limestone while the heads were carved from marble. In front of the remaining carved heads are vertical panels with dedicatory inscriptions that served as plinths for statues.

Along the shorter, southwestern side of the forum was a temple to the imperial Severan dynasty. Roman emperors were deified and their subjects, while believing in their divine status, also undoubtedly saw great political benefits in treating their leaders as gods. Only the staircase, platform and underground storage room remain. Some of the red-granite columns around the forum once belonged to the temple.

SEVERAN BASILICA

The Severan Basilica, 92m long and 40m wide, ran along the northeastern side of the Severan Forum. The basilica, originally a judicial basilica rather than a church, contained two apses at either end, a nave, aisles divided by red-granite columns and possibly a wooden roof. It was started by Septimius Severus and completed by his son Caracalla in AD 216 (read the dedicatory inscription on one of the panels of the nave). The relative austerity of the main hall stands in marked contrast to the extravagantly sculpted pillars at either end, many of which honour Liber Pater (Dionysius) and Hercules. In the 6th century AD, Justinian converted the basilica into a Christian church, with the altar in the southeastern apse. From the top of the stairs off the northwestern corner are good views of the remainder of the ancient city, although it's not always open.

BYZANTINE GATE

Northwest of the basilica, a track leads to Via Trionfale (the Cardo) and the Byzantine Gate. Note the phallic reliefs to the right of the gate – one of many at junctions around the city – which suggest the existence of prostitutes in the ancient city. Also watch out for what look like bullet holes but which in fact were where supports affixing marble to the streets' walls were hammered into the walls – Leptis Magna's streets may not have been paved with gold, but they were lined with marble.

OLD FORUM

The old forum of Leptis Magna was the centre of the first Punic settlement on the site (from the 7th century BC) and the early Roman era. The barely excavated remains of Punic houses are off to the northeast. This square was allowed to fall into neglect after the shift of the city centre to the south, so little remains. Nonetheless, as the monumental heart of the building projects by the Emperor Augustus, it remains an important signpost to life in the ancient city. Paved in AD 2, it was surrounded by colonnaded porticoes on three sides.

On the left, as you enter the forum if coming from the Byzantine Gate, were three temples. The Temple of Liber Pater dates from the 2nd century AD, but the high podium is all that remains. The Temple to Rome & Augustus (AD 14–19) was built of limestone and may also have been used as a platform for speakers addressing crowds in the square. Next to nothing remains of the Temple of Hercules. On the right as you enter the square, the grey-granite columns mark the site of the Civil Basilica, which was built in the 1st century AD and then rebuilt in the 4th century. It was later converted into a Byzantine church of which the apse, aisles, narthex and seriously eroded columns are discernible. The Curia (Senate House; 2nd century AD) was nearby. In the centre of the forum is a small baptistry in the shape of a cross, as well as a particularly unreligious exedra that local guides like to call the casino.

PORT

The port was another key element of Septimius Severus' vision. The **lighthouse**, of which only the foundation remains, was once more than 35m high. Some historians believe that it was not that different from the more famous Pharos of Alexandria. The best-preserved sections of the port are the **eastern quay** with warehouses, the ruins of a watchtower and some of the loading docks. Look also for the imposing staircase of the **Temple of Jupiter Dolichenus**. Jupiter Dolichenus was a little-known Syrian deity at the time of Septimius Severus. It is believed that the appearance of a temple in his name at Leptis Magna was attributable to the fact that Septimius' wife was Syrian.

Don't be fooled by the lack of water. The reason the buildings of the eastern quay are still relatively intact is that the port was hardly used. Soon after its construction, the harbour silted up and is now covered by vegetation.

MARKET

As you're returning from the port, detour northwest past the Severan Basilica to the market, one of the most unusual and attractive of the Leptis monuments. In its two reconstructed octagonal halls (approximately 20m in diameter) stalls were set up to sell the bounty of Leptis farmers and merchants. The northern hall is believed to have been the section for fabrics; next to it is a copy of a stone measuring tablet from the 3rd century AD. The top length equates to a Roman (or Punic) arm (51.5cm), the middle was a Roman (or Alexandrine) foot (29.5cm), while the bottom length was known as the Greek (or Ptolemaic) arm (52.5cm). The other hall was reserved for trading in fruit and vegetables. There were more stalls in the colonnaded portico that surrounded the perimeter.

The market was built in 9–8 BC and rebuilt during the reign of Septimius Severus; some of the columns with marble capitals date from this latter period. Of the richly decorated façades, the best that remains is of two ships (in celebration of the seafaring merchants of Leptis). Look also for the stone benches with deep lines gouged by ropes used in moving large amounts of produce.

MONUMENTAL ARCHES

Just outside the southern corner of the market, on Via Trionfale, is the **Arch of Tiberius** (1st century AD). A short distance southwest is the **Arch of Trajan** (AD 109–10), possibly commemorating the accession of Leptis to the status of a colony within the Roman Empire. Both arches are of limestone.

CHALCIDICUM

This monumental porch is in the block immediately west of the Arch of Trajan. Built in the early part of the 1st century AD under Augustus, its colonnaded portico was reached via steps from Via Trionfale. It contained a small temple, honouring Augustus and Venus, of which statue bases remain. There are also some cipolin columns and Corinthian capitals from the 2nd century AD. Look for the elephant base in the eastern corner (fronting onto the arch).

THEATRE

Leptis' theatre is one of the oldest stone theatres anywhere in the Roman world and is the second-largest surviving theatre in Africa (after Sabratha). It was begun in AD 1–2, although many adornments were later added, and was built on the site of a 3rd- to 5th-centuries BC Punic necropolis. The

READER'S TIP

A rather trivial thing concerning Leptis Magna, which, however, made my visit to the site even more exciting and memorable. Our Polish guide recommended to us to do one simple thing when visiting the Theatre in Leptis Magna – you should climb to the top of the theatre (upper stalls) without looking back as you go up. Then when you've reached the highest part, you should turn back and admire the view of the Theatre and the panorama of the city against the background of the turquoise waters of the Mediterranean – an unforgettable experience.

Malgorzata Januszko, Poland

most striking feature of the theatre is the stage with its façade of three semicircular recesses surrounded by three-tiered fluted columns dating from the era of Antoninus Pius (r AD 138–61). The stage was awash with hundreds of statues and sculptures that included portraits of emperors, gods and wealthy private citizens. Two remain – Liber Pater (decorated with grapes and leaves) and Hercules (his head is covered with a lion skin).

The VIP seats just above the orchestra were separated from the paying customers by a solid stone bannister that was added in AD 90, while the lower seats were actually carved out of the existing rock at the time of construction. Atop the upper stalls of the *cavea* (seating area) were some small temples and a colonnade of cipolin columns.

HUNTING BATHS

If you head northwest from the Arch of Septimius Severus, you pass under the Oea Gate, or **Arch of Antoninus Pius** (2nd century AD). You eventually come to the superb **Hunting Baths**, recognisable by their consecutive, barrel-domed roofs in light sandstone. These baths never rivalled the Hadrianic Baths, but the frescoes and mosaics throughout the building are superb. The *frigidarium* contains the fresco that gave the baths their name – showing hunters and animals in the Leptis amphitheatre. There are also some fine frescoes in the adjoining vaults. On the walls of the bath is an exceptional Nilotic fresco; watch out for the good marble panelling. The baths, constructed in the 2nd century AD, were used for almost three centuries.

Before you make the reasonably long trek out here, check that the baths are open as they were temporarily closed when we last visited.

AMPHITHEATRE

Around 3km east of the centre of Leptis Magna (you'll need to get here by car), the evocative **amphitheatre** (adult/child 3/1LD, camera/video 5/10LD; 8am-6pm) once held 16,000 people and was hollowed out of a hill in the 1st century AD. The upper stalls may have once been encircled by a colonnaded portico. Note that as the amphitheatre is separated from the main site, you'll have to pay an additional entry (fine) and camera (excessive) charge. There's a model replica of the amphitheatre in Room 10 of the Leptis Museum (opposite).

CIRCUS

The circus (or hippodrome) is reached via a side passage on the western side of the amphitheatre. Dating from AD 162 during the reign of Marcus Aurelius Antoninus, it was home to chariot races attended by up to 25,000 people. The long side of the track ran for 450m while the short sides were only 100m in length. As such, it was one of the largest known circuses outside Rome. Acrobatic performances were sometimes used in the central area to keep the crowd

THEY CALLED IT SPORT

The entertainment on offer in Roman amphitheatres was not for the faint-hearted. A typical programme consisted of people hunting rabbits and small rodents in the arena in the morning, followed by shackled criminals being left to the mercies of the lions. At least the Christians, who followed the criminals, were allowed into the arena free of shackles, although few escaped. All of this operated as the pre-match entertainment for the main event – the epic contests of the gladiators.

entertained in between races. A normal race programme included numerous races of seven laps, each run in an anticlockwise direction. These days, the circus consists of not much more than low-lying foundations, but for a fine mosaic representation of a day at the circus, make sure you visit Villa Sileen (p107), west of Al-Khoms.

LEPTIS MUSEUM

The **Leptis Museum** (adult/child 3/1LD, camera/video 5/10LD; 8am-6pm Tue-Sun) is like a smaller version of the outstanding Jamahiriya Museum (p76) – expansive in scope, beautifully laid out and very well organised with informative posters in each room detailing the history of the relevant period – although here many of the individual exhibits are labelled in both English and Arabic. Allow a minimum of two hours to see the museum properly.

The rooms on the ground floor run in an anticlockwise direction.

Room 1 deals with Libya's prehistory, and has examples of petrified trees from the Libyan desert, an evocative model-map reconstruction of Leptis and stone carvings from the Jebel Acacus. **Room 2** is devoted to the Punic/Phoenician era and includes pottery pieces from the 5th and 6th centuries BC that were found in the Punic necropolis under the theatre. **Room 3** is also dominated by Punic pottery. The representation of the goddess Tarnit is of special interest, as are the descriptions of Punic town planning and a dedicatory slab from the market place.

Room 4 is the chamber of Roman triumphal arches, including an imposing two-level relief from inside the Arch of Septimius Severus depicting Septimius and his wife; between them is the head of Hercules draped with a lion's head. **Room 5** has another statue of Hercules draped as a lion, some Roman pillars, dedicatory inscription tablets and, on the northern wall, the symbol of Aesculapius, the god of healing, whose symbol is used by modern medical practitioners. Many of these items were found in the Temple of Jupiter Dolichenus in the port (see (p115). **Room 6** is given over to busts, including a particularly fine one of Neptune.

Room 7 is one of the museum's most impressive rooms, with superbly sculpted marble statues dating from the Severan age. Clockwise from the left, the statues represent an athlete, an elegant marble woman of Leptis Magna, a young Marcus Aurelius, Serapis in the form of Aesculapius, a partial black-stone Serapis, Isis and a Leptis woman from the first half of the 3rd century AD. Note especially the exceptional skill used in sculpting the folds in clothes. The glass cabinet on the right as you enter contains the many faces of the goddess Isis.

Room 8 contains excavations from the Hadrianic Baths (p112), including the huge hand of Septimius Severus and an incredibly skilful marble representation of a seated (and now headless) Mars. There is also a modern painting of the *frigidarium*.

Room 9 is dedicated to the Nymphaeum (p113) and port, and includes a possible (unlabelled) statue of Isis (note the tail of the cornucopia).

Room 10 is another fine room, this time with the theatre (p115) as its theme. Items to look out for include representations of Mercury and Venus and a huge dedicatory inscription tablet in Roman and Punic – both languages were used until the 2nd century AD. Note also the statue of a woman with a portly child holding poppies, thought to be a representation of the family of the Roman emperor Hadrian. There is also a model reconstruction of the amphitheatre (opposite).

Room 11 showcases the Severan Forum (p113) and Old Forum (p114) with Medusa and Gorgon heads high on the wall, two column bases from the temple to the Severan dynasty in the Severan Forum. **Room 12** is a ghostly room of headless and handless statues (body parts were often carved separately to increase the statues' resale value). There are also Latin inscriptions commemorating the reconstruction of the market porticoes and five portrait busts found in the market (p115). **Room 13** also has an interesting collection of busts representing the diverse faces of Leptis, a pompous statue of a magistrate and an attractive marble panel inscription to a 2nd-century governor of Africa.

On the 1st floor, where the rooms are arranged in a clockwise pattern, **Room 14** showcases the ancient trade activity of Leptis and includes the original measuring tablet used in the market. **Room 15** is devoted to the coins of the Misrata Treasure (see p119). **Room 16** fronts onto the open staircase and contains items of everyday Roman life. **Room 17** houses funerary objects, a small statue of a sleeping, winged Eros and ornate urns (alabaster for the wealthy) used to store ashes after cremation. Note also the poignant pottery coffin of a child in one of the glass cases. **Room 18** has more funerary urns and small coffins, as well as a two-faced Janus (Roman god of doorways, passages and bridges) relief and big stone reliefs from the fortified farms of Ghirza (p121). **Room 19** has similar reliefs, this time from Qasr Gilda.

Room 20 marks the transition to the Byzantine period with a dusty but attractive mosaic from a church 60km south of Leptis, as well as tablet reliefs from the four churches that were in Leptis during the Christian era. **Room 21** covers the Islamic period and has beautiful pottery bowls and unimaginative models of a mosque, madrassa (school), mihrab (niche in a mosque) and *minbar* (pulpit in a mosque). **Room 22** commemorates Libyan resistance to Italian rule with weapons and a woodcarving of the battle of Al-Mergeb. **Room 23**, near the staircase, is given over to a reconstruction of a traditional Bedouin tent (note the separation of men and women), with dolls showing traditional outfits. **Room 24** has gifts given to Colonel Muammar Qaddafi. Highlights of this quirky collection include a map of an undivided Palestine, a huge book made of palm trunk lauding the colonel, and a document of homage written in blood by an Iraqi traveller. **Room 25** has some anticlimactic photos of the Great Man-Made River (Al-Nahr Sinai; p122). The stairs lead back down to the exit, past the towering painting of Colonel Qaddafi being adored by the masses in the central skylight area.

Sleeping & Eating

Most people choose Al-Khoms (p108) or Zliten (right) as a base for exploring Leptis. It's also possible to visit as a day trip from Tripoli or, if you're heading east, to visit Leptis and then continue on to Misrata for the night or, at a stretch, Sirt.

Inside Leptis itself, it's possible to **camp** (5LD) in car park No 1 under the pine and eucalyptus trees; it's a quiet spot at night and guarded by police from the station opposite. There's another small camping ground opposite car park No 2.

Inside Leptis, between the ticket office and museum, is **Mat'am Addiyafa** (☎ 621210; meals 15LD; 🕑 lunch), which has an agreeable atmosphere and a good set lunch.

Getting There & Away

Leptis Magna is 3km east of Al-Khoms and 123km east of Tripoli. If you're coming from Tripoli and plan to bypass Al-Khoms, the turn-off to Leptis Magna is 3.5km east of the main turn-off into Al-Khoms and is marked by a yellow sign with a small painting of the ruins. Zliten is 31km east of Leptis, Misrata 91km. Shared taxis run regularly along the coastal road to Al-Khoms from both directions; there are reasonably frequent shared taxis to Leptis from Al-Khoms.

ZLITEN زليطن

☎ 0571 / pop 101,900

The coastal oasis of Zliten sprawls along the coast 34km east of Al-Khoms. It's a largely unattractive town although it is redeemed by three things: the proliferation of palm trees along the main highway, its stunning mosque and mausoleum and a hotel that makes a reasonable base for Leptis Magna (p110). Before the revolution it was renowned for its wine-making, but it now has a large fishing port.

In the streets of the old town, most of the houses are derelict and earmarked for destruction but the occasional door has traces of the town's former elegance. Villa Dar Bu Kammara, a ruined villa in the area, has fallen into disrepair, but its mosaics will one day be on show, probably in the Leptis Museum (p117).

Sights

MAUSOLEUM & MOSQUE OF SIDI ABDUSALAM

This is one of the finest modern Islamic buildings in Libya and was reportedly decorated by the same artisans who worked on the Hassan II Mosque in Casablanca. Its distinctive green dome is surrounded by a multitude of minarets and smaller domes. The external panels of the façade contain some superb ceramics with floral and arabesque motifs. The tiled pillars are most attractive, particularly the unusual small, tiled pillars around the minaret's balconies. There is some fine Arabic calligraphy in sandstone on top of the outer pillars of the building saying 'Al-Mulk-'illah' (Everything to God).

Non-Muslims are not permitted inside the mausoleum's inner sanctum but the gilded tomb is clearly visible from the door, as are the marvellous stucco ceilings. Please be especially discreet during prayer time. The tomb belongs to the pious Sidi Abdussalam, who died in Zliten in the 16th century AD. There is also a madrassa on the site.

Sleeping & Eating

Funduq Zliten (☎ 620121; zlitenhotel@lttnet.net; Sharia al-Jamahiriya; s/d/ste 35/45/75LD) When we first visited this place in 2001 in the days when Libyan government hotels were pretty grim, we thought Funduq Zliten was like paradise. The rooms are still quite good, but they're starting to show their age, many of the bathrooms could be cleaner and most of the staff learned their service skills at the government school of disinterest. The disconcerting smell of Dettol in the corridors was also not a highlight of our visit. The restaurant (meals 15LD) is fine but nothing special.

There is a handful of cheap eateries close to the post office and between the highway and main roundabout.

Getting There & Away

Shared taxis connect Zliten with Misrata, Al-Khoms and Tripoli.

AROUND ZLITEN

The area around Zliten is renowned for its **marabout tombs** (*turba;* also known as *zawiyas*), which attract a steady stream of pilgrims. A visit to the holy tombs is said to bestow a greater fertility upon pilgrims; many women come here to ask for help in having a child. Local taxi drivers know where to find the tombs. There's also a good **beach** at Souq al-Khamis.

MISRATA مصراتة

☎ 051 / pop 406,800

Misrata is Libya's third-largest city and has a distinctive feel with its well-ordered and relatively clean streets and, remarkably for Libya, 'no smoking' signs in many buildings. There's little to see in town, but as the last major town before the long trek east to Benghazi, it makes a decent overnight stop. Some people also use it as a base for visiting Leptis Magna (p110), although it's 100km away.

History

In ancient times, Misrata was an important port for the caravan trade and traders from Misrata were famed throughout the Sahara. Its carpet industry is also one of the longest standing in Libya. Two Arab families, the Muntasir and the Adgham, dominated the city's life and led the local tribes in their disputes with the Turkish overlords during Ottoman times when Misrata was an important administrative centre and was considered the second city in Turkish Tripolitania. Under the Italians it was again a centre for settlement and administration – a time when the relatively structured layout of the streets was completed.

Orientation & Information

The centre of town and the main square (Maidan an-Nasser) are around the intersection of Sharia Abdul Rahman Azem (which runs all the way from the highway to the centre of town, north-south all the way) and Sharia Ramadan Asswayhli (which runs east-west through town).

The **main post office** (Sharia Ramadan Asswayhli) is 500m north of Maidan an-Nasser, while there are internet cafés dotted around the centre of town; one of the better ones is in the street behind Funduq al-Diyafa.

Sights

The town's **souq**, in the lanes off Maidan an-Nasser, has a thrice-weekly market for local clothing and carpets. The only other sight of note is the **Quz al-Teek** (Tower of

THE MISRATA TREASURE

In 1981 more than 100,000 coins of unknown origin were discovered in an underground chamber not far from Misrata by archaeologists doing routine excavations. The coins, dating from AD 294–333, are thought to have been the property of a garrison rather than a private individual, so immense was the haul. Some of the coins are in the Misrata museum, although the largest collection is on display in Room 15 of Leptis Museum (p117).

Dunes), west of the town centre. This sky-piercing, space-age tower is a monument to the Libyan resistance. Beneath the tower is a small **museum** (adult/child 3/1LD; 9am-1pm & 3-6pm Tue-Sun) containing some pottery artefacts of minor interest, photos of prehistoric Saharan rock art and parts of the Misrata Treasure (p119).

Sleeping

Buyut ash-Shabaab (Youth Hostel; ☎ 624880; dm 5LD) Not up to the standard of other youth hostels in Libya, this place seems to be rarely cleaned.

Funduq as-Siyahe (☎ 619777; Sharia Ramadan Asswayhli; s with shower 20LD, d with shower & toilet 25LD) This grand old hotel is a friendly if run-down place very close to Maidan an-Nasser. The clean rooms have high ceilings, a touch of old-world charm and many overlook a courtyard.

Funduq al-Diyafa (☎ 629620; Sharia Ramadan Asswayhli; s/d with shared bathroom 15/20LD, s/d/tr with private bathroom 20/30/45LD) Funduq al-Diyafa is in a similarly good location as Funduq as-Siyahe, a couple of hundred metres south of the main square but set back behind a shady open square. The rooms are simple but well-kept and better than the exterior or the lobby suggests. It also wins the prize for the cleanest bathrooms (shared and private) in Misrata. It also has a coffeehouse and a restaurant (meals from 10LD) that serves reasonable Turkish food.

Funduq al-Kabir (Grand Hotel; ☎ 620178; grandhotel@maktoob.com; Sharia Sana Mahidly; s/d/ste from 30/35/45LD, studios/villas 55/85LD;) This professionally run hotel is excellent value and has a much more intimate feel to other hotels in town. It's central, but on a quiet street, and the rooms are spacious and comfortable. It also has a good restaurant (meals 15LD).

Funduq Quz at-Teek (☎ 613333; fax 610500; Sharia Dar al-Ry; s/tw/ste 35/42/90, s/d studio 38/45LD, villas without breakfast 50LD;) If you've slept in Tobruk at the Funduq al-Masira (p154), you'll do a double-take here because the resemblance is uncanny: from the tapestries in the lobby to the signs of decay in the bathroom. Once Misrata's best hotel, the rooms are still worth the asking price although it's in increasing need of an overhaul. The hotel is next to the Quz al-Teek tower, about 2km west of the city centre.

Eating & Drinking

There are a couple of good patisseries on Sharia Ramadan Asswayhli, about 400m south of Maidan an-Nasser; look for the sign brandishing a chef. Almost next door to the patisseries is a simple, unnamed restaurant doing hearty servings of half a barbecued chicken *(djeaj mahama)* with soup and beans (8LD, including drinks).

Misrata's contribution to café culture comes in the form of a swish, semicircular and glass-walled coffeehouse overlooking the main intersection on the western side. About 100m to the west, just off Sharia Abdul Rahman Azem, is a small pizza restaurant that serves, not surprisingly, pizzas (4LD to 8LD) and hamburgers (from 1LD).

Getting There & Away

There are regular shared taxis and micros from Misrata to Tripoli, Zliten and Sirt. You might also find an early-morning shared taxi or bus heading for Benghazi. The taxi station area is adjacent to the main square.

AROUND MISRATA

About 17km west of Misrata (31km east of Zliten) are some of the largest **coastal sand dunes** in the world. If you've spent any time in the sand seas of southern Libya, you may wonder what all the fuss is about. Nonetheless if these are the only dunes you're likely to see in Libya, they're worth a small detour. They're 5km north of the highway via a good road. If you can't find them, ask for *'tanaret zray'* (the nearby tuna factory), which is the name by which locals know the dunes.

TAUORGA تاورغاء

Tauorga, 53km south of Misrata by road, has the unusual distinction of being the only town on the Libyan coast where most of the inhabitants are as dark skinned as sub-Saharan Africans – some locals claim to be the descendants of freed slaves, while others argue they are related to Libya's original indigenous inhabitants.

Tauorga is renowned for its palm-woven products, including bags, baskets and mats. Many of these items are offered for sale from roadside stalls along the main highway, opposite the turn-off to Tauorga (41km south of Misrata). Here you'll also find the colourful pottery of Gharyan for sale.

After passing the turn-offs to Tauorga, you start crossing the Sahel as-Sirt (Sirt Plain), a flat, scrubby and featureless expanse of nothingness that stretches all the way to Ajdabiya.

GHIRZA غرزة

The monuments of remote Ghirza are considered to be some of the most important indigenous contributions to Libyan civilisation. These 3rd-century-AD public buildings include temples and tombs (3rd to 5th centuries AD) as well as a series of **fortified farms**. To get an idea of what to expect, some examples of Ghirza stonework is on display in Galleries 1 and 5 of Tripoli's Jamahiriya Museum (p76) and stone reliefs from the fortified farms in Room 18 of Leptis Museum (p117).

Ghirza is believed to have been a 3rd-century settlement on the southern fringes of Roman Tripolitania. It was built by Romanised Libyans and the architecture was heavily influenced by the Roman style of the day. When Arab travellers passed through the area in the 11th century AD, the temples were still in use.

At the far (southern) end of the site are the three **tombs** that are the highlight of Ghirza's remains. There are distinctive, sandstone pillars encircling these elevated, squat mausoleums, each adorned with relief carvings of scenes from everyday life, including evidence of harvests that are now difficult to imagine in such a barren landscape. The central tomb has some detailed animal and flower motifs around the façade, while the northernmost tomb features particularly fine stonework atop some of the pillars, and Latin inscriptions flanked by two Roman eagles.

Getting There & Away

It's a hard slog to get to Ghirza and there is no public transport to the site; we picked up one local who had been waiting patiently at the checkpoint for hours. The best option is a very long day trip from Misrata or a detour as you head east towards Sirt. It can get fiercely hot here in summer, so bring plenty of water with you.

In case your driver or guide doesn't know the way, take the main highway from Misrata towards Sirt. After 82km, take the turn-off for As-Sadaada to the south. After 18km, you reach another road junction with a checkpoint. Ghirza is off to the east, 91km away, along a partially asphalted road. The road is shadowed for almost the entire distance by the Great Man-Made River. At a fork in the road about 80km after the checkpoint, turn right (there's a sign to Ghirza in Arabic). The ruins are a further 11.5km and reached through the bleak modern village of Ghirza; take the stony tracks leading out from the eastern end of the village.

SIRT سرت

☎ 054 / pop 133,900

Sirt is a custom-built city waiting impatiently for the day when it can be declared the capital of the United States of Africa. Colonel Qaddafi was born, and spent part of his childhood around Sirt and he has transformed it from a small village into a central pillar of his ambitious scheme for an economic and political community of African states.

Built on the site of the ancient city of Euphranta, Sirt was later an important land communication point with the south and an embarkation point for many caravans. Under the Italians it was an administrative centre.

Sadly, this supposed showpiece of the revolution is a city without soul, a lifeless place of few charms. It's a friendly enough town but the only reason for travellers to spend any time here is to break up the long journey between Benghazi and Tripoli.

Orientation & Information

The town's main thoroughfare, Sharia al-Jamahiriya (also known as Sharia 1st September), sweeps from the southeastern entrance to the town to the western perimeter. About 3km from the highway, at the point where Sharia al-Jamahiriya turns west, are most of the facilities you'll need – the main post office, pharmacy and a good grocery store underneath the town's best restaurant. Also on this bend is a bank, Masraf al-Jamahiriya. Between Sharia al-Jamahiriya and the highway are the headquarters for the General People's Congress (GPC; p40). The modern, sprawling parliamentary complex runs along the western side of Sharia al-Jamahiriya.

Sights

Not a lot really. If you're an aficionado of **revolutionary murals**, the posters of Colonel Qaddafi may qualify as Sirt's only tourist attraction (there are some particularly fine examples of the genre). Without any apparent attempt at irony, one proudly proclaims in Arabic that 'The best thing about Sirt is that it is in the centre of Libya'. Most of the billboards laud African unity and the Great Man-Made River.

Sleeping & Eating

Sirt arises from its customary slumber whenever parliament sits (usually close to the end of the year) or the city hosts one of its pan-African conferences. Sirt is also home to large celebrations commemorating the 1 September revolution. Finding a bed at these times is near impossible.

Buyut ash-Shabaab (Youth Hostel; ☎ 61825; off Sharia al-Corniche; dm 5LD) The youth hostel is a friendly, down-to-earth place without pretensions to luxury; it's often full if you arrive late in the day. Staff can arrange simple meals from 1LD. It's a small block north of the corniche, opposite a college and next to the Red Crescent building.

Funduq al-Mehari (☎ 60100; fax 61310; Sharia al-Jamahiriya; s/tw/d 35/45/50LD, ste 90-120LD) Funduq al-Mehari is a bit out on a limb, just north of the road almost 6km west of the post office, but the rooms are comfortable, spotless and excellent value and some even have traces of elegance. Some bathrooms are a little rundown, but if the showers are an indication of the achievements of the Great Man-Made River, then it is (literally) a roaring success.

Funduq Qasr Mutamarat (☎ 60165; fax 60959; www.sirtgulfhotel.com; info@sirtgulfhotel.com; north of GPC; s/d/q with private bathroom 48/70/128LD, standard/presidential ste 128/430LD) This is Sirt's showpiece hotel with large, extremely comfortable rooms spread over four buildings. After five years of trying, it has finally allowed us to see one of the six presidential suites – extravagant, mock-Louis XIV furniture, enormous rooms and serious questions about whether African dollars are being well-spent. The hotel is just north of the parliament buildings, about 300m west of Sharia al-Jamahiriya.

Mat'am al-Aseel (☎ mobile 0927011018; Sharia al-Jamahiriya; meals 10-12.50LD; ⏰ lunch & dinner) Far and away the best restaurant in Sirt, this Turkish restaurant is all most visitors see as they rush on to Tripoli and Benghazi. Fortunately the food (grilled meats and Turkish bread are a recurring theme) is good and the service likewise.

Getting There & Away

At 592km to Sebha, 561km to Benghazi and 463km to Tripoli, Sirt is a long way to anywhere. The main shared taxi station is just north of the post office.

GREAT MAN-MADE RIVER (AN-NAHR SINAI) لنهر الصناعي العظيم

Although you may see the mounds, pumping stations and construction work of the Great Man-Made River throughout Libya, the reservoir 17km east of Sirt offers an opportunity to take a closer look, if only for the symbolism attached to Colonel Qaddafi's grand vision. The gravel track leading south off the highway leads to the reservoir 2.2km away; you may be escorted to the dam's edge by a friendly, machine-gun-toting soldier.

The large reservoir is filled with water pumped from wells via underground pipes, some of which are visible beneath the iron grille on the viewing platform. Note the map showing the various stages of the GMR project although it won't necessarily include the latest stages. For more information on what Colonel Qaddafi dubbed the 'Eighth Wonder of the World', see p64.

MEDINAT SULTAN مدينة سلطان

Medinat Sultan, 50km east of Sirt, was an important Fatimid site but is now dusty and derelict, scarcely managing to relieve the monotony of the long road east to Ajdabiya. The excavations include the rubble of the old Fatimid mosque, a couple of kilometres inside the main gate, but you'd require lots of imagination to make any sense of it. Of greater interest are the two muscular **Philaeni brothers**, cast in bronze and lying in a walled compound just inside the gate. The hollow statues, one facing west towards Tripolitania, the other facing east to Cyrenaica, once formed part of a more-than-5m-tall Italian-built arch (Arco Philaeni) demarcating Tripolitania from Cyrenaica at Ras Lanuf, 200km to the east. The point where the arch once stood was where the Phoenicians and Greeks divided the land between them in a novel way; turn to See How They Run (opposite) for details. When Colonel Qaddafi and his revolutionary government came to power in 1969, they saw the arch as a symbol of the fractured nation they

> **SEE HOW THEY RUN**
>
> In the mid-4th century BC, the Greeks and the Phoenicians decided that it was high time that they divided Libya between them on an official basis. An agreement was reached that Greek runners should set out from Cyrene in eastern Libya and Punic (Phoenician) runners from their capital at Carthage (in modern-day Tunisia). Where they met, the border would be drawn. When the runners met at Ras Lanuf, the Greeks accused the Phoenicians, the Philaeni brothers, of cheating. They were offered the choice of either being buried alive or allowing the unsporting Greeks to progress. They chose martyrdom.

were trying to unite and, in the early 1970s, tore it down.

Across the other side of the dirt track that runs through the site, on an open patch of ground 50m to the north, are some scattered **stone reliefs**. These once adorned the façade of the arch with carved scenes of Italian soldiers. The closest one to the gate shows Mussolini (second from left) being saluted by his soldiers. The dusty and unlabelled museum on the site is not worth any of your time.

The entrance to the site is through a pair of green iron gates on the northern side of the highway. There are no regular opening times although it's usually open from around 9am until just before sunset daily; there's an on-site caretaker, so simply bang on the gate.

MEDINAT SULTAN TO AJDABIYA

The coastline from Sirt to **Ajdabiya** (see p131) runs past a large area of salt basins and the towns along the way are of interest to travellers only as petrol, toilet or food stops. The gulf region, known as Al-Khalij, is nonetheless the heart of Libya's most prolific oil-producing areas and the towns along the dip in the gulf – especially **As-Sidra**, **Ras Lanuf** and **Brega** – are little more than adjuncts to overgrown oil terminals.

Just 19km east of the main turn-off to Ras Lanuf and 197km west of Ajdabiya is the old border between Tripolitania and Cyrenaica. The only evidence of this historically significant spot (for details check out See How They Run, left) is a flattened area of around 5 sq metres on either side of the road. If you look closely, you can just see the foundation outline of the Arco Philaeni.

One town of particularly grim notoriety is **Al-'Aghela**, 87.4km east of Ras Lanuf. A concentration camp was based to the south of here during the Italian occupation. Thousands of Bedouin died here with over 10,000 people crowded in at any one time. A famous Libyan poem of lament by the popular poet Rajab Buwaish speaks powerfully for a generation of Libyans: 'I have no illnesses but the illness of the concentration camp of Al-'Aghela'; an English translation is available on www.libyana.org.

Note that the town of Al-'Aghela is actually part of Cyrenaica, but we have included it here for ease of navigation – the Colonel would be proud of us for disregarding the border between the two ancient provinces.

Cyrenaica

Cyrenaica is wholly unlike anywhere else in Libya. There are faint reminders of Libya's desert geography in the far southeast, where Tobruk, one of the world's premier WWII sites, provides a gateway to the little-visited oasis of Al-Jaghbub and the remote Great Sand Sea. But for the most part the region is physically different to the rest of the country. Cyrenaica is Libya's greenest corner, home to the Jebel al-Akhdar (Green Mountains), which closely shadow the coastline creating some spectacular landscapes, particularly around Ras al-Hillal.

Cyrenaica's main difference, though, is cultural. Although the Romans left their mark, Cyrenaica was more strongly influenced by the ancient Greeks. Nestled in its narrow strip of coastline are three outstanding cities of Greek antiquity – Cyrene, Apollonia and Tolmeita. Pockets of Byzantine culture, such as Qasr Libya and L'Atrun, round out the picture.

During the Islamic period Cyrenaica was often ruled from Egypt. When the rebellious Cyrenaicans refused to yield to Egyptian rule, hundreds of thousands of families belonging to the Bani Salim tribe from Arabia were transplanted to Cyrenaica. Their descendants remain here, giving rise to the claim that Cyrenaica is, linguistically and culturally, the most Arab region in the world outside of the Arabian Peninsula. It is often said that the Middle East begins at Ras Lanuf.

Cyrenaica's distinctiveness from the rest of Libya also finds expression in the region's cuisines, and its people's reputation for being gregarious storytellers and poets. Indeed, clamorous cities, such as Benghazi are more evocative of Egypt than the rest of Libya.

HIGHLIGHTS

- Marvel at the aesthetic vision of the ancient Greeks at **Cyrene** (p141) and **Tolmeita** (p134)
- Examine at close quarters the skilled mosaic artistry of the Byzantines at **Qasr Libya** (p136)
- Enjoy the old-world charm of Freedom Sq and the clamour of Souq al-Jreed in **Benghazi** (opposite)
- Take in the panoramic sweep where the Jebel al-Akhdar meets the Mediterranean at **Ras al-Hillal** (p149)
- Pause to reflect on the wartime tragedy of **Tobruk** (p151)
- Get a taste of the Sahara at the dune-framed lake of **Buhairat al-Fredgha** (p155) near Al-Jaghbub
- Drive the desert road from **Tobruk to Ajdabiya** (p154) without falling asleep at the wheel

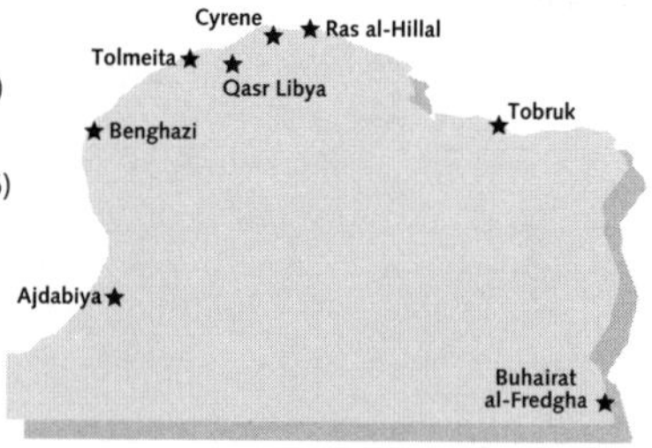

WESTERN CYRENAICA

Cyrenaica's west is more a place to pass through on your way somewhere else, although Benghazi is an agreeable city with great hotels and restaurants and enough sights to warrant half a day's exploration. Awjila is a long way from anywhere, but its exceptional Al-Kabir Mosque and the old city may just be worth the detour.

BENGHAZI بنغازى

☎ 061 / pop 665,689

Libya's second city and the principal city of eastern Libya, Benghazi is a mix of busy commercial centre and rundown Mediterranean charm, although it lacks the obvious appeal of Tripoli. All but the merest traces of Benghazi's antiquity are buried beneath the modern city, and much of the old town was destroyed during WWII.

Nonetheless, if you know where to look Benghazi is worth exploring. It can also make a good base or staging post for touring the Jebel al-Akhdar, as well as the Greek cities of Tocra, Tolmeita, Cyrene and Apollonia. The climate is also one of the more pleasant in Libya; even in summer, you've a good chance of catching a sea breeze. Benghazi is at its best around sunset and early evening, when the streets are often alive with people and the city lights provide the perfect backdrop to the waters of Benghazi's double harbour.

History

The original settlement here was just east of modern Benghazi and was founded by Greek settlers from Cyrene, although some archaeologists argue that the settlers came directly from the islands of the Aegean. Called Eusperides, it was first mentioned in historical records in the 6th century BC and was thought to be the site of the legendary garden of Hesperides, from the Greek myth of the golden apples. The only reminder of this site of myth is the lake surrounded by reeds, picnic areas and water slides alongside the road to Al-Bayda, around 4km northeast of town.

Eusperides was abandoned in the mid-3rd century BC and a new settlement grew up on the shores of the Mediterranean in what is now modern Benghazi. By around 249 BC the new settlement was named Berenice (see p126), named after a Cyrenaican princess and wife of Ptolemy III of Egypt. Like other formerly Greek cities of northeastern Libya, Berenice fell under the sway of the Romans in the 1st century BC. By the time that the Byzantines arrived, the city was in decline and although they made some repairs, it fell into obscurity.

After the Arab invasion, Benghazi was again neglected in favour of other cities of more strategic importance, such as Ajdabiya. It was only in the 15th century AD that Benghazi was rediscovered by Tripolitanian merchants, taking the city into a new and prosperous phase. Benghazi is named after Ibn Ghazi (also Bani Ghazi), a local holy man renowned in the 15th century AD for his good deeds.

The Turks took Benghazi in 1578, but their attempts to make it a centre for tax collection drove traders to other towns. Benghazi recovered its fortunes during the mid-19th century, but this was not to last. In 1911 the Italians laid siege to the city from the sea. The city subsequently became an Italian fortress in the face of fierce resistance by the surrounding tribes. With the resistance finally subdued during the 1930s, Benghazi virtually became an Italian city.

During WWII the city constantly changed hands. More than 1000 bombs rained down upon the city and by the time the war ended there was little left. After the war, many settlers from trading families from western Libya, especially from Misrata, came to the city. After independence the development of the city began again, and the harbour was enlarged to accommodate commercial shipping.

Benghazi was bombarded by the missiles of the US Sixth Fleet in April 1986, causing considerable damage and killing as many as 30 people (see p41).

Orientation

Benghazi's hotels are spread far and wide. The older part of the city stretches out from the northern shores of the harbour and covers an area roughly bounded by Sharias Ahmed Rafiq al-Mahdawi, 23 July and Al-Jezayir. The heart of the 'medina' is the partly Italianate Freedom Sq; to the northeast is the covered Souq al-Jreed.

CYRENAICA

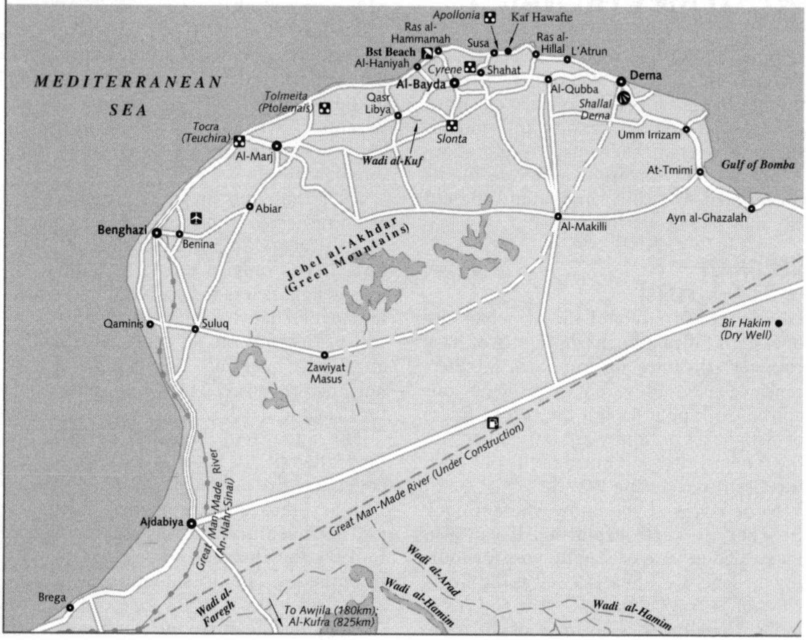

Benghazi's two harbours divide the northern sections of the city from the road south to the university suburb of Qar Yunis.

Information

INTERNET ACCESS

Internet cafés (🕑 10am-midnight Sat-Thu, 6pm-midnight Fri) are found on almost every street of the city centre, although many places come and go. Look for the blue Internet Explorer sign or red Yahoo! sign on the window. The more convenient places are along Sharia Jamal Abdul Nasser and along Sharia Qasr Ahmed; each of these is marked on the map. Hotels also have internet access, including **Funduq al-Fadheel** (per hr 1LD; 🕑 3pm-midnight) and **Funduq Tibesti** (per hr 2LD; 🕑 10am-midnight).

JAWAZZAT

The **jawazzat** (☎ 9098765; Sharia al-Corniche) is at the western end of Benghazi harbour.

MONEY

There are plenty of banks in the central area. The Masraf al-Tijara Watanmiya (Bank of Commerce & Development), where you can get Visa cash advances, has branches at the airport, Islamic Call Building, Funduq Uzu and Funduq Tibesti; the latter has an ATM that serves Visa and Visa Electron, with a maximum daily withdrawal of 200LD.

A small and relatively open black market of moneychangers operates between Freedom Sq and the southern entrance to Souq al-Jreed.

POST & TELEPHONE

The **main post & telephone office** (Sharia Omar al-Mukhtar; 🕑 10am-10pm Sat-Thu) is about 300m north of the harbour.

Sights

OLD BERENICE

Just set back from the water and next to the old lighthouse are the low-lying remains of the old Greek (and later Roman) settlement of Berenice (see p125). There's not a whole lot to see, but what there is, in outline, includes a broad range of historical eras – a trace of the 3rd-century BC **Greek city wall**, four **Roman peristyle houses** and six **wine**

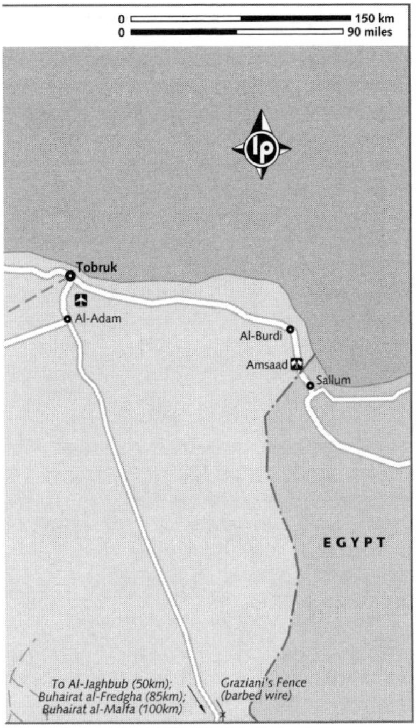

vats and a **Byzantine church** with a mosaic in desperate need of restoration. These ruins formed the northern part of the ancient city, which extended south and east but now lies buried beneath modern Benghazi.

FREEDOM SQUARE

Benghazi's **Old Town Hall** runs along the western side of Freedom Sq. Built during the period of Italian occupation, the town hall is now derelict, rubbish-strewn and closed to the public, although traces of its former elegance remain nonetheless. The decaying, whitewashed Italianate façade is unmistakably grand, with some lovely arched doorways and pillars. The large balcony once played host to its share of important orators – Mussolini addressed the crowds, German field marshal Rommel reviewed his troops and King Idris spoke to his subjects from here.

At the northern end of Freedom Sq is the **Atiq Mosque** (also known as Al-Jame' al-Kabir, or the Great Mosque). The original mosque on the site was built in the early 15th century, but had many later renovations.

Behind the mosque is another square surrounded by modern porticos and off to the northwest is the **Osman Mosque** with its distinctive Ottoman-style minaret.

SOUQ AL-JREED

The covered market of Benghazi, Souq al-Jreed, stretches for over 1km from Freedom Sq to Al-Funduq Market. It's not the most evocative bazaar in the Arab world but its liveliness and colour are among the highlights of a visit to Benghazi.

Like any Middle Eastern market worth its salt, Souq al-Jreed offers just about anything you could want and plenty that you don't. This market exists primarily for locals, which is what makes it so worthwhile. There are watches, cheap clothes, elegant gold jewellery, *galabiyyas* (men's robes) of alternately questionable and refined taste, henna, Levis and 'anything you want, one dinar', all displayed to the accompaniment of the music of Umm Kolthum crooning out from the latest Sony sound systems. Also visible through the cloud of overbearing perfumes are pharmacies, felafel stalls, mosques and glossy pictures of Mecca. The nearer you get to Al-Funduq Market, the greater the noise and general clamour, and the more the lines between an Arab bazaar and an African market become blurred. For many reasons, this is a place to wander through slowly, not least because the floor is quite uneven in parts.

COMMONWEALTH WAR GRAVES CEMETERY

Benghazi is home to a small but well-kept cemetery for Allied soldiers killed in WWII. It contains the graves of Australian, British, Greek, Indian, Jewish, Libyan, Norwegian, South African and Sudanese soldiers. The cemetery is 5km southeast of the city centre. Take the First Ring Rd from Funduq Uzu, passing under the road to Tripoli. The cemetery is on the right behind a fence of iron railings. If you're taking a taxi (3LD), ask for *'maqbara australiya'*.

OTHER SIGHTS

On the waterfront, next to Old Berenice is the square-sided **old lighthouse**, which was built during the Italian occupation and remains in use. The waterfront here runs southeast from here for around 700m and

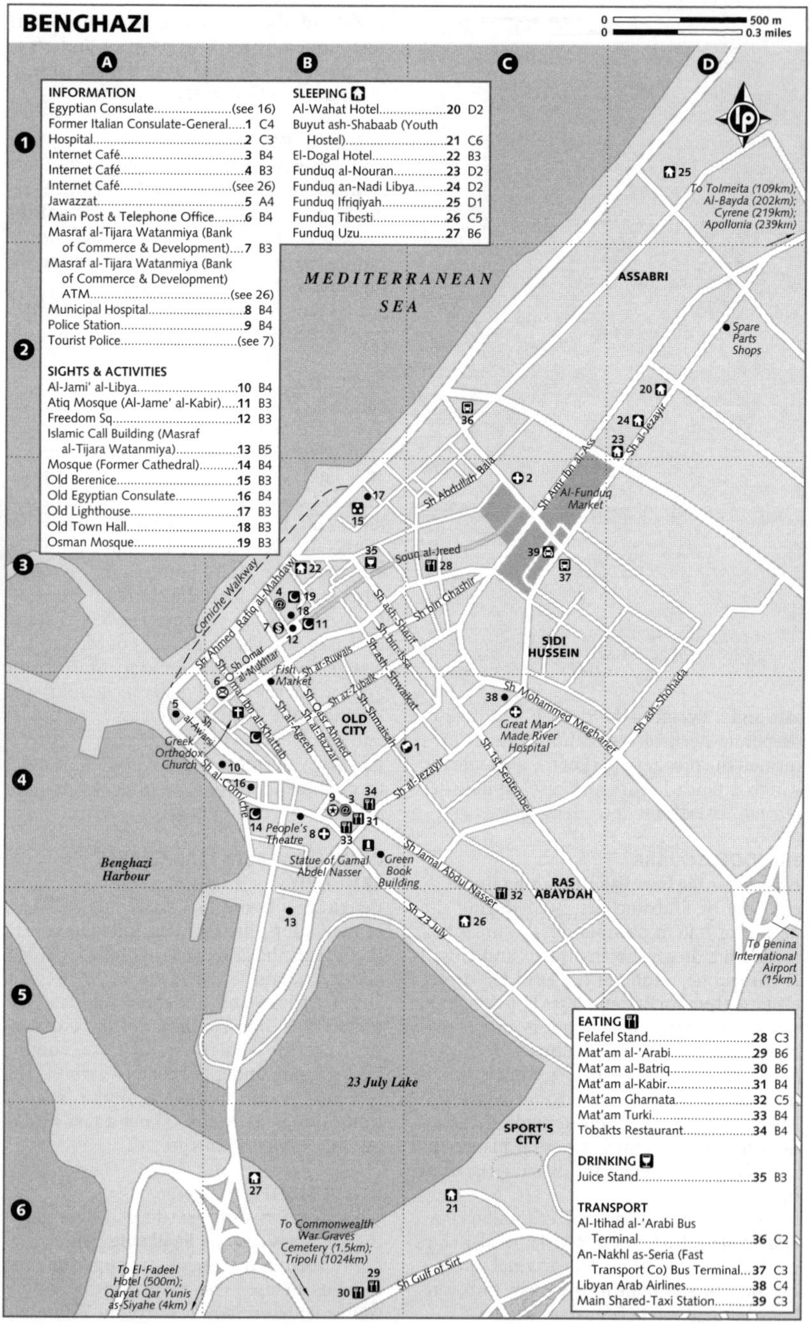
BENGHAZI
0 500 m
0 0.3 miles
INFORMATION
Egyptian Consulate......................(see 16)
Former Italian Consulate-General.....1 C4
Hospital..2 C3
Internet Café.....................................3 B4
Internet Café.....................................4 B3
Internet Café...............................(see 26)
Jawazzat..5 A4
Main Post & Telephone Office.........6 B4
Masraf al-Tijara Watanmiya (Bank of Commerce & Development)....7 B3
Masraf al-Tijara Watanmiya (Bank of Commerce & Development) ATM.......................................(see 26)
Municipal Hospital...........................8 B4
Police Station....................................9 B4
Tourist Police................................(see 7)
SIGHTS & ACTIVITIES
Al-Jami' al-Libya.............................10 B4
Atiq Mosque (Al-Jame' al-Kabir).....11 B3
Freedom Sq......................................12 B3
Islamic Call Building (Masraf al-Tijara Watanmiya)..................13 B5
Mosque (Former Cathedral)...........14 B4
Old Berenice.....................................15 B3
Old Egyptian Consulate..................16 B4
Old Lighthouse................................17 B3
Old Town Hall..................................18 B3
Osman Mosque................................19 B3
SLEEPING
Al-Wahat Hotel...................20 D2
Buyut ash-Shabaab (Youth Hostel)............................21 C6
El-Dogal Hotel.....................22 B3
Funduq al-Nouran...............23 D2
Funduq an-Nadi Libya.........24 D2
Funduq Ifriqiyah..................25 D1
Funduq Tibesti.....................26 C5
Funduq Uzu.........................27 B6
EATING
Felafel Stand...............................28 C3
Mat'am al-'Arabi.........................29 B6
Mat'am al-Batriq.........................30 B6
Mat'am al-Kabir...........................31 B4
Mat'am Gharnata.........................32 C5
Mat'am Turki................................33 B4
Tobakts Restaurant.....................34 B4
DRINKING
Juice Stand...................................35 B3
TRANSPORT
Al-Itihad al-'Arabi Bus Terminal...................................36 C2
An-Nakhl as-Seria (Fast Transport Co) Bus Terminal...37 C3
Libyan Arab Airlines....................38 C4
Main Shared-Taxi Station...........39 C3
MEDITERRANEAN SEA
ASSABRI
Spare Parts Shops
To Tolmeita (109km); Al-Bayda (202km); Cyrene (219km); Apollonia (239km)
Sh al-Jezayir
Sh Amr ibn al-Ass
Al-Funduq Market
Sh Abdullah Bala
Souq al-Jreed
Sh bin Ghashir
Sh ash-Sharif
Sh bin-Issa
Sh ash-Shwaikat
SIDI HUSSEIN
Sh Mohammed Megharief
Sh ash-Shohada
Great Man-Made River Hospital
Sh 1st September
Corniche Walkway
Sh Ahmed Rafiq al-Mahdawi
Sh Omar al-Mukhtar
Sh Omar ibn al-Khattab
Sh ar-Ruwals
Fish Market
Sh az-Zubalk
Sh Shmaisah
Sh al-Ageeb
Sh Qasr Ahmed
Sh al-Bazzar
OLD CITY
Sh al-Awarsi
Greek Orthodox Church
Sh al-Corniche
People's Theatre
Statue of Gamal Abdel Nasser
Green Book Building
Sh Jamal Abdul Nasser
Sh 23 July
RAS ABAYDAH
Benghazi Harbour
To Benina International Airport (15km)
23 July Lake
SPORT'S CITY
To Commonwealth War Graves Cemetery (1.5km); Tripoli (1024km)
To El-Fadeel Hotel (500m); Qaryat Qar Yunis as-Siyahe (4km)
Sh Gulf of Sirt

CYRENAICA

THINGS THEY SAID ABOUT... BENGHAZI

Benghazi's Medina is nearly as large as that of Tripoli – one square, whitewashed house after another, and in every street small Arab cafés where for a halfpenny you can get coffee and hookah. The market was closing. The tradesmen had fastened their booths with shutters; the camels from the country stood with their loads on their backs ready to leave; only the cafés were open, and the monotonous Arab gramophone music sounded from them all.

Knud Holmboe, Desert Encounter *(1931)*

has been repaved as a pleasant waterfront **corniche**.

The pastel shades and wooden shutters of the **Old Egyptian Consulate**, just off Sharia Jamal Abdul Nasser, exude a certain decaying elegance amid the palm trees and are strongly evocative of its Italianate origins.

Along Sharia al-Corniche, the grand whitewashed and arched faced is home to **Al-Jami' al-Libya**, Libya's first university. From here you should be able to see the twin domes of the **former cathedral** (now a mosque) off to the east. This was once the largest church in North Africa. From a distance, its imposing grandeur is impressive; up close, it stands forlorn and disused.

Sleeping

Benghazi's accommodation gets better all the time, although most places are spread out across the city.

BUDGET

Buyut ash-Shabaab (Youth Hostel; ☎ 2234101; dm 5LD) Behind the sports stadium, Benghazi's well-run youth hostel is basic but most rooms are well-maintained. Men and women are housed in different parts of the building and there are a few family rooms. It's a popular place, so book ahead.

Funduq Ifriqiya (☎ 3380444; fax 3386698; Sharia al-Jezayir; s/d/tr 15/20/25LD; ❄) Funduq Ifriqiya is streets ahead of the other budget options in Al-Funduq Market area, with simple but tidy rooms (with satellite TV) that have been renovated in the not-too-distant past. It's little used by tour groups, an attraction in itself.

Qaryat Qar Yunis as-Siyahe (Qar Yunis Tourist Village; ☎ 9096903; www.tourist-village.com; Sharia Qar Yunis; s/d/ste incl breakfast from 27/38/60LD, chalet/apt/villa from 20/25/50LD; ❄ 💻 🏊) Six kilometres south of Benghazi, this enormous tourist village has a range of high-quality accommodation, from spacious hotel rooms (some with renovated bathrooms) to recently built villas by the beach. There's also a children's funfair. It's a terrific base for Cyrenaica, although it's overrun in summer, when you'll need to book ahead.

MIDRANGE

Prices in this section include breakfast and all rooms come with private bathroom.

Funduq an-Nadi Libya (☎ 3372333; fax 3372334; Sharia Ahmed Rafiq al-Madawi; s/d 25/40LD; ❄) Funduq an-Nadi Libya, 3km north of the centre, is run by the Automobile Club of Libya and has comfortable, quiet and spacious rooms with satellite TV. The hotel is in a complex of office buildings behind a large iron gate with a security guard; the sign in Arabic outside reads Al-Mujame as-Siyahe (Tourist Complex).

El-Dogal Hotel (Funduq el-Dogal; ☎ 9091579; fax 9097613; Sharia Ahmed Rafiq al-Mahdawi; s/tw/d 30/45/50LD; ❄) One of the newer hotels in Benghazi, El-Dogal has large rooms that won't win any style awards. However all except one per floor have views over the Mediterranean, while the corner single rooms here are better than solo travellers will find elsewhere. Breakfast is also above average.

Al-Wahat Hotel (Funduq al-Wahat; ☎/fax 3372766; alwahat_hotel@yahoo.com; Sharia al-Jezayir; s/d 30/45LD, ste 55-100LD; ❄) This outstanding new privately run hotel is hard to beat, with sparkling, spacious rooms. OK, some of their style choices may not be to your taste – pink bathrooms and floral flourishes – but value like this is rare and everything from the service to the levels of comfort make this one of our favourite places in town.

El-Fadeel Hotel (Funduq el-Fadeel; ☎ 9099795; elfadeelhotel@hotmail.com; Sharia el-Shatt; s/d/ste from 40/50/70LD; ❄ 💻) Built in 2003, this is one of the best packages in town, with pleasant, large and well-appointed rooms. The hotel also has facilities for which you'd pay triple the price elsewhere: balconies, some with seaviews; a barber; laundry service; two restaurants; computers with wi-fi internet (7.50LD per 24 hours) in all suites; and an internet café. There's also a swimming pool under construction. Service is professional and you can pay with Visa. Welcome small touches include a detailed city map for each guest.

Funduq al-Nouran (☎ 3372091; info@alnouranhotel.com; Sharia al-Jezayir; s 50-60LD, d 60-75LD; ❄) Due to open in early 2007, they were still applying the finishing touches to this new four-star hotel when we were there, but they're a friendly lot and gave us a sneak preview. The rooms we saw were large and tasteful, with clean lines, balconies and an almost European sense of style. It's always risky to recommend places before they open, but we've no hesitation in doing so on this occasion.

TOP END

Funduq Uzu (☎ 9095160; www.uzuhotel.com; Sharia al-Jezayir; s/d with lake view 60/75LD, without 50/65LD, ste 100-220LD; ❄ 💻) One of Benghazi's top hotels, Funduq Uzu has superbly appointed rooms with all the requisite bells and whistles. Suite No 534 wins our vote for the best room in Benghazi, with its plush leather couches, cosy sitting area and views across the lake to the city centre (especially stunning at night). The buffet breakfasts are among the best in town.

Funduq Tibesti (☎ 9090017; fax 9098029; Sharia Jamal Abdul Nasser; s/d with lake view from 80/115LD, without view 75/100LD, ste from 150LD; ❄) On the northern side of the harbour, this is another classy hotel with a luxurious ambience; look for the grass waterfalls adorning the façade. Facilities include a patisserie, health club, business centre, coffeehouses and restaurants.

Eating

Benghazi has some terrific restaurants, ranging from quick eats to places serving Turkish, Italian and Libyan food.

RESTAURANTS

Mat'am Turki (☎ 9091331; Sharia 23 July; sandwiches from 1LD, pizza 2-6LD, meals 12LD; 🕑 10am-1am) The most recent addition to the burgeoning population of Turkish restaurants in Benghazi, Mat'am Turki has fast become one of the most popular places to eat for Libyans and travellers alike. Partly it's because of the outdoor tables, but the cheese bread is divine, the mixed grills are enormous and the atmosphere is bright and breezy.

Tobakts Restaurant (☎ 0925334425; Sharia Jamal Abdul Nasser; meals 13-18LD) For a break from North African or Turkish food, Tobakts is one of the few Italian restaurants still in town.

Mat'am Gharnata (☎ 9093509; Sharia Jamal Abdul Nasser; meals 15-17LD; 🕑 lunch & dinner) The food and service are both good. The banquet includes five salads, fish and a choice of cakes.

Mat'am al-'Arabi (☎ 9094468; Sharia Gulf of Sirt; meals 16.50LD; 🕑 lunch & dinner Sat-Thu, dinner Fri) This is one of Benghazi's finest restaurants, but with an eminently reasonable price tag. The banquet meals come with flat Arab bread and are excellent value. The upstairs eating area has a delightful atmosphere, with a mosaic floor, tented roof and soft lighting. Not surprisingly, it's a popular place with locals, tour groups and expats alike.

Mat'am al-Kabir (☎ 9081692; Sharia Jamal Abdul Nasser; meals 18LD; 🕑 lunch & dinner) Mat'am al-Kabir offers a similar deal to Mat'am al-Turki, with friendly service and excellent banquet-style meals, which have all the usual accompaniments.

QUICK EATS

Mat'am Al Batriq (Sharia Gulf of Sirt; 🕑 lunch & dinner) Here you'll find fast food that's so original and tasty that we always try to stop by whenever we're in town. It does a range of food, but the chicken filled with cream is just the ticket if you've arrived from long hours on the road.

For cheap shwarmas and sandwiches, there are numerous cheap restaurants along Sharia Jamal Abdul Nasser and in the streets surrounding Al-Funduq Market. The north side of the vegetable market is where you'll find stalls selling *ta'amiyya* (the Egyptian variety of felafel). There's also a felafel stand halfway through Souq al-Jreed on the east side of the lane.

Drinking

The souq is also one of the rare places in Libya where you'll come across a juice stand selling freshly squeezed juices and milkshakes. In the souq and a few doors north of Sharia ash-Sharif, it sells excellent banana milkshakes *(moze halib)* for 1LD, mango shakes *(manga halib)* for 1.50LD and fruit cocktails for 2LD.

DOMESTIC FLIGHTS FROM BENGHAZI

destination	airline	one way/return (LD)	frequency
Al-Kufra	Libyan Arab Airlines	37/74 2 weekly	
Sebha	Libyan Arab Airlines	41.50/83	2 weekly
Tripoli	Libyan Arab Airlines	37.50/75	3-4 daily
	Al-Buraq Air	45.50/91	5 daily

Getting There & Away

Benghazi's Benina International Airport handles both international and domestic flights. **Libyan Arab Airlines** (☎ 9092064; Sharia al-Jezayir; 8am-7pm Sat-Thu, 9am-noon & 3-7pm Fri) and **Al-Buraq Air** (☎ 2234469; Benina International Airport) operate a range of domestic flights.

There are daily buses and shared taxis to Tripoli, Sirt, Al-Bayda, Sebha and Tobruk from Al-Funduq Market.

Getting Around

TO/FROM THE AIRPORT

Benina International Airport is 18km east of the city. A private taxi to the airport costs 10LD.

TAXI & MICRO

Most micro journeys around town cost 0.25LD, while a shared taxi costs around 0.50LD. Most private-taxi journeys will cost 2LD to 3LD, although drivers may ask up to 5LD for destinations outside the city centre.

AROUND BENGHAZI

Suluq, 55km south of Benghazi, is where the Italians hanged Omar al-Mukhtar in front of 20,000 of his imprisoned supporters (see p138). The great man's body has been buried here since his execution, but the commemorative shrine was not moved from Benghazi to Suluq until early 2001.

AJDABIYA اجدابيا

pop 140,558

The best thing that can be said about Ajdabiya is that there are roads from here to everywhere – Benghazi, Al-Kufra, Tobruk and Sirt – and it was this role as a crossroads town that made it a historically significant as a key destination for traders arriving from the Sahara. The town was also important during the Fatimid period – you can see the rubble of a Fatimid mosque and fortress (ask for 'qasr Fatimid'), which has stones bearing a few Roman inscriptions. If you stay longer than it takes to fill your car with petrol, however, you'll soon discover that it's a place of little charm. The promising Amal Africa Hotel, north of town just off the road to Benghazi, will soon be the only habitable hotel in town, while the simple eateries around town are uniformly unappealing.

AWJILA أوجله

pop 6790

Awjila, one of the Jalu oases, is something of a surprise packet. It sees far fewer tourists than the lovingly restored remnants of its old town deserve. Awjila's old mosque is the finest oasis mosque in Libya. Sadly, the trickle of tourists is unlikely to increase until they improve the road south to Al-Kufra.

Awjila is also famous as a centre of Berber culture and, rarely for Libya, some people speak only Berber.

There's a small internet café, next to the mosque on the west side of the highway about halfway through town.

History

Awjila was mentioned in passing by Herodotus in *The Histories* in the 5th century BC. Much later, some historians believe that when the all-conquering Arab armies of Islam arrived here in the 7th century AD, many Berbers headed southwest into the Sahara, thereby giving birth to the Tuareg people (see p48). In the 8th century, Awjila became a prosperous commercial centre renowned for exporting high-quality dates. Later, it became an important staging post for trans-Saharan caravans and pilgrims.

Sights

The flurry of travellers passing through Awjila for the March 2006 solar eclipse encouraged the local authorities to restore sections of old Awjila, and they've done an

THINGS THEY SAID ABOUT...AWJILA

Augila, a town well known in the time of Herodotus, covers a space of about one mile in circumference. It is badly built, and the streets are narrow and not kept clean. The houses are built of a limestone, dug from the neighbouring hills, and consist only of one story or ground floor. The apartments are dark...The public buildings are yet more mean and wretched.

Journal of Frederick Hornemann's Travels from Cairo to Mourzouk 1797–8

outstanding job. They've also produced an informative little DVD on the city's history, *Awjila: History and Civilisation.*

The **old city**, west of the main highway close to the centre of Awjila, has a still-active well and some small gardens, as well as two houses, which have been transformed into museums. The restored rooms include looms for making traditional blankets, kitchens, living quarters, farming and hunting implements; look in particular for the doors made from local palm trees and the mixture of covered rooms and open courtyards. Also in the old city is an old mosque with the conical domes that are so distinctive to Awjila.

Visible from the entrance to the old city is the extraordinary **Al-Kabir Mosque**, easily the best example in Libya of the old oasis mosques that once greeted Muslim travellers and pilgrims crossing the Sahara. Originally built in the 7th century and restored in the 1980s, the mosque's appeal is only partially told by its dimensions: at 456 sq m, it contained nine doors, 21 beehive domes, dozens of arches and walls 40cm thick. But it is the overall effect of space and light that give the mosque its unique charm. The domes, built from mud-brick and local limestone, are akin to something conjured from a child's imagination, while the small openings in each dome allowed in light to the otherwise dark interior. The palm-trunk main door leads into a warren of columns and arches that are cool and in perfect harmony with the sense of respite and refuge from a harsh desert climate. Even if you're not going as far as Al-Kufra, many travellers will consider the mosque alone worth the long detour south from the Tripoli-Benghazi highway.

Behind the mosque are some ruined mud buildings that mark the location of Awjila's former **Turkish fort**.

Not far away to the south – look for the cylindrical modern minaret in earth tones and without windows – is the **Mosque and Mausoleum of Abdullah ibn Ali al-Sarah**, the last resting place of a leader of the Islamic conquest, and companion of the Prophet Mohammed. The modern tomb is mildly interesting, but the cemetery that forms part of the mosque compound includes more evocative beehive domes; steps lead down beneath the domes into a semi-subterranean mosque that is like a smaller version of Al-Kabir Mosque.

Elsewhere in town, watch out for the pyramidal **pigeon towers** riddled with small holes for pigeons for enter and feed.

Sleeping & Eating

Awjila would make for an excellent overnight stop if the Funduq Awjila al-Siyahe (Awjila Tourist Hotel) was even vaguely habitable. We were offered a prison-like room without bathroom (not a shared bathroom, *without* bathroom) and without breakfast for 15LD per person. We chose to sleep in our driver's home.

On the main highway through town, the Ojala Restaurant serves basic fare such as chicken and rice and sandwiches.

Getting There & Away

Awjila is the only town (apart from neighbouring Jalu) between Ajdabiya (250km to the northwest) to Al-Kufra (625km to the southeast).

THE ROAD TO AL-KUFRA

The long, lonely road from Ajdabiya to Al-Kufra stretches for over 900km, punctuated only by the twin oases of Awjila (p131) and Jalu, the occasional checkpoint, oil fields, electricity pylons and signs of the Great Man-Made River (see The Eighth Wonder of the World, p64). Otherwise it's unrelieved monotony of sand plains stretching to the horizon with scarcely a sand dune for the entire length of the road.

The road surface here is patchy all the way, although the last 200km into Al-Kufra is

THE CYRENAICA OF HERODOTUS

The earliest historical mention of Cyrenaica comes from the Greek historian Herodotus. In *The Histories*, an epic of history and storytelling which Herodotus wrote almost 2500 years ago, the names of the Greek cities of ancient Libya are littered throughout the text, among them Tocra, Apollonia, and Eusperides; Herodotus describes the latter as having 'good soil' and as being the westernmost point in Libya reached by an invading army of Persians. Of 'the fortunate people of Cyrene', Herodotus has much to say, including an encounter with some travellers who had passed through the region. 'Being asked if there was anything more they could tell him about the uninhabited parts of Libya, these declared that a group of wild young fellows, sons of chieftains in their country, had on coming to manhood planned among themselves all sorts of extravagant adventures, one of which was to draw lots for five of their number to explore the Libyan desert and try to penetrate further than had ever been done before' (*The Histories*, Book 2:32). These young men from Cyrene succeeded in their aim of crossing the desert and returned to tell a suitably fantastical tale of attacks by tribes of little people and visiting a land inhabited by wizards.

atrocious and easily the worst road in Libya. This stretch of road alone – a rutted tarmac riven with axle-breaking potholes, where the soft desert sand on either side is often preferable to the road itself – will take a minimum of four to five hours in a 4WD and wins our vote as Libya's worst. Yes, they're repairing (or rather, rebuilding) it but it will take a long while before things improve. Unless you're planning to visit Awjila en route, consider flying from Benghazi to Al-Kufra.

NORTHERN CYRENAICA

It's difficult to imagine a richer concentration of ancient sites anywhere in the world than the northern Mediterranean coast of Cyrenaica and its hinterland. Glorious Cyrene is the undoubted highlight, although both Apollonia and Tolmeita are spectacular in their own right. Further east along the coast, the precipitous landscapes of Ras al-Hillal share the shore with ancient Byzantine churches, particularly at L'Atrun. Inland, the green hills of the Jebel al-Akhdar conceal the astonishing Byzantine mosaics at Qasr Libya, the important if small ruins at Slonta and the historically poignant canyons of Wadi al-Kuf. Shahat, Al-Bayda and Susa, which all have excellent accommodation and make good bases for your explorations.

TOCRA (TEUCHIRA) كرة تو

pop 23,688

Tocra was one of the five cities of the Greek Pentapolis (Five Cities; see p31). Although we know we'll be in trouble with the enthusiastic caretaker, whose love of the site exceeds our own, we have to say that Tocra is historically significant rather than aesthetically satisfying and it's easily the least evocative of Cyrenaica's ancient sites.

Founded around 510 BC, Tocra (Teuchira) was one of the first ports settled from Cyrene. It was renamed Arsinoe, after the wife of Ptolemy II, and later known as Cleopatris, after the daughter of Cleopatra and Mark Antony. From the time of the Ptolemies, the city shared a similar history with its sister city, Ptolemais (Tolmeita). Tocra was built using soft sandstone, which proved unable to withstand the earthquakes and other vagaries that the centuries have wrought upon the Cyrenaican coast.

Sights

After passing through the gate into **Tocra** (admission 3LD, camera/video 5/10LD; 7.30am-5pm Oct-Apr, 7.30am-7.30pm May-Sep), you pass between Greek and Roman columns, while over the wall to your right are the excavated remains of **Roman tombs** cut into the rock wall of a sunken pit.

The **fort**, no more than 100m from the gate and overlooking the water, is compact and attractive; the current structure dates from the Turkish and Italian eras. There was a fort (and possibly a temple) on this site in the Greek period. The structure was later embellished by the Romans and Byzantines, although there are no obvious traces of these buildings.

Well signposted behind the castle is the **museum** (admission 3LD, camera/video 5/10LD;

CYRENAICA

(⌚ 7.30am-5.30pm), with a site map of Tocra, dusty pottery exhibits and (if restoration is complete) a fine mosaic taken from the site – but only archaeologists are likely to consider it worth of the extra expense. Outside the gate and to the west, a small archaeological railway runs west to the **Eastern Basilica**, in which the skeleton of the main sanctuary, apse and baptistry are visible, as are some ancient Greek inscriptions. Also worth looking out for are the **Greek Gymnasium**, the **Islamic Quarter**, the remains of the **city walls**, another **church** with a mosaic floor, the remnants of the **Roman baths** and **necropolis**, all of which are nearby. Most are littered with **Greek inscriptions**.

Getting There & Away

Tocra is 70km northeast of Benghazi and is well-signposted off the coastal road. We hope that en route you don't encounter the man we saw taking pot-shots at birds with his rifle from his car window.

TOLMEITA (PTOLEMAIS) طلميتة

The ruined city of Tolmeita (formerly Ptolemais) doesn't rival Cyrene or Leptis Magna, but its palm-fringed setting, and easily identifiable signs of the transition from Greek to Roman occupation, make this an essential stop on your Cyrenaica tour. If time allows, the beaches have good bathing and soft sand, especially to the west of town near the Italian fort.

History

Tolmeita was founded in the 4th century BC and its privileged position as one of the cities of the Pentapolis continued under the Romans. The city fell into decline with the arrival of the invading Arab armies in the 7th century, although Tolmeita was the last city of the Pentapolis to fall.

The excavated areas of the city mostly date from the 1st and 2nd centuries BC, when Tolmeita covered 3 sq km and was a thriving Hellenistic city. Only 10% of the ancient city has been excavated, with further excavations proceeding at a snail's pace.

Information

There are many **guides** (50LD) who know Tolmeita well, but it's worth mentioning the knowledgeable Abdusalam Bazama, who worked on the original excavations.

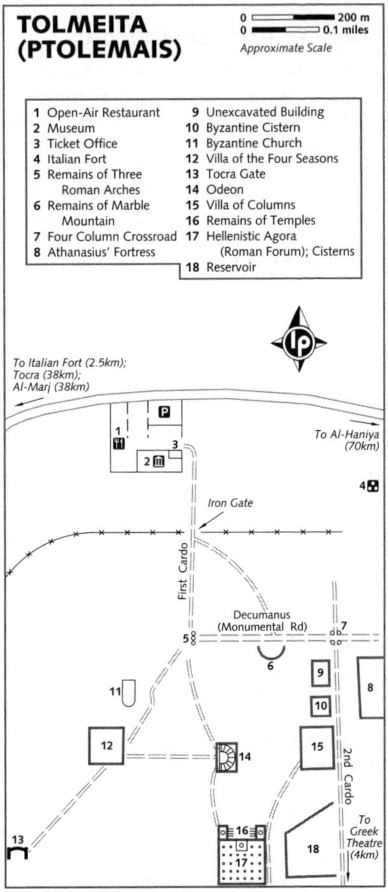

Although the museum (p136) is next to the **ticket office** (admission 3LD, camera/video 5/10LD; ⌚ 7.30am-5pm), we suggest that you leave it until the end, when the exhibits will be more easily understood in their historical context.

Sights

A dirt track runs up behind the ticket office towards the Jebel al-Akhdar and leads into the site. About 200m from the iron gate you can see two **Italian forts** off to the east and southwest, dating from 1923. You may also be able to see the skeletal traces of the ancient **Greek city walls** along the northern face of the Jebel al-Akhdar.

The trail continues up the hill, shadowed on the left by the rubble of the **first cardo** (main north-south road), which ran from the water's edge to the mountains. After 250m, there are bases of three **Roman arches** which, in the 3rd century AD, stood with four columns each and marked the crossroads of the first cardo (unusually, Tolmeita has two cardos) and the **decumanus** (main east-west road). This was one of the most important crossroads in the city and stood at the heart of ancient Tolmeita. The *decumanus*, also known as the Monumental Road, was once lined with colonnaded arched porticos running either side along its length.

Away to the southeast is the compact **Byzantine Church**, which dates from the 5th century AD and is notable for the fact that its domed apse remains largely intact, unlike many in Libya. A further 100m southwest are the remains of the **Villa of the Four Seasons**, which was built in the 4th century AD. Belonging to a wealthy Roman notable, it contained the beautiful Four Seasons mosaic, which is in the museum. The northeastern corner of the villa was a *frigidarium* (cold room). Close to the centre of the villa was a courtyard which was, unusually, semicircular on one side; the floor was covered with mosaics. From the villa, you can see the ancient **Tocra Gate**, about 300m to the southwest.

Around 300m to the east is the enchanting **Odeon**, a small theatre, which was once covered by a roof and large enough to seat up to 500 people. Performances of Greek music were accompanied by dancers in the sunken pit. In the 3rd century AD, the Roman love of water won out and they transformed it into a swimming pool; traces of the pipes running to the nearby cistern are visible on the southeastern side of the building. The front of the stage was adorned by three statues – Claudius, Marcus Aurelius and Archimedes – which you'll now find in the museum.

A short walk up the hill takes you to the Greek **agora** (marketplace), which later served as the Roman forum. Along the northern side were three temples, each with four Doric columns. The column bases remain; those of the northeastern temple are particularly fine. As you climb up to the raised area of the agora, be careful of the many small shafts, which drop 6m to the cavernous **cisterns** beneath the floor, which were once the largest cisterns in North Africa.

A staircase just off-centre leads down into the cisterns, which received water from mountain springs 25km east of Tolmeita via an aqueduct. The long, eerie caverns with arched ceilings suggest that a sense of style prevailed even for underground water storage. At shoulder height along the walls, note the clearly discernible dividing line between the ceiling height during Greek rule (when stone slabs were used in construction) and that of the 2nd century AD, when the thirsty Romans enlarged the cisterns by raising the ceiling using bricks and cement.

The path running northeast from the agora skirts the former **reservoir walls**, which also show the transition from Greek to Roman occupation – the bottom half marked with lines is Greek, while the top section is Roman.

After about 300m, you come to the **Villa of Columns**. The original structure was destroyed in AD 115–18 during the Jewish Revolt (see p31). The later villa belonged to a wealthy Roman local. One of the rooms on the southern side contained an exquisite Medusa mosaic on the floor. Next to it was the dining room; its floor still contains mosaic fragments and its wall traces of marble. In the centre of the villa is the sunken swimming pool. The pool was lined by two small gardens, while the pedestal in the centre once supported a small animal fountain in granite. On the northern side of the villa was the *frigidarium*.

Along the eastern side of the villa runs the **second cardo**, which was lined with shops and ran all the way up the hill to the south to the **Greek Theatre**, the remains of which are barely visible halfway up the mountain. North along the cardo is a **Byzantine cistern** and an **unexcavated building** with a mosaic peeping out from beneath the soil. Off to the northeast is **Athanasius' Fortress**, which dates from the 5th century AD.

Continuing north along the cardo, you reach the **Four Column Crossroad**, another significant intersection in the ancient city. Only the bases remain, but the columns once provided an important counterpoint to the three arches that lay west along the *decumanus*. Halfway between the two junctions are the base remains of a **marble fountain**, which depicted Bacchus. The gate by which you entered the site is not far off to the northwest.

As you leave the site, don't miss the **museum** (admission 3LD, camera/video 5/10LD; 7.30am-5pm). The central room is dominated by the superb Four Seasons mosaic from the villa of the same name; clockwise from the top left is summer, spring, winter and autumn. On the left wall is the wonderful Medusa head mosaic from the Villa of Columns; to the right of it is a plan of the Villa of Columns. On the right of the Four Seasons mosaic are the three statues from the Odeon.

The highlights of the western room are the 3rd-century AD tablets of gladiators (found in the theatre) and a mosaic of Orpheus (western wall) taming the wild beasts (2nd to 3rd century AD).

In the eastern room are raised column pieces adorned with the faces of Mars and Jupiter, as well as a number of interesting sarcophagi-and-grave covers. There are also 6th to 7th century BC statues from the city of Barce (now Al-Marj; see below), and along the northern wall is the granite animal fountain from the Villa of Columns.

Eating

Bringing a picnic lunch can be a good idea; the third Italian fortress (about 4km along the road to Tocra) would be an excellent spot. There's also an open-air restaurant, in the car park in front of the museum, which serves simple food (around 10LD) and drinks.

Getting There & Away

Tolmeita is 37km northeast along the coast from Tocra. If you're coming from the east, a good road leads down off the mountains from Al-Bayda, Al-Marj and Qasr Libya.

AL-MARJ المرج

☎ 067 / pop 87,089

The modern town of Al-Marj marks the site of the ancient city of Barce, which was an important Greek city founded in 560 BC. Unfortunately, there's nothing left to see because it, along with the modern town which was the centre of much Italian settlement, was consigned to history by an earthquake in 1963.

QASR LIBYA قصر ليبيا

If you come to Cyrenaica and don't visit Qasr Libya, you've missed one of northeastern Libya's signature sights. It may be small but this fine museum has one of the most extraordinary collections of Byzantine mosaics that you'll find in North Africa. The story of their discovery also has a Dead Sea Scrolls quality about it – when Libyan dam workers unearthed the two Byzantine churches in 1957, the exceptional preservation of their floor mosaics caused a great stir among archaeologists.

The mosaics were laid in AD 529–40, during the reign of Justinian I (527–65), in the village of Olbia, which lay in the hinterland of Cyrene. The ceramic pieces that make up each panel are less than 1cm in diameter and thus follow the Hellenistic school of mosaic. The craftsmen drew inspiration from natural and folk scenes of daily life, with pagan influences being incorporated into the Christian panoply.

Orientation

In the centre of the town of Qasr Libya is a small service road running parallel to the main road up a slight incline. At the top of the incline take the road leading under the boom gate. After 1.2km you reach a junction with a red, white and green sign in Arabic. Take the road running down the hill to your left; the Turkish fort should be visible on the hilltop to your right.

Sights

MUSEUM

Viewed alone, each of the 0.5-sq-metre mosaic panels that adorn the walls of the **museum** (admission 3LD, camera/video 5/10LD; 7.30am-5pm) is impressive. But when you realise that all 50 covered the floor of a single room of the Eastern Church it all seems extraordinary. To see them as they appeared, look for the small black-and-white photo reproduction on the wall to the right after you enter, alongside an informative article from the site's excavator.

The panels, which cover a wide range of subjects and seem to have links with early Christian beliefs, are numbered, well-labelled and grouped into often diverse sets of five. Among those depicting the gods, panels seven (the river god Geon), nine (the river god Physon), 17 (the river god Euphrates) and 19 (the river god Tigris) form a set representing the Four Rivers of Paradise, with the mischievous nymph Kastelia of Delphi (18) in the middle. There are also some fine Nilotic river scenes – panels six and 10 are especially good, with waterfowl, lotus flowers and fish. Some of the animals are also exquisite, especially the snakes (panel 11), deer (five), horses (29) and birds (42). Also stunning are the buildings including a brilliant evocation of the New City of Theodarius (three) and a wonderful church façade with columns (28).

Yet it is **panel 48** that aroused the most excitement when the church was uncovered. It contains one of the few representations of the legendary Pharos lighthouse of Alexandria. Atop the roof on the left is the dark-green (to indicate bronze) figure of the naked Helios with a downward-pointing sword in his right hand. The circular object at the tip of his sword is believed to be the famous iron mirror of the lighthouse. On the right of the panel is another human figure, standing on the mainland and depicted as a naked, bronze colossus. Nicely juxtaposed to the main image is panel 49, which represents a boat with a passenger whose hand is stretched out towards Pharos.

Also of great importance is **panel 23**, a Byzantine inscription stating that the mosaics were laid in AD 539. This panel lay in the centre of the church floor. The much larger mosaic on the museum floor lay at the eastern end of the church's northern aisle. This mosaic of panoramic scale includes a variety of plants and animals, a hunting scene, and the Nile with crocodiles and lotus flowers in the centre. Two of the three inscriptions are religious, invoking God's protection and referring to Christian martyrs, while the third (closest to the museum door) records the laying of the mosaic.

As you leave the museum, note the mosaic fragment on the wall to the right of the door. This forms part of the mosaic frieze that ran between the evenly spaced panels.

OTHER SIGHTS

Directly opposite the entrance to the museum is the tranquil **Western Church**, which is shaped like a cross. Its large, dusty mosaic in the centre of the floor, though reconstructed in keeping with its original state, seems quite dull in comparison to those in the museum.

Next to the museum and Western Church is a small **Turkish fort**, which has fine ramparts that obscure the view from this hilltop perch.

The **Eastern Church**, where the mosaics were found, is east of the museum, about 100m down a dirt footpath. Given the splendour of its former contents, the modern building, with its aluminium roof and reconstructed walls, is a disappointment. The now-empty squares do, however, provide some context to the original layout of the mosaics.

Getting There & Away

Qasr Libya is about 45km west of Al-Bayda and 59km east of Al-Marj.

WADI AL-KUF وادي الكوف

Wadi al-Kuf, east of Qasr Libya on the road to Al-Bayda, was the scene in 1927 of some of the most bitter and defining battles between the Libyan resistance and Italian forces. As a result, Wadi al-Kuf holds huge historical significance for many Libyans. It also has some of the finest scenery in the Jebel al-Akhdar.

One tributary of the wadi is spanned by a striking modern bridge, but try to take the detour that leads down through the wadi proper, rejoining the main road after 8km. You can also hike through the wadi, but to do the latter you would need to be self-sufficient in food and water and, in winter, warm clothes.

Coming from the west, the road twists through the picturesque landscape of wooded areas down through the increasingly towering cliffs. The further you descend, the more the cliffs are pockmarked with caves. The resistance retreated to these caves after each ambush to hide from the retaliatory bombardments of the Italians. The greatest concentration of caves is near the bottom of the valley after about 6km.

Around 7km down into the valley an iron bridge spans the road. Built by the Italian army in an attempt to ferry troops and supplies through the valley, it marks the spot where the forces of Omar al-Mukhtar halted, albeit temporarily, the southwards march of the Italian army, which was on the move from the Mediterranean to Al-Kufra. It was not until the infamous General Graziani surveyed countryside from a cliff-top and pinpointed the caves where the guerrillas were hiding that the Italians, supported by targeted bombing, were able to break through (see p138).

THE CAPTURE, TRIAL & EXECUTION OF OMAR AL-MUKHTAR

In early September 1931, the Italians received word that a party of Libyan rebels was planning a livestock raid on Cyrene. Not long after, the small raiding party was sighted near Slonta. Italian soldiers closed in and 11 rebels, close to starvation, were killed. The horse of the 12th was shot and its rider overtaken as he tried to escape on foot. He was about to be shot until one of the soldiers recognised him as Omar al-Mukhtar, the leader of the Libyan resistance. Al-Mukhtar was taken to Apollonia and later transported by ship to Benghazi. There was great rejoicing in colonial ranks.

Upon receiving the news, Marshal Badoglio told his underlings to 'make immediate arrangements for a criminal trial which can only end with the death sentence'. The trial on 15 September was a farce, with the dignified bearing of Al-Mukhtar in stark contrast to the unseemly bloodlust of the Italian prosecutor and audience. Al-Mukhtar took full responsibility for his actions and calmly accepted his fate with the words: 'From God we have come and to God we must return'. His Italian defence lawyer was imprisoned for performing his role too sympathetically. The next day Al-Mukhtar was hanged in the Suluq concentration camp (see p131) in front of 20,000 eerily silent prisoners. The Italians had their man, the rebellion petered out and a Libyan legend was born.

Throughout Wadi al-Kuf, you may recognise many scenes from *Lion of the Desert* (see p37), the film about the life of Omar al-Mukhtar, which was partly filmed here.

AL-BAYDA البيضاء

☎ 084 / pop 121,533

Al-Bayda is a pleasant city on the northern fringe of the Jebel al-Akhdar. Although its only sight of note is the rarely visited Temple of Aesculapius, Al-Bayda's good hotels make it one of the most important bases for travellers in this part of the country with Cyrene, Apollonia, Qasr Libya and Slonta all within striking distance. The area also has one of the mildest climates in Libya and is famous for its apples, grapes and, in November, *shmari* (a very sweet berry).

Al-Bayda was one of the main strongholds of the Sanusi Movement during the Ottoman period. After the Italians seized the town, the resistance movement moved south to Al-Jaghbub and to Al-Kufra. In the years after independence, King Idris effectively used Al-Bayda as his administrative capital and spent much of his time here, alienating the powerbrokers in Tripolitania.

Orientation & Information

The easiest landmark in town to use to get your bearings is the telecommunications mast of the main post office. Sharia al-Ruba, Al-Bayda's main thoroughfare, runs straight through the centre of town and continues as the main coastal highway to Shahat (Cyrene) and beyond. West of the post office, on the opposite side of Sharia al-Ruba, is a small **internet café** (per hr 1LD; 🕑 10am-midnight Sat-Thu, 5pm-midnight Fri).

A further 1km east along Sharia al-Ruba, another road leading north boasts banks and the distinctive local parliament building with its large bronze dome. Behind the parliament is a compound of white buildings containing the **jawazzat** (☎ 633925). Another 1km east towards Shahat, you pass the Masraf al-Tijara Watanmiya (Bank of Commerce & Development) where you can get cash advances on your Visa card.

Sights

Al-Bayda's premier sight is the little-visited **Temple of Aesculapius**, the god of healing. Although nowhere near as well preserved as nearby Cyrene, its columns and temple outline derive from the little-known Greek city of Ballagrai. The temple, which dates from the 4th century BC, is also notable for the extremely rare representations of silphium (plant similar to wild fennel; see p144) atop some of the columns in the southwestern corner of the site. The temple is around 2km west of town, just north of the main road in from Benghazi. The turn-off is opposite the Omar al-Mukhtar University and marked by a sign to the always-closed 'Albeida Museum'. If you need directions, ask for *'zawiyat al-bayda'*.

On the other side of the main highway, on the western edge of town, is the huge

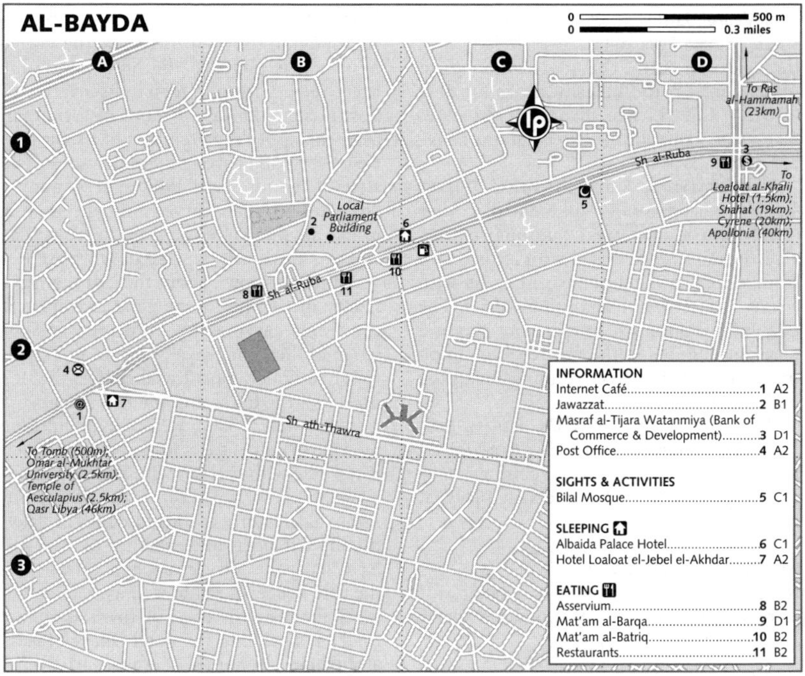

sandstone clock tower and dome of **Omar al-Mukhtar University**. Formerly an Islamic university, it's now a multidisciplinary institution that is usually open to casual visitors. West of the main post office the road is lined with cypress trees, beneath which is a simple white **tomb** topped by a green dome, the last resting place of Rawayfa al-Ansari (one of the friends of Mohammed).

At the other end of town, you can't miss the striking, white **Bilal Mosque**. This modern mosque has an attractive onion-like dome flanked by four smaller domes, as well as two piercing minarets.

Sleeping

Hotel Loaloat el-Jebel el-Akhdar (☎ 630968; fax 630971; Sharia al-Oroba; s/d/ste with private bathroom 30/40/70LD; ❄) This welcome addition to Al-Bayda hotel scene has attractive rooms, friendly management and is in a central location. A standard Libyan-style tourist restaurant here provides ample banquet-style meals (15LD). There is also a 24-hour internet café (1LD per hour) located just next door.

Albaida Palace Hotel (☎ 633455; qaseralbida@yahoo.com; Sharia al-Ruba; s/d with private bathroom 30/40LD; ❄) Now faced with competition, this erstwhile favourite of tour groups has improved. The rooms in this large, white, Art Deco building in the centre of town are fine and the service far more helpful than it used to be.

Loaloat al-Khalij Hotel (☎ 631977; fax 631981; Sharia al-Ruba; s/d 40/50LD; ❄) Probably the pick of Al-Bayda hotels, this private hotel opened in August 2006 and has good, partly carpeted rooms that could be larger if they didn't lose so much space with an entrance hallway for each room. But that's being picky – the rooms are excellent, the service good, modern local artworks adorn the public areas and there's a large and pleasant coffeehouse.

Eating

There is a handful of decent restaurants in town, as well as plenty of snack bars the length of Sharia al-Ruba for 2km east of the post office. Sharia ath-Thawra, parallel to Sharia al-Ruba two blocks to the south, has some decent grocery stores.

Mat'am al-Batriq (☎ 638450; Sharia al-Ruba; meals 3-10LD; noon-11pm Sat-Thu, 2-11pm Fri) Right in the centre of town, this place serves great pizzas for 5LD to 9LD, shwarmas for 3LD to 5LD, and chicken dishes; it also does take-away. Look for the two penguins above the door.

Asservium (Sharia al-Ruba; meals from 10LD; lunch & dinner Sat-Thu, dinner Fri) This cool place has trendy music and great outdoor seating. The upstairs terrace is a wonderful place from which to watch the world go by with a *shay* (tea; 1LD) or a *nargileh* (1LD). The affable Mustapha will ensure your stay is a pleasant one. It's in the centre of town, on the corner of the street running up to the parliament building.

Mat'am al-Barqa (☎ 635328; Sharia al-Ruba; meals 15LD; lunch & dinner Sat-Thu, dinner Fri) At the eastern end of town, Mat'am al-Barqa serves good-quality banquets in pleasant surroundings.

Getting There & Away

If you need a shared taxi to Shahat (for Cyrene), white minibuses run along Sharia al-Ruba every few minutes.

AROUND AL-BAYDA

Ras al-Hammamah (known locally as Hammamah) is a tiny village 22km north of Al-Bayda. The beach, which is a mixture of soft sand and rock pools, is a great place to swim, although there's no shade. There's a summer-only tourist village.

Further along the coast, southwest from Ras al-Hammamah, are other good beaches. About 5km west of the Hammamah Tourist Village is **Bst Beach**, a sheltered cove and home to a small fishing community. It's a good place for a picnic or campfire. A further 10km southwest is **Al-Haniya**, another small town with good beaches. The views towards the west are quite picturesque.

On Friday, families flock to these beaches from Al-Bayda, so they can get pretty overcrowded, although that makes it the best day to meet the locals.

At the turn-off to these beaches from the main highway, just east of Massah, is a high-walled compound which marks the former **Palace of King Idris**. With more than a hint of revolutionary humour, the compound has been turned into a mental hospital.

SLONTA سلنطة

About 24km south of Al-Bayda, the village of Slonta is home to the only significant pre-Greek Libyan artefact discovered in northeastern Libya. Of more historic than aesthetic appeal, the remains of a **stone temple** (admission 3LD) cover a mere five sq m. The style of the often-childlike figures, human faces and animals carved into the rock is unlike anything else you'll see in Libya. The site was obviously a place of worship, but very little is known about the cult that gave rise to the temple. Some good examples of the Slonta carvings are on display in Gallery 5 of the Jamahiriya Museum in Tripoli (p78), although most travellers feel that it's no substitute for seeing the real thing.

The temple is 500m west of the sandstone mosque in the centre of town, behind a green metal gate with chicken wire around the perimeter. Ask for directions at the checkpoint immediately north of the mosque. The gate's usually left open and whether or not you have to pay the entry fee depends on whether the gate-keeper is in the vicinity.

At the western edge of town, a minor road runs north to the small village of **Omar al-Mukhtar**, so-named because the rebel leader was finally captured by the Italians near here.

SHAHAT شحات

☎ 084 / pop 44,391

The modern village of Shahat has nothing of interest but it serves as the gateway to the spectacular ancient city of Cyrene.

Sleeping & Eating

Buyut ash-Shabaab (Youth Hostel; ☎ 637371; camping 5LD, dm 5LD) The hostel is a stone's throw from the gate leading down to the ruins. It's clean, friendly and has been recommended by a number of travellers; the hot water is reliable.

Cyrene Resort (☎/fax 0851-64391; s/d 35/45LD;) This former Winzrik Hotel, about 2km northeast of the police station, is set in the fields around Cyrene. It has simple rooms, some of which have some nice touches like bay windows. Best of all is the quiet atmosphere, the personal satellite receivers in most rooms and the atmospheric café and restaurant cut into one of the caves.

Cave Restaurant (☎ 635206; meals from 15LD; lunch) Living up to its name, this is another eatery hewn from the rocks around Cyrene. It's an atmospheric place offering tasty food, friendly young waiters and good views down towards the coast from the terrace.

Barqa Restaurant (☎ mobile 0926224490; meals 13LD; 🕑 lunch & dinner) Not far from the Temple of Zeus, this cosy little place can get a little overrun by tour groups, but the food (the usual fare of tajine, couscous or rice along with the soup-salad ensemble you've come to know so well) is fine and it's the closest recommended restaurant to the ancient city.

Getting There & Away

Shahat is 17km east of Al-Bayda and 74km west of Derna. Shared taxis between Al-Bayda and Shahat arrive and leave from under the eucalyptus trees, just short of the pillars marking the gate leading down to Cyrene.

CYRENE

Cyrene is glorious, a worthy Cyrenaican rival to Tripolitania's Leptis Magna both for the splendour of its monuments and for its setting, looking out over the not-so-distant Mediterranean from an elevated rocky perch. Cyrene is Libya's most complete ancient Greek city; it was and remains the poster boy for the more than five centuries of sophisticated Greek rule in northeastern Libya. The site has many levels, geographically and temporally, in the sense that later Roman buildings overlay many of the Greek temples and public buildings.

In short, don't miss Cyrene.

Information

Visiting **Cyrene** (admission 3LD, camera/video 5/10LD; 🕑 7.30am-6pm May-Sep, 8am-5pm Oct-Apr) requires a compulsory **guide** (50LD). In the days when good guides were scarce we used to recommend specific guides to Cyrene, but both the quality and quantity of guides has increased to the point where there are dozens of excellent guides and we've no reports from travellers of sub-standard ones.

Entrance to the site is via the southeastern gate, which is on the upper level of the site next to the road which leads through the trees from Shahat. There are stalls selling snacks, drinks and a moderate selection of expensive books opposite the northern gate (exit).

History

In the early 7th century BC, settlers set out from the Greek island of Thera (modern Santorini). They were led by Battus, a man chosen for the task by the oracle of Apollo at Delphi. The reason for their journey was both demographic and political – the island had limited resources for a growing population, but their departure was also seen as a means of reducing the political tension caused by the prevailing power struggles on Thera. The small band of less than 100 people first landed on the island of Platea, south of Crete in the Gulf of Bomba, before heading off again to a spot just east of modern Derna. They quickly discovered that their new home was not suitable for the colony they hoped to establish. The wily Giligami tribe convinced the Greeks to

CYRENAICA

THE FOUNDING MYTH OF CYRENE

Cyrene's founding myth places the gods at centre stage in an epic tale of romance, betrayal and renewal.

Cyrene, a Thessalian nymph known in Greek as Kurana, was a princess and a very modern woman, preferring to hunt animals at Mt Pindus while refusing to undertake the domestic chores that were the lot of her contemporaries.

One day, Apollo saw her wrestling a lion and immediately fell in love with her. Clearly used to getting his own way, Apollo abducted Cyrene and took her in a golden chariot to the site that would one day bear her name. The Temple of Apollo was founded to commemorate Cyrene strangling a lion to make the region safe for settlers.

But this family epic which came to define Cyrene had a postscript. When Aristaeus, the bee-keeping son of Apollo and Cyrene, pursued Eurydice in a clumsy rite of seduction, the unfortunate woman was killed by a snake. Aristaeus' bees died in a plague of divine retribution. Only after Aristaeus conducted the ceremonies of atonement and the bees were born again from the carcasses of sacrificed animals was Cyrene freed from the titanic struggles of the gods.

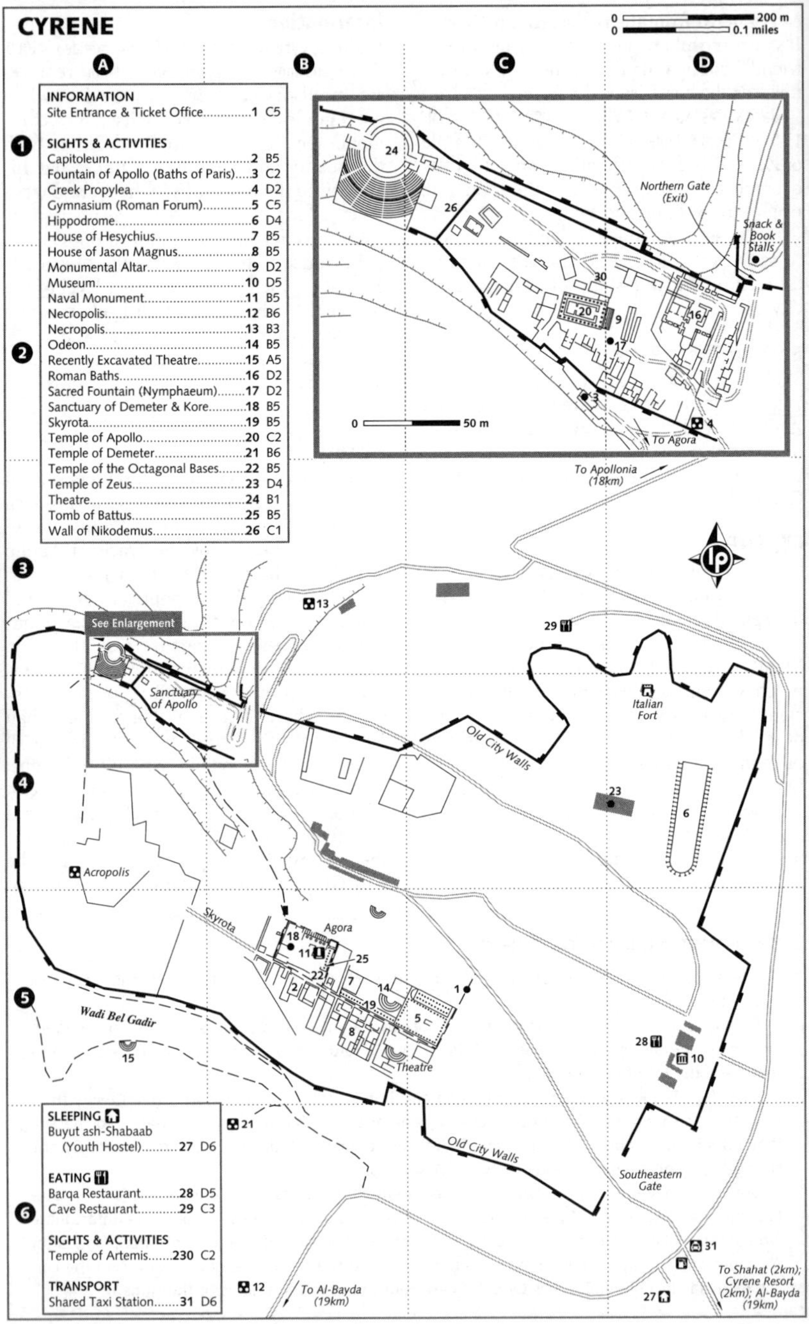
CYRENE
0 200 m
0 0.1 miles
A
B
C
D
1
2
3
4
5
6
INFORMATION
Site Entrance & Ticket Office............1 C5
SIGHTS & ACTIVITIES
Capitoleum......................................2 B5
Fountain of Apollo (Baths of Paris)....3 C2
Greek Propylea...............................4 D2
Gymnasium (Roman Forum).............5 C5
Hippodrome....................................6 D4
House of Hesychius.........................7 B5
House of Jason Magnus...................8 B5
Monumental Altar............................9 D2
Museum..10 D5
Naval Monument............................11 B5
Necropolis.....................................12 B6
Necropolis.....................................13 B3
Odeon...14 B5
Recently Excavated Theatre............15 A5
Roman Baths..................................16 D2
Sacred Fountain (Nymphaeum)........17 D2
Sanctuary of Demeter & Kore..........18 B5
Skyrota..19 B5
Temple of Apollo.............................20 C2
Temple of Demeter..........................21 B6
Temple of the Octagonal Bases.......22 B5
Temple of Zeus...............................23 D4
Theatre..24 B1
Tomb of Battus...............................25 B5
Wall of Nikodemus..........................26 C1
Northern Gate
(Exit)
Snack &
Book
Stalls
0 50 m
To Agora
To Apollonia
(18km)
See Enlargement
Sanctuary
of Apollo
Old City Walls
Italian
Fort
Acropolis
Skyrota
Agora
Theatre
Wadi Bel Gadir
Southeastern
Gate
To Al-Bayda
(19km)
To Shahat (2km);
Cyrene Resort
(2km); Al-Bayda
(19km)
SLEEPING
Buyut ash-Shabaab
(Youth Hostel)..........27 D6
EATING
Barqa Restaurant...........28 D5
Cave Restaurant............29 C3
SIGHTS & ACTIVITIES
Temple of Artemis.......230 C2
TRANSPORT
Shared Taxi Station.......31 D6

CYRENAICA

THE EARTHQUAKE OF AD 365

If one event signalled the final decline of the Roman Empire in North Africa, it was the earthquake and tsunami of AD 365. There had been earthquakes before – in AD 306 and AD 262 – but this one brought centuries of civilisation crashing down. With its epicentre in the Mediterranean near Cyprus, its devastating power wrought havoc from Sabratha in the west to Apollonia in the east. So powerful was the quake that parts of these cities, including Apollonia's entire port, disappeared into the sea and the great cities of Cyrene and Leptis Magna were reduced to rubble. The empire that had conquered the world was brought to its knees and never recovered.

return the stolen land with a promise to lead them to a more fertile site where there was a 'hole in the heavens'. Cleverly, the tribesmen marched them through the night, concealing the more fertile areas en route. They took them to land occupied by a different tribe and Cyrene was founded, in 631 BC.

Cyrene soon expanded and more settlers arrived from Greece on a promise of prime agricultural land. Not surprisingly, the local tribes resented the intrusion and asked the Egyptian pharaoh for help, but the Greeks won out in 570 BC. The leader of the first colonists, Battus, ruled as king for 40 years. His dynasty lasted from 631 BC to 440 BC – a period of eight kings, great stability and territorial expansion.

During the city's golden age in the 4th century BC, Cyrene was considered by many as the pre-eminent city of the Greek world. Its wealth and agricultural abundance enabled it to save Greece from famine in 390 BC through a massive export of grain. Plato, who had been sold as a slave by Dionysius, was liberated by a citizen of Cyrene, Annikeris, in 388 BC. Cyrene was at this time a great cultural centre, home to Aristippus (a philosopher of renown who founded the Cyrenaic school of philosophy), Theodorus (a contemporary of Socrates and famous for his skill in arithmetic, geometry, astronomy and music) and Eratosthenes (mathematician, astronomer and the third librarian of the great library of Alexandria).

In 331 BC, Cyrene came under the rule of Alexander the Great. When Alexander's empire collapsed, the Greek world fragmented and the federation of the Pentapolis (of which Cyrene was the premier city) became a largely autonomous entity. In the 3rd century BC, Cyrene and the other cities of the Pentapolis fell under the umbrella of the Ptolemies, who ruled Egypt. Instability ensued and Ptolemy I sent his stepson Magas to Cyrene in an attempt to restore their dominance. The ambitious Magas, reading from a different script, severed his ties with the Ptolemaic dynasty which was by then ruled by Ptolemy Philadelphus, son of Ptolemy I. It was not until 260 BC, with the engagement of Magas' daughter, Berenice, to the son of Philadelphus that Cyrene was again incorporated into Egypt and the period of independence came to an end.

In 96 BC Ptolemy Apion generously bequeathed Cyrenaica to the Romans and by 75 BC Cyrene had become an important Roman capital. Successive Roman proconsuls favoured an approach that recognised the Greek heritage of Cyrene, and the city remained essentially Greek in character until the 1st century AD, when the Jewish Revolt of AD 115–17 saw the city's destruction. The emperor Hadrian, often referred to as Cyrene's second founder, sought to re-establish the pre-eminence of Cyrene. His rebuilding program gave the city's architecture a more Roman flavour – temples were elevated onto platforms and columns were left smooth and unfluted.

By the middle of the 3rd century AD the city was in decline, in keeping with the general malaise of the Roman Empire. From then on it was a downward spiral, with a devastating earthquake in AD 262, a shift of the Roman capital from Cyrene to Tolmeita as part of the administrative reforms of Emperor Diocletian, and another massive earthquake in AD 365. Unfortunately, subsequent restoration work did little more than paper over the cracks.

In the centuries that followed, Cyrene became a Christian city subject to frequent droughts and predatory raids from the nomadic tribes of the interior. Much weakened, Cyrene was in no position to resist the westward march of the Islamic armies of Amr ibn al-Ass in AD 643. There is evidence of ongoing settlement for a few centuries after then, but Cyrene's day had passed.

Sights

GYMNASIUM/FORUM

The large open square on your right a few hundred metres after the entrance gate was originally built by the Greeks in the 2nd century BC as a gymnasium. As the major sporting building of Cyrene's upper terrace, it was surrounded on four sides by Doric columns and the open palaestra (exercise area) was the scene of races and other sporting contests. In the second half of the 1st century AD, it was converted by the Romans into a forum, or caesareum (Forum of the Caesars), where political meetings were held. In its Roman manifestation, the compound contained a civil basilica and a temple. Access was through two monumental gateways with four Doric columns. Now stripped of their main adornments, the open spaces wear a decidedly abandoned air.

SKYROTA

The road running along the southwestern perimeter of the forum was the **Skyrota**, the main road through the Greek city. It's still lined with impressive columns bearing graven images of Hermes and Hercules. This section was once known as the Portico of the Hermas and the road was to become in Roman times a monumental passageway linking the forum to the agora. Behind the western wall of the gymnasium was the **Odeon** (theatre) and the Xystos, a track used by athletes training for races. Across the thoroughfare was another small theatre for musical performances, which was probably abandoned after the earthquake in AD 262.

HOUSE OF JASON MAGNUS

Also across the path from the Xystos is the impressive private residence of Claudius Tiberius Jason Magnus, high priest of the Temple of Apollo in the 2nd century AD. The floor of the main entrance is covered with marble. A number of rooms, including the large dining room or banquet hall, feed off the main inner courtyard. Around the courtyard are a few Corinthian capitals (one bearing the bearded face of Battus, Cyrene's founder and first king) and there are some well-preserved female figures draped with finely sculpted marble clothes. The best example of the house's mosaics is the superb Four Seasons mosaic, which is now kept under an unattractive aluminium roof. From the site, look down across the valley to the southwest, outside the site's perimeter, to see the small, recently excavated theatre.

HOUSE OF HESYCHIUS

On the hill overlooking the agora is the home of Hesychius, a Christian who returned to Cyrene after the AD 365 earthquake in a bid to restore the glory days of the city. Hesychius was a friend of the philosopher and bishop Sinesius. There is a fine mosaic of an angel on the northwestern side showing clearly recognisable Byzantine iconography, alongside an inscription imploring God to protect the women and children of Cyrene. In the compact, three-sided courtyard are the remains of a small fountain, or nymphaeum.

AGORA

The agora was the heart of ancient Cyrene, serving as a public square, a forum for ora-

SILPHIUM

The great wealth that fed Cyrene's growth as a metropolis of monumental grandeur was fed in part by its agricultural abundance. Primary among its crops was the indigenous silphium plant, which was much sought after in the ancient world. Now extinct, this plant, similar to wild fennel, was harvested on the highlands of the plateau inland from Cyrene. The list of claimed properties for silphium is quite extravagant, but there is little doubt that its sap was used as a medicine (a purgative and antiseptic) and as a dressing added to food. There is also some suggestion that silphium was a highly effective aphrodisiac – which may explain its almost-mythical importance. The plant was so highly prized that its image appeared on the city's coinage. Carved representations of the plant are rare and one of the few remaining examples is on some of the capitols atop the columns of the Temple of Aesculapius (p138) in Al-Bayda. There is also a modern drawing in the museum at Susa (p147).

tors, a market and a magnet for the powerful people of the day. Many civic and religious buildings were clustered around the agora. Many still bear the traces of Roman influence, superimposed onto the fine monumental constructions begun by the Greeks. During the reign of Septimius Severus (r AD 193–211), porticoes were added.

The **Temple of the Octagonal Bases** (2nd century AD) lies in the southeastern corner of the agora, with the base of four columns remaining. It may have replaced an earlier Greek temple. However, the Roman temple is believed to have been built in honour of Aesculapius, the god of healing. The rubble also contains a poorly preserved floor mosaic.

The most distinctive of the agora's monuments is the reconstructed **Naval Monument**, originally built by the Ptolemies in the 3rd century BC in celebration of a naval victory. This stunning statue features a wingless (and now headless) Victoria standing on the prow of a ship, flanked by two dolphins and holding the tritons of Neptune. The female form is wonderfully rendered, with clothing elegantly carved into the marble.

The **Tomb of Battus**, the leader of the settlers from Thera and first king of Cyrene, is now thought to lie behind the naval monument on the eastern side of the agora, although there remains some disagreement about this among archaeologists. The founder of the colony has the rare honour of being buried not only within the city walls but also in the principal square.

The **Sanctuary of Demeter and Kore**, an unusual circular structure, was the scene of a riotous, women-only, annual celebration and feast. As part of the festivities, the women of Cyrene proceeded from here to the **Temple of Demeter**, which is outside the city walls and visible in the distance from the House of Jason Magnus. The statues represent goddesses of fertility. The cavities alongside the statues of the seated goddesses (3rd century BC) were used for offerings to the goddesses; the standing figures were added by the Romans.

Outside the agora's southern wall is the **Capitoleum**, the customary temple to the Greek trinity of Zeus, Hera and Athena (or, if you were Roman, Jupiter, Juno and Minerva).

From the northern side of the agora, a path leads down off the plateau and there are some superb views over the Sanctuary of Apollo towards the coastal plain to the Mediterranean.

SANCTUARY OF APOLLO

This rich collection of temples, baths and other public buildings sits on a ledge overlooking the plain.

The path down from the agora leads to the **Fountain of Apollo (Baths of Paris)**. This delightful spot under the cliff is a good place to rest in the shade to the accompaniment of a particularly vocal colony of frogs. This small thermal complex at the outlet of a natural spring was built in the 5th century AD. Note that around some of the pools are some small niches used for the personal possessions of the bathers or for oil lamps.

The sanctuary's ancient gateway is marked off to the east by the four Doric columns of the reconstructed **Greek Propylea** or Monumental Gateway (3rd century BC).

The **Temple of Apollo** was one of the earliest temples at Cyrene, with the foundations dating from the 6th century BC. The initial structure was little more than an open courtyard, but was soon enhanced by rows of six columns along two sides and 11 on the other two. Fragments of the temple's pediment suggest a representation of the nymph Cyrene strangling a lion. A statue of Apollo playing the lyre was found here and now resides in the British Museum in London. The temple was rebuilt during the 4th century BC, again with 34 columns. It was destroyed during the Jewish Revolt and what you see now is essentially a 2nd-century AD Roman building in the Greek Doric style (the columns are smooth, not fluted).

Immediately in front of the temple is the **monumental altar** (6th century BC), which is 22m long and made from limestone covered by marble slabs. Religious rites, including animal sacrifices, were carried out here. The great Greek poet of the age, Callimachus, describes in his famous Hymn to Apollo scenes of sacrificing bulls, the altar adorned with flowers and crowds of dancing young people. Note also the reconstructed **Sacred Fountain**, or nymphaeum, with its attractive lions and columns.

On the northern side of the Temple of Apollo is the **Temple of Artemis**. The foundation was laid in the 6th century BC and is thought by some archaeologists to pre-date the Apollo temple. It consisted of a room, or cella, with columns in the centre. It may once have celebrated both Apollo and Artemis. Most of what you see now, including the marble portal, derives from the temple's rebuilding in the 4th century BC. In the remainder of the sanctuary are the barely visible remains of temples to Isis, Hecate and Latona, and the tomb of Hercules.

THEATRE

Just west of the sanctuary is the spectacularly situated theatre, which could once seat 1000 spectators. Its original construction was by the Greeks and probably dates from the 6th century BC although it was much modified in subsequent centuries. In the 2nd century AD, the Romans transformed it into an amphitheatre in which the oval-shaped arena measured 33m by 29m. Seats, supported by struts built into the cliff, were constructed on the Mediterranean side. The slabs down the hillside are all that remains of this ambitious idea. The theatre affords a superb view over the sheer drop, and of the hillsides with glimpses of the old necropolis and the sea.

WALL OF NIKODEMUS

Separating the Sanctuary of Apollo from the theatre and built during the Roman era, this wall protected the much-frequented public buildings in the sanctuary from the wild animals in the amphitheatre. The wall is named after one of the priests of the Temple of Apollo.

ROMAN BATHS

The Roman baths are the last buildings as you leave the site via the northern gate. Built in AD 98–99 under the emperor Trajan and restored by Hadrian, these baths contain some good mosaics and cipolin columns. The *frigidarium* is the best preserved room of the baths complex and contains a Latin inscription honouring Hadrian. There is also a *apodyterium* (changing room), where the statue of the Three Graces now in Tripoli's Jamahiriya Museum (p78) was found, as well as the *tepidarium* (warm room) and *calidarium* (hot room). In December 1913, during a violent storm, a famous statue of Venus (or Aphrodite) of Cyrene wringing out her hair was unearthed; it now stands in the Museo Nazionale Romano in Rome.

NECROPOLIS

Cut into a cliff face along the old road down to Apollonia and in the countryside in all directions for miles around Cyrene are the more than 2000 tombs of the old necropolis. Originally built by the Greeks in the 6th century BC, they were used and added to by the Romans and Byzantines right up until the 6th century AD. Many of the tombs were later used by nomads for habitation, some of them being quite spacious. Some contain traces of the original architectural façades. The hollows in front of some Greek tombs once held likenesses of Persephone, the goddess of death, while the Roman tombs held carved portraits of the deceased. On the hillside there are also some sarcophagi with lids.

TEMPLE OF ZEUS

A steepish climb up the hill from the rest of the site is the famed **Temple of Zeus**, one of the highlights of Cyrene. Reflecting Cyrene's importance in the ancient Greek world, the Temple of Zeus was larger than the Parthenon in Athens. Constructed in the 5th century BC, the sanctuary measured 32m by 70m and was surrounded by two rows of eight and two rows of 17 columns. In the sanctuary itself there were two rows of Doric columns as well as two columns in the porch. On the main platform in the sanctuary was a statue of a seated Zeus holding Victory in his right hand and a sceptre in his left. Animal sacrifices were carried out in the temple. The ancient entrance was from the east. Under the Romans the temples was used to honour Jupiter; it also served the Greek/Libyan hybrid deity, Zeus Ammun.

The temple was restored under the emperor Augustus (r 27 BC–AD 14), but was then destroyed in AD 115 during the Jewish Revolt. Like many of Cyrene's public buildings, it was rebuilt in AD 120 by the Roman emperor Hadrian. After it was reduced to rubble by the AD 365 earthquake, it was ransacked by Christian zealots who called it a 'den of demons' in reference to the statues to ancient gods.

The temple is being comprehensively and painstakingly reconstructed by Italian archaeologists.

The rubble of the **Hippodrome** or racetrack area, which once had tiered seating, is on the same plateau to the east.

MUSEUM

The one-room Cyrene's **museum** (adult/child 3/1LD, camera/video 5/10LD; 8am-1pm Tue-Sun) is not a match for the museum at Leptis Magna (p117) or Tripoli (p76), but it nonetheless contains a fine collection of Roman statues, tablets and a small gathering of mosaics. Many of the statues are accompanied by useful explanations in English, Italian and Arabic.

All of what you'll see are fine examples of the marble finery that once adorned Cyrene's major buildings, but the statues of Jupiter (found in the Capitoleum; p144), Alexander the Great (from the Roman Baths; opposite), one of the best remaining representations of the Three Graces, a portrait bust of Marcus Aurelius and another male bust from the Severan era and found in the Temple of Apollo (p145) are especially finely rendered.

Also of great importance are the tablets that mark the great landmarks of Cyrene's history: the Cyrene Decree of Augustus that sets out the Roman laws for protecting the Greek inhabitants when Cyrene passed into Roman hands; the Diagramma or Constitution for Cyrene by Ptolemy I dating from 332 BC; the Founders' Decree (4th century BC), which records Cyrene's origins; a tablet recording Cyrene's gift of corn to Greek cities during the famine in the 4th century BC; and the will of Ptolemy VII, which bequeaths Cyrene to the Romans should he die without an heir. For a historical overview of these events, see p141.

Other highlights include mosaics from the House of Jason Magnus (p144) and surrounding area and the glass cabinet in the centre of the room, which contains gigantic fingers from a statue of Zeus that once stood in the centre of the Temple of Zeus.

SUSA سوسة

084

The small town of Susa is the gateway to the pretty Greek-Byzantine city of Apollonia. The modern town was first established in 1897 by a group of Muslim refugees from Crete.

The road down off the mountain from Shahat and Cyrene to Susa is shadowed by the ancient road between Cyrene and Apollonia, and deep ruts mark the tracks left by the chariots of old. Halfway between the two sites stands a simple, white monument to the memory of Libyans who died in the war against the Italians. The last part of the journey involves a spectacular descent as the road winds down off the northern rim of the Jebel al-Akhdar with great views along the coast.

Susa has a petrol station and some grocery stores along the main street, close to the main post office. It is about 20km from Shahat.

Sights

Apollonia's **museum** is a short distance southwest of Al-Manara Hotel, but it has recently closed (reportedly due to a lack of interest among travellers). Before it closed, it wasn't Libya's finest museum, with poorly labelled, dusty exhibits. That said, it contained some interesting artefacts, including: a 2nd- to 3rd-century AD Roman tomb, which was found in front of the Western Church in Apollonia; a drawing of the silphium plant; mosaics from the Byzantine church at Ras al-Hillal; an 1825 line drawing of the Greek Theatre; elegant tablet reliefs from L'Atrun Church; the exquisite door frame from the Byzantine Duke's Palace; and four mosaics found in the Eastern Church. Let's hope it has reopened by the time you read this.

Sleeping & Eating

Al-Manara Hotel (Map p148; 5153001; fax 5152188; www.manarahotel.com; s/d/ste 45/60/95LD;) One of the new breed of private hotels sweeping Libya, Al-Manara Hotel is exceptional. It has outstanding rooms, a prime location just 50m from the site entrance, fine views from most rooms with some overlooking the ruins, a good restaurant (meals 15LD), good buffet breakfasts and professional service.

APOLLONIA سوسه

Apollonia, the former port for Cyrene, spreads along the Mediterranean shoreline in a reminder of how the ancient Greeks and Romans always chose beautifully located sites for their settlements. It's one of the top five ancient cities in Libya, with a wealth of Roman, Greek and Byzantine buildings. It gives an unmistakeable sense of walking amid the accumulating splendour of the great civilisations of the ancient world.

History

Apollonia was the harbour for Cyrene, 18km to the west, and because of this it played a critical role in the prosperity of Cyrene and the other cities of the Pentapolis. Archaeological evidence gathered to date suggests that the city was operating as a port as early as the 7th century BC. It served a similar purpose under the Romans and even came to rival Cyrene in significance in the late Roman period, as it was considered to be less vulnerable to attack than cities further inland. After Diocletian, the city was for a time the seat of Roman Governors in the province of Libya Superior.

Most of what remains today dates from the Byzantine era (from the 5th to 6th centuries AD) when Apollonia was known as the 'city of churches'. It had five basilicas and 19 towers.

Sights

The ruins of **Apollonia** (admission 3LD, camera/video 5/10LD; 7.30am-7pm May-Sep, 8am-5pm Oct-Apr) run along a narrow strip of land for around 1km east from the site entrance to the Greek Theatre. As such it's an easily negotiable site.

Of the Byzantine city's five churches, four are within the city walls and the fifth is just outside the walls to the south. The **Western Church** is just near the entrance, with the western wall of the city running around the apse. The four green columns in the sanctuary are of Roman origin and, like much of Apollonia, were used by resourceful Byzantines in the later construction; the four white columns are wholly Byzantine. The church was originally covered with a wooden roof and the floor was entirely marble. The cisterns at the eastern end lead to the baptistry in the northeastern corner and there are some mosaic fragments on the floor.

A short distance east is the **Central Church**. Its marble floor is better preserved; in the main sanctuary are some fine pillars adorned with Byzantine crosses and the globe of Atlas. Outside the main sanctuary on the western side, you should note the bench reserved for the bishop to rest on after the strenuous task of presiding over communion and, to the north, the tiny

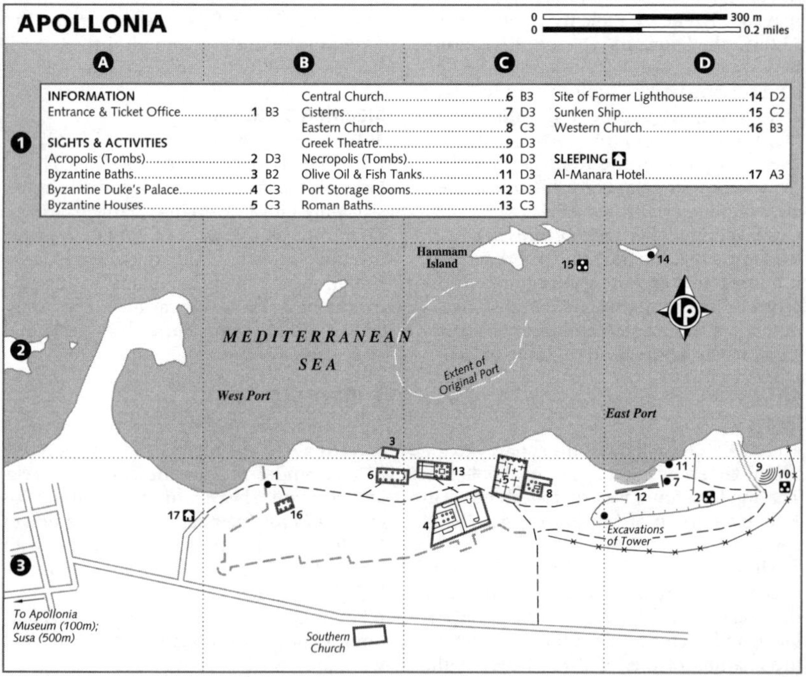

child's baptistry. North of the church is the rubble of **Byzantine baths**.

The **Roman baths** just east of the Central Church date from the 2nd century AD. The columns lining the eastern side have Roman capitols dating from AD 138, while the drums, clearly visible within the columns, are Greek. In the northeastern corner of the main building is the **gymnasium** – pottery from the Greek (black) and Roman (red) eras is scattered about. Immediately south of the gymnasium is the *frigidarium*.

Above the baths on the hill is the **Byzantine Duke's Palace**, once one of the biggest palaces in Cyrenaica. The first room after you enter from the north was a waiting room and library; note the huge stone shelves reserved for large books. The western section of the palace was the domain of the duke and his family. The private chapel (one of the city's five churches) is reached by passing under some well-executed stone arches. In the chapel, the elegant curve of the apse is a feature as is the throne room leading off the main room. There were 83 rooms in the eastern wing, used as quarters for servants and soldiers. A small staircase leads up to the highest point, formerly the home of the leading officer, which enabled him to keep an eye on his troops and the remainder of the palace. Close to the foot of the staircase is a large, black stone, once used by the Romans to seal their wells.

Northeast of the palace and down the hill are **Byzantine houses** and the **Eastern Church,** in its heyday the biggest church in Cyrenaica. Huge columns of cipolin marble once divided the nave and aisles, forming transepts; many are still standing. The marble was shipped from the Greek island Paros, while the granite slabs used to close off the nave came from Egypt. Although this was among the earliest of the churches (5th century AD), some mosaics remain. Other features to watch out for are the two sacrificial altars and baptistry.

After you've explored the church, follow the path above the beach to the storage rooms cut into the wall – goods being shipped awaited distribution or loading here. In the rock wall are two arched **cisterns**. On the beach itself the two stone-tower bases protruding from the sand were once used as pottery and amphora stores. Into the beach's southern wall are wedged hundreds of pottery shards. It is believed that this was the site of a pottery factory; the blackened sections indicate that there was a kiln here. The ancient harbour, now underwater, lay out to the north. Visible offshore, Hammam Island was, before the earthquake, connected to the mainland and home to a **lighthouse**. The underwater ruins, including a ship of 22 hands, would make for fantastic snorkelling, but the authorities are understandably reluctant to allow it for fear of damage from treasure seekers. The beach is nonetheless a good place for a swim.

From the small hill above the cisterns, you can see down to the five perfectly circular holes cut from the rock. These were the **olive oil tanks** of the Byzantine city. To their right is an enormous **fish tank** (4th century AD) from where the townsfolk could come to choose their evening meal.

The remains of the Greek **acropolis** (tombs) are to the southeast, and over the hill to the east is the plunging **Greek theatre**, which stood outside the walls of the ancient city. The views are wonderful from the upper stalls. There are also remains of the Roman **necropolis** off to the east and south.

RAS AL-HILLAL رأس الحلال

☎ 081

Plunging hillsides dropping down off the Jebel al-Akhdar into the Mediterranean. A perfect arc of bay that shelters an ancient Byzantine church with a spectacular panorama. Welcome to Ras al-Hillal, home to the most dramatic scenery along the Libyan coast.

Coming from the west, from where the cinematic sweep of the landscape is best appreciated, a small road leads off the coastal highway to the Byzantine-era **Ras al-Hillal Church**. Apart from the views, which are themselves reason enough to come here, the church is simple with the clear outline of the main sanctuary and apse and a few dusty mosaics on the floors.

Before the Byzantines arrived, Ras al-Hillal was, for a time, the second port of Cyrene after Apollonia, although nothing remains to suggest this. At the eastern end of town is a nice small beach, behind which is a fresh water spring.

The road behind the town climbs into the mountains, with some fine views en route. After 14km, the picturesque **Shallal Ras al-Hillal**

> **THINGS THEY SAID ABOUT... RAS AL-HILLAL**
>
> It was a marvellous morning, and I have rarely seen anything so beautiful as this mountainous country. Colour was everywhere, from the sky which formed a deep blue arch over my head, to the thousand shades of green in the woods all around. The ground was thickly strewn with all kinds of flowers, and black and brownish-red butterflies fluttered among the gaily coloured blooms. Here the rocks, even where they were bare, were not grey, but displayed a wealth of colour.
>
> *Knud Holmboe,* Desert Encounter *(1931)*

waterfall, which flows virtually year-round, is visible on the left. The valley shelves are an excellent place for a picnic. Climbing still further, you reach a plateau, which is also a good place to rest and then to set off exploring the Jebel al-Akhdar on foot. Around 2.5km beyond the waterfall is a fork in the road. The left branch leads up towards the **Greek Tombs**, which are on either side of the road for about 1km. A few of these lonely sentinels are surrounded by sunken graves as well as ancient wheel ruts hewn into the rock.

Sleeping & Eating

Apart from the ageing, summer-only tourist village at the western end of the bay, which was undergoing renovations when we were there, the **Rainbow Resort** (☏ 634714; 2-/4-bed bungalows 80/85LD, apt 90LD; meals 15LD) is a great place to wind down for a day or so. Formerly a university agricultural project, its good rooms, palm trees and proximity to such beautiful vistas make it one of the best choices along the Cyrenaican coast. It's well signposted off the coastal highway, up the hill to the south at the eastern end of town.

Getting There & Away

Ras al-Hillal is 30km east of Susa, along the coastal highway that leads to Derna.

L'ATRUN الأثرون

The small town of L'Atrun, 9km east of Ras al-Hillal and 29km west of Derna, contains better-preserved Byzantine churches than those at Ras al-Hillal. The **Western Church** stands on a bluff above the Mediterranean and must have been a spectacular place to worship. The walls of the church are still intact and the sanctuary is strewn with marble pillars, some of which are marked with a carved Byzantine cross. Just outside the sanctuary walls are abandoned grave covers, with carved crosses, snakes and other motifs.

The less dramatic **Eastern Church** lies over the hill 150m to the east. To reach it, you skirt a steep, rocky cove with cave tombs gouged into the rock.

L'Atrun is around 350m north of the main road, while the modern village is on the south side of the road.

DERNA درنة

☎ 081 / pop 79,860

The shabby apartment blocks of Derna sprawl along the coast and into an attractive wadi that spills out from the Jebel Akhdar. We struggle to come up with too many reasons to linger here but there's a moderately interesting old quarter, a waterfall, a good restaurant and a reasonable hotel to break up the journey between Tobruk and Susa.

Sights

The main square of the **old town**, which lies about 1km south of the corniche, is surrounded by small cafés. There is also a covered **souq**, which is well worth a look around for its local colour. Dominating the skyline in the old town is the **Masjed as-Sahab**, a fine example of modern Islamic architecture. Built largely of sandstone, it has two fine minarets with lattice windows halfway up the tower, a large open courtyard and lovely red calligraphic motifs above the archways.

If waterfalls float your boat, you haven't much to get excited about in Libya – so you may want to head around 8km south of town, through the narrow wadi that cuts like a gash into the jebel, to the small waterfall of **Shallal Derna**, which is fed by a series of springs further up the wadi. For everyone else, it's probably not worth the effort.

Sleeping & Eating

Funduq al-Ferdous (☎ 633570; fax 623979; Sharia Rafal Ansari; s/d/tr 25/35/45LD; ✈) There are other places to stay in town but this is the only one we feel comfortable recommending. Once you're past the unimpressive façade, the rooms are simple but well kept and the management has been praised by some travellers as the friendliest in Libya – we're inclined to agree. This hotel is signposted at the western end of the Corniche, although it's about 1km inland – ask for 'Nadi Darnus' (Derna Club), which is very close by.

Mat'am Salsabil (☎ 624863; Sharia al-Corniche; meals 15LD; ⏲ lunch & dinner) This restaurant, 450m west of the harbour, is easily Derna's best with good food (standard tourist set meals or grilled mains) and above-average service. We assume that the 'heart' on the menu is a mistranslation, or at least we hope so.

Getting There & Away

The shared-taxi station is about 2km east of the town centre. Taxis run to Tobruk, Al-Bayda and Benghazi.

EASTERN CYRENAICA

Libya's northeastern corner has just three sites of interest and it's a long journey to get here, but the name of Tobruk will resonate for travellers with any interest in the WWII North African campaign. And for those whose time in Libya is restricted to the coast, Al-Jaghbub also makes an interesting and reasonably accessible Saharan detour.

TOBRUK طبرق

☎ 087 / pop 124,340

Tobruk was the scene of some of the most important battles of WWII, and it's a name known around the world even if many people don't know that it lies in Libya. It's home to poignant Commonwealth, German and French war cemeteries and a host of other WWII sites. It's clear, however, that they weren't fighting over Tobruk for its beauty – let's be honest: modern Tobruk is one of Libya's least inspiring towns – but for its strategic significance.

That said, a recent governor – Tobruk local and now Libyan prime minister, Al-Baghdadi Ali al-Mahmudi – oversaw a massive public works campaign that has made the city's roads much more manageable and its waterfront a touch more appealing.

As the last major Libyan town on the road to the Egyptian border 139km away, many travellers end up passing through here and some reasonable hotels and a good restaurant at least break up the journey.

Orientation & Information

All roads in Tobruk lead to the harbour. The road from Egypt enters the town at the western end of the harbour, next to Funduq al-Masira. From the west, the main road from Derna passes the turn-off to the Knightsbridge (Acroma) Cemetery and then cuts through the centre of town to the harbour. The compact city centre is around the square surrounding the main post office on the hill overlooking the harbour's northern side. Here you'll find most of the banks, including the **Masraf al-Tijara Watanmiya** (Bank of Commerce & Development; off Sharia al-Jamahiriya) – where you can get Visa cash advances – a

VISITING TOBRUK'S WWII SITES

Tobruk's **WWII cemeteries** (⏲ 9am-5pm Sat-Thu, 2-5pm Fri) are well maintained. There are cemeteries for most of the major participating nations, except for Italy (its government repatriated all the bodies of slain Italian soldiers). Cemetery registers are kept in a safe at the gate of the two Commonwealth cemeteries (Knightsbridge and Tobruk); these list the names of fallen soldiers, in alphabetical order, with a corresponding row number and letter to assist in finding a specific grave. Sadly, many Muslim graves are not listed.

The Knightsbridge (Acroma) Cemetery and the Australian (Fig Tree) Hospital are west of town, off the road to Derna, while the German Cemetery, Tobruk (Commonwealth) War Cemetery, French Cemetery and WWII trenches are all on, or just off the road to the Egyptian border south or southeast of town. The museum and Rommel's Operations Room are both located in Tobruk itself.

If you want to see every one of the WWII sites listed in this section, expect to pay around 20LD and take a minimum of three to four hours.

couple of hotels, the town's best restaurant and two **internet cafés** (Sharia al-Jamahiriya; per hr 1LD) where connections can be slow. The **Libyan Arab Airlines office** (☎ 622681) is on the east side of the square, diagonally opposite Funduq al-Jebel al-Akhdar.

Sights

KNIGHTSBRIDGE (ACROMA) CEMETERY

The Knightsbridge Cemetery, 20km west of town, is the largest in Tobruk. Contained within its walls are 3649 graves. Of these 2663 are of known soldiers and 986 unknown (most of these have headstones marked 'Known unto God'). The nationalities represented highlight the massive loss of life in this tragic period of history: UK (1584/703 known/unknown); New Zealand (435/61); South Africa (363/47); Australia (240/63); India (8/3); as well as Canada (15 known), France (two), Greece (12), Poland (two) and Yugoslavia (two). Among the graves are the bodies of two soldiers who were awarded the prestigious Victoria Cross.

Unlike most of the other cemeteries, Knightsbridge is on the site of an actual battleground. The large white cross overseeing the thousands of headstones lends the place an air of tranquillity.

AUSTRALIAN (FIG TREE) HOSPITAL

Between the Knightsbridge Cemetery and Tobruk, this former Australian field dressing station is often known simply as the Fig Tree. This shady spot on the now-peaceful plains surrounding Tobruk was an ideal location for a hospital, with its deep natural caves (now heavily silted up) and shelter offered by fig trees a few kilometres from the front line. It was also connected by a ridge to the battlefields of Knightsbridge. An offshoot of one of the original fig trees, which still stands, was taken to Australia and planted in the gardens of Melbourne's Shrine of Remembrance.

To reach the sight from Knightsbridge Cemetery, travel east along the main road to Tobruk for 12km, then take the turn-off to the south for 1.7km.

GERMAN CEMETERY

The closest cemetery to central Tobruk, the forbidding German cemetery overlooking Tobruk harbour, was built in 1955 to resemble a Libyan fort. It contains the names of 6026 German soldiers inscribed in mosaic slabs lining the inside walls of the sandstone fort. It's often closed but there's usually someone around who can help find the key *(miftah)*. The cemetery is signposted east off the road to the Egyptian border, 3km south of the harbour; it's reached via an 800m dirt track. Ask for '*maqbara al-manya*'.

TOBRUK (COMMONWEALTH) WAR CEMETERY

The Tobruk (Commonwealth) War Cemetery, 6km south of the harbour on the road to the Egyptian border, also has an air of simplicity and dignity. This cemetery contains 2479 graves – not all are from Commonwealth countries, but simply those who fought for the Allied cause. The countries most represented include Australia, India, New Zealand, South Africa, the UK and Poland. There are also two soldiers buried here who were awarded the Victoria Cross.

FRENCH CEMETERY

Most of the over 300 soldiers buried here died in the Battle of Bir Hakim, 80km southeast of Tobruk, in May and June 1942. The graves are marked with simple crosses inscribed with each soldier's name and regiment. The bodies of Muslim soldiers who fought alongside the French are also buried here.

The French Cemetery is behind a sandstone gate and walls, 8km south of the harbour and on the corner of the road to Al-Jaghbub.

WWII TRENCHES

During the Siege of Tobruk, the city was completely encircled by 25km of defence lines or trenches. The most easily accessible are just north of the road to the Egyptian border, 18.4km from the harbour; the trenches are not signposted and are just past the huge factory to the north, which sends up great clouds of white dust.

The four lines of concrete trenches were built by Italian and Australian soldiers. The Australians and Germans, who rarely fought in Tobruk itself, faced off in a bloody war of attrition here. The trenches have silted up over the years, but some key elements are still visible, including large, sunken tank platforms as well as smaller Browning gun emplacements. In places,

THE RATS OF TOBRUK

The Rats of Tobruk are among the best-known soldiers in Australian military history and an integral part of the country's mythology. Some 14,270 Australian soldiers (out of a total 24,000 Allied troops) participated in the Siege of Tobruk, which lasted from 10 April 1941 until 10 December 1941 (240 days spanning a fierce Libyan summer). It was here that the Allies inflicted the first major defeat on the Wermacht.

The aim was to halt the advance into Egypt of the German Afrika Korps, to buy time for the Allied forces in Egypt to resupply and reinforce their ranks. The besieged Allies were supplied by a motley array of seafaring vessels – known as the Tobruk Ferry Service, or the Junks or the Scrap Iron Flotilla – which made the highly dangerous Spud Run into Tobruk Harbour.

At the time of the siege, a Radio Berlin announcer denounced the Australians as the 'rats of Tobruk', comparing them to rats burrowing underground and caught in a trap, in a bid to destroy their morale. Instead, the Australians turned the name into a badge of honour and source of amusement. A famous photo shows a Bren gun carrier with the words 'Rats to you' painted on the side and an unofficial medal with a rodent on it was struck from the aluminium of a downed German plane.

On 20 June 1942, seven months after the Australians were finally evacuated, German field marshal Rommel's army launched a fresh assault and retook Tobruk in a day.

stairs lead to underground bunkers, some of which are still quite deep.

On the north side of the trenches is Wadi Dalia, a shallow valley whose walls are riddled with caves. It was in this wadi that hundreds of Australians died from aerial bombardment.

It's a good idea to wear boots or shoes, rather than sandals, when visiting, as the area is strewn with rusted WWII-vintage barbed wire.

TOBRUK MUSEUM

Tobruk Museum (admission 3LD) is in a converted church around 500m north of Sharia al-Jamahiriya. It reportedly contains a moderately interesting collection of WWII memorabilia but, as the man at the shop next door said, the caretaker doesn't show up very often and he was nowhere to be found while we were in town. We were told to go to the offices of the Ministry of Tourism, adjacent to Rommel's Operations Room, to ask for the key *(miftah)*, but the person responsible had left town and the key had gone with him. We hope you have better luck.

ROMMEL'S OPERATIONS ROOM

This poorly maintained site in the heart of Tobruk, 600m north of the western end of the harbour, includes the bunker from where Rommel directed operations. In the same square is an assortment of WWII memorabilia.

Behind the white wall immediately to the east are the rusting remains of a bomber which crashed in the Libyan Desert south of Tobruk in 1943. For the full story, see The Last Journey of the *Lady Be Good*, p156.

Sleeping & Eating

Funduq al-Jebel al-Akhdar (☎ 626128; Sharia al-Jamahiriya; s with sink & shared bathroom 10LD, s/d/tr with shared bathroom 15/20/30LD) We have to confess that we've included this place only so that we can tell you that Rommel, clearly a man of simple tastes, stayed in Room 319 here, albeit for only four hours. That's also about how long most travellers would be able to withstand the grubby bathrooms and bleak rooms. Nothing seems to have changed, or been cleaned, since the great man graced the hotel's corridors.

Funduq Qartaj (☎ 620442; ferasfly79@yahoo.com; www.qartagehotel.com; Ring Rd; d with/without air-con & TV 25/20LD, tr 40LD; ❄) When we first visited here six years ago, we thought it the best hotel in town. In truth, the rooms here are unexciting but tidy and large enough to swing a suitcase. The main drawback is the location, on a busy road about 2km northwest of the harbour, which leaves it a long way from anywhere.

Funduq el-Jaghbub (☎ 628260; hot-jag@yahoo.com; Sharia Jamahiriya; d with/without private bathroom 35/25LD, with private bathroom & balcony 40LD) The newest of Tobruk's hotels, this would probably be our pick as the best place to stay. The rooms are fine with some of Tobruk's modern bathrooms, while you're in the centre of town, close to the post office, internet cafés and best restaurant.

Funduq al-Masira (☎ 625761; fax 625769; s/d 43/53LD) You have to admire the bravado of a place that has aged terribly but still raises its prices. The lobby is one of the finest examples of the genre of 1970s-era Libyan government hotels and the service seems wearied The lifts don't work (and if they do, don't trust them), the restaurant is grim and the bathrooms are a study in decay. That said, the rooms themselves aren't bad at all, you'll get BBC on the dial and the breakfasts are better than most.

Mat'am al-Khalij (☎ mobile 0925785344; Sharia al-Jamahiriya; meals 10-12LD; lunch & dinner) If you spend any time in Tobruk, you'll end up eating here every night as it's easily the best place in town. Take a table on the upstairs terrace with views over the harbour and order from a range of pizzas, grilled meats and fish dishes. The service is friendly and usually English-speaking.

Getting There & Away

Given that Tobruk is about as far east as you can go in Libya, those returning to Tripoli may want to consider flying one way. Or at least you might once they finish repairing the runway, which could take a few months or a few years. When services resume, tickets cost 51/102LD one way/return.

If you're driving and you need to get to Benghazi or Tripolitania in a hurry, consider taking the gun-barrel-straight desert road to Ajdabiya (372km). There is a petrol station at around the halfway point, a checkpoint and nothing else to relieve the monotony.

Getting Around

Tobruk is a sprawling city and taxis are everywhere, but you need to know what you're looking for – not the clearly painted taxis as elsewhere in Libya but a private car with a cup or pipe attached to the roof. Strangely, these technically illegal private taxis are all you'll find in town.

AL-BURDI

Set on a beautiful arc of bay watched over by two headlands close to the Egyptian border, Al-Burdi is many travellers' first or last experience of Libya. There's a reasonable beach here, but the town was largely destroyed by Allied bombing of Italian defensive positions during WWII. The only place of interest to detain you as you pass through is **John Brill's Room** – a small room high on a bluff overlooking the Mediterranean where the British soldier John Frederick Brill painted an extraordinary tableau in 1942. His interpretation of the war includes finely rendered female dancers, a violinist, novels by Dickens, human skulls and the use of black and white to symbolise war and peace. John Brill died three months after completing the painting at the age of 22. He is buried in the cemetery at El-Alamein in Egypt.

AL-JAGHBUB الجغبوب

pop 400

Rich in historical associations – it was one of the most important Saharan oases of ancient times – and closer to the Egyptian oasis of Siwa (150km) than it is to Tobruk (285km), remote Al-Jaghbub is a quiet place where nothing happens in a hurry. It's a long way to come and is probably not worth the journey on its own. But if you're planning to cross the Eastern Sand Sea to Al-Kufra, Al-Jaghbub is your starting point. If your time in Libya is restricted to the Cyrenaican coast but you want to see the desert, the countryside around Al-Jaghbub will also give you a small taste.

History

The remote oasis of Al-Jaghbub was for centuries an important staging post for pilgrims and trans-Saharan traders on their way to Siwa, Cairo and Mecca. In 1856, Sayyid Mohammed Ali al-Sanusi, the Grand Sanusi (see p36) moved the headquarters of his Sanusi movement from Al-Bayda to Al-Jaghbub, and its *zawiya* (Islamic college or monastery) became of the most important of the 146 Sanusi lodges. The Grand Sanusi transformed Al-Jaghbub into a fortress town and a symbol of the enduring Sanusi hostility towards Libya's Ottoman (and later Italian) rulers. Al-Jaghbub's Sanusi university became so important that it was considered Africa's second most important Islamic university after Cairo's famous Al-Azhar University. Mohammed al-Mahdi, the Grand Sanusi's son, moved the Sanusi headquarters to Al-Kufra in 1896. The *za-*

GRAZIANI'S FENCE

In February 1931, the Italian Government decided to build a barbed-wire fence stretching from the Mediterranean port of Bardia to the oasis of Al-Jaghbub, a mere 270km away. Supervised by armoured patrols and the air force, the fence sought to cut off the rebels from their supply sources and contacts with the Sanusi leadership in Egypt. Construction began in April and was completed by September. This move, along with the deportation of almost the entire population of the Jebel Akhdar, was decisive and precipitated the end of the rebellion. This extraordinary barbed-wire monstrosity still runs close to the Libyan-Egyptian border from near Tobruk, finishing at Al-Jaghbub – whereupon the desolate Great Sand Sea begins.

wiya was torn down just two decades ago as part of an attempt to rewrite Libya's pre-revolution history.

Sights

Visible from the checkpoint as you enter town, the enormous pile of bricks and rubble was the former Zawiya Sanusi. This was once a world-renowned seat of Sanusi learning. Reports of the *zawiya* at its peak tell of famous scholars and the finest building materials, including wooden beams imported from India. Sadly, it didn't survive the revolution.

Of less historical significance but more aesthetically evocative is **Qasr Athani**, the brick, Italian-era fort that's visible from all over town. It's rubbish-strewn but largely intact with a warren of rooms and arched porticoes surrounding the interior courtyard.

Sleeping & Eating

There are no hotels in town, although travellers planning to spend the night will usually be provided with a room in a private home. Restaurants are also nonexistent, but there's a small supermarket in the centre of the newer part of town. Some nearby stalls also serve local dates that are much-loved throughout Libya.

Getting There & Away

The road from Tobruk to Al-Jaghbub receives little traffic and the surface is, therefore, generally quite good. Unusually, the *953 Michelin* map is incorrect, listing the distance as 230km – the correct figure is 285km.

AROUND AL-JAGHBUB

For the last 50km into Al-Jaghbub if you're coming from Tobruk, the barbed-wire monstrosity known as **Graziani's Fence** (see left) shadows the highway to the east.

All of the following sights, with the exception of Buhairat al-Malfa, require a local guide and a 4WD. One local guide with knowledge of all the sites listed here is Abd al-Salam az-Zintani (☎ satellite 008821633399329).

There are two salt lakes *(buhairah)* within striking distance of Al-Jaghbub. **Buhairat al-Malfa** is the only one accessible in a 2WD vehicle, some 30km east of town along the road to the Egyptian border. If you've been to the Ubari lakes (p187) in Fezzan, Malfa is nothing to get excited about, but the water is turquoise and the lake covers a considerable area. On a rock ledge above the lake on the western side are some ancient **engravings** of cattle that are at least 3000 years old (see Periods of Saharan Rock Art, p200) and worth the climb. The area is also strewn with **fossilised shells**. The Egyptian border is 5km beyond the lake.

Closer to Al-Jaghbub (18km), but accessible only by 4WD, **Buhairat al-Fredgha** is an altogether more evocative desert lake, situated as it is alongside the sand dunes that mark the commencement of the **Great Sand Sea**. In addition to the lake itself, millennia-old **graves**, complete with bones, are carved into the nearby rock, while the **twisted palm tree** is famous for the contorted shape of its trunk.

Around 35km west of Al-Jaghbub town, you'll find some outstanding examples of upright **fossilised tree trunks**.

INTO THE SAHARA

One of the most evocative desert journeys in Libya – not least because it's a route traversed by very few travellers – is to cross the Great Sand Sea from Al-Jaghbub to Al-Kufra (p207). This 800km, three-day, two-night desert crossing enters the sand sea south of Al-Jaghbub and involves difficult driving through high sand dunes for most of the route to Al-Kufra. The exceptions

THE LAST JOURNEY OF THE LADY BE GOOD

On 5 April 1943, an American B-24 bomber named *Lady Be Good* took off from the Suluq Airfield, south of Benghazi, part of a 25-strong squadron on a routine bombing raid against Naples in southern Italy. Forced by a sandstorm to abort the mission, the pilot turned for home. The pilot radioed Benghazi's Benina International Airport, but in the severe weather conditions the radio went dead. With no radio contact and with fuel running low, the nine crew members parachuted from the plane, which subsequently crashed over 700km southeast of Benghazi (600km south of Tobruk). One parachute failed to open. The remaining eight crew members began a desperate walk north. Five crew members gave up after an epic 104km. In his diary, which was found with his corpse, Robert Toner wrote on 12 April: 'There is no hope whatsoever and the night is cold'. The remainder of the crew refused to give up, with one walking a further 44km before collapsing and dying.

None of this was known to the outside world until 1958 when a team of British geologists prospecting for oil found the wreckage of the plane. Eight of the bodies were found by an American search team two years later. The body of the last crew member, Vernan Moore, has never been found.

The wreckage of the *Lady Be Good* remained at the crash site for 51 years until graffiti and treasure-hunters forced the Libyan authorities to take custody of the plane. It can now be seen next to Rommel's Operations Room (p153) in Tobruk.

are flatter country for about 130km about halfway through – it was in this area that an American B-24 bomber crashed in 1943 (see The Last Journey on the *Lady Be Good*, above) and black, rocky mountains for the last 100km into Al-Kufra. Once there, remember that it's a further 350km from Al-Kufra to the southeast's main attractions of Jebel al-Uweinat (p209) and Jebel Arkno (p208).

An experienced local guide is essential for this journey. We highly recommend the English-speaking **Ali Hamed** (☎ mobile 0913754088; alihamed64@yahoo.co.uk), while **Abd al-Salam az-Zintani** (☎ satellite 008821633399329) has also been recommended.

The Jebel Nafusa & Ghadames

The barren Jebel Nafusa (Western Mountains) is Libya's Berber heartland and one of Libya's most intriguing corners, a land of stone villages on rocky perches and otherworldly Berber architecture. The fortress-like architecture of the jebel reflects the fact that this is a land of extremes. Bitterly cold winters – snowfalls are rare but not unheard of – yield to summers less punishing than elsewhere in Libya, though the southern reaches of the Jebel Nafusa merge imperceptibly with the scorching Sahara.

It was to here that many Berbers retreated from invading Arab armies in the 7th century, and the Jebel Nafusa remains one of the few areas in Libya where Berber culture still thrives. Consequently, the jebel's human landscape is as fascinating as its geography and architecture.

The Jebel Nafusa merits as much time as you can spare. From the underground houses of Gharyan in the east to the crumbling *qasr* (fortified granary store) and old town of Nalut in the west, imagination and necessity have fused into the most improbable forms. Nowhere is this more true than in Qasr al-Haj and Kabaw where the wonderful *qasrs* look like a backdrop to a *Star Wars* movie. Elsewhere, the abandoned stone village of Tarmeisa surveys the coastal plain from its precipitous rocky perch, while Yefren makes an agreeable base.

Beyond the jebel on Libya's western frontier lies one of the world's best-preserved oasis towns. Ghadames is an enchanted spot, a labyrinthine caravan town of covered passageways, intricately decorated houses, beautiful palm gardens and a pace of life perfectly attuned to the dictates of the desert. Ghadames one of our favourite places in Libya.

HIGHLIGHTS

- Lose yourself in the labyrinthine lanes of the magical old city in **Ghadames** (p164)
- Imagine yourself in a galaxy far, far away in the perfect Berber granary store of **Qasr al-Haj** (p160)
- Pick your way through the best preserved old town in the Jebel Nafusa at **Nalut** (p162)
- Picnic amid the enchanted troglodyte *qasr* at **Kabaw** (p162)
- Crawl to the edge of the precipice at the abandoned stone village of **Tarmeisa** (p161)
- Watch the sunset from the terrace (or your balcony) in the **Yefren Hotel** (p159)

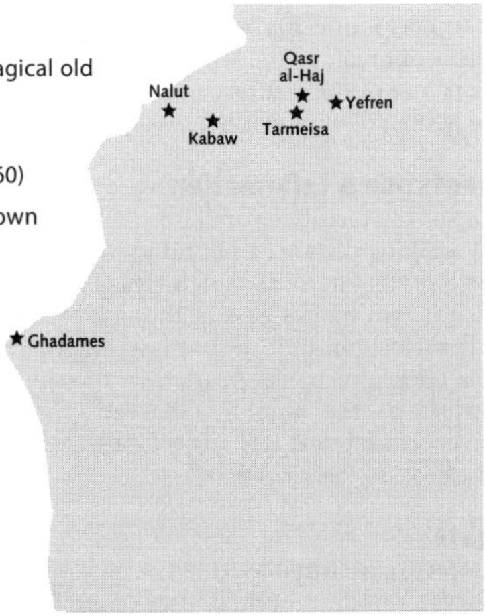

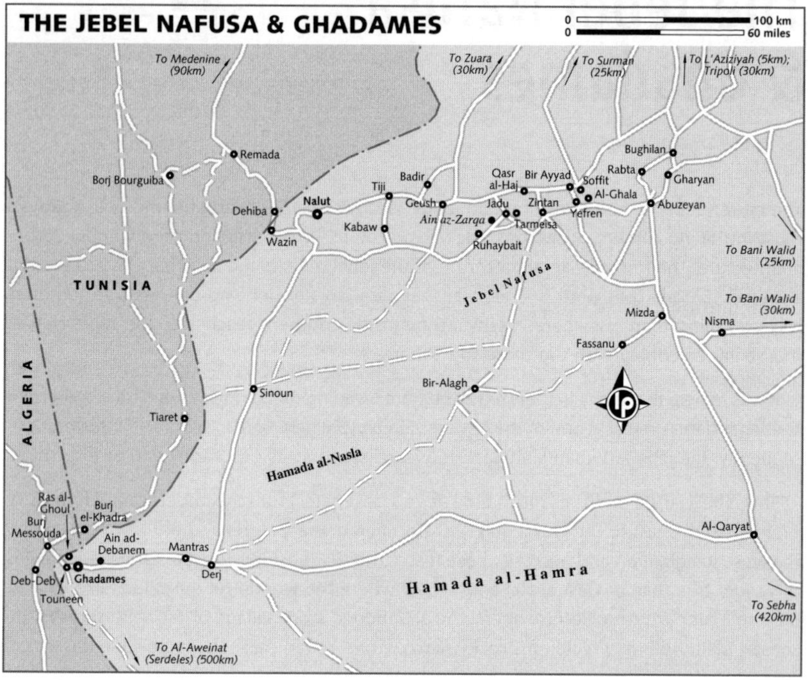

GHARYAN غريان

☎ 041 / pop 87,142

Gharyan sprawls across the top of the plateau at the eastern end of the Jebel Nafusa. Although not the region's most picturesque town, it's worth a quick stop to see one of the underground Berber houses, buy some pottery or break up the long journey south – this is one of the last towns of any size before Sebha, 690km south across the desert.

Orientation & Information

Most of the facilities you'll need are within easy walking distance of Funduq Rabta (see opposite) on Sharia al-Jamahiriya. The post office is two blocks east of the hotel (look for the telecommunications mast) and there are a couple of banks nearby. In the same complex as the hotel is Gharyan's most convenient **internet café** (per hr 0.75LD; 9am-midnight Sat-Thu, 5pm-midnight Fri).

Sights

DAMMOUS (BERBER HOUSES)

Gharyan's underground houses *(dammous)* were built by the ancient Berber inhabitants of the area and provided a refuge from cold winters, hot summers and invaders – the houses were invisible to all but those within a few hundred metres. All of Gharyan's houses have been abandoned by their owners for modern housing and some are now used as storage pens for animals. Sadly many have also fallen into disrepair.

To reach the best preserved **dammous** (admission 5LD), walk 400m south from Funduq Rabta (right as you leave the hotel) and then turn right again. One is about 50m along on the left behind a 3m-high wall with two decrepit pottery amphorae atop the gate. Back where you left the main road, ask for the key *(miftah)* at the coffeehouse.

The living quarters are at the base of a dramatic circular pit, with a radius of about 10m, cut three storeys deep into the earth; the depth of the houses varied as the inhabitants dug until they found sufficiently hard rock. The wooden door at ground level opens to a tunnel that leads down into the house, which consists of living rooms, a kitchen, bedrooms and storage areas that were cut into the base of the walls. Animal bones were once placed into the well in the centre of the courtyard; the worms that emerged from the bones assisted drainage. The house was once home to as many as six families.

There's another well-preserved **dammous** (☎ mobile 0912106859) near the Shima Mosque in the town of Abu Hamam, close to Bughilan.

POTTERY

Gharyan and neighbouring **Bughilan** are famous throughout Libya for their pottery. Stalls line the road in from Tripoli selling everything from huge serving bowls to small storage jars. To see the pottery (*fakhar* or *gilal*) being made, head to the crafts school in the small street south of the Funduq Rabta. You should be able to see pottery-making and carpet-weaving demonstrations.

Sleeping & Eating

Funduq Rabta (☎ 631970; fax 631972; Sharia al-Jamahiriya; s/d/ste 25/35/50LD) Good news: Funduq Rabta hasn't aged in five years and it's even lowered the price. The bad news is that five years ago it was already run-down and had (and still has) 'government hotel' written all over it. Rooms are simple but adequate for a night. The **restaurant** (meals 15LD) is cavernous and forlorn and the food reasonable.

Funduq Dar Gharyan (☎ 631483; fax 631415; s/d 35/45LD) Off the main highway near the town entrance as you arrive from Tripoli, Funduq Dar Gharyan is similar to the Rabta with tired, 1970s-era décor that has been kindly left unaltered. The **restaurant** (meals 15LD) here is like that at Funduq Rabta – uninspiring banquet-style meals (15LD) that will fill but not excite you. The problem here is that you're a long way from anything else.

There are cheap restaurants dotted around town, especially lining the main roads into town.

Getting There & Away

Gharyan lies on the main road between Tripoli (84km) and Sebha (595km). Shared taxis to/from Tripoli leave throughout the day from 6am, with less regular departures to Yefren, Sebha and Nalut.

YEFREN يفرن

☎ **0421 / pop 69,291**

Yefren is one of the more appealing towns in this mountainous region. It sits high on a series of rocky bluffs, overlooking the flat coastal plain, and is surrounded by attractive wooded areas. It's a relaxed place and nothing happens here in a hurry. There is, however, **internet access** (per hr 1LD) at a few places along the main street; look for the blue Internet Explorer sign.

Sights

The deserted **old town** is over 500 years old and there are a few ruined remains scattered around the hillsides. To gain an appreciation of Yefren's remarkable location, wander out to Yefren's only hotel (see below), which has superb views from its back terrace. The nearby **Turkish mosque** also has an attractive minaret, overlooking the plains below.

Over the hill east of the town centre are the remains of an ancient **Jewish synagogue** (*ma'abed al-yehud* or *kanisat al-yehud*) that served a Jewish community of up to 2000 people until 1948. There had been a synagogue on this site for almost 2000 years. The ramshackle interior contains six arches and six windows (the number represents the points of the Star of David) surrounding a raised platform. The ceilings are adorned with ancient Hebrew inscriptions. The main entrance was via the east door through a short, arcaded passage. It's impossible to find this place under your own steam; ask for directions at the hotel. The caretaker is usually nearby with the key, and although there is no formal entry fee, a donation of around 5LD is appreciated. He can also point you in the direction of some **dammous** nearby.

Around 12km east of the town centre is **Qasbat Suffet**, a hilltop Roman mausoleum that's visible from miles around. A possibly apocryphal story which we were unable to confirm tells of how, during the Italian occupation, General Rodolfo Graziani (see p36) visited here, found a Roman coin and duly dispatched it to Mussolini with words to the effect of 'we have returned'. The road leading to Qasbat Suffet is next to the petrol station – take the first turn-off if you're coming into Yefren along the main road from Gharyan, the third if you're coming from the west.

Sleeping & Eating

Buyut ash-shabaab (Youth Hostel; dm 5LD) The pleasant youth hostel is behind the police station, up the hill from the post office.

Yefren Hotel (☎ 60278; www.yefrenhotel.com; s/d/tr 30/50/60LD; meals 15LD) Welcome to the best hotel in the Jebel Nafusa. The rooms may be spacious and attractive and the staff friendly, but the views from some rooms and from the hotel terrace are without parallel, especially at sunset. If you're fortunate to snaffle one of the west-facing rooms, peel back the carpet (!) and contemplate the sweeping panorama. All in all, it's outstanding.

Getting There & Away

Shared taxis run reasonably regularly to Gharyan and Zintan and beyond.

ZINTAN الزنتان

The inhabitants of this pleasant but unspectacular town, 34km west of Yefren, are renowned throughout Libya for their quick wit – they're certainly a friendly lot. There are a few **dammous** (underground and in caves) dotted around the town. There are also a couple of petrol stations (one in the centre of town and another on the road from Nalut), a **buyut ash-shabaab** (youth hostel; dm 5LD) and well-stocked grocery stores, it's a reasonable place to break up a journey. Zintan really starts to bustle around sunset.

The main Gharyan-Nalut highway runs through the southern outskirts of town, and the surrounding fields are covered with olive and almond groves. The road to Qasr al-Haj (below) is spectacular, with a ruined **fortress** on a nearby bluff and a palm-fringed **spring** down in the valley.

QASR AL-HAJ قصر الحاج

This village is home to Libya's largest, most spectacular example of Berber architecture; a must-see even if you're just passing through en route to Ghadames. The circular and completely enclosed fortified granary is wonderfully preserved; recent landscaping at the entrance and renovation work on some of the houses in the surrounding old town, which fell into disuse in the 1950s, mean that this site will get even better in the coming years. There's a public toilet just outside the *qasr*.

This extraordinary **qasr** (admission 2LD) was built to store the harvests of the surrounding area in the second half of the 12th century by the formidably named As-Sheikh Abd-'Allah ibn Mohammed ibn Hillal ibn Ganem Abu Jatla (Sheikh Abu Jatla).

When the *qasr* was first built, Sheikh Abu Jatla, a deeply religious man, extracted rent from each interested party in the form of barley and wheat, then distributed it among the poor and haj pilgrims or sold it for money for the upkeep of the mosque and to pay Quranic teachers in the madrassa.

You enter the *qasr* from the eastern side. After passing through the main door, the passageway is flanked by two spacious alcoves where you'll see displayed the huge latches for securing the doors.

The main courtyard is breathtaking, and like wandering into a self-enclosed, manmade canyon. The walls are completely surrounded by cave-like rooms. In all, there are 114 storage rooms in the *qasr* – exactly the same number as there are suras (verses or chapters) in the Quran – although many are now subdivided into pens for different crop types or for various families who share the same space. The *qasr*'s area is 1188 sq metres, with each storage area about 5m 'deep' from the door to the back wall. There are three storeys of rooms above the ground and another 30 rooms underground.

If you arrive after good rains, many of the stores may be filled to overflowing,

THE BERBER QASRS OF JEBEL NAFUSA

Berber architecture in the Jebel Nafusa is like something out of a *Star Wars* film set. Most of the fortified granary stores, known as *qasrs,* date from the 12th century and have stood the test of time remarkably well.

Despite their name (*'qasr'* means castle), these structures were rarely used as a form of defence. Instead they offered protection for the local crops needed for the community's survival. Constructed from local rock, sun-dried mud brick and gypsum, the cool storage areas, sealed with doors made of palm trunks, warded off bugs, thieves and inclement weather. Their purpose was akin to that of a modern bank, with the system of enforced saving and stockpiling preventing the cropholders from squandering their resources.

Rooms below ground were used to preserve olive oil; the above-ground rooms customarily housed barley and wheat. You'll often see animal horns on the ramparts; these served as amulets of good fortune. Also evident are the remains of ancient winches used for hoisting produce from ground level to the upper storage rooms.

although those on the top floor are no longer in use. When we visited, some crops had been stored for as long as 12 years and looked as fresh as if recently harvested. Please note, however, that these crops represent people's livelihoods, so don't venture inside without permission.

Some of the rooms still boast the original palm-trunk doors, which have aged remarkably well. Note also the holes on either side of each door for threading the latch (usually made from the wood of olive trees).

Viewed from any angle, the *qasr* is spectacular. For a different perspective, climb the stairs leading up above the entrance. A ledge (1m wide in most places) circles the *qasr*'s top level.

Today, the site is usually kept closed, not least because many of the storage rooms are still in use. The caretaker will usually get wind of your arrival, but any of the villagers know where to find him. Your entry fee goes towards efforts to preserve the *qasr* from heavy rains and vagaries of time.

JADU جادو

pop 6160

The modern hilltop town of Jadu is a mixed Berber-Arab settlement overlooking the Sahel al-Jefara (Jefara Plain) from the barren escarpments of the Jebel Nafusa. Built on the site of an older town, Jadu has lost much of its charm and the few old buildings that remain are in a sorry state. The post office and petrol station are both on the road running southwards out of town and there are no banks that change money.

Sights

The **museum** (admission 3LD, camera/video 5/10LD; 9am-1pm & 3-6pm Tue-Sun) contains an oil press, a model reconstruction of Qasr al-Haj, examples of building materials traditionally used in the area, local costumes and agricultural implements. You'll often find the museum closed during its official opening hours, but if you ask around for the key someone will usually let you in, except at prayer time. The museum is in the stone building 100m north of the main roundabout in the centre of town (ask for *al-mathaf*).

Sleeping & Eating

Jadu's only hotel is the simple **Funduq Jadu as-Siyahe** (Sharia al-Jamahiriya; per person 15LD) in the pink building just east of the main roundabout. Expect basic but habitable rooms.

For food, take what you can get in Jadu. There are the usual grocery stores selling biscuits and tins of tuna, as well as a few cheap restaurants that do hamburgers and liver sandwiches for 1LD to 2LD each.

Getting There & Away

Jadu sits atop the plateau 146km east of Nalut. There are infrequent departures by shared taxi to Tripoli, Nalut, Gharyan and Zintan.

AROUND JADU

Ain az-Zarqa

One of many natural springs or wells dotted throughout this stretch of mountains, this small, crystal-clear pool fringed by palm trees is stunningly located at the bottom of cliffs that surround it on three sides. It's a great spot for a picnic and particularly popular with locals on Friday.

To get there, take the road southwards out of Jadu for 4.5km, from where a dirt track runs off to the right (west). The turn-off is marked with a maroon-and-blue sign in Arabic. After about 1km, you come to an open picnic area. For those with limited time, a short walk takes you to the edge of the cliffs that overlook the pool far below; be careful of loose stones, as it was here that one Lonely Planet author nearly took a high dive. Alternatively, follow the road down the canyon – about a one-hour walk going down and twice that coming back up.

Tarmeisa

This abandoned and ancient stone village, 10km southeast of Jadu, clings to a narrow, rocky outcrop overlooking the Sahel al-Jefara and is one of the most evocative of the ancient Berber settlements in the Jebel Nafusa.

The only entrance to the town is from the car park at the road's end across a dirt 'bridge' with a deep trench on either side. This was once the town gate, with a drawbridge surrounded on three sides by plunging cliffs. The bridge was opened every morning at 6am and closed again at 6pm, effectively sealing off the town. The first house you come to on your left was one of the last to be abandoned in the late 1950s. Look for the **tunnels** leading underground to the houses, one of which contains a huge oil press.

Entering the village proper, there are plenty of small doorways and passageways to explore. About halfway through the village, one house on the eastern side contains a well-preserved **bridal room** (for use on the wedding night), which has traces of relief-carving patterns and attractive storage alcoves. Elsewhere, note the roofs reinforced with a multitude of palm or olive tree trunks.

The buildings at the northernmost (and narrowest) end of the village include a **mosque** with a squat, pyramidal minaret. Most of the structures in this section were rebuilt in 1205, suggesting that the original construction of the village took place much earlier. There are fantastic **views** from here, and a stunning vista down off the escarpment over the Sahel al-Jefara, with its hundreds of snaking wadis heading northwards. Be very careful as there are no rails to prevent unsuspecting travellers from falling.

KABAW كاباو

The quiet Berber town of Kabaw, 9km north of the Gharyan–Nalut road and around 70km west of Jadu, is set among rolling hills and is home to another stunning *qasr*. This stretch of countryside is one of the more fertile areas of the Jebel Nafusa; the sight of shepherds with their flocks in the surrounding fields is not uncommon.

Sights

The **qasr** (also known locally as the *ghurfas*) is over 700 years old and, while smaller and less uniform than the one at Qasr al-Haj, is still captivating, with a wonderful medieval charm. None of the storage rooms remain in use and the door is permanently left open. The *qasr*'s impregnable hilltop position highlights how, in such an unforgiving landscape, the protection of grains was almost as significant as guarding water.

The rooms surround an open courtyard, with some sections climbing four- or five-storeys high. Many of the doors are made of palm trunks and most of the structure is a combination of rock, gypsum and sun-dried mud bricks. In the centre of the courtyard is a white tomb belonging to a local religious notable. Pottery storage jars are scattered around the courtyard's perimeter. Most of the time you're likely to have the place to yourself, except on Thursday afternoon and Friday, when it comes to life as a favourite picnic spot for local families.

Outside the *qasr*'s walls, the ruins of the old town tumble down the hillside. Most of the houses are sadly derelict.

Festivals & Events

In April most years, Kabaw hosts the **Qasr Festival**. The festivities celebrate the unique heritage of the Berber people of the area, with particular emphasis on Berber folklore. Important local ceremonies (weddings, funerals and harvests) are re-enacted by people in traditional dress.

Eating

Hannibal (☎ 0912123957; meals 10-12LD; 🕑 lunch & dinner) This is the only restaurant, 11km southeast of town on the Gharyan-Nalut road, 2km east of the Kabaw turn-off. The soup is hearty, the chicken dishes tasty and the service willing. It also does a tasty fruit cocktail.

NALUT نالوت

☎ 0470 / pop 68,865

At the western end of the Jebel Nafusa, the regional centre of Nalut is home to yet another exceptional *qasr*, as well as an old town tumbling down the hill. Unlike others in the region it occupies its own rocky bluff, which makes for some wonderful photos.

The road from Tripoli winds up off the plain to the east and meets the Ghadames road (which approaches across the plateau from the south) at the main roundabout in the town centre. The large white *baladiya* (municipal or town hall) and post office are west of the roundabout; along this road are a number of shops and a mosque. There's a petrol station along the road to Ghadames.

Sights

OLD TOWN

The qasr was once the old town's centrepiece and is now almost completely surrounded by the uninhabited remains of the stone-and-gypsum village that cling to the edge of the steep hillside. The views over the mountains and plains from any of the elevated areas around the *qasr* are superb.

There are three mosques, only one of which (the white mosque) is still in use. The white mosque between the car park and the *qasr* is the most recent; it's closed to visitors and rarely used. Down the hill immediately be-

THINGS THEY SAID ABOUT...NALUT

[Nalut is] the chief town of the Jebel Nefusah, on the brow of the mountain which dominates the desert. The dwellings – with the exception of the Turkish fort and a few government dwellings – are some of the most curious in the world....But the grottoes of Nalut were typical of this mountain country; everything here was rock: there was not a plant or a tree to be seen. On the highest point of the promontory rose the castle, almost part of the rock itself.

Alberto Denti di Pirajno, A Cure for Serpents *(1955)*

hind the white walls is Nalut's oldest mosque, **Alal'a Mosque**. Its low arches and stone mihrab suggest that it was once a fine, if simple, place of worship. There is also a functioning well in one of the rooms off the compact main sanctuary. The walls just inside the entrance are marked with Arabic relief inscriptions stating that the mosque was rebuilt in 1312. Old Nalut's third mosque is beyond the *qasr* on the eastern end of the outcrop.

Also near the *qasr* are two old **olive oil presses**. One is about 30m back towards the car park from the caretaker's tent, off the northern side of the path; look for the huge circular platform and crushing stone. There's another, equally impressive example of an oil press around 150m west of the *qasr*, off the southern side of the path. In use until 2000, this one is kept locked so you'll need to ask the *qasr*'s caretaker for the key – ask to see the '*ma'sered zeytoun*' (olive press).

QASR

Like the other *qasrs* of the Jebel Nafusa, the main section of this ancient troglodyte **granary** (admission 2LD; daylight) is reached through a covered tunnel that used to regulate entry to the inner sections. The walls of the entrance tunnel are lined with Arabic inscriptions carved in relief, which record that the *qasr* was rebuilt over the ruins of an earlier structure in 1240.

The *qasr* of Nalut is quite unlike those at Kabaw and Qasr al-Haj. While the same principles are in evidence – small storage rooms carved into the rock and self-enclosed within high walls from a perch on a rocky bluff – the *qasr* at Nalut has the feel of a small, fortified village. Rather than facing onto an open courtyard, the rooms with their palm-trunk doors are tightly packed and overlook two narrow thoroughfares without any hint of uniformity.

The structure's interior is strewn with old pieces of pottery once used to store dates, wheat, oil and barley. As well as the palm-trunk doors and holes used for latches, look for the small wooden struts protruding from the walls – these provided reinforcement to the walls, which look fragile but have proved remarkably resilient. The larger rooms belonged to richer merchants or farmers, while some were subdivided for families unable to justify a room all to themselves. There were 400 chambers, but the keeper always knew how much each family had in storage at any given time. The last rooms fell vacant in 1960.

For the best view of the *qasr*, head for Funduq Winzrik (below).

Sleeping & Eating

Buyut ash-Shabaab (Youth Hostel; ☎ 2858; Sharia Ghadames; dm 5LD) Close to the petrol station, this small hostel is basic but as cheap as you'll get in Nalut, and it's rarely crowded.

Funduq Winzrik (☎ 2204; s/d/ste with private bathroom 25/40/50LD; meals 15LD) Built in 1933 by the Italians and magnificently located across the valley from the old town, Funduq Winzrik has been restored – although not with much imagination. Design features include carpet on the floors, carpet on the walls, carpet on the bedside table… The rooms are spacious and simple but the bathroom plumbing is in need of attention. Its best feature is the terrace, which has unrivalled views of the old town and *qasr*, especially just before sunset.

Like in any Libyan town, there are small sandwich and hamburger bars along the road in from Ghadames and just down the hill on your right from the roundabout.

Mat'am Ajweiba (☎ mobile 0913705327; meals 10-12LD; lunch & dinner) Located 8km south of town at the petrol station on the turn-off into Nalut from the Gharyan-Ghadames road, this is one of the better restaurants in this part of the country. It has a pleasant dining room, good food and friendly service.

Getting There & Away

Occasional shared taxis and one daily bus leave from next to the *baladiya* for Tripoli and nearby towns.

NALUT TO GHADAMES

Shortly after you leave Nalut, the landscape loses the last tinges of green. About 125km from Nalut is the bleak settlement of **Sinoun** which has a tiny stone-and-mud-brick old town with a crumbling fort.

Just before reaching the checkpoint outside Derj, a turn-off to the east leads to Al-Qaryat (312km) and Sebha; this road shares the prize with the road from Tobruk to Ajdabiya for Libya's most unexciting road.

The sleepy town of **Derj**, 210km south of Nalut, is little more than a place to stop and refuel. The road bypasses much of Derj itself, which has a post office and a mud-brick old city that is rarely visited but worth exploring if old cities are your thing.

The road from Derj to Ghadames is quite bumpy in patches. Wind-blown sand can encroach onto the road and wandering camels can be a hazard.

GHADAMES غدامس

☎ 0484 / pop 17,092

There's nowhere on earth quite like Ghadames, which could just be our favourite place in Libya. The Unesco World Heritage–listed old city is a magical evocation of an idyllic caravan town of the Sahara – a palm-fringed oasis, the sense of an intricate maze, stunning traditional houses huddling together for company amid the empty spaces of the Sahara, and extensive covered walkways that keep the desert heat at bay. Around seemingly every corner is a world of wonder, a sense that here, at last, is a place where the cliché rings true and time truly has stood still. Now abandoned although increasingly well preserved, Ghadames may be drawing ever-greater number of tourists, but when you're lost in its labyrinth it can feel like you're the only person in a city of ghosts.

History

The stories of Ghadames' past are safeguarded by the old men of the community who keep the oral history alive.

It is believed that there was a town near Ghadames' current site around 3000 BC, but little is known of the area's history prior to Roman occupation in 19 BC. The Romans fortified the town, which they called Cydamus, and turned it into a regional centre that provided the coastal cities with olive oil. Under the reign of Septimius Severus (AD 193–211), Ghadames became a garrison town for the Third Legion. The Roman occupation of Ghadames lasted for over two centuries, during which time the

THE GREAT CARAVANS OF GHADAMES

Remarkably, for one of the principal trading centres of the Sahara, Ghadames produced only one product of note, and a not very lucrative one at that – embroidered slippers. Instead, Ghadames became one of the great entrepôt towns for goods from all over Africa; the merchants of Ghadames were famous throughout the Sahara. So prolific were the Ghadames caravans that when caravans arrived in towns across the Sahara, they were often assumed to be Ghadames caravans.

The town was also unique in that the main traders rarely travelled themselves but relied on a network of agents across Africa who, when a Ghadames caravan arrived, would check loads and undertake transactions on behalf of the real owners, the entrepreneurs of the desert. The influence of the agents stretched from Mauritania to Egypt, from Lake Chad to the Mediterranean – and their descendants can still be found living across Africa. Many cities such as Timbuktu still have a 'Ghadames St'.

Goods from the interior of Africa that passed through the gates of Ghadames en route to the coast included an exotic array of precious stones, gold and silver, ivory, Tripolitanian horses, dates and ostrich plumes. In the other direction, glass necklaces and Venetian paper (for use in religious texts), pearls from Paris and linen from Marseille passed through on their way south.

The arrival of a caravan in Ghadames was quite an event. The camels bearing great chests were unloaded and the goods almost immediately offered for sale in the markets of the town. These were heady days of celebration in Ghadames, with the caravans also bringing mail, loved ones, stories of desert adventures and news of a wider world from across the sands.

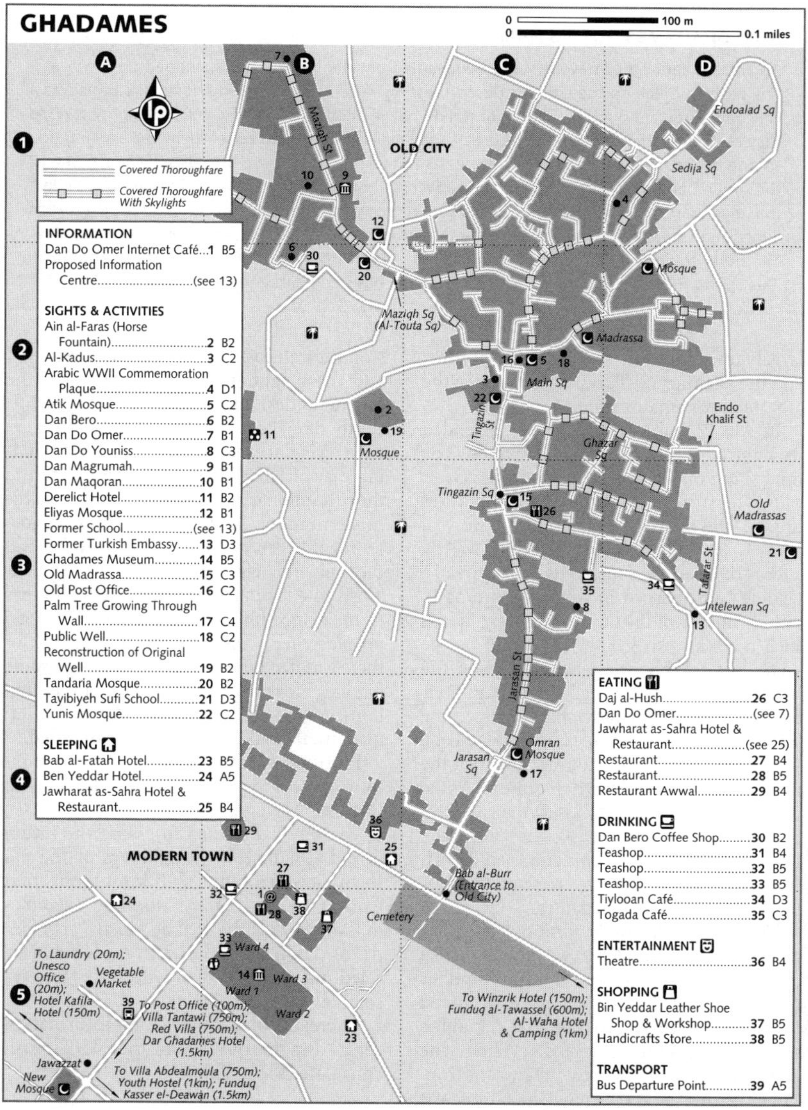

ancient idols of the traditional religions lost influence in the town.

In the 6th century AD, the Byzantine armies of Justinian I brought Ghadames under the empire's jurisdiction, while Greek missionaries who followed in the army's wake effectively turned the town into a Christian settlement. With the arrival of the Islamic armies in Libya, the town was overrun in 46 AH (AD 668) and most of the Berber inhabitants converted to Islam (see Ras al-Ghoul, p175).

Although dates of any precision are difficult to come by, it is believed that the site of the old city was founded around 800 years ago. It is the third town in the area now known as Ghadames. The town remains

HOW GHADAMES GOT ITS NAME

An ancient caravan of travellers and merchants from the Nemrod tribe stopped for lunch at a tiny oasis to break up the arduous desert crossing. With the sun beating down, the oasis was a welcome sight, although they thought it didn't have enough water to warrant a lengthy stay. As they continued their journey the next day, they realised that they had left behind a cooking pot, so one of the men was sent to retrieve it. As he was about to leave the oasis, his horse pawed the ground and fresh water rose to the surface. In honour of the occasion, but with a little less romance than some of us would have liked, the party combined the words *ghad* (which means 'lunch') and *ames* (which means 'yesterday') to produce the name Ghadames, or 'lunch yesterday'. The other traditional name of Ghadames is Ain al-Faras (Well of the Mare, or Horse Fountain). This spring formed the foundation of the original oasis and subsequent settlements.

largely unchanged in design since that time, and the Islamic and Turkish character of the architecture remains intact.

In AD 1228 the Hafsid dynasty extended its control southwards to Ghadames. The imposition of taxes by far-distant rulers later caused tension and, with the Ghadamsis' taxes unpaid, the rulers in Tunis sent an army of some 10,000 men to collect their dues. Met by a force of Ghadames men outside the town, a terrible battle ensued in which, according to one chronicler of the day, the fighting 'raised such a black dust that the sky could not be seen'. Remarkably, the Ghadamsis won the battle and, their point made, duly paid their taxes. Not long afterwards, the town became largely independent. Ghadames remained one of the most important caravan towns of the northern Sahara until the 19th century. As the colonial powers began to assert their control over the Sahara, in the 1840s the slave trade was abolished first in Tunis and then French Algeria, with devastating consequences for the economic life of Ghadames.

The Ottomans loosely administered Ghadames after 1810. When squabbles broke out between the semi-autonomous families of the city in 1874, the town was occupied by a full Ottoman garrison that remained until the Italians arrived. When the Allied forces sought to eject the Italians from Libya during WWII, even Ghadames was not spared. On 11 November 1943 French pilots flew US-registered B-17 bombers in an assault on Ghadames, launched from neighbouring Algeria. Although lasting for only 10 minutes, the intense bombardment killed 40 Ghadamsis (their names are listed in Arabic in the museum), including 12 children, destroyed 70 houses and damaged a further 200. The Atik Mosque, which had stood for almost 1300 years, was destroyed and the neighbouring Yunis Mosque (the second oldest in Ghadames) was significantly damaged. No Italians were killed.

In recent decades, Libya's old cities, including that of Ghadames, have fallen victim to the revolutionary government's push towards modernisation. In 1982–83, the Libyan government began building a new town beyond the walls and new houses were given to Ghadamsis to encourage them to leave the homes of their ancestors. In 1984, there were 6666 people living in the old town; four years later there was just one family left. Although some families move back into the cool of their old houses during summer (especially during Ramadan), the old city is effectively deserted.

Fortunately, the potential windfall from tourism and the involvement of the United Nations Development Program (UNDP) since 1999 has helped to assure the future of old Ghadames, with surveys of the old town, new maps and significant renovation work. One of the most stunning examples of their work is the well of Ain al-Faras (see p173). Until 2005 the well was a rubbish-filled pit; now it's filled with water and resembles its original state.

There are plans to open an information centre for the old city in the old Turkish consulate (see p171).

Orientation

Ghadames is an easy place to find your way around. Entering town from the east, the road forks just before entering the built-up area. The right fork runs past the cemetery on your left while the old city fans out beyond the walls on your right. About 1.5km after the fork, the main road of new Ghadames runs off at right angles to the south.

Information

GUIDES

A **guide** (half/full day 40/60LD) is essential for your first visit to the old city. There are now a number of local guides speaking English, French and Italian, all of whom are, in our experience, excellent.

If you're launching an expedition south into the desert (see p176), the following two Tuareg guides are recommended:

Al-Sheikh Bahous (☎ 63230; al,sheikhbah@hotmail.com) A hugely experienced French-speaking guide who's great company in the sands.

Bilal S Aghali (☎ 62956; bilal_aghali@yahoo.com) A friendly English-speaking guide who comes highly recommended by travellers.

INTERNET ACCESS

Dan Do Omer Internet Café (☎ 62300; dandoomer@yahoo.com; per hr 1LD; 9.30am-midnight) Also offers international phone calls and fax.

JAWAZZAT

Passport office (☎ 62437; 9am-noon & 5-8pm Sat-Thu) Almost opposite the New Mosque.

LAUNDRY

If your clothes are in danger of exploring the old city without you, there's a good **laundry** (9am-1pm & 6-9pm Sat-Thu) a small block west of the New Mosque. Your clothes will be dry-cleaned and ironed (sometimes including your underwear!). Shirts and pants cost 1.5LD each, and underwear is 0.5LD each. If you're having trouble finding it, ask for 'Ash-Sharouk Maasella' or 'Launderie'.

> **THINGS THEY SAID ABOUT... GHADAMES**
>
> Enclosed within their oasis and isolated in the vast desert, the Ghadamese nevertheless maintain contacts all over the world; they combine the flabbiness of sedentary people with the broad vision of the nomads. The Ghadamese tradesman, huddled in his little hovel stuffed full of goods, will talk with the greatest simplicity of his stays in Paris and London, or of the letter he has just received from his representative in Marseilles or New York.
>
> *Alberto Denti di Pirajno,* A Cure for Serpents *(1955)*

POST & TELEPHONE

Post office (8am-1pm & 5-8pm Sat-Thu) South of the New Mosque – look for the usual telecommunications mast.

Sights

OLD CITY

The original families still retain ownership over the houses in the **old city** (adult/child 5/1LD, camera/video 5/10LD) and many return regularly to carry out maintenance. Many of the gardens surrounding the covered areas of the city are still in use. In total, the old city consists of around 1600 buildings, which includes almost 1250 houses, 21 mosques and 17 *zawiya* (religious colleges).

The covered alleyways rely entirely on natural light and in most places there are evenly spaced skylights – some are as high as 10m – which can be surprisingly effective. Areas where the skylights are not as prevalent can be quite dark, so it's worth bringing a torch. Almost every thoroughfare is lined with sitting benches that are good places to rest – even on the hottest summer day the covered areas are remarkably cool. Most of the houses and other buildings are not open to the public (except at festival time), although an increasing number, possibly up to 30, are opening. Some of these are listed in the Walking Tour, p169.

The old city of Ghadames was a city of loosely configured concentric areas. The inner circle consisted of residential and commercial districts and covered around 10 hectares. As you moved further away from the city's heart, the densely packed houses gave way to gardens. Beyond the gardens was the city wall.

The built-up areas of old Ghadames were divided into two main sections to represent the two major tribes of the region: the Bani Walid and the Bani Wazid (named after the sons of one of the first Berber leaders of Ghadames). The Bani Walid occupied the quarters north of the main square, with their sector subdivided into three subgroupings of families, while the Bani Wazid area to the south was home to four distinct sub-families or tribes.

Each of these seven sections were known as 'streets'. There are, therefore, seven main streets in old Ghadames. Each 'street' used

THE TRADITIONAL HOUSES OF GHADAMES

Nothing can quite prepare you for your first visit to a Ghadames house, another world of pristine white walls, exquisite decoration and deceptively large living areas that make maximum use of vertical space. The design of the houses – which were built from gypsum and sun-dried mud brick with ceilings reinforced with palm trunks – is uniform, although they sometimes vary in terms of size and the richness of decoration depending on the wealth of the owners.

After entering the palm-trunk doors at street level, you'll pass through a small reception or entrance room where guests were greeted. A short corridor runs past a storage room on the same level, then a staircase leads to the next level, at the top of which was often a 'dry toilet'.

The small landing at the top of the stairs leads onto the main living room. This large room (generally around 3m by 4m) was where a family would take its meals, entertain guests and spend most of its time. It was also the centre of the social life of the women of the house. The ceiling may be as much as two-storeys high with a skylight at the very top; note the strategically placed mirrors throughout the house to reflect the only source of external light. At night, oil lamps were used. Adorning the walls are intricately painted decorations, including the four-fingered hand of Fatima that was believed to ward off evil. The decorative flourishes were done largely by women, often as a means to prepare the house for married life.

Another feature of the living room was the large number of painted cupboards, each serving a specific purpose – cooking implements, women's clothes, the father's possessions, a toy cupboard or gifts for a boy on reaching manhood. Smaller niches were repositories for sugar and tea, while the small, circular hole at ground level was the place to throw date seeds when you'd finished with them (like most things in Ghadames, these were later recycled for animal feed).

On the same level as the living room are usually two smaller rooms. One was a bedroom but the other had an arched doorway with the Al-Qubba canopy, formed by two pillars with a pointed roof. This was where a woman received her husband on their wedding night (see A Woman's World, opposite).

Two sets of stairs usually leads up from the living room to more bedrooms, and storage and food preparation rooms. One staircase ultimately takes you to the roof. In the wall of an upper room there was often a small door that connected to a neighbouring house. This door served a dual purpose of being a fire escape and a pathway for women passing from house to house. Five or six houses were often joined in this way and neighbouring houses often belonged to close relatives. The roof area often contained the kitchen and more storage areas reached via more stairs – Ghadames houses were clearly not for the infirm.

With help from Unesco and driven by Ghadames' popularity among tourists, an ever-growing number of the old houses have been restored and opened to the public; some of the most accessible are covered in the Walking Tour (opposite). The best idea is to combine your visit with a meal (p174).

to be like a self-contained town, with its own gate that was closed at sunset each night, and a mosque, houses, schools, markets and a small communal square. The square was used for weddings, celebrations and funerals.

Although the rhythms of daily life were largely played out within the seven streets, and conflicts between the different quarters were frequent, there was also a strong sense of belonging to a wider Ghadames community. Whenever the whole town was under threat from an external enemy or a collective decision was needed, the families of the seven streets would congregate in their respective squares to agree on a response. The oldest man or most respected elder from each of the seven families would then be sent to the central square of the whole town where the seven representatives would organise a communal defence or come to a collective decision. These councils of elders would also handle internal community disputes, discussions around ancient customs, criminal issues and irrigation. Punishment for indiscretions often comprised of exclusion from festivities or market activities.

All events of city-wide importance took place in the central square. At other times, it was where news was passed from one

A WOMAN'S WORLD

In Ghadames, women led a life of concealment in keeping with the dictates of traditional Islamic society. Although the public world of Ghadames life was traditionally dominated by men and they made major decisions relating to family life, the women's domain was the house and women made many important decisions regarding life within the four walls.

One of the central features of any traditional Ghadames house was Al-Qubba, a canopy set up in a room where a wife received her husband on their first night of marriage.

When her husband died, the wife was confined to the house for four months and ten days (a Quranic principle known as Ar-Ridda), after when she was free to remarry and resume a normal life, as there would be no doubt as to whom was the father of her children. A bereaved husband was, of course, free to remarry immediately. Although the mourning woman was free to move within the house, tradition demanded that she receive any visitors in Al-Qubba.

Men would attend the funerals in the public squares, while women performed the mourning ceremonies, attended only by women, inside the house. Other public ceremonies were similarly held in the town squares for men and either in the houses or on the rooftops for women – the city was designed in such a way that Ghadames women could conceivably walk across the entire city without being seen by men. In matters of inheritance, a wife received one-eighth of her husband's property and her daughters half that of her sons.

Whenever a decision was made or judgment passed down by the town's elders, the women of the city were informed by two specially appointed, freed, female slaves. A weekly women-only market was held on the interconnected rooftops of the old city.

sector of the city to another. The main square also reflected Ghadames' position as a trans-Saharan caravan town – caravans from throughout Africa would enter the city through here, bringing news of shifting tribal allegiances, battles and the wellbeing of loved ones far away; for more information see The Great Caravans of Ghadames, p164. Staring off at each other across the main square are the two main mosques of the old city, one for the Bani Walid (the Atik Mosque) and one for the Bani Wazid (the Yunis Mosque).

In addition to the two primary subdivisions of the town, a third (outside the old city walls) began to spring up to the west of the old city in the 1960s. This area, known as *fogas,* was home to the Tuareg who had started to move away from a purely nomadic lifestyle and chose to settle in Ghadames.

GHADAMES MUSEUM

The town **museum** (☎ 62225; adult/child 3/1LD, camera/video 5/10LD; ⏲ 9am-1.30pm) is housed in an old fort that began life as a police station under the Italians. It has five sections; only those of greatest interest are listed here. There are old black-and-white photos of Ghadames.

Ward 1 contains some informative posters about Ghadames' history and a range of ethnographic exhibits. Highlights include the famous embroidered slippers of Ghadames made by the Bin Yeddar family, huge copper keys and padlocks, the like of which are still used in the old city, and a large selection of folk medicines – the remedy for constipation (top row on the left) looks particularly nasty.

Ward 2 contains artefacts from the Roman era, including the remains of Roman pillars from the town's Triumphal Arch.

Ward 3 has a decent collection of Tuareg items, while Ward 4 has architectural drawings from a Libyan-Italian archaeological team, building materials, fossils and a few stuffed animals.

OTHER SIGHTS

Modern Ghadames is a pleasant town whose skyline is dominated by the attractive **New Mosque** with its marble pillars and towering minaret; non-Muslims are not allowed inside. The old **cemetery** opposite Bab al-Burr, the main gate to the old city, is filled with thousands of what appear to be unmarked gravestones. However, true to the Ghadames tradition of oral history, the precise identity and location of each grave is passed down from father to son.

Walking Tour

The following walking tour takes you through the seven sectors of the city. If you

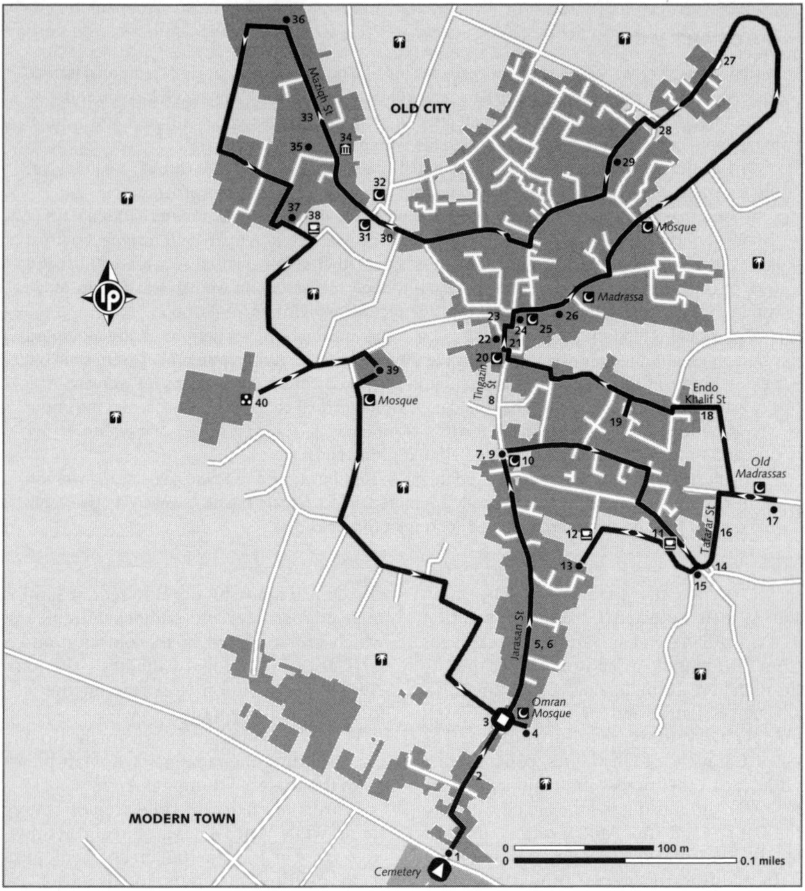

WALK FACTS

Start Bab al-Burr
End Jarasan Sq
Distance 5km
Duration 3 hours

want to fully explore the old city, you could easily take an entire day, although this walking tour can be completed in three hours.

The best place to start is at the main gate of the old city, **Bab al-Burr (1)**. This was once used by the city's inhabitants; strangers usually entered the main square via Ain al-Faras (see p173), meaning that the residential districts were spared from the arrival of unwanted intruders. Immediately after passing under the arches, you find yourself in a covered passageway lined with benches.

Continue to the end of the **passageway (2)**, turn left and then right. This is the start of one of the seven major streets, Jarasan St, which runs deep into the heart of the city. The lovely whitewashed walls are a taste of things to come and, during the time when the city was inhabited, their height must have offered residents significant privacy. A short distance further on is **Jarasan Sq (3)**, entered through an attractive archway framing the minaret of the white Omran mosque. This compact square was the meeting place for one-seventh of the city's men and, as such, is surprisingly small. Note that in the four corners are the remains of Roman pillar bases – these were taken from the old Roman city nearby and used for building materials by residents of the later Islamic city.

Take a short detour to the southeast from Jarasan Sq for the famous **palm tree (4)** growing through the wall and then return to Jarasan St. The street leads into the covered section of the city, where the cool walls can provide welcome respite from the heat. Note the skylights that climb up in narrow shafts between the houses. The natural light enables you to both find your way and admire the distinctive **Ghadames doors (5, 6)**. Made of sturdy palm trunks split in half to form planks, the larger doors lead into houses while the smaller ones indicate chambers used for storage. Note also the improbably large padlocks used to secure the rooms. Another feature of the doors are the small leather studs in bright red, green and yellow (the colours of Ghadames), which partially cover some doors; these indicate that the owner has made the haj pilgrimage to Mecca.

After about a 300m walk north of Jarasan Sq, you reach **Tingazin Sq (7)** which also represents the start of **Tingazin St (8)**. Although similar in size to the earlier square, the feel is entirely different. This delightful square is completely covered from the sun and is lit by a soft light from nearby skylights. On the western wall are some **decorative patterns (9)** carved in relief. Taking the road running east off the square, you pass the shell of an **old madrassa (10)** on the right. Head east for approximately 200m, then turn right and then left. The covered area continues for a short distance before you again come out into the open air – the start of the garden area.

Almost as soon as you come out into the light, the **Tiyloaan Café** (11; p175) is on your right. You could also double back to **Togada Café** (12; p175), behind which is the **Dan Do Youniss** (13; ☎ 62724; admission 2LD; ⏰ daylight), one of the traditional Ghadames houses that has opened to the public; unusually, it has helpful English-language labels in most rooms. There are also good views from the roof.

A little further to the southwest, you come to another open area, **Intelewan Sq (14)**, where you'll most likely find a few souvenir sellers. On the right as you enter is a whitewashed building that was the first non-Quranic **school (15)** in Ghadames. Modern sciences were studied in the building, which was later used as the Turkish consulate. If you turn north, the path is lined with gardens enclosed behind walls. This thoroughfare is **Tafarar St (16)**, another of the seven main streets. At the next junction, turn right to the white domed building 50m along on the right. This is the **Tayibiyeh Sufi School (17)** and is worth visiting for its intimate courtyard and splendid views from the roof.

Return the way you came and take the first right, into **Endo Khalif St (18)**, which once again leads you undercover and turns left. The roof is, typically, covered by palm leaves with struts made from palm trunks. Winding your way left, right, right again and then left brings you into **Ghazar Sq (19)**. This lovely uncovered square is surrounded by alcove niches and a balcony encircling the square on the 1st floor. This balcony enabled children to watch the public ceremonies played out in the square below; wedding festivities sometimes lasted for up to 14 days!

The path heading west soon leads to the main square. Just before entering the square, you can visit the **Yunis Mosque (20)**, built in 1422 and the main mosque of the Bani Wazid part of town. This simple mosque makes use of pillars from the old Roman triumphal arch. Upon entering the square, you leave the Bani Wazid part of town.

The **main square (21)** of Ghadames is, like the seven tributary squares, surprisingly small in size given its importance in the public life of the city. With two mosques overlooking its open courtyard, the square is simple and lacks the charm of some of the smaller squares. In a niche on the northwest wall of the square, built into the back wall of the Yunis Mosque, is **Al-Kadus (22)**, the unlikely headquarters of Ghadames' water supply regulator (see Al-Kadus & the Art of Water Management, p172).

If you exit the main square under the northern arch, you enter the **Bani Walid (23)** districts of Old Ghadames. If you turn right at the first opportunity, the **Old Post Office (24)** is on your right. Above the path immediately outside the door hangs a chain from one of the palm struts. This is where bags of mail were hung. The appointed man from each departing caravan could sort through the bag to see whether any letters could be delivered along his caravan route, while arriving caravans could check whether any mail had been sent to them during their long absences.

By all accounts, the old men who loitered around the main square made a point of knowing everybody's business, so it usually wasn't necessary to check the mailbag.

Next door to the post office is the **Atik Mosque (25)**. This was once the oldest mosque in Ghadames, if not all of Libya. The original mosque on this site was built in 44 AH (AD 666) and, incredibly, survived until 1943, when it was destroyed by Allied bombing (p164). The sanctuary is off-limits to non-Muslims, but from the door you can see the attractive row of arched pillars, running across the centre of the rectangular hall, and the mihrab.

To get to the women's section of the mosque, return to the main thoroughfare outside the door and take the door immediately to the east. The next opening, again, leads into the **public well (26)**, which served as a public water-gathering point.

After leaving the well, follow the covered street to the east for about 400m. The uncovered path running east through the gardens is divided by a shallow canal which still serves as an irrigation channel. Winding your way north and then west between more gardens, you re-enter the built-up areas of the old city at the very small and partially covered **Endoalad Sq (27)**.

To the southwest is **Sedija Sq (28)**, which is surrounded by some superb three-storey, mud-brick Ghadames houses. Note the pattern of alternating upright and inverted triangles running along the top of one of the walls. The design is found across the Sahara of western Libya (as far south as Ghat) – one legend claims it represents the crown of an ancient Berber queen who ruled over the desert.

Taking the right fork of the two lanes running southwest, you pass a **plaque (29)** in Arabic which commemorates the bombing of Ghadames during WWII. You'll soon return to the covered lanes, where you can fully appreciate the value of skylights (and a torch), as there are fewer of them. At the T-junction, turn right, follow the curving arc of a lane to the southwest and then turn right again; watch out for jutting walls in the darkness. Continue west then northwest through a light passageway that is one of the most lovely in the old city. The benches along its side are a nice place to sit and rest.

The passage leads into **Maziqh Sq** (**30**; also known as Al-Touta Sq). This open courtyard has a tree just off-centre; if you're game, try one of the small white berries, which are tasty, not to mention perfectly safe. On the western side of the square is **Tandaria Mosque (31)**, while **Eliyas Mosque (32)** fronts onto the eastern side. The perimeter is lined with the usual arched alcoves.

Maziqh St (33) continues across the square. Not long after leaving the square, just after

AL-KADUS & THE ART OF WATER MANAGEMENT

Ghadames was renowned on the caravan routes for the plentiful water from its well, and the city authorities recognised the need to carefully manage their most precious resource. The egalitarian system they devised was ingenious.

The main water supply was connected to all points in the city via a network of underground canals. Water users were divided into three categories: private homes were the first to be supplied; followed by the mosques, which required water for ablutions and general distribution; and then the gardens.

To precisely calculate and distribute the water, a man would occupy the niche in the main square into which water was fed from the spring and into canals. This guardian of the waters ensured that the large bottle *(al-kadus)* that hung underneath the outlet was filled each time. A hole in the bottle then released the water into the canal. The time it took to empty (approximately three minutes) represented a unit of measurement – one *kadus*. Each *kadus* was noted by making a knot in a palm leaf. Two men helped the main regulator by telling him how much water each district or garden was permitted. Each garden was fed off the main canals – when they had received the correct amount, a stone was placed over the opening to ensure that no-one took more than their fair share.

So regular was this process that time was measured for the whole city by calculating how many *kadus* had passed since sunrise. Anyone could find out the time by visiting the main square and asking in the *al-kadus* niche, thereby making Ghadames one of the few places to have devised its own independent system of time and water management.

veering to the right, is **Dan Magrumah (34)**, a traditional Ghadames house open to the public. **Dan Maqoran (35)** is in the street running off to the west, while a further 250m, at the far northwestern end of the city, is **Dan Do Omer** (**36**; see p175).

Maziqh St continues to the outer reaches of old Ghadames. At the end, turn left where a few twists and turns between walled gardens and mud-brick houses, past **Dan Bero (37)** and the **Dan Bero Coffee Shop (38)**. You'll finally reach **Ain al-Faras** (**39**; Well of the Mare, or Horse Fountain), the site of a deep well that gave birth to the creation myth of Ghadames (see How Ghadames Got Its Name, p166). Unesco has recently realigned and reactivated the spring, making it a delightful spot; steps lead down behind the water to an underground reconstruction of the old well and photos of how it once looked.

Immediately west of the well is the place where caravans and other outsiders could come to tether and water their camels; they could gain access to the town via the nearby main square to receive mail, news and provisions. Also nearby is the elegant façade of a **derelict hotel (40)**; Sophia Loren slept in Room 10 while filming *The Road to Timbuktu*. This was also the area for strangers who were not to be privy to the secrets of the magical old town.

From the mosque on the south side of the square, an arch leads to an irrigated path that twists away to the southeast and back to Jarasan Sq.

Festivals & Events

In October/November, Ghadames' annual **three-day festival** brings the old city alive in a riot of colour and activity. Ghadamsis return to their family homes in the old town and throw open the doors for singing, dancing and public festivities, most of which are performed in traditional dress. It's a great chance to see re-enactments of ancient celebrations in their traditional environment.

On the first day of the festival, some public events are held in the modern city. On the morning of the second day, the festivities move to the old city, with weddings and ceremonies to celebrate the rite of passage of young men to adulthood. Up to thirty of the old houses are used – where some events would once have lasted seven days, seven houses are used to represent each day. On the third day, the festival moves to the Tuareg part of town (west of the old city) and into the desert, concluding in the evening in a Tuareg camp amid the sand dunes.

During the tourist high season (October to April), you'll find traditional performances by local dance troupes somewhere in town on most nights. Tuareg groups perform in the sands west of town, while traditional Ghadames performances take place in the theatre (see Map p165) close to the main junction.

Sleeping

Accommodation in Ghadames is improving all the time, ranging from stays in family homes to a top-notch hotel – with more of the latter already on the drawing board. All accommodation is in the new town.

BUDGET

Youth Hostel (Buyut ash-Shabaab; ☎ 62023; dm 5LD) Ghadames' youth hostel is basic, has small rooms and is plagued by problematic plumbing, but for this price you can hardly complain.

Jawharat as-Sahra Hotel & Restaurant (Funduq Jawharat as-Sahra; ☎/fax 62015; bed in 4-bed r 5LD. Run by the avuncular Ahmed at-Tunisi, this small hotel is a stone's throw from the entrance to the old city and has basic rooms. See also p174.

One solution to Ghadames' shortage of beds is the prevalence of villas – homes that operate like B&Bs. All are simple, well-kept and far more personal than the hotels. They also offer kitchen facilities and charge 20LD (including breakfast) per person.

If the ones listed here are full, the owners are usually happy to ring around and find you a bed.

Red Villa (☎ 0912133524; ⌘) Simple rooms but most have private bathrooms.

Villa Abdealmoula (☎ 62844; villa_moula@yahoo.com; ⌘) Run by the energetic Othman Elhashhashie, this is the most homely of the villas and is very well run.

Villa Tantawi (☎ 62205; ⌘) Friendly place with ornate, over-the-top rooms and a resident cat.

MIDRANGE & TOP END

All of the following places have air-con and private bathrooms (unless stated otherwise) and prices include breakfast.

Winzrik Hotel (Funduq Winzrik; ☎/fax 62485; camping 5LD, s/d 30/40LD;) This comfortable place has 16 spotlessly clean rooms with bath and air-con. The splashes of traditional decoration in some rooms is a nice touch and the location, a short walk east from the entrance to the old city, is also better than most. You can pitch a tent in the hotel's walled compound; the cost includes use of the shower and toilet.

Funduq al-Tawassel (☎ 62971; fax 021-3601374; s/d 30/40LD;) Although the rooms at this intimate little hotel are simple, they're spacious and nicely kept. Best of all, the staff exude a gentle desert charm and seem genuinely pleased to see you, in an unobtrusive way. If you're here as a group, you'll probably fill the place and it will feel like your own private house.

Kafila Hotel (Funduq Kafila; ☎ 021-3609990; kafilahotel1969@hotmail.com; s/d from 30/40LD) In the streets behind the New Mosque, this is one of the longer-standing hotels in town and it remains a popular place for groups. Perhaps that's because the rooms are enormous, although it has to be said that most are uninspiring and careworn.

Al-Waha Hotel & Camping (Funduq al-Waha; ☎ 62569/70; wah.2000@yahoo.com; camping 5LD, s/d 30/40LD;) Another of the oldest hotels in Ghadames, Al-Waha is popular with tour groups, but the truth is that all rooms are simple and some are showing none-too-graceful signs of age; most beds sag and the bathrooms in particular are in need of an overhaul – one traveller reported that their bath took 45 minutes to fill. Breakfast here is also no great thing.

Funduq Kasser el-Deawan (☎ 63350; fax 041-634115; s/d 35/50LD;) Almost as far south as you can go in Ghadames (which isn't far), this new place is excellent, with spacious, well-appointed rooms with satellite TV. It's a popular place and our only complaint is that some rooms could be cleaner when things are busy, but don't let that put you off because there's no better place for the price in Ghadames.

Bab al-Fatah Hotel (Funduq Bab al-Fatah; ☎ 63356; fax 021-3615262; s/d/tr 35/50/75LD;) At last a new hotel from where you can see the old city from your room, at least if you have a north-facing room. The rooms themselves are well-sized, clean and comfortable, if a touch overpriced, but we've no hesitation in recommending a stay here because the location is easily the best in town.

Ben Yedder Hotel (Funduq Ben Yedder; ☎ 63410; yedder@hotmail.com; s/d 35/50LD;) Another easy-to-recommend new hotel close to the town centre, Ben Yeddar has rooms that are the merest cut above others in a similar price range, and excellent bathrooms. Although we visited when it was still new and yet to age, we suspect that the attentive staff will keep it in good nick.

Dar Ghadames Hotel (Funduq Dar Ghadames; ☎ 021-3621414; fax 63408; www.darsahara.com; s/d/ste 100/110/150LD;) Now here's something special. One of just a handful of traditionally styled hotels in Libya, Dar Ghadames recreates the clean lines and tranquil air of the old city, using traditional architecture in the public areas – note the palm-wood roof above reception and the arched corridors which feel like an old, if somewhat polished Ghadames laneway. The rooms are large, supremely tasteful and as comfortable as anywhere you'll find in Libya. Most also have an outdoor terrace, there are plans for a swimming pool and the restaurant (below) is excellent. If you splurge once in Libya, make it here.

Eating

For a cheap meal of meat, chicken or liver sandwiches or a hamburger (each 0.75LD), try the two small restaurants either side of the internet café.

Restaurant Awwal (☎ 62429; meals 12-15LD; lunch & dinner) Almost every tourist who comes to Ghadames eats here at least once. The food – mainly chicken and lamb dishes, including *tajeen* (a lightly spiced dish with a tomato and paprika-based sauce) – is fairly standard tourist fare but the food is tasty and the service attentive.

Jawharat as-Sahra Hotel & Restaurant (☎ 62015; meals 5-15LD; lunch & dinner Sat-Thu, dinner Fri) This pleasant place does good couscous, barbecued meat and shish kebab and is all the better for the fact that it doesn't get too many tourists. The chilled atmosphere goes perfectly with the macchiato (1LD) and thick Arabic coffee (*qahwa*; 1LD). See also p173.

All the hotels also have restaurants serving set meals that are good if unexciting. **Dar Ghadames Hotel** (Funduq Dar Ghadames; ☎ 021-3621414; fax 63408; www.darsahara.com; lunch 20LD,

DINING IN TRADITIONAL HOUSES

An Italian visitor to Ghadames during the 1920s remarked that 'the delicate sensibility of these people delights to place beautiful things before guests and then to leave them the joy of discovering them for themselves'. Many such pleasures remain and the best eating experience in Ghadames – lunch or dinner in one of the **traditional houses** (meals incl soup & drinks 15LD) of the old town – is a case in point. The most frequently prepared meal is the delicious local speciality of *fitaat* (lentils, mutton and buckwheat pancakes cooked together in a tasty sauce in a low oven and eaten with the hands from a communal bowl). Some places also do camel couscous. Eating this wonderful meal amid an evocative atmosphere is one of Ghadames' must-dos.

Your tour company will most likely make the arrangements and most of the nearly 30 houses open to the public offer this service, including **Dan Do Omer** (☎ 62300; dandoomer731@yahoo.com) and **Daj el-Hush** (☎ 62004), although all of them are excellent.

dinner 25LD) is an exception with outstanding buffets. See also opposite.

Drinking

A number of traditional teahouses have opened in the gardens of the old town and are wonderful places to break up your ramble through the old town. They usually open early in the morning and close just before sunset. The better ones include two places just northwest of Intelewan Sq: Tiyloaan Café has a pleasant courtyard, while **Togada Café** (☎ 63377) is set in an ample garden. Another good choice in the northwest of the old city is the shady palm garden of Dan Bero Coffee Shop, although it was closed for renovations when we visited.

For more information on finding these places see the Walking Tour, p169.

In the modern town, outdoor cafés and teahouses abound; they're marked on the map. The greatest concentration is along the road running between the main intersection and the new mosque.

Shopping

Ghadames' most famous handicrafts are the striking embroidered slippers in bright colours. Unique to Ghadames, they've been produced by the local Bin Yeddar family for centuries. The family has a shop and workshop in the small market north of the museum. Prices start at around 43LD.

Most of the shops scattered around Ghadames sell a range of Tuareg handicrafts, especially leather items, replica camel saddles, cloth for Tuareg turbans and silver jewellery. You can also pick up palm-woven products and tacky items such as long-dead desert scorpions and snake skins in glass cases.

Getting There & Away

AIR

There are no regular scheduled flights between Tripoli and Ghadames, although there's always talk of this changing and one-way/return prices for these nonexistent flights are listed by Libyan Arab Airlines as 26.50/53LD. The airport is 19km east of town.

BUS & SHARED TAXI

There are at least two buses daily from Ghadames to Tripoli; both leave from the main street, 50m northeast of the new mosque. Shared taxis for the Jebel Nafusa require a change in Nalut.

CAR & MOTORCYCLE

Ghadames is 611km southwest of Tripoli. For information on the road between Ghadames and Nalut, see p164.

AROUND GHADAMES

Ras al-Ghoul

About 10km northwest of Ghadames is the lonely desert castle of Ras al-Ghoul (Mountain of Ghosts), perched on a rocky bluff rising up from the plains. This dramatic fort predates the arrival of Islam and was once part of a chain of desert castles across North Africa that communicated with each other through messengers and smoke signals. When the forces of Islam swept through Ghadames in 668, the majority of Ghadamsis converted. Those who didn't were driven from the town and took refuge at Ras al-Ghoul. The Islamic soldiers encircled the castle and placed it under siege, not realising that a secret well within the remote redoubt could keep the rebels alive indefinitely. After negotiations took place, a compromise was reached and the siege was lifted.

The castle originally consisted of three concentric walls and the stone skeletons of the castle's rooms remain visible. Be very careful when climbing up as the deep shaft of the ancient well is uncomfortably close to the top of the path. From the eastern side you can see (100m away to the east) the barely visible low remains of a camp used by Islamic fighters during the siege; a further 100m east are the remains of the camp's cemetery, containing 13 graves. Perhaps not surprisingly, given their losses, the Arabs also called the site Jebel ash-Shohada (Mountain of the Dead). It was from the camp that the ghostly legend of Ras al-Ghoul was born as the soldiers reported seeing strange lights coming from the castle.

Elsewhere from the summit, the views are simply superb. The undulating sand dunes to the north and west lie within Algerian territory, while just 7km away to the northeast is the Tunisian town of Burj el-Khadra. It's one of the most accessible places in Africa to watch the sunset in three countries.

To the west, you can see a sandy track running over a low ridge of uniform hills, along which are a series of Algerian border posts. Beyond the ridge, the track leads to a large sand dune (about 4km away) which is in a small finger of Libyan territory surrounded by Algeria. The sunsets here can be stunning.

If you've hired a guide for Ghadames, the full-day service usually includes a sunset trip to Ras al-Ghoul.

Touneen

The small village of Touneen, 3.5km west of Ghadames, has a mud-brick old city and, in terms of style, is like Ghadames in miniature – with some covered areas and far fewer tourists. That said, the village is in far worse condition than Ghadames, save for its mosque, which remains in use.

Ain ad-Debanah (Ain M'Jazzam)

Some 39km east of Ghadames along the road to Derj, a rough track leads for 9km to the two salt lakes of Ain ad-Debanah (also known as Ain M'Jazzam). The lakes in the Idehan Ubari in the Fezzan are more beautiful but if you won't be venturing that far south, this may be your only opportunity to swim in a desert (salt) lake.

INTO THE SAHARA

Although you could take the paved road from Ghadames to Sebha and beyond, well-frequented desert trails head south and southeast deep into the Sahara across the forbidding Hamada al-Hamra. Such deep-desert expeditions are not to be undertaken lightly and definitely not without an experienced local guide. If you're crossing in winter, night-time temperatures can plunge well below zero, so come prepared. For many, however, it's worth it. As one traveller wrote to Lonely Planet after crossing from Al-Aweinat to Ghadames:

> The sand is orange pink, the mountains high and out of HG Lovecroft's books. Out of this world. After three days of Garamantian graffiti...and caves containing drinkable rainwater, on to Al-Aweinat. Four days pass as we drive northwards along the Algerian border. The medina of rocks and sand, with streets and avenues made by solid high rocks takes our breath away. The Tuareg call it Madrgat. Teas in the desert, bread baked in the sand, the full moon. At the end we reached Ghadames, the jewel of the desert.
>
> *Christina Koutoulaki, Greece*

Ghadames to Al-Aweinat

There are a number of reasons to take the direct route south from **Ghadames**, not the least of which is that, at journey's end, you're at the gateway to the Jebel Acacus (p198), Wadi Meggedet (p193), and Ghat (p194) without needing to double back via Ubari and Sebha. Far more romantically, there's the cachet of crossing a largely uninhabited stretch of the Sahara. That said, the landscapes, though harshly beautiful, lack the epic scale of routes further east and elsewhere in the Libyan Sahara.

The main route – which no longer crosses or shadows the Algerian border due to a dispute between Libya and Algeria – leads south across the **Hamada al-Hamra** (roughly 310km), the western reaches of the **Idehan Ubari** (Ubari Sand Sea; 80km) and then a rocky landscape (210km) into Ghat. Within these broad designations there are a variety of landscapes. When we crossed, recent rains had left the shallow wadis of the Hamada bathed in a tinge of green, and

THE HAMADA AL-HAMRA

The Hamada al-Hamra – the Red Plain of northwestern Libya – is an unrelenting void, as emptied of landmarks as of signs of life. Nothing catches the eye. Perspective is difficult to grasp. But there are moments of absolute clarity when eternity begins just beyond the car door.

And yet, the Hamada owes its existence to water. When the rains ceased and the Sahara began to dry out around 4000 years ago, the rivers which once flowed from the mountains of the central Sahara to the sea dried out. They left behind mountain debris carried down onto the plateaus, eroded landscapes and gravel plains like the Hamada. This great tableland of sedimentary limestone, newly exposed to unimpeded Saharan winds, was thereafter polished smooth as all loose debris was scoured away by wind and sand.

The dimensions of the Hamada are impressive, stretching almost 500km from west to east and 300km from the foothills of the Jebel Nafusa in the north to the cliffs of the Jebel Hasawinah in the south, a total area of around 90,000 sq km. Sand seas get all the attention, but in actual fact barely one-ninth of the Sahara rises as sand dunes, and sand covers just one-fifth of the desert's surface. As such, gravel plains like the Hamada are the Sahara's truest terrain.

To see the Hamada at its most extreme, the route from Derj to Idri (below) perfectly catches that sense of uninterrupted emptiness, while the western reaches of the Hamada between Ghadames and Al-Aweinat (opposite) have more subtle variations of topography.

there were isolated sand dunes and the occasional prehistoric **rock engraving** littered along the route. In the northern Hamada, local shepherds roam from November to March with their flocks of sheep; as spring approaches, large family groups join them for ritual shearing of the sheep and festive feast.

There's a natural gas field in the western reaches of the Hamada (from where gas is piped to a refinery on the coast near Zuara and on to Italy) so don't be surprised if you come across large trucks crossing a semi-paved road on your first day (if you're coming from the north). The last stretch of the journey into **Al-Aweinat** is becoming easier by the day as an oil company grades the road to its oil camps and rigs.

A couple of points worth watching out for as you travel south are the eerie vestiges of a **petrified forest** (N 28° 25′ 06.42″ E 10° 36′ 43.47″) and, further south, the fresh-water well of **Bir Helou** (N 26° 42′ 09.49″ E 10° 18′ 29.06″) which has a resident cat and a caretaker who appreciates gifts of cigarettes or bread.

To make this crossing requires a minimum of three days and two nights, although you may spend three nights sleeping in the desert if you leave after lunch from Ghadames on your first day. The drivers of the Paris–Dakar Rally, of course, routinely make the journey in one day.

Derj to Ubari

Although you can also begin this route in Ghadames, we like to begin the crossing from **Derj**. That's because it takes you through the heart of the **Hamada al-Hamra**, one of the most extreme desert territories on earth (see above). Unlike the more undulating western reaches of the Hamada on the Ghadames to Al-Aweinat route, here the Hamada is unrelentingly flat and an extraordinary evocation of the Sahara's vast, featureless plateaus.

We suggest that you camp the first night in the Hamada to truly appreciate the epic scale of this empty land. On the second day, you drop down off the western ridges of the Jebel al-Hasawinah; at one point a sign warns: 'Your vehicle must be safe before go'. You'll also pass by a windswept **well** surrounded by abandoned mud dwellings en route to **Idri** (p183) at the eastern end of the Wadi ash-Shatti. From Idri, trails enter the **Idehan Ubari** (Ubari Sand Sea). This enormous sand sea has some of the most spectacular dune-scapes in the Libyan Sahara. On your second night, you should definitely camp in this wonderful cathedral of shifting sand.

The 'easier' route across the sands heads roughly southwest to **Ubari** (p191), although more challenging routes abound. From Ubari, most people head along the Wadi al-Hayat to **Tekerkiba** (p186) and sleep the third night close to the **Ubari Lakes** (p187).

Fezzan & the Sahara

The Sahara is nowhere more beautiful (or accessible) than in Libya. It's possible that no other Saharan country has such a stunning variety of desert landscapes.

In the far southwest, the Jebel Acacus is at once hauntingly beautiful and one of the most important open-air galleries of prehistoric rock art on earth. Nearby, at least in relative desert terms, are the unearthly rock formations of Wadi Meggedet. Further east, the sand seas of Wan Caza, Murzuq and Ubari are enchanted showpieces of nature's artistry. Hidden among the dunes of the latter are the Ubari Lakes, which carry more than a whiff of fantasy. And then there are the unique, black volcanic sands of Waw al-Namus or, as far southeast as you can go in Libya, the gloriously remote wadis of Jebel al-Uweinat.

But this is also a land with a fascinating human history. The trade routes of the Libyan Sahara had strong links to the great empires of central and west Africa. The oases of the interior – small explosions of fertility in the midst of great expanses of desert wasteland – spawned towns such as Ghat, which endure to this day, holding out as redoubts against the vast Sahara. Improbably it was in the Fezzan, close to the modern settlement of Germa, that the great civilisation of the Garamantians flourished and, for almost 1400 years, made the desert bloom.

The Sahara is also the land of the Tuareg, the former nomads of the central Sahara. This proud and hardy people, once the feared protectors and pillagers of caravans, continue to inhabit the remotest of areas, eking out a harsh existence from animal husbandry, small crops and, increasingly, tourism.

HIGHLIGHTS

- Watch the sunset from above the south bank of **Umm al-Maa** (p188), one of the most beautiful of the Ubari Lakes
- Explore the glorious rocky monoliths and millennia-old rock art of the **Jebel Acacus** (p198)
- Discover the dark heart of the Sahara at unforgettable **Waw al-Namus** (p206)
- Escape the crowds amid the bizarre rock formations of **Wadi Meggedet** (p193)
- Get so far off the beaten track that there is no track at **Jebel al-Uweinat** (p209)
- Find the perfect sand dune and thousands more just like it in **Idehan Murzuq** (p203)
- Contemplate a campfire alongside a silent Tuareg while shooting stars light up the sky close to **Wadi Methkandoush** (p204)

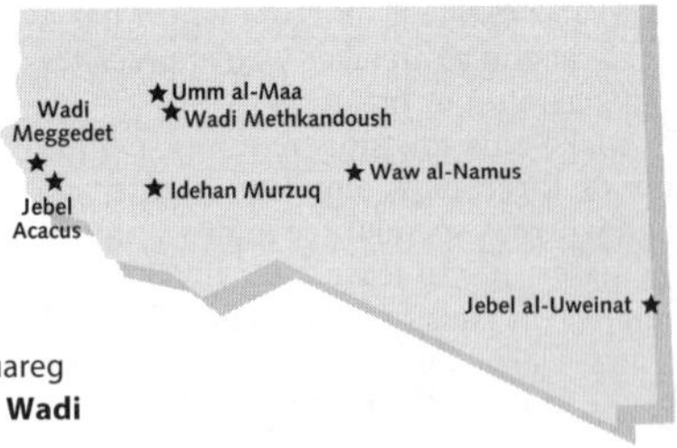

Maps

Navigating the Sahara requires good maps and an experienced local guide. A satellite-generated Global Positioning System (GPS) can also come in handy, but it's no substitute for good local knowledge – a GPS can point you in the right direction but can't tell what lies in between, and hence the most appropriate route.

Maps of the Sahara are notoriously inexact and, with two exceptions, most are insufficient for navigating. For the Jebel Acacus, the outstanding *Jebel Acacus – Tourist Map & Guide* (1:100,000), published by **EWP** (www.ewpnet.com), is based on satellite maps, is exceptionally detailed, locates most rock art sites and has commentary in both English and French. It can be purchased for UK£10 from **West Col Productions** (☎ 01491-681284; Copse House, Goring Heath, Reading RG8 7SA, UK).

The Jebel Acacus map is based on the old Russian survey maps (1:200,000) from the 1970s. They may be in Cyrillic but they're still the best maps for Saharan navigation. They can be difficult to track down; try **Stanfords** (☎ 020-7836 1321; www.stanfords.co.uk).

The other, larger-scale maps that cover the Sahara give a vaguely accurate picture although few tracks or topographical features are shown. The better-ones include

THE ERA OF EUROPEAN EXPLORATION

Of the most important expeditions to discover the true course of the Niger or Nile Rivers, or to reach fabled Timbuktu, many began in Tripoli and crossed the Libyan Sahara. With much of the funding coming from Britain, the British Consulate in Tripoli (see p86) became the scheming hub from which many of the following explorers radiated.

A theological student from Germany, **Frederick Hornemann** left Cairo in 1798 posing as a Muslim in a caravan of merchants. He passed through Al-Jaghbub, Awjila and Tmissah before reaching Murzuq on 17 November 1798, about 10 weeks after leaving Cairo. He became very ill, was forced to stay in Murzuq for seven months, before finally joining a caravan to Katsina (Nigeria). He wrote a letter to the Africa Association on 6 April 1799 in which he told them not to begin searching for him for three years. He was never heard from again. To get a more detailed picture of his Libyan adventures, read *Journal of Frederick Hornemann's Travels From Cairo to Mourzouk 1797–8*.

Hugh Clapperton, a naval lieutenant from Edinburgh, set out from Tripoli in early 1822. Accompanied by Walter Oudney and Dixon Denham, his plan was to reach the kingdom of Bornu (Lake Chad). Clapperton was laid low by malaria in Murzuq but during his recovery made forays to Germa and Ghat. The party laboured on to Lake Chad and two of them returned to tell the tale of a journey that was 'distressing beyond description to both camels and men'. Oudney died while trying to reach the Niger River. His Journals are published as *Difficult and Dangerous Roads*.

Major Alexander Gordon Laing started out from Tripoli in 1825 headed for Timbuktu. His route took him through Ghadames and then across the Algerian Sahara. He was the first Western traveller to reach the former city of riches, but was murdered soon after leaving Timbuktu on his return journey. His notes were never found.

Travelling under the banner of the British Bible Society, **James Richardson** left Tripoli in August 1845 and travelled from Ghadames due south to Ghat, where he was warmly welcomed by the sultan who presented him with gifts for Queen Victoria. His second expedition, in 1850 on behalf of the British Government, included a young Heinrich Barth (see below). Richardson was, however, a difficult man and the party members travelled separately and slept in separate camps. Barth and Richardson travelled together to Murzuq and Ghat before going their separate ways.

Arguably the doyenne of European Saharan explorers, most of **Heinrich Barth's** travels from 1849 to 1855 took him beyond Libya, especially to Agadez and Timbuktu. He was one of the first Europeans to report rock carvings in the Tassili-n-Ajjer, very close to the Jebel Acacus. But he nearly didn't make it that far (see The Legends of Kaf Ajnoun, p194).

Alexandrine Tinné, a wealthy Dutch heiress, arrived in Murzuq in 1869 with a large caravan (she travelled in style) and a bodyguard of two Dutch sailors. An Ahaggar Tuareg chieftain promised to escort her from Murzuq to Ghat, but a few days into the journey he attacked her, slashed off her hand and left her to slowly bleed to death.

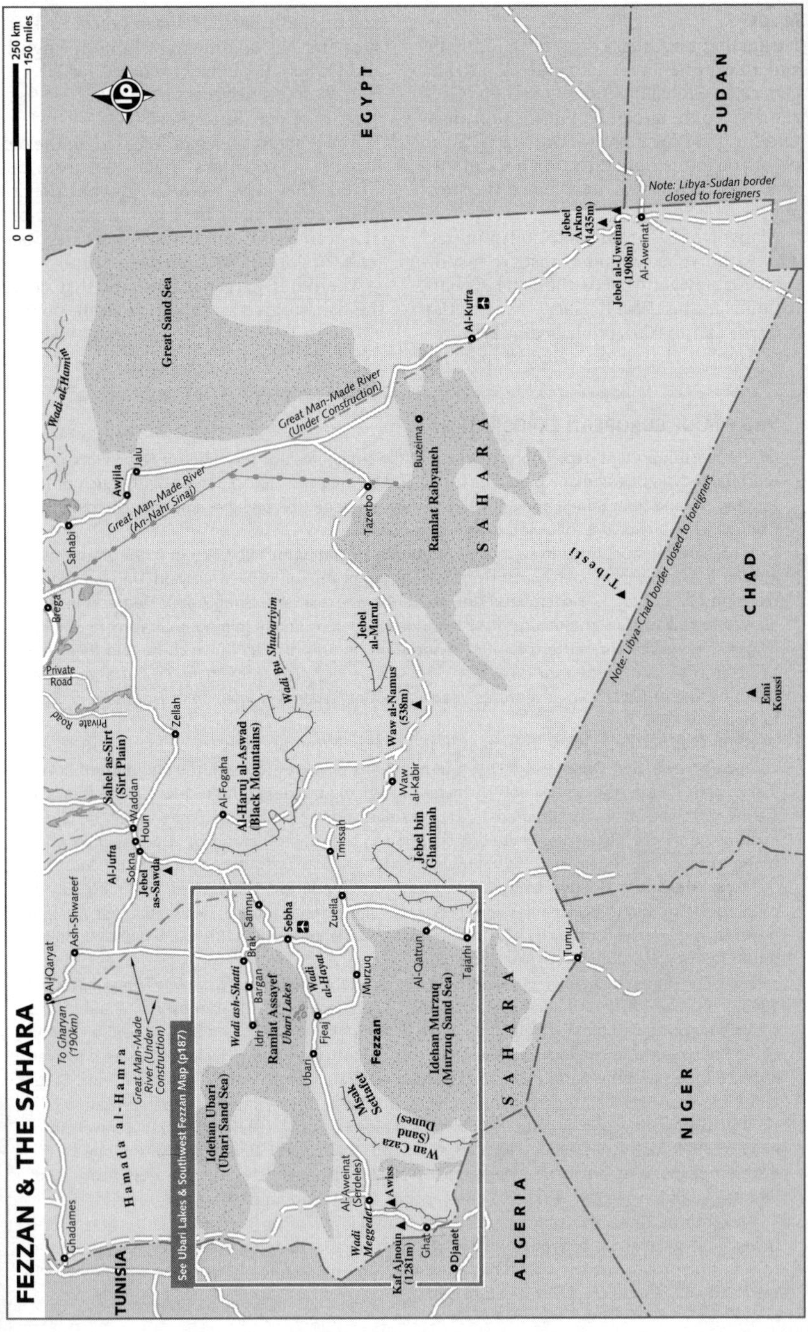
FEZZAN & THE SAHARA
0 250 km
0 150 miles
EGYPT
SUDAN
CHAD
NIGER
ALGERIA
TUNISIA
SAHARA
SAHARA
Note: Libya-Sudan border closed to foreigners
Note: Libya-Chad border closed to foreigners
Great Sand Sea
Wadi al-Hamim
Great Man-Made River (Under Construction)
Great Man-Made River (An-Nahr Sinai)
Great Man-Made River (Under Construction)
Jebel Arkno (1435m)
Jebel al-Uweinat (1908m)
Al-Aweinat
Al-Kufra
Buzeima
Ramlat Rabyaneh
Tazerbo
Jalu
Awjila
Sahabi
Brega
Tibesti
Emi Koussi
Private Road
Private Road
Zellah
Sahel as-Sirt (Sirt Plain)
Waddan
Houn
Sokna
Al-Jufra
Jebel as-Sawda
Al-Fogaha
Al-Haruj al-Aswad (Black Mountains)
Wadi Bu Shubariyim
Jebel al-Maruf
Waw al-Namus (538m)
Waw al-Kabir
Tmissah
Jebel bin Ghanimah
Ash-Shwareef
Al-Qaryat
To Gharyan (190km)
Hamada al-Hamra
Ghadames
See Ubari Lakes & Southwest Fezzan Map (p187)
Samnu
Sebha
Zueila
Brak
Bargan
Wadi ash-Shatti
Idri
Ramlat Assayef
Ubari Lakes
Wadi al-Hayat
Murzuq
Al-Qatrun
Tajarhi
Fjeaj
Ubari
Fezzan
Idehan Murzuq (Murzuq Sand Sea)
Idehan Ubari (Ubari Sand Sea)
Msak Settafet
Wan Caza (Sand Dunes)
Al-Aweinat (Serdeles)
Awiss
Wadi Meggedet
Kaf Ajnoun (1281m)
Ghat
Djanet
Tumu

FEZZAN & THE SAHARA

Sahara & Environs (1:2,200,000) by International Travel Maps and *953 – Africa North & West* by Michelin (1:4,000,000).

Another excellent resource for Sahara expeditions is *Sahara Overland – a route and planning guide* by Chris Scott. Its section on Libya includes seven detailed route descriptions (including GPS coordinates).

SEBHA REGION

Sebha is most people's gateway to the Libyan Sahara and although the most evocative Saharan landscapes lie further south, some rarely visited sites in the vicinity allow you to escape the crowds that converge on the Sahara's better-known sights. According to some sources, this is the most arid place on earth. But don't let that deter you.

SEBHA سبها

☎ 071 / pop 130,244

Sebha is the largest settlement in the Libyan Sahara and now serves as a sprawling garrison town. It's also an important transit point for Saharan travel, whether by tourists or heavily laden trucks bearing human and other cargo for destinations as far afield as Chad, Niger and Algeria. As a result, it's an incongruous, sometimes fascinating mix of tour buses with digital-camera-toting tourists, dusty sub-Saharan Africans waiting in the shade for passage north or south and cheap (often smuggled) goods that have arrived from across the desert.

It's a bit too far from the action to make a convenient base for exploring the southwest of the country, but overnighting here enables you to break up the long journey to or from the coast, have a hot shower, check your internet and change money.

Orientation & Information

It's unlikely that you'll need to stray beyond the two main streets, Sharia Jamal Abdul Nasser and Sharia Mohammed Megharief, which run parallel to each other through the heart of town. Sharia Jamal Abdul Nasser is the extension of the road in from Murzuq and Germa.

The *jawazzat* (passport office) is in the unpaved street north of Sharia Mohammed Megharief, just north of Mat'am Acacus. **Masraf al-Jamahiriya** (Jamahiriya Bank; Sharia Jamal Abdul Nasser) and **Masraf as-Sahari** (Al-Sahari Bank; Sharia Mohammed Megharief) both change money.

The post office is in a small street connecting the two main streets not far from Funduq Kala; look for the huge telecommunications tower. Private telephone offices, some doubling as internet cafés, abound along the two main streets. There's also an internet café in Funduq Fezzan (see p182).

Sights

Not much really. The **Italian fort** that overlooks the town doubles as a military base and anywhere in town you should be very wary of pointing a camera in its direction.

The **Point of Light School** (Sharia Mohammed Megharief) is where a young Muammar Qaddafi studied secondary school before being expelled, probably for organising demonstrations against government inaction during the 1956 Suez crisis. The school is at the eastern end of Sharia Mohammed Megharief and, as it's still in use, not open to visitors. Local students are, however, constantly reminded of their famous forerunner by oil paintings depicting scenes from his life in his old classroom.

Sleeping

Sebha has a reasonable range of accommodation, although service with a smile is difficult to find at any of the hotels in town; staff are usually civil at best, but don't expect to be bowled over by the warmest of welcomes.

Buyut ash-Shabaab (Youth Hostel; ☎ 621178; off Trigh al-Tarablus al-Katib; dm 5LD) After a bright start a few years back, this hostel has not been very well maintained and can be quite grubby. It's often filled with dusty sub-Saharan Africans recovering from their ordeal of crossing the Sahara.

Fezzan Park (☎/fax 632860; mobile 0925131967; Sharia al-Jamahiriya; huts per person with shared bathroom 10LD, ste 50LD;) Arguably the best of the Sahara's camps, this appealing place is 10.8km southwest of Sebha off the road to Ubari. It offers the usual huts, which are generally airtight, but most of the beds will have you longing for the comfort of a sand bed amid the dunes. The suites will seem like paradise after dusty desert trails. If we have one complaint it's that the high volume of tourist traffic that passes through

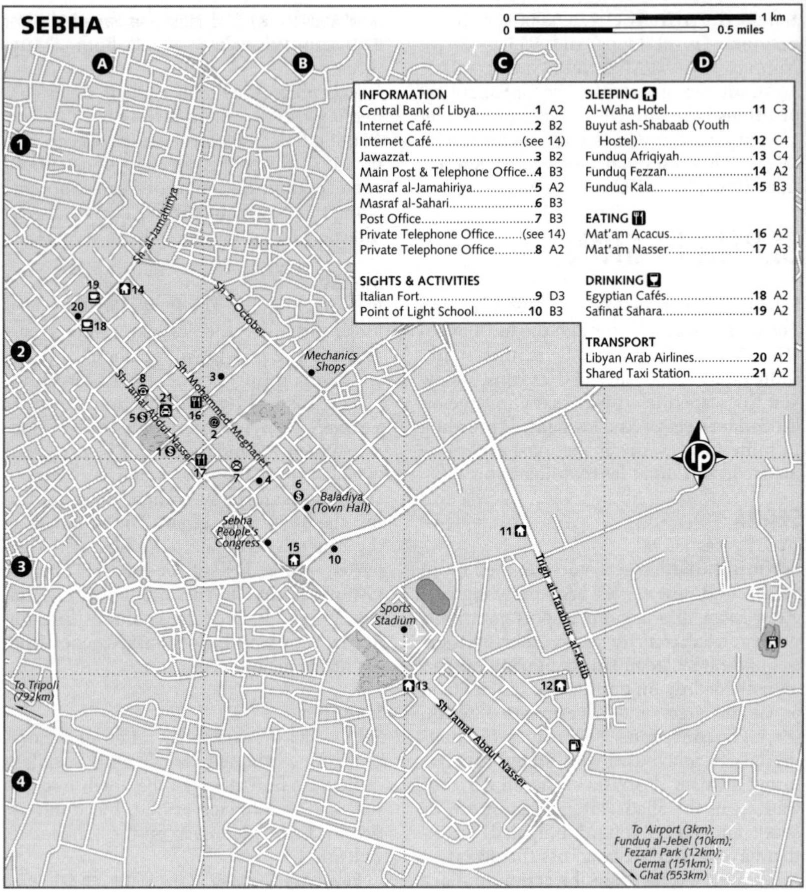

here is taking its toll on the service which is not as efficient as it once was. There's also a swimming pool and a zoo with desert animals. The roaming ostriches are more inquisitive than dangerous. Breakfast costs 5LD.

Funduq al-Jebel (☎ 629470/9; s/d 25/35LD; ❄) This fully renovated hotel of long standing occupies a hilltop location around 10km from town, with sweeping views over the barren plains and palm groves – sunset is the time you'll most appreciate staying here. The rooms aren't all that exciting, but they're comfortable. The corners of each floor are best for views from the balconies. Check a few rooms if you can, as some of the bathrooms are a bit iffy. The **restaurant** (meals 12-15LD) isn't bad if you can't face the long drive into town.

Funduq Fezzan (☎ 631910, fax 628549; Sharia al-Jamahiriya; s/d/tr/ste 25/35/45/60LD) Originally built for Libyans in town for government business, Funduq Fezzan (formerly Funduq al-Mehari) has changed its name but left the rooms as they were. Perhaps it did so out of nostalgia, but we would prefer to see an overhaul. The rooms are run-down, tired and not everything works, but the suites could easily sleep four and are large, airy and fine for a night. Service has improved since we were last here, but that's not saying much.

Funduq Afriqiya (☎ 623952, fax 631550; Sharia Jamal Abdul Nasser; s/d/tr/ste with private bathroom 25/40/65/80LD; ❄) The recently renovated Funduq Afriqiya has large rooms that are unexciting but comfortable. There are some fine views over town from the upper floors.

Funduq Kala (☎ 637181; alkalaa@winzrik.com; Sharia Jamal Abdul Nasser; s/d/ste with breakfast 40/55/90LD;) Don't be put off by the cavernous, 1970s-era public spaces of this hotel, because, thankfully, it has spent most of its renovation dollars on the rooms, which are among the best in Sebha. Rooms are semi-luxurious, at least by the standards of southern Libya. All are spacious and some have balconies overlooking a lovely shady courtyard.

Al-Waha Hotel (Funduq al-Waha; ☎ 636424; alwaha_hotel@yahoo.com; Trigh al-Tarablus al-Katib; s/d/ste with breakfast 50/65/125LD;) Sebha's newest hotel is also its best, with excellent rooms, friendlier staff than at most Sebha hotels and bathrooms that sparkle. Not surprisingly, it's often full. Hopefully, if it keeps doing what it's doing, it might encourage other hotels in town to lift their game. Meals here cost 15LD to 25LD.

Eating & Drinking

Aside from the hotels, most eating places are along Sharia Jamal Abdul Nasser or Sharia al-Jamahiriya. Don't expect fine dining, but at least Sebha is generally cheaper than other Libyan cities.

Mat'am Acacus (☎ 634934; Sharia Mohammed Megharief; meals from 6.50LD; lunch & dinner) It's hard to see why you'd eat anywhere else in Sebha, because this is one of the few places in town that seems to understand tourists. The dining area and bathrooms are spotless, the service is welcoming and the quality of the food is first-rate, if not particularly imaginative. Great coffee is another bonus. In short, it's an oasis in what is otherwise an uninspiring town.

Mat'am an-Nasser (☎ 628220; Sharia Jamal Abdul Nasser; meals from 10LD; lunch & dinner) Although not quite as impressive as the Mat'am Acacus, Mat'am an-Nasser is also good; the atmosphere in the upstairs air-con dining room is a bit plain, despite the eerie blue aviary. However, it produces reasonable food and the service is well intentioned if a little quirky at times. It also serves up a range of sweets, such as baklava (4LD per kilogram), and snacks such as chicken *shwarma* (1LD) in the bright and breezy downstairs dining area.

Safinat Sahara (Sharia al-Jamahiriya; hamburgers 1LD; 11am-3pm & 6pm-1am) Open late, Safinat Sahara is usually filled with locals. It's more a tea and *tawle* (backgammon) kind of place, but it does snacks, too.

Egyptian cafés (Sharia Jamal Abdul Nasser; 11am-1am) On the corner opposite Libyan Arab Airlines are two wildly busy cafés that attract a lively group of Egyptian and Libyan workers in the evenings. It's an all-male crowd; Western women will attract initial looks but little else. Options include *tawle* (free), nargileh (1LD to 2LD), tea (0.5LD) and oily *ta'amiyya* (felafel; 1.5LD). The café closest to the corner is the more appealing. As Sebha's only real nightlife, it's a good earthy place to spend an evening, although your conversation will have to compete with Egyptian movies blasting from the TV.

Getting There & Away

AIR

Libyan Arab Airlines (☎ 623875; cnr Sharia Jamal Abdul Nasser & Sharia al-Jamahiriya; 7am-2pm Sat-Thu May-Sep & 8am-3pm Sat-Thu Oct-Apr) has nightly flights to Tripoli (37.50LD) and to Benghazi (46.50LD) as well as a twice-weekly flight to Ghat (28LD), although check that the latter is indeed operating. Sebha airport is 5km southeast of the town centre.

BUS & SHARED TAXI

The bus and shared-taxi station is along Sharia Jamal Abdul Nasser in a small yard about 400m southeast of the Libyan Arab Airlines office. There are evening and morning departures to Tripoli, as well as more frequent cars to Ubari.

Getting Around

TO/FROM THE AIRPORT

Private taxis into town shouldn't cost more than 2LD to 3LD, but drivers often ask for, and won't budge from, 5LD.

WADI ASH-SHATTI وادى الشاطىء

The 139km-road through Wadi ash-Shatti is shadowed by the Jebel Hasawinah to the north and the sand dunes of the Idehan Ubari (Ubari Sand Sea or, as it is also known here, the Ramlat Assayef) to the south. Some locals claim to be descended from the ancient Garamantian people (see p30). In small villages you may see interesting, deserted mud-brick houses, although most have been reduced to rubble. There are more beautiful wadis, but as few travellers take this route it has an appealing, out-of-the-way character.

Idri, at the far western end of the wadi, is most travellers' only experience of the Wadi, lying as it does at the convergence of trails between the Hamada al-Hamra and Idehan Ubari. Historical accounts suggest that Idri was once a beautiful place of gardens, springs, date trees and a dramatic castle. Things have definitely changed. The town was destroyed in 1836 and it now has an abandoned, end-of-the-road feel to it; all the rubbish from the wadi seems to have blown here. The castle exists only as rubble, and distant views of the sands are the town's only redeeming feature.

Expeditions south across the dunes to the Ubari lakes are possible from the villages of **Missaan** or **Al-Gurda**.

There are no tourist facilities in the wadi, although a number of basic camps were being built when we passed through.

SEBHA TO GHARYAN

The 595km road north-south from Sebha to Gharyan (see p158) is one of Libya's most monotonous. Crossing the road at two points and running alongside it in a few places is the Great Man-Made River (Al-Nahr Sinai; see The Eighth Wonder of the World, p64 – a decidedly unremarkable bump in the landscape. Elsewhere only the cursory checkpoints relieve the boredom. The road is in an appalling condition close to Sebha with canyon-like potholes and ridges of asphalt that will slow your car to a careful crawl.

The dusty settlement of **Brak**, around 75km north of Sebha where the Tripoli-Sebha highway passes the entrance to Wadi ash-Shatti, is unlikely to detain you for long. It does have a 19th-century **Turkish fort**, a 20th-century **Italian fort** and a dilapidated mud-brick **old town** beyond the palm groves, but they're hardly worth your time as you speed somewhere else more interesting. If you're heading south and hungry, wait for Sebha.

The nondescript town of **Ash-Shwareef**, 277km north of Brak, has petrol and eating facilities. Mat'am Al-Qala'a isn't bad for couscous and chicken (6LD).

Al-Qaryat, a further 90km to the north, is similarly uninspiring. At the checkpoint just south of town is the turn-off for the desert road that leads across the plains to Derj (313km) and Ghadames (408km). South of the checkpoint is a petrol station and a few scattered restaurants and teahouses.

The town of **Mizda**, 130km north of Al-Qaryat (about 70km south of Gharyan), has some old mud houses that mark the **old town** and locals can usually point the way to the **House of Heinrich Barth**, where the celebrated German explorer stayed on his way south. Mizda also has a petrol station and a few sandwich and chicken restaurants along the highway. Signposted in Arabic just off the main road is **Funduq Mizda al-Siyahe** (☎ no phone; s/d/ste 25/35/45LD), which has big, airy rooms, ornate curtains and carpet that doesn't quite reach the wall. It's nothing special, but the rooms are fine for a night if you want to break up the journey.

AL-JUFRA الجفرة

Halfway between Sebha and the coast, east of the Tripoli-Sebha highway, are the three adjacent towns of the Al-Jufra oasis – Houn, Sokna and Waddan. Bizarrely, Al-Jufra was announced as the capital of Libya in 1987, but the idea never caught on and Libyans love to say that this is a great place to buy a house because the building boom that followed the announcement was not matched by subsequent demand.

If you're coming from Sebha, the last part of the journey passes through the **Jebel as-Sawda** – a wild, rocky landscape of black basalt. In contrast, the road northwest from Waddan to Abu Nijayn is lined with more than 100km of palm and olive trees, which form part of the Wadi al-Lout agricultural project.

Dates from the Al-Jufra oases are highly sought-after throughout Libya. Another reason to come is that very few travellers make it here.

Houn هون

☎ 057 / pop 19,373

Houn, 345km from Sebha, is the main town in Al-Jufra. Houn is often referred to as the migrating town, as the modern town is the fourth settlement in an area that has been occupied for the last 700 years.

The bank, post and telephone offices are along Sharia al-Jamahiriya, Houn's main street, as is the museum.

SIGHTS

The original town, called Miskan, is buried beneath the dunes 4km northwest of Houn and the second town, about 500 years old, is nearby although next to nothing remains. The third city is the **medina** of the current town and is 150 years old; it was abandoned for modern housing during the 1950s and 1960s. There is one large, typical **medina house** that was built in 1842 and has been restored.

Houn's sweet little museum, **Thakirat al-Medina** (admission 3LD; 9am-1pm & 3-6pm Tue-Sun), has a collection of local artefacts and memorabilia. It's the warehouse-like building opposite the turn-off to the old medina; ask for *'al-Mathaf'*.

FESTIVALS & EVENTS

If you happen to be in Houn at the end of February or beginning of March, you may happen upon the annual **Sweet-Making Festival**. The celebrations to herald the end of winter see the town's best cooks vie to make the most outlandish sweets and cookies. The results are later consumed by all and sundry in a wonderfully indulgent way to mark the beginning of spring.

SLEEPING

Buyut ash-Shabaab (Youth Hostel; ☎ 2040; dm 5LD) Next door to the school and run by one of the teachers, this small hostel is about 500m from the highway. The place is simple and friendly, although a bit noisy when school is in.

Funduq al-Haruj (☎ 3067, 3381; s/d 25/35LD) This oasis of relative comfort, on the main highway near the Houn hospital, is the only hotel for hundreds of kilometres in any direction. The rooms are enormous and the private bathrooms are good. Lunch or dinner costs 10LD to 20LD.

Sokna & Waddan سوكنة & ودان

pop 28,313

Sokna, a few kilometres south of Houn, became an important regional centre in the 19th century when its Arab traders and financiers were active as far afield as Murzuq and the central Sahara. In the process they often formed allegiances with the powerful Fezzan tribes of the Awlad Suleiman and Awlad Muhammad, as well as Al-Qaddhafa who were Colonel Qaddafi's forebears. The landscape around Sokna is very attractive, with palm trees and sand dunes.

Waddan, north of Houn at the crossroads where the highway splits to Misrata and Sirt, is a small and quite charming town with a picturesque ruined brick castle on the hill in its centre; it provides a panoramic view over the town and oasis. Close to the castle are some old mosques built in the local style.

AL-HARUJ AL-ASWAD الهروج الأسود

If Waw al-Namus (p206) is the dark paradise of the Sahara, then Al-Haruj al-Aswad is the black heart of Libya. Covering about 45,000 sq km in the geographical centre of Libya, 'The Black Haruj' is an immense extinct volcano that has erupted six times down through the millennia and left behind a landscape closely resembling that of Mars. A black, brooding world of granite and basalt with the occasional wadi, it's a fascinating place, although at midday it can feel like labouring across the Devil's Anvil. It's heavy, slow going and the scenery is more compelling than beautiful. Occasional gazelle, waddan and Houbara bustard (see p63) hide from local and international hunters in isolated valleys. A few prehistoric engravings dot the rocks.

There are reportedly quite extensive **petrified forests** on the east side of Al-Haruj, close to **Wadi Bu Shubariyim** off the route between Tazerbo (p207) and Zellah, although we can't confirm this.

The most easily accessible gateway town to Al-Haruj is Al-Fogaha, a sleepy village around 325km northwest of Sebha. It has a modern town with a post office and a few small grocery stores, and a mud-brick **old town** down amid the palm trees behind low sandstone buttresses. There were once 22 **freshwater springs** in Al-Fogaha and 18 remain in use. They are on the fringes of the reasonably extensive old town, which has a time-worn air, a fine white vernacular mosque and traditional houses in various stages of disrepair. Look out for the occasional black stone from Al-Haruj al-Aswad which was used in the construction of some buildings. You're likely to be the only tourist here, which is part of the town's moderate charm. One of our highlights was sitting down in the sand with the elders of the village and listening as they patiently told us their memories of the town, all the while drawing lines in the sand as they told of the arrival of Islam, the dynasties of the sultans of Fezzan and other dates of local importance – ask your guide if they can do the same.

When we visited, the mayor showed us to what he called the Funduq as-Siyahe (Tourist Hotel), but it had yet to become fully operational. It was unclear whether it would actually become a hotel, or more accurately an occasional guesthouse for travellers, but it was super-clean. The multiple mattresses were heaven after 10 days sleeping in the desert (although we did miss the stars) and even the shower produced by the problematic plumbing was as enjoyable as it was necessary.

At least one French tour company, Point Afrique (p233), offers tours to Al-Haruj; you're unlikely to come across any other travellers – something which is becoming increasingly rare in the Libyan Sahara.

IDEHAN UBARI & WADI AL-HAYAT

The most accessible of the great sand seas that give so much depth and beauty to the Libyan Sahara, the Idehan Ubari (Ubari Sand Sea, also known as the Ramlat Assayef or Ramlat Dawada) and the lakes hidden behind its dunes are Libya's most popular desert experience. You won't have the lakes to yourself, but it's nonetheless a landscape of rare beauty. And such is its scope, there are ample opportunities to escape the madding crowds when it comes to a camp site all your own.

Wadi al-Hayat, the Valley of Life, which ranges from 2km to 12km wide, is wedged between the sand sea's southern border and the brooding ridges of the Msak Settafet (Msak Setthaf). The wadi is one of the most fertile, and hence habitable, areas of the Fezzan. The underground water table lies close to the surface, allowing palms to flourish unirrigated. Once also called the Wadi al-Ajal (the Valley of Death), this is the former home of the Garamantes, a fabled civilisation that ruled the desert and made it bloom (see p30). The wadi's strategic location made an import axis of communications along the caravan routes. These days, the wadi is home to a string of towns, especially Germa, Ubari and Tekerkiba, which can provide a base for exploring the region. The main highway from Tripoli to Ghat runs through the heart of the wadi and there are good hotels and camps as well as well-stocked grocery stores ideal for kitting out your desert expedition.

FJEAJ الفجيع

☎ 0728

Fjeaj, 133km southwest of Sebha, has little to see, although a colourful **Thursday market** and the prehistoric **rock-carved giraffe** on the rocky wall across the highway from the youth hostel could detain you for a short stopover.

The **Buyut ash-Shabaab** (Youth Hostel; ☎ 2827; main highway; dm or camping 5LD) is just back from the main highway. It's a friendly place with basic though clean rooms. Guests can use the kitchen and meals are available from 6LD. Some of the staff speak French.

TEKERKIBA تكركيبة

Tekerkiba, the main gateway to the Ubari Lakes, is where you survey the steep ascent of what could be your first sand dune and, depending on your state of mind and level of experience, either get a rush of adrenaline or wonder what you've let yourself in for. Don't worry, it's nowhere near as scary as it looks and many would say not at all. There are three camps (signposted in English off the main highway) that face the wall of dunes on the northern fringe of Tekerkiba. We recommend using them just for a (usually) hot shower and a soft drink, because sleeping in a straw hut alongside the tyre-marked ramp of sand is no substitute for finding an isolated and perfectly sculpted sand valley of the Ubari Sand Sea beneath a canopy of stars. But some travellers don't agree. When Hugh Clapperton passed through Tekerkiba in the 1820s he remarked, 'We found a great deal of trouble getting anything to eat'. There are no such problems these days, provided you're not expecting haute cuisine.

The busy **Camping Africa Tours** (☎ 071-625594; camping/thatched hut 5/15LD, motorcycle/car 5/10LD, meals 10-15LD) has the best facilities but can get a little overrun with 4WDs and people. It's run by the alternately funky and offhand Abdul Aziz, who serves cappuccino for 1LD

UBARI LAKES & SOUTHWEST FEZZAN

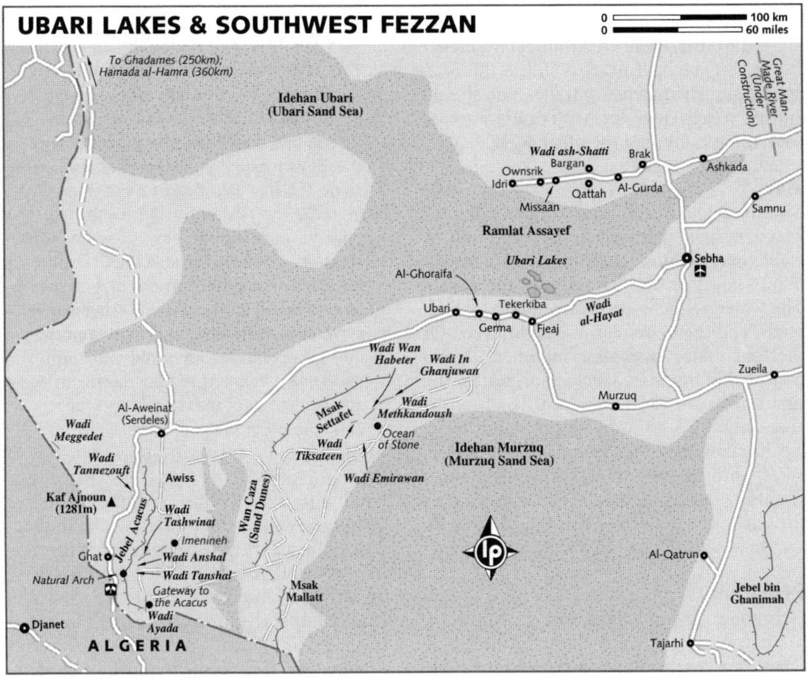

if he can be bothered. There's usually no charge to use the shower or toilets.

Also nearby are the quieter Camping Fezzan and Tekerkiba Tourist Camping; the latter in particular tends to avoid the convoys that stream off the dunes during peak season.

THE UBARI LAKES أوبارى بحيرات

Whether you travelled to Sebha by plane or passed long days across monotonous desert plains, your first sight of the Ubari Lakes is not one you'll ever forget. It's the aesthetic relief of the deepest blue in a land engulfed by sand, the miracle of the sound of water lapping at the shore in the desert's heart, the sense that our childhood imaginings of the Sahara's beauty were not misplaced. If you've spent time in other Saharan towns and become disillusioned with how humankind has tamed the beauty of the oases with sprawling towns of no discernible beauty, the Ubari Lakes are an evocative antidote. Yes, the lakes are salty – so salty, in fact, that swimming here is a buoyant experience almost as curious as Jordan's Dead Sea – but there are freshwater wells in the vicinity and the stunning visual effect is everything. And yes, the lakes can get overrun with convoys of tourist-bearing 4WDs, but the combination of sand dunes, waters of the deepest blue and palm trees will more than compensate.

There are at least 11 lakes in this eastern section of the sand sea, although many have dried up as a result of evaporation and lowered water tables from intensive agriculture in the nearby Wadi al-Hayat. One of the most celebrated lakes, Mandara (p189), has also all but disappeared. But Mavo, Gebraoun and Umm al-Maa remain as picturesque as ever. The four lakes are clustered in pairs, with Mavo and Gebraoun separated from Umm al-Maa and Mandara by a massive ridge of sand – crossing from Gebraoun to Umm al-Maa requires an exhilarating steep descent and plenty of fine photo opportunities.

Although the lakes are splendid places by day, resist the temptation to sleep here by night as mosquito swarms are an unpleasant feature.

For those of you driving your own vehicles, note that there are a number of smaller ridges that you have to cross and, as this is an area of surprisingly heavy traffic, you should approach each ridge-line with caution in case something is coming the other way.

Mavo مافو

The closest lake to Tekerkiba (about 40km), Mavo nestles against a high ridge-line of sand, overlooking countless small undulations away in the distance to the north. The water's edge is also surrounded by high reeds, and there are plenty of palm trees. Of the four major lakes described here, Mavo is probably the least spectacular, but as the first one most travellers reach, you'll probably only think so in hindsight. With tourists has come another feature of visiting the lakes, with unobtrusive Tuareg silver merchants laying out an array of jewellery pieces for sale at the eastern end of the lake. There are three other lakes, now dry, in the area.

Gebraoun قبرعون

Gebraoun, around 3km east of Mavo, is many travellers' favourite among the Ubari Lakes, not least because an abandoned village fans out from the western shore and the wall of sand rising precipitously up from the southern bank is one of the highest in the region. Gebraoun is also one of the largest of the Ubari Lakes, measuring about 250m by 300m, and is supposedly deep; when we asked some locals how deep it was, their answer was no more enlightening than 'very deep'.

The ruins of the town of Old Gebraoun (whose name means the Grave of Aoun) are slowly returning to the sands with gaping doorways and a generally abandoned air. In 1991, after centuries of habitation, the population of Old Gebraoun was relocated by the Libyan Government to the bleak settlement of Gebraoun al-Jadid (New Gebraoun), which is on the main highway in Wadi al-Hayat. Among the few recognisable buildings are two mosques with squat minarets, and a school. On the dune overlooking the town and the lake is a small tomb marked with a flag; this is the last resting place of the local notable Aoun, who gave the area its name.

Gebraoun lake is the best Ubari Lake for a swim and there are plenty of access points around the shore-line. Once immersed, you'll notice the curious sensation of water at an agreeable temperature close to the surface with scalding temperatures just a few feet below. If you do decide to swim, please be discreet about your bathing costume (preferably a T-shirt and shorts) to avoid transgressing local sensibilities. Another reason why Gebraoun is most swimmers' destination of choice is the freshwater well in the camp on the north side of the lake – use its water in moderation, but enough to avoid spending the rest of the day caked in salt. And one final piece of advice to would-be swimmers: don't even think of shaving on the morning of your visit.

There's a small camp at the western end of the lake where you can get tea, buy local souvenirs and rest in the shade as the day heats up. Camp Winzrik, the larger camp on the northern shore, also has a kitchen which can be used by visitors, simple meals (around 15LD) and soft drinks and, wait for it, skis and a snowboard (5LD). If it's your first time, practise on some of the smaller dunes nearby before attempting the main hurtling descent behind the lake. Camp Winzrik's friendly Tuareg caretaker, Sheikh, loves to serenade visitors.

> **THE WORM-EATERS OF GEBRAOUN**
>
> The inhabitants of Old Gebraoun were members of the Dawada tribe who went by the none-too-charitable name of 'Worm-Eaters'. The epithet has been in use since the British explorer, Walter Oudney, became the first European to visit the lake in 1822. The reason for the name is that their diet once included tiny red shrimp-like creatures that were found in the lake's shallows and that thrived in the high salinity levels. Fishing for the shrimps was the preserve of women who pounded their catch into cakes, which they sun-dried. Surplus cakes were exchanged, along with dates and other fruits of the oasis, for the tobacco and olive oil of passing Tuareg.

Umm al-Maa أم الماء

It's time to come clean: this is our favourite of the Ubari Lakes. Umm al-Maa (the name means 'Mother of Water') is magnificent, a narrow, elongated stretch of water surrounded by closely packed palm trees and with a backdrop of perfectly sculpted sand dunes in the vicinity and small clusters of palm trees petering off to the horizon. As a smaller lake and much less open-sided than the others, it has an intimate feel to it and is an idyllic spot. After a number of visits where our photos didn't quite match the beautiful reality that we remembered, we've finally worked out the trick – the best photos are to be taken just before sunset from the steep ridge of sand that runs the length of Umm al-Maa's southern shore. Breathtaking.

As this is one of the more popular lakes, plenty of Tuareg handicraft sellers spread out their wares not far from the eastern shore.

Mandara مندره

Mandara, once one of the most stunning of the Ubari Lakes, is now almost entirely devoid of water. This seemingly irreversible process is a shame for many reasons, not least because the lake was not so long ago renowned for the changing colour of its water: from brilliant shades of green and blue to red, depending on the time of day. Like Gebraoun, it used to be surrounded by a small village, but the inhabitants were forced to leave in 1991. The buildings are now derelict and, with the receding water line, contribute to the sad sense of a dying place. The dry lakes of Umm al-Mahsan and Atroun are also in the same area.

The views towards the densely clustered palm trees of Mandara remain picturesque, especially from the sand ridges to the north and west. For now, Mandara remains on most travellers' itineraries, but that's really only because it lies on the main route from Umm a-Maa to Wadi al-Hayat.

THINGS THEY SAID ABOUT... THE SAHARAN CLIMATE

> The climate of Fezzan is at no season temperate or agreeable. During the summer the heat is intense; and when the wind blows from the south is scarcely supportable, even by the natives. The winter might be moderate were it not for the prevalence of a bleak and penetrating north wind during that season of the year, and which chilled and drove to the fire not only the people of the place, but even myself, the native of a northern country.
>
> *Frederick Hornemann,* Travels from Cairo to Mourzouk 1797–8

GERMA جرمة

☎ 0729

Almost everyone who visits the Libyan Sahara ends up passing through Germa at some point. Although the main section of town along the highway is largely unattractive, the city has a rich history. This was once the capital of the Garamantian Empire (p30) which bequeathed it the mud-brick ruins of the ancient capital of Garama, and subsequently a terrific museum. With an excellent hotel and a few good camps dotted around town, Germa can also make a good base for exploring the area.

Orientation & Information

The residential area of Germa is north of the Tripoli-Ghat highway, although most of the facilities are along the highway. At the turn-off to the paved road running south over the Msak Settafet to the desert is a petrol station and nearby are a couple of hotels, basic restaurants and the museum.

Germa is not a good place to change money as the town's handful of banks aren't always willing to do so.

Sights

GARAMA

Ancient **Garama** (adult/child 3/1LD, camera/video 5/10LD; 🕓 8am-7pm May-Sep, 9am-5pm Oct-Apr), the ancient city of the Garamantians, is one of the most significant archaeological sites in Libya.

The initial Garamantian settlement was at Zinchecra (see p191), high on the hills of the Msak Settafet overlooking Wadi al-Ajal, as the wadi was then called), 2km south of Germa. In the 1st century AD the Garamantians moved to Garama, a new city made of stone, clay and animal dung at the foot of the sand dunes. This new location took full advantage of the natural fortifications offered by the Idehan Ubari and the mountains of the Msak Settafet. There was a lake and natural spring nearby. Garama originally had six towers within the city walls; most of the buildings that remain were added in subsequent centuries.

About 50m after entering the site is an open **square** on the left where wild horses were brought from the desert to be domesticated and then exported to Rome; the Garamantians were famous as horse breeders and herders of long-horned cattle. The square also functioned as a starting point for caravans, which carried dates, barley and wheat to exchange for Roman goods, such as wine. In their heyday, the voracious Garamantian traders controlled most central Saharan caravan routes from their base in Garama.

The newer-looking sandstone structure on the southwest side of the square was a wealthy **merchant's home**. When Islam came to Garama, Muslims moved into the old town and remodelled it. The buildings behind the merchant's house made up the **Islamic Quarter**. In this section is the modern reconstruction of the mosque and madrassa.

The **western sector** of the ruins is the oldest part of town and at least some of the buildings are believed to show traces of the original settlement. The rubble immediately northwest of the junction was once thought to be the remains of a bath built in the Roman style, but the British archaeologists excavating the site now believe it was more likely an ancient **temple**. The ramshackle **lanes** that twist out from behind the temple through the old quarter were built just wide enough to enable camels laden with saddle bags to pass through.

The old city is dominated by the large castle-like structure at the western end. This building may once have been a **Garamantian palace** containing a harem section on the far western side of the enclosed compound. When the Byzantines moved in, it was inevitably converted into a church. Little remains of either manifestation, but there are good views over the old town from the walls.

Old Garama is about 1km north of the main highway. There's a sign in English pointing to the 'Old City' opposite the petrol station on the highway.

THINGS THEY SAID ABOUT... THE GARAMANTES

> The territory is encircled by sand but this does not prevent the Garamantes from easily finding wells at a depth of about two cubits, for the waters of Mauritania flow through this region. The Garamantes build their houses from salt extracted from their mountains like stone... In the middle lies Phezania facing the solitary reaches of Africa...it seems scorched or, or else it flames as it reflects the rays of the sunup. Till now it has been impossible to trace the route leading into the territory of the Garamantes. If our reconnaissance is correct, the brigands of this nation cover their shallow wells over with sand.
>
> *Pliny the Elder,* Natural History *(1st century AD)*

MUSEUM

Germa's small but excellent **museum** (admission 3LD, camera/video 5/10LD; ⏰ 8.30am-2pm & 3-6.30pm Tue-Sun) is 50m west of the petrol station on the Tripoli-Ghat highway. It's especially notable for a good time graph showing the various eras of rock art in the region; a dramatic satellite photo showing Wadi al-Hayat wedged between the Ubari and Murzuq Sand Seas; an ancient Garamantian mummy found near Germa; photos of the prehistoric carvings from Wadi Methkandoush; a map of the region carved in rock; improbable organic shore deposits from Wan Caza; a few broken ostrich eggs from the Jebel Acacus; and a model of the cemetery of Mohammed's companions in Zueila. Some of the exhibits are illuminated by informative English labels.

Festivals & Events

In some years in March the town hosts the **Germa Festival**, which is a colourful occasion. Inhabitants of Wadi al-Hayat don traditional dress and perform local dances, all contributing to a highly festive atmosphere. Many of the children from Germa and the surrounding areas also dress up and in some performances occupy pride of place. Unfortunately no-one seems to know from one year to the next when the next festival will take place.

Sleeping & Eating

Germa's cosy little camping grounds are generally better for showering (2LD for non-guests) and eating (breakfast 5LD, lunch or dinner 10LD) after emerging from the sand than for sleeping, as night-time mosquitoes are a problem. That said, many travellers do stay here and the camps are well-equipped with simple straw huts and kitchens that can be used for a small fee.

Eirawan Camping (☎ 642413; camping 5LD, huts per person 10LD) This long-standing camping ground consists of whitewashed mud huts with thatched roofs. It has the advantage of being down a quiet side road and hence escapes the unappealing ambience of the highway. There are shared showers (with geyser-sourced hot water) and squat toilets. The covered eating area is quite pleasant. It's 250m north of the Tripoli-Ghat highway and the turn-off is 1.5km west of the petrol station. On the same side road as Eirawan Camping and closer to the highway, **Timbuktu Camp** (☎ 2416) promises to be similar once the building work has finished.

Old City Tourist Restaurant (☎ 0722-642245; camping 5LD, huts per person 10LD, meals 8-12LD) Next to the gate of ancient Garama, this laid-back restaurant has added a number of simple huts to its repertoire which makes it a good overall package, especially given its location. You can use the kitchen (4LD) and smoke a nargileh (1LD) while you wait for the afternoon heat to pass.

Tassilie Tourism Camping & Restaurant (☎ 642299; Tripoli-Ghat highway; s/d 10/20LD) The accommodation here is a tad run-down and there are only seven rooms (with private bathroom) set around a compact courtyard. The owner is friendly and there's a small restaurant doing simple meals. It's about 200m east of the museum.

Funduq Germa (☎ 642276; Tripoli-Ghat highway; s/d 15/30LD; ❄) The friendly management of Funduq Germa has gone for the utmost simplicity in its pricing system – prices are the same whether or not you have a room with air-con or a private bathroom (some with a mosaic tiled floor). It's not bad value if you can get both. The rooms are otherwise jaded.

our pick **Funduq Dar Germa** (☎ /fax 642396; www.darsahara.com; s/d 40/50LD) If you're arriving from the desert, Funduq Dar Germa will feel like the Garden of Eden. The rooms are very comfortable and the squeaky-clean private bathrooms come with, wait for it, a bathtub. The restaurant is easily the best in town and it can also arrange a picnic lunch for excursions to the lakes or elsewhere for 10LD. There's a gift shop, a small teahouse and the front terrace is most pleasant, especially when bedecked with sunflowers. It's the maroon building 50m south of the petrol station on the road to Wadi Methkandoush.

Getting There & Away

Germa is 150km southwest of Sebha; there are regular shared taxis to Ubari and Sebha.

AROUND GERMA

Almost 13km west of Germa, just after Al-Ghoraifa on the south side of the road, are the best-preserved examples of the curious square-topped pyramid Garamantian tombs known as **Ahramat al-Hattia** (admission 3LD, camera/video 5/10LD; 🕑 9.30am-1.30pm Sat-Thu, 3-5pm Fri). When the tombs were first excavated some interiors contained offering tables, stellae (stone slabs bearing a commemorative inscription), amphorae, pottery dishes and even gold and ostrich eggs. Some tombs have been reconstructed to something resembling their original form. There were once 100 tombs in the area and all are thought to have belonged to the dynasties of the Garamantian royal family, although some archaeologists claim they were first built in 3000 BC by the Garamantes' forerunners.

Other tombs that look like they are melting back into the earth lie hidden amid the palm trees on either side of the main highway between Germa and Ubari.

Alongside the road from Wadi Methkandoush as it crosses the Msak Settafet and descends into the Wadi al-Hayat are all that remains of the ancient Garamantian capital of **Zinchecra**, the forerunner to Garama. As the wadi began to dry out, the Garamantians moved their capital down into the valley and Zinchecra was thereafter used as a place of burial; the tombs that are all that remain of Zinchecra are among 50,000 that once dotted the area.

UBARI أوباری

☎ 0722 / pop 44,500

Ubari is an important regional centre and the town where many travellers emerge after crossing the Ubari Sand Sea from Idri. As such the first sight of it – a forest of palm trees of the Wadi al-Hayat set against the backdrop of the black Msak Settafet (also known here as the Jebel al-Aswad, or Black Mountains) can be quite picturesque. That

THINGS THEY SAID ABOUT...UBARI

Oubari is situated amidst well-cultivated fields and Gardens surrounded by a higher wall and in better condition than any other town in Fezzan. The houses are also in good condition as is the Castle which like all other buildings in this country is built of mud or clay though the foundation of this castle is built of rough stones. The inhabitants appear to be more plentifully supplied with the good things of this world than the rest of their countrymen.

Hugh Clapperton, Difficult & Dangerous Roads *(1822)*

said, away to the west in the sand sea and visible in the distance as you approach the descent into Ubari is an oil field. Look a little closer at the town itself and you'll soon be longing for the solitude of the sands – it's a dusty, wind-blown place lined with mechanics' workshops; sand stained black with crank grease and oil. Water shortages are a periodic problem here and palm trees have seen more fertile days.

Ubari does, however, have at least one good hotel, a couple of internet cafés and well-stocked grocery stores, and is the only town of any size between Germa and Al-Aweinat.

Orientation & Information

Ubari sprawls either side of the highway, but most of the facilities you'll need are along the main road. There's a bank just east of the fort, almost opposite the road to Ghat. The petrol station is at the eastern end of town, while the main post and public telephone office is at the western end of town; for the latter, take the highway until it reaches a T-junction, 100m west of where it branches off towards Ghat, and it's along on the right.

There are two **internet cafés** (per hr 1.50LD) 50m west of the roundabout in the town centre. Connections can be slow.

Sights

If you're here in the morning or late afternoon, the **old market** is still in use; it's just north of the main roundabout. The hybrid Turkish-Italian **fort**, 50m west of the Ghat turn-off, is worth a quick look, as is the **Tuareg Mosque**, which dates from the 19th century and is named in honour of the town's Tuareg heritage.

Sleeping & Eating

Wat Wat Camp (☎ 642471; south of Germa-Ghat highway; tents 5LD, huts with/without breakfast 13/10LD, meals 8-15LD) Reasonable huts, outdoor eating and friendly staff are the order of the day here, but like most oasis tourist camps, sleeping can mean a plague of mosquitoes.

Funduq Ubari (☎ 623095; s/d 30/35LD, meals 15LD; ❄) It's difficult to decide whether the pervasive smell of disinfectant here is reassuring or disconcerting. The beds also sag prodigiously and the atmosphere is that of a typical government hotel – adequate but depressing.

Funduq Qala'a (☎ 626000; castle_obari@hotmail.com; Germa-Ghat highway; s/d with shared bathroom 30/40LD; ❄) Ubari's most atmospheric choice, this converted castle has tidy rooms that are extremely comfortable for this region. The castle origins can mean some rooms are a little cell-like but it's very well maintained and the courtyard's an antidote to the bleakness of the town surrounds. The meals (15LD) are arguably the best in town although nothing that will live too long in the memory.

Apart from the camp and two hotels, basic restaurants are found all along the highway. They serve couscous, (sometimes scrawny) chicken and not much else.

Getting There & Away

Germa is 60km west of Germa and 262km northeast of Al-Aweinat (Serdeles). From the shared-taxi station, about 100m east of the fort, taxis run infrequently to Ghat (four hours, 362km) via Al-Aweinat (three hours) and to Sebha (2½ hours, 190km) via Germa (30 minutes).

SOUTHWEST FEZZAN

Home to the extraordinary natural wonders of Jebel Acacus, Wadi Meggedet, Idehan Murzuq and Wan Caza, the old caravan towns of Ghat and Murzuq and some of the finest open-air galleries of prehistoric rock art anywhere in the Sahara, Libya's far southwestern corner is where the Libyan Sahara comes alive. Spend as long here as you can.

AL-AWEINAT (SERDELES) العوينات

☎ 0716

The small town of Al-Aweinat (which also goes by the lovely Tuareg name of Serdeles) is one of the more pleasant oasis towns of the Libyan Sahara. It's not that there's anything to see here, but its tree-lined streets, excellent camp and convenient location give it a more welcoming feel if you're arriving from the desert than larger oasis towns like Germa, Ubari or Murzuq.

Most travellers who've crossed the Hamada al-Hamra and Ubari Sand Sea coming from Ghadames (p176) rejoin civilisation here. Al-Aweinat has always been the most important gateway into the Awiss region (p199) in the north of the Jebel Acacus, but the uncertain situation at the time of research regarding the road south of Ghat (see p195) also means that Al-Aweinat has also become the most important entry and departure point into the Jebel Acacus as a whole.

Al-Aweinat has a **fort** that is built on the spring of Al-Aweinat. According to the British explorer Hugh Clapperton in the 1820s, the local Tuareg believed it to be inhabited by ghosts and, as a result, they wouldn't enter the site. The Libyan police clearly don't have any such qualms for they now occupy the site; entry is not permitted and nor are photos of the exterior. It was built as a castle during the Arab/Islamic period.

Alfaw Camp (☎/fax 021-3340770; mobile 0912140678; alfawtravel@yahoo.com; Tripoli-Ghat highway; s/d/tr per person 15/25/37.50LD) This place has become an essential staging post on the road into or out from the Awiss region of the Jebel Acacus and, as such, can get very crowded with cars, campervans and all manner of travellers. The mud-thatch huts are fine and how much you enjoy the simple meals (8LD to 10LD) of chicken, couscous and salad probably depends on whether you're arriving from the desert or about to enter. It also has a travel agency onsite (and camps at Awiss) and it's therefore a good place to trade stories and get advice from locals and other travellers.

WADI MEGGEDET وادى ماغد يت

As you wind your way along the sandy valleys of Wadi Meggedet, close to the Algerian border, you'll find yourself shaking your head in disbelief. Wadi Meggedet is like nowhere else in Libya: pinnacles emerge from the sand, like a city of rock skyscrapers in miniature, taking on the strangest shapes and causing even the most experienced desert traveller to marvel at nature's eye-catching artistry. It could be Mars, it could be the moon but it's the sort of place that leaves one lost for words. Although most of the area known as Wadi Meggedet is flat, the northeastern reaches drop down quite steeply and are wonderful places to explore as footprints of gazelle, waddan and fennec fox lead into a world as labyrinthine as any North African medina. Not many travellers make it out this way. Get here before that changes.

Wadi Meggedet is separated from the Al-Aweinat–Ghat highway by a long ridge of sand dunes It is possible to cross the dunes in a 4WD, although the sand is soft in many places, or you can take the longer route – driving north until the dunes peter out, then heading south. Wadi Meggedet is most easily visited from Al-Aweinat (Serdeles, 80km; left), but to avoid doubling back after visiting the wadi, continue south between the sand dunes and the Algerian border before turning east to rejoin the highway next to Kaf Ajnoun.

KAF AJNOUN كهف الجنون

The end-of-the-earth landscapes of the Sahara lend themselves easily to myths and legends, but few places have attracted quite so many as 1281m-high Kaf Ajnoun, also known as Idinen. Rising up alongside the most important ancient paths that led from Fezzan and Ghadames to Ghat, this strange rock formation appears as if from nowhere around 25km north of Ghat (from where it's visible on a clear day).

Its name, which means the Mountain of Ghosts, is a reminder of how Kaf Ajnoun's otherworldly aspect has always played on the minds of travellers. The local Tuareg have a treasure-trove of ghost stories about the place (see The Legends of Kaf Ajnoun, p194). The mountain bears an uncanny resemblance to a haunted desert citadel, with a fortress-like summit complete with pinnacles of rock that could easily be watch-towers. To truly appreciate the strangely disturbing symmetry of Kaf Ajnoun, take the trail shadowing the Algerian border from Wadi Meggedet to Ghat; it is from the west that Kaf Ajnoun really makes you

THE LEGENDS OF KAF AJNOUN

Kaf Ajnoun was once known among the Tuareg as the Devil's Hill, a 'mountain hall of council where djinn [genies] meet from thousands of miles around'. Not surprisingly, such stories lured many a sceptical European explorer. In 1822, Hugh Clapperton claimed that 'we had been told many wonderful stories about this hill, that there were people with red hair living in it, that at night when encamped near it you would hear them beating on their drums, see their fires and hear them firing on their musquets'. Mind you, the appearance of white men among the locals was almost as strange as Kaf Ajnoun itself, and the two naturally coalesced – white strangers were feared as the children of Idinen (Kaf Ajnoun).

Clapperton recounted the story of a merchant travelling from Ghadames to Algeria. The traveller had been stopped by one of these red-haired djinns who then demanded a gun, for which it paid with a piece of paper inscribed with writing the merchant could not understand. The djinn told the merchant that on arriving in a town in Tuat (Algeria), the paper was to be given to a black dog that would come to meet him at an appointed place. The merchant was surprised to receive the payment from just such a dog at the appointed place in exchange for the paper; he was blessed with riches for the rest of his life.

Legends such as these ensured that no Tuareg would climb the hill or even get too close, although European explorers just couldn't resist the temptation. Walter Oudney climbed the hill without any adverse effect. But before you dismiss the legends as superstition and set off to climb to the top, remember the difficulties of two other explorers. In 1845, James Richardson became lost and was unwell for days after attempting to climb Kaf Ajnoun. Just five years later, Heinrich Barth reached the summit, but was exhausted and dehydrated by the time he got there. On the way down, he lost his way and collapsed. To stave off thirst he cut open a vein to drink his own blood. A mere 27 hours after setting out, he was found by a local Tuareg man, feverish and close to death.

wonder. It's possible to camp close by, if you dare, and some travellers have scrambled up to the summit without suffering any adverse effects. But it's an eerie place, and there are those who claim to have heard strange night-time noises while camping here.

Beyond the sand dunes across the highway is the broad **Wadi Tanezrouft** which offers fine views of the western wall of the Jebel Acacus and contains the hot springs of **Al-Fawar**. Some travellers journey from here by camel into Ghat.

GHAT غات

☎ 0724 / pop 25,172

Perhaps the most attractive of the oasis towns in Libya's south, Ghat has always been a travellers' favourite, and not just because it has served as one of two main gateway towns to the Jebel Acacus. The mud-brick medina in the heart of town is probably the finest of its kind in Libya. The setting is superb, with a backdrop of stunning sand dunes, the dark ridges of the Jebel Acacus to the east and the distant peaks of the Tassili-n-Ajjer (in Algeria) to the west. It is also notable as one of the few permanent Tuareg settlements in the Sahara.

History

Ghat's medina was built by the Garamantes in the 1st century BC atop of the ruins of an earlier settlement known as Rana, although it has been much modified and most of what's now visible dates from the 12th century. In Garamantian times, Ghat was one link in a chain of fortified oases that afforded protection to Garamantian caravans as they crossed the desert. It also served as part of the defence system of Garama: a bulwark and early warning system against hostile forces from the south. Although it never rivalled Ghadames in size, its strategic location as the only significant town in the region ensured that it played a critical role in the ebb and flow of Saharan trade and war. This role as a natural hub of Saharan communications brought it considerable prosperity.

The Tuareg came to know the area as the 'Land of Peace'. It was also known in the old Libyan language as the 'Land of the Sun'. It was not until the 14th century that the name Ghat began to appear in the accounts of geographers and travellers. Throughout this period and until relatively recently, the town came under the aegis of the Tuareg of the Tassili-n-Ajjer. They used their influence to set up a free-trade zone of sorts, although caravans only remained free of peril if they paid protection money to local Tuareg tribes. By the early 19th century, Ghat was said to be on the verge of supplanting Ghadames and Murzuq as the principal town of the Libyan Sahara.

The Sultan of Ghat (a hereditary position passed down through the female line) was subservient to the sultans of the Ajjer Tuareg, but always enjoyed a significant degree of autonomy. In the 19th century, however, the Ottomans extended their reach into the Sahara. Ghat's age of autonomy came to an end in 1875, with the first full-scale Ottoman occupation of the town. This, combined with the decline of the slave trade and the shift away from trans-Saharan trade routes, saw Ghat fall into decline. Ghat later came under the rule of the French and Italians, although both maintained little more than a token presence in town. Cross-border trade ensured that the town did not disappear entirely, and Ghat's remoteness ensured that non-Muslim visitors were rare – until Libya's recent tourist boom.

THE ROAD SOUTH OF GHAT

Like so many old Saharan caravan towns, Ghat was at the time of writing passing through a difficult historical moment. In early 2006 the Algerian army occupied a major wadi south of Ghat, thereby closing off the routes from Ghat into the Jebel Acacus and leaving the town marooned. Travellers began to leave the road and enter the Acacus at Al-Aweinat, 100km away to the northwest. We still think Ghat is worth the effort, but judging by the empty camps and hotels when we visited, not too many travellers were willing to come this far to find out. Although by the time you read this the Libyan and Algerian authorities have probably sorted things out and re-opened the route south of Ghat, check the latest information before setting out.

In case the southern route has reopened, we have included a route description based on an earlier visit; see p202.

Orientation & Information

Ghat is a compact town. It has one main street – the highway in from the north, which sweeps past the medina, the police station, **jawazzat** (passport office; ☎ 7102308) and a number of cheap restaurants, then on past the main post office, Masraf al-Safari (bank) before heading south towards Algeria.

There are a couple of **internet cafés** (per hr 1LD) in the centre of town.

Sights

MEDINA

Ghat's medina is a fine example of vernacular Saharan architecture, with a tangle of lanes weaving between crumbling mud-brick buildings that bear the merest traces of their former glories. The medina is compact but you could easily spend a couple of hours wandering through it.

The old city has, like many of its kind, only been deserted quite recently (for more details see Out With the Old, p59). The last of the medina's old inhabitants only moved out, into modern housing, in 1991. Although some families are reported to have moved within the medina's walls, these are recent immigrants from Niger rather than townsfolk.

The main entrance to the **medina** (adult/child 3/1LD, camera/video 5/10LD; ⏰ sunrise-sunset) is via the small open square opposite the *baladiya* (town hall). There's no ticket office, but once you've entered, word will get around and the friendly Tuareg ticket seller will find you soon enough. By the roadside just outside the square is a wonderfully well-preserved ancient **well**.

In the medina proper, the first square you come to after passing under the low arch was used for weddings and is still used for festivals (see p197). This western area of the medina *(agrum wusharan)* is the oldest part of town.

The medina's **old mosque**, which is not generally open to the public, has a distinctive squat minaret in the Sudanic style and was built in 900, although next to nothing remains from this time. Given the hotch-potch of alterations, it shows a surprising unity of style.

The ziggurat-like structure in the heart of the old town served as the **old congress building**, where public meetings were held and from where the people of the town could be

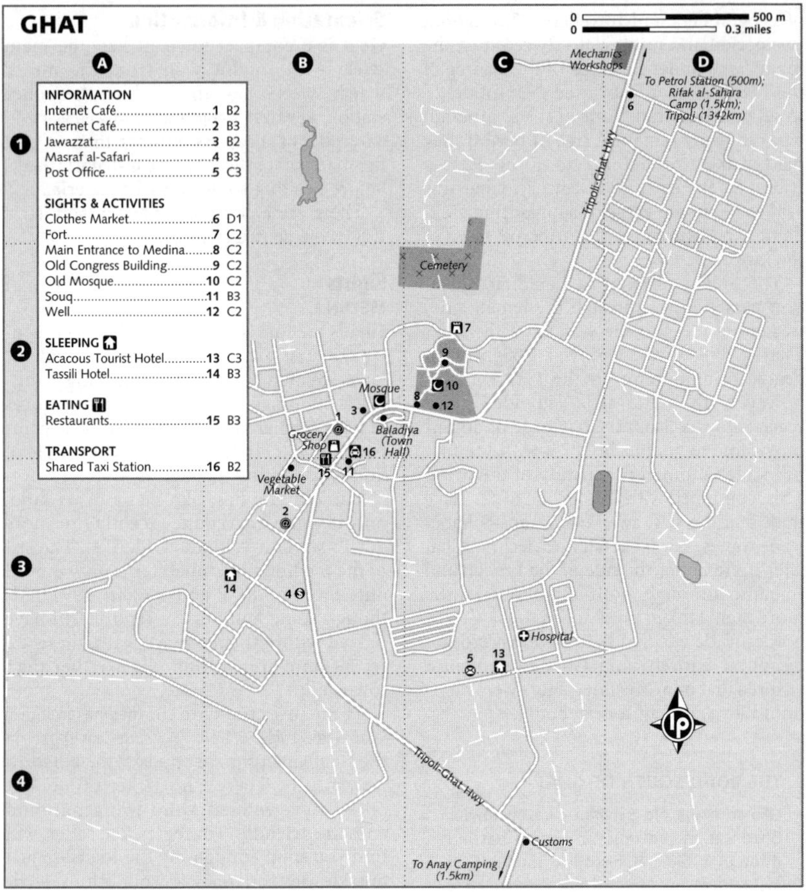

addressed. Climbing to the top affords excellent views over the roofs of the medina.

On some of the small flat platforms surrounding the lanes are indentations caused by the ancient process of crushing date seeds.

The houses, and indeed most of the public buildings of the medina, were built from a durable mixture of animal dung, sun-dried clay, mud-brick and straw, while roofs were often supported by wooden beams and laced with palm fronds for added protection. Carved into some interior walls are some nice relief façades. Watch out also for the tiny palm-trunk doors; the passing centuries have seen the level of sand rise, raising the ground level of the town. Atop some houses are mud adornments of alternately upright and inverted triangles. While no-one is certain, one local legend (which is also believed in Ghadames) claims that their resemblance to a crown is to remind the inhabitants of a much-loved Berber queen who ruled the desert.

Overlooking the medina is the **fort**. The Turks started its construction, but it was not finished until Italians arrived and converted it into a barracks. There are some superb views of the Jebel Acacus from the roof and you may be able to make out Kaf Ajnoun (p193) to the north. The best views over the medina itself are from the path that climbs up to the fort from behind the old town.

TYING A TUAREG TURBAN

The Tuareg turban (known as *ashaersh* or *tagelmoust*) has puzzled ethnographers for centuries. The Tuareg are one of the few people in the world for whom men, but not women, must wear the veil. One functional purpose is as protection against wind and sand. However, it also serves a social purpose in the rigid hierarchy of social relationships. A Tuareg man is not supposed to show his face to one of higher status, and Tuareg who still follow the traditional way of life will rarely expose the lower half of their face in company. When such men drink tea, they are supposed to pass their glass under their *tagelmoust* so as not to reveal the mouth.

There are many ways of tying the *tagelmoust*. Although it's likely to take a while for you to muster the casual ease with which Tuareg men accomplish the daunting task, one relatively easy way to do it is as follows:

Step 1 Fold the cloth so that it remains the same length but half the width.
Step 2 Drape the folded cloth flat over your head so that three-quarters of its length hangs down in front of your right arm and the shorter length over your left.
Step 3 With your right hand, hold the cloth about halfway down its length.
Step 4 Place your left hand across your body, tense it so that your four fingers are pointing out to your right and your thumb is pointing to the sky.
Step 5 Holding your left hand just below your right shoulder about chest high and about six inches out from your body, rest the nearest fold of the long length of cloth on your left hand between the thumb and flattened forefinger.
Step 6 With your right hand, quickly take the length of cloth in a full circle in front of your face and around the back of your head until you return to where you started.
Step 7 Repeat as many times as necessary.
Step 8 Tuck any remaining strands of cloth into the folds on the top or back of the head.
Step 9 Ask your Tuareg guide to sort it out.

There, we told you it was easy.

SOUQS

Ghat has a busy, open-air **souq** (Tue) that's worth delaying your departure for if you're in town. It has a delightful feel and you can hear a mix of Arabic, Tuareg and French being spoken. Most of the stalls sell clothes, but there are also watches, sunglasses and fruits on offer. This is the place to purchase your Tuareg turban *(ashaersh)* for protection against the sun and sand of the Sahara. The standard cost is 3LD per metre and although some Tuareg take up to 10m, three should be sufficient. Another good buy are Tuareg pants *(akerbai)*, with their exquisitely brocaded hems. These loose-fitting pants (expect to pay around 15LD) are very comfy and ideal for minimising the chafing of riding a camel. On days when the market is not open, try the **clothes market** on the main highway 1.7km northwest of the medina.

Festivals & Events

New Year is a great time to visit Ghat. The **Acacus Festival** is one of Libya's more regular festivals and sometimes includes a spectacular sunset concert against the cathedral-like backdrop of the Jebel Acacus. The festival is also an excellent (and possibly the only) opportunity to see performances of Tuareg dancing (p60).

Sleeping & Eating

Ghat is not blessed with an abundance of accommodation, but most travellers only stop here long enough to refuel and head out into the desert. Like most camps across Fezzan the two camps suffer from an abundance of hungry mosquitos, so bring repellent or buy a spray in town.

Anay Camping (☎ 7102587; mobile 0925357308; tents 5LD; thatch huts per person 10LD, campervans 10LD) Some 2km south of town off the main road to the Issayen, this place has the usual cute, simple thatched huts, although they're not particularly airtight and the mattresses are somewhat dusty. The hot showers are wonderful if you've just come in from desert. Ramadan, your host, is an amiable chap;

there's a small artisan's shop in the compound and the kitchen can be used by guests.

Rifak as-Sahara Camp (☎ 7102362; mobile 0912146091; Tripoli-Ghat highway; cabins per person 20LD, camping 10LD; ⊠) Strange place, this. The newly built and airtight cabins are very impressive, but only three of them have air-conditioning; absurdly, the price remains the same. The cabins also belong to the architectural genre of toilet blocks, while the adjacent older, now-closed thatch-and-stone huts were far more in keeping with local architecture. It has also built a new restaurant. It's the first building you come to on the left as you enter Ghat.

Tassili Hotel (☎ 7103001; s/d 15/20LD) You'd have to be desperate. In fact, we only include it here for two reasons: to award it the prize as the worst tourist hotel we came across in Libya and to warn you to mutiny if your tour guide tells you you're staying here. Nothing works, the smells are years old and the whole place looks like it was built as an afterthought and could fall down any day.

Acacous Tourist Hotel (☎ 7102769; hotelacacous ghat@ghat.gov.ly; d with/without TV 30/20LD, ste 45LD, meals 15LD) Ghat's only habitable hotel is, fortunately, very comfortable and quite new. OK the carpet doesn't always quite reach the walls, but the furniture is new, the rooms are spacious and are all-in-all very comfortable. You can also walk to the medina from here.

Cheap restaurants serving chicken and rice or sandwiches are along the main drag west of the medina. Expect to pay 5LD to 8LD for soup, salad, drinks and main dish.

Getting There & Away

Although timetables for Libyan Arab Airlines list twice-weekly flights from Tripoli to Ghat (one way/return 51/102LD), services are unreliable and were suspended at the time of research.

You're a long way from anywhere here – Ghat is 100km southwest of Al-Aweinat, 552km southwest of Sebha and 1342km from Tripoli. Shared taxis congregate at the entrance to the souq on the main road; most only go as far as Ubari.

THE JEBEL ACACUS جبل اكاكوس

The Jebel Acacus (pronounced A-ka-kous) is not the most famous massif of the Sahara, but that can only be because Libya was for so long closed to the outside world. Dark basalt mountains with sand dunes piled high into many of the cliffs, sandstone buttresses fashioned by the wind interspersed with golden rivers of sand, rock formations that seemed to have been crafted by an experimental artist alongside rock art brilliantly executed by the hand of the ancients – these are the secrets of the Acacus. This Unesco World Heritage–listed area deserves as much time as you have and probably more.

This was once purely the domain of the Tuareg; settled and nomadic Tuareg families ranged across the whole Acacus region. Most of the Tuareg families have in recent years moved to the towns, especially the oases around Ghat, and only 13 families remain in the Acacus and Awiss region – it's not uncommon to find old Tuareg men wandering the wadis blissfully alone. Theirs is a disappearing world. Many Tuareg who have left the Acacus now return as guides and drivers, and to have a Tuareg companion show you the land of his ancestors is one of Libya's highlights.

THE DISCOVERY OF SAHARAN ROCK ART

Although the indigenous Tuareg inhabitants of the Sahara have known about the rock art in their midst for centuries, it has only recently captured the attention of the outside world. The German explorers Heinrich Barth and Gustav Nachtigal reported their findings and even made sketches of some of the pieces. On 6 July 185, Barth wrote, 'No barbarian could have graven the lines with such astonishing firmness, and given to all the figures the light, natural shape which they exhibit.' But it was not until 1955 that a team from the University of Rome, led by Professor Fabrizio Mori (whose name has become synonymous with the rock art of the Acacus), undertook a serious study of the art. This tradition continued through the 1990s when another Italian team recorded over 1300 sites in the Acacus alone. Their findings, and the modern threats to the art, have contributed to the area being added to Unesco's World Heritage List of Endangered and Protected Sites.

The landscapes and people of the Jebel Acacus are themselves reason enough to visit here, but it is the astonishingly enduring rock art that gives it a special dimension. Their whimsical beauty reflects an almost child-like simplicity, but they were created by extremely skilful artists. The rock-art's appeal is also enhanced by an understanding of what it represents: the local Tuareg believe that the ancient artists saw their art as a school for their descendants, leaving behind a history book cast in stone of what they saw and how they lived.

It is not known who was responsible for the art. Some archaeologists attribute the images to the ancestors of the modern Tuareg, a people who remained in the Sahara as the climate dried around 4000 years ago. Others claim that the Garamantes people, who inhabited Wadi al-Ajal to the north, were responsible. Both claims may indeed be true, but the fact that much of the art predates these groups suggests that they were merely following a tradition set in motion by earlier indigenous inhabitants of the region.

For information on the different types of Saharan rock art, see p60.

Permits

Permits, obtainable from the police stations in Ghat, Al-Aweinat or Ubari, are required to visit the Jebel Acacus, but your tour company will take care of this probably without you realising it's been done. For the record, permits must be obtained for each tourist (8LD), Libyan-/foreign-registered car (5/20LD), and local guide, driver and/or cook (5LD).

Entering the Acacus

The main gateway towns to the Jebel Acacus are Al-Aweinat (p193) and Ghat (p194), while many travellers also arrive from the desert to the east after visiting Wadi Methkandoush (p204), Idehan Murzuq (p203) and Wan Caza (p203). However, given that entering the Acacus from Ghat was not possible at the time of writing (see The Road South of Ghat, p195), our coverage runs from north to south.

Many travellers have told us that not all Libyan guides know the precise locations of the rock-art sites in the Acacus. For that reason we have included GPS points for some of the more important sites.

JEBEL ACACUS – THE TOP TEN

- **Afozedzhar Arch** (p202)
- **Adadh** (below)
- **Painting of wedding scenes** (Wan Melol; p201) in Wadi Tashwinat
- **Painting of hunting scene** (Wan Traghit; p201) in Wadi Tashwinat
- **Elephant carving** (p201) in Wadi Tashwinat
- **Canyon and ghelta** (Wadi Tashwinat; p201) in Wadi In Ferdan
- Panoramic view of the Acacus in **Wadi Am'raka** (Wan Imlal; p201)
- Panoramic view of **Awiss** (below)
- Watching the sunset over the Acacus from **Wan Caza** (p203)
- Your first shower in days at **Aminaner well** (p201)

In addition to this guide, the 1:100,000 *Jebel Acacus – Tourist Map & Guide* (see p179) is a must-have companion for exploring the Acacus, covering the mountains in exceptional detail, including many more rock-art locations than we can cover here.

Awiss

The northern Awiss region of the Jebel Acacus has some wonderful rock paintings, although it's more famous for its weird and wonderful landscapes. There's no finer example of this phenomenon of nature imitating art than one of the first sites you come to in the north of Awiss– **Adadh** (N 25º 31′ 18.77″ E 10º 35′ 58.70″). This so-called 'Finger Rock' somehow seems to defy the laws of gravity, and at almost 20m high you can't help but think that it just has to fall soon. Around 350m east of Adadh are some quite impressive engravings of lovemaking.

Having started with one of the Acacus' signature sights, it's time to get an overall perspective of the landscape that defines the Acacus. Not far south of Adadh, a **panoramic view** (N 25º 30′ 24.41″ E 10º 34′ 22.51″) opens up after a short climb. Better at sunrise than sunset, it's a stunning location with views of Adadh away to the north. Further south you'll come across a range of **rock art** (N 25º20′ 00.49″ E 10º31′ 19.52″) providing an excellent introduction to

PERIODS OF SAHARAN ROCK ART

The rock art of North Africa is thought to have its origins almost 12,000 years ago (10,000 BC) in the central Sahara. There is a belief among some archaeologists that it was from here that such art spread to Ethiopia, Kenya and Egypt, the latter possibly drawing on the Saharan art for inspiration in the great subsequent flourishing of Egyptian art. Although centuries of exposure to the elements have made it difficult to precisely date much of the rock art, most of the examples to be found in the Libyan Sahara fall within five relatively discrete historical periods.

The first of these is most commonly known as the **Wild Fauna Period** (10,000–6000 BC) but the period is also called the Early Hunter Period and the Bubalus Period after a species of giant buffalo that became extinct 5000 years ago. This era is characterised by the portrayal of elephants, giraffes and Barbary sheep from the time when the Sahara was covered by the plentiful savannah.

The **Round Head Period** (8000–6000 BC), overlapping for a time its forerunner, is known for human figures with formless bodies and painted, circular heads devoid of features. During this period, the people of the central Sahara are believed to have been foragers in the era prior to the appearance of domesticated stock. Its later stages feature more decorative figures adorned with headdresses and unusual clothing.

The next era was the **Pastoral Period** (5500–2000 BC) or Bovidian Period, which coincides with the gradual transition from a temperate to arid climate. Accordingly, human figures are shown in positions of dominance over the natural world, with spears, domesticated cattle and ceremonies in keeping with more settled communities. Experts also believe that this was when the skill of the artists began to decline.

The **Horse Period** (1000 BC–AD 1) followed, with many images of horses or horse-drawn chariots, some seemingly propelled through the air, reflecting the fact that transport and movement became more sophisticated and enabled relatively long-distance travel. Cattle are by far the dominant forms. Human figures from this period are represented by two triangles, one upright and one upside down, joined at the apex with a circular head on top. Much of the Tuareg writing (Tifinagh) alongside the paintings is from this period.

The final era of Saharan rock art was the **Camel Period** (200 BC–present). Camels became the Sahara's beast of burden and they are shown in abundance during this period. Paintings from the earliest part of this period are of the highest quality while more recent ones are nowhere near as finely conceived.

the genre. Most periods of Saharan rock art (see above) are represented with good paintings of a giraffe (minus its head), ostrich, a stick-headed human figure and a hunter with a bow and arrow; there's also an enormous carving of a man wearing a mask which signifies that we've caught him in the act of making love. Dog or jackal masks are a feature of lovemaking scenes in Saharan rock art; some experts believe them to be an invocation of the Saharan fable of a jackal's wedding, symbolising fertility and rain.

You're now venturing into the heart of the Awiss region and just north of Wadi Tiheden are some exceptionally rendered carved **elephants** (N 25°19′ 37.16″ E 10°32′ 25.03″), with giraffe and cattle carvings in the vicinity. Also nearby are some of the clearest examples of painted stick-head **human figures** (N 25°19′ 32.64″ E 10°32′ 16.22″). Not far south, in Wadi Udhohen, there is a clear painting of a **chariot** (N 25°17′ 12.88″ E 10°34′ 53.12″). Before leaving Awiss, pause to take in the outstanding **fighting scenes** (N 25°16′ 01.25″ E 10°35′ 45.13″) in Wadi Tiheden, complete with dead bodies and fighters wearing horned helmets; note the one about to attack from behind.

Note that there are vehicular routes between Awiss and the rest of the Jebel Acacus to the south. As a result, you'll need to head west towards the well of Bir Talwawat and journey south between the dunes of Wan Caza and the eastern ridges of the Acacus.

Wadi Tashwinat & Around

The main access point for Wadi Tashwinat if you're coming from Awiss is the well of **Aminaner** (N 24°51′ 34.21″ E 10°39′ 38.59″) at the northern end of Wadi Wan Millal. This is one of the Acacus' most popular wells, where water is pumped out in generous quantities for travellers and local Tuareg alike. Situated on a broad, barren plain, Aminaner strongly highlights the miracle of water in the desert. You can have a bucket shower and give those clothes a much-needed wash; drying is not a problem.

You could easily devote an entire day to exploring the 101 wadis that make up the main valley of Wadi Tashwinat (also known as Wadi Tashween). As one local Tuareg told us, Tashwinat is the capital of Acacus.

Close to the entrance of Wadi Tashwinat is **Awanini**, a small mountain whose name means 'Go Up and See', so named after a legendary figure did precisely that, but was unable to climb down and hence died there. On a wall facing Awanini to the south, and signposted as Wan Traghit, are some of the finest and most famous paintings in all the Acacus. The most beautiful is the **hunting scene** (N 24°51' 21.52" E 10°32' 25.09") in ochre and white, with the hunter and his prey (possibly waddan or mouflon) appearing to dance across the rock. Also present on the same rock face are giraffe and a Garamantian chariot. This wonderfully varied collection spans a number of periods, ranging from around 10,000 BC (the giraffe) to the more recent chariot. Sadly, the best giraffe has been defaced by souvenir hunters.

Approximately 300m around the corner to the west is a superbly carved **elephant** (N 24°51' 36.69" E 10°32' 16.95") represented in a skilled line-carving of perfect proportions. Next to it is a smaller elephant, which has been less well preserved due to water damage. These engravings are unusual for the Acacus, which is dominated by paintings.

Also not far into the main wadi, behind a sign saying Takdhalt, a series of tablets, sheltered by an overhang of rock, show remnants of what must have been an enormous and ancient **rock-carved map** (N 24°51' 07.58" E 10°31' 09.16") of Wadi Tashwinat. The tributary wadis are marked by lines and the wells by small depressions in the rock. Next to the map are some fine human figures and Tuareg Tifinagh letters.

In the main Wadi Tashwinat, is one of the Acacus' famed painted **wedding scenes** (N 24°50' 25.89" E 10°30' 09.35"), designated by a yellow Department of Antiquities sign as 'Wan Melol', where the 6000-year-old detail is exquisite, especially the women washing hair and the women trying on dresses. If only all wedding photography was so originally rendered.

Nearby, and signposted as Wan Mughjaj are the **excavation pits** of Professor Mori where a child's skeleton from 5400 years ago was found (it's now in Gallery 4 of Tripoli's Jamahiriya Museum; p78). There's also a smaller, three-columned **natural rock arch** (N 24°51' 24.45" E 10°34' 41.12"), shown as **Tin Khilqa**, at the entrance to a small valley. The columns are as finely fluted as any Roman column in Leptis Magna. At the end of the arch are some more paintings, including a unicorn.

Also within striking distance is Wadi In Ferdan, a tributary wadi off the southern end of Wadi Tashwinat. Here you'll find a **desert mosque** (N 24°49' 17.20" E 10°29' 20.47"), which consists of a collection of stones facing Mecca that have served desert travellers for centuries. High above the mosque is a rock ledge, the walls of which have **hunting scenes** with human figures pursuing animals with bows and arrows, as well as **giraffe** and a faint representation of what may be a **panther**. Above the ledge and visible from the 'mosque', there is a rock formation shaped like a camel. Further into Wadi In Ferdan, a narrow, steep-sided **canyon** (N 24°47' 33.36" E 10°29' 59.20") which leads to three **ghelta** (natural springs), which once provided an invaluable water source for the Tuareg; they're now only used for animals.

The highest point (1506m) of the Jebel Acacus is behind the wall of mountains almost due west.

Southern Acacus

The southern reaches of the Acacus receive fewer visitors than they used to before the closure of the road south of Ghat (see p195), but it's every bit as spectacular down here as elsewhere in the Acacus. If anything, the mountains rise more steeply here than further north.

As you work your way south from Wadi Tashwinat – the easiest way is to leave close to where you entered near the **Aminaner well** – look out for the elevated ledges on the eastern side of **Wadi Am'raka** or **Wan Imlal**. From one of these, there are signature **panoramic views** (N 24°47' 40.80" E 10°40' 10.76") over the Acacus for miles around. Further away to the southwest are the adjacent wadis of Anshal and Tanshal, which are home to some of the best rock art in the southern Acacus.

The southernmost of the two is **Wadi Tanshal**, where the first site you come to

THE CLIMATIC CONTEXT

When the Ice Age peaked in the northern hemisphere around 20,000 years ago (18,000 BC), it ushered in a period of low rainfall and barren landscapes across the Sahara – much the same as prevails today. With the thaw of the Ice Age 12,000 years ago (10,000 BC), the climate of the Sahara again became temperate and animals and people returned to occupy most of the region. Another possible dry spell approximately 8000 years ago (6000 BC) saw the introduction of domesticated cattle from the West, but for the next 3000 years the Sahara was covered with savannah, year-round lakes, pastureland and acacia trees. The temperate, often humid, climate continued until 4500 years ago (2500 BC) when the last transition commenced and the Sahara began to become the vast, arid desert it is today, a process that was drawn out over 1500 years. Perennial lakes were replaced by more-seasonal water sources and as the region became progressively drier, oases replaced lake-side and mountain villages as the sites of settlements and agricultural or pastoral activity. It was also the period in which trans-Saharan trade became the dominant economic activity fostered by an increased reliance on chariots, then horses and finally camels that were introduced to the Sahara 2200 years ago (200 BC).

The rock art from these periods is an invaluable resource depicting humankind's changing relationship with nature. Professor Mori's tracing of the transition from the dominance of animals over human beings towards domestication and a taming of the natural environment through food production still holds true. Indeed, it remains the most enduring legacy of the art – a deeper understanding of the ancient world.

includes a cow, camels and a number of ancient Tuareg letters, most of which date from the time when domesticated beasts of burden had replaced wild animals as the predominant wildlife of the Sahara. There's also a very faint giraffe from an earlier period. The second site, also on the west side of the wadi, shows cows as well as a fine, stylised human figure. From here, a cave leads into the rocks and comes out on a ledge affording fine views back down the wadi.

The third site, on the other side of the valley, involves a bit of a climb, but is worth it for the very faint image of an elephant, of which the top half is missing, and the superb representation of **three women dancing** (N 24°42′ 03.51″ E 10°37′ 08.83″); it stands almost half a metre high although it has sadly been damaged by recent rains.

Wadi Anshal is almost 13km long. At the far end of the wadi are some fine paintings of **women** (N 24°43′ 27.49″ E 10°31′ 52.66″), with good **elephant and giraffe carvings** (N 24°43′ 34.84″ E 10°33′ 11.44″) about 2km before you reach the women. A further 2km back towards the entrance of the wadi, you'll see some tyre tracks leading into a cleft in the rock. If you follow them, you'll discover more recent carvings of camels and human riders superimposed on an earlier and much more sophisticated carving of female cattle.

Almost due south of the entrance to the two wadis is the most famous (and largest) of many natural arches in the Jebel Acacus, the towering, 150m-high **Afozedzhar Arch** (N 24°41′ 04.16″ E 10°37′ 57.74), which stands watch over the junction of three wadis. This massive stone gateway is nature at its most creative and easily the most spectacular natural rock formations in the Acacus. Although there are others, none is as impressive as this one.

Coming from Ghat

Although the road south from Ghat was closed at the time of research (see p195), it is likely to reopen at some time during the life of this book. The following route description is based an earlier visit.

From Ghat, the paved road continues south as far as **Issayen**, literally the town at the end of the road. From here the trail descends into a rocky and sandy series of tracks and, soon after Issayen, one of these branches off to the Algerian border. Alongside the main track approximately 5km past Issayen is a white **monument** to the Libyan and Algerian mujaheddin who died fighting the French. Also next to the main trail are a number of **overturned French military vehicles** marking the spot where the French occupying army lost a battle. Until the Algerians and Libyans reopen this route, this was as far south as you could go at the time of writing.

Thereafter, the road runs roughly parallel to the Algerian border as it heads south and then east. The border is marked by evenly spaced white markers and you must be careful not to stray into Algerian territory – even in this remote area, a border is still a border.

After encountering the picturesque **Takharkhuri Dunes**, trails lead north into the Jebel Acacus via **Wadi Ayada** (Tuareg for 'leg'), a broad wadi lined with uneven cliffs rising to towering rocky bluffs. As you make your way through the wadi, you may come across an army checkpoint which marks the official **Gateway to the Acacus**. A few kilometres after the checkpoint, the trail leads over a deceptive ridge that is followed by an exhilarating descent of almost 100m. This is the southern Acacus' point of no return.

WAN CAZA وان كازة

The golden sand dunes of Wan Caza run in a narrow, roughly north-south chain from close to the Ubari–Al-Aweinat highway almost to the Libya–Algeria border. They shadow the Jebel Acacus all the way, with the Msak Mallat running parallel to the dunes to the east. Wan Caza may lack the epic scope of the sand seas elsewhere (it's all relative), but they're as beautiful as any dunes in Libya. Most travellers encounter them when travelling between the Jebel Acacus and the Idehan Murzuq or Wadi Methkandoush.

At the main crossing point, the valley is famous for its multicoloured sand beneath the surface, including black and white. The valley is thought to have been the site of a **Neolithic cemetery** and pottery shards, fragments of ostrich eggs and the ash-coloured sand provide considerable weight to this theory. Organic shore deposits found by geologists at Wan Caza (there are examples in the Germa Museum; p190) also suggest that this was once the shore of a large lake or inland sea; it's hard to escape the impression that Wan Caza still wears the aspect of a graduated shoreline, albeit this time of a desert as vast as any ocean.

Visible from the eastern reaches of the Jebel Acacus, Wan Caza also makes a wonderful campsite after leaving the southern Acacus and before entering the Awiss region (p199) to the north. The panoramas from the sand dunes at sunset towards the silhouetted peaks of the Acacus is the stuff of legend. In particular, we like the view from N 25°12' 11.47" E 10°48' 58.08", not far from the well of Bir Talwawat.

IDEHAN MURZUQ أدهان مرزق

The Idehan Murzuq (Murzuq Sand Sea) is the desert of which you've always dreamed. This incomprehensibly vast mountain range (over 35,000 sq km – not much smaller than Switzerland) made entirely of sand is simply breathtaking. It's home to as beautiful desert scenery as you'll see anywhere – dunes rise hundreds of metres high and myriad wave-like ridges, sculpted by the wind, ascend to

THE FORMATION OF SAND DUNES

Sand dunes are among the great mysteries of the Sahara. In the desert, sand particles are relatively heavy so even the strongest winds can rarely lift them much higher than an adult's shoulders. The slightest bump in the landscape can cause a phenomenon known as cresting, where an accumulation of drifting sand builds up. The slopes facing the wind are generally more compacted and less steep than those that lie on the other side of the ridge-line. The actual formation takes place where there were originally favourable land formations (often surprisingly small) and a constancy in the direction of the winds. Over time, with a base of ever more densely compacted sand, they become a 'permanent' feature of the landscape. Individual or small groups of dunes inch forward with time, pushed by consistent winds, although sand seas are relatively stable, having formed over millennia as rock is scoured and worn down to individual grains of quartz or sand.

One of the most common types of dune are barchan or crescent dunes (the shape of the ridge-line), *seif* (Arabic for sword) which have long, sweeping ridges and *akhlé*, a haphazard network of dunes without any discernible pattern. Unique combinations of all of these can be found in both the Idehan Ubari (p187) and Idehan Murzuq (above).

For more information on sand dune formation, *Geomorphology in Deserts* (1973) by Robert Cooke and Andrew Warren is dense but comprehensive, while Ralph Bagnold's *Libyan Sands – Travels in a Dead World* (1935) is more accessible.

razor-sharp summits. The northern face of the sand sea rises up from the impossibly barren Murzuq Plateau. From a distance during the heat of the day, the Idehan Murzuq shimmers pale yellow in the heat haze. In the midst of the dunes as the sun lowers, the undulations change into subtle yet magical plays of light and shadow.

The Idehan Murzuq is far less frequented than the Idehan Ubari further north. Indeed, if you venture deeper into the Idehan Murzuq beyond the northern reaches of the sand sea, you'll likely travel for days without seeing another vehicle and the choice of sand valleys in which to camp are seemingly endless. This is a place to soak up the solitude of the desert, sleeping under the stars and surrounded on all sides by moonlit sand dunes.

Ask your Tuareg guide to tell you stories about one of the northeastern valleys of the sand sea. It is said that at night, those camping there will hear the sounds, carried eerily by the wind, of ghosts at a wedding party, singing and dancing in order to lure the inquisitive to their deaths. This is also one of the places where it's possible to hear the curious desert phenomenon known as the Drumming Sands – the interplay between the wind and the sand's surface. As one guide who has heard the phenomenon told us, 'it sounds just like an aeroplane'.

WADI METHKANDOUSH & AROUND وادى متخندوش

Barren and inhospitable **Wadi Methkandoush** (adult/child 3/1LD, camera/video 5/10LD; 8am-5pm), where the Msak Settafet meets the Murzuq Plateau, has one of the richest concentrations of prehistoric rock carvings in the world. Most of the carvings in the soft sandstone date back at least 12,000 years, making this one of the oldest rock-art sites in Libya. This open-air gallery contains hundreds of wonderful carvings of giraffe (including a bullet-scarred engraving of a giraffe herd), hippopotamus, elephant, crocodile, ostrich and rhinoceros. The most spectacular carving, of two catlike figures sparring on their hind-legs alongside four ostriches, is astonishing – the most spectacular single rock carving in Libya; it adorns a large flat boulder about halfway along the wadi and requires a moderately easy climb to reach.

The proliferation of animals represented at Wadi Methkandoush is all the more remarkable because of the barren, nightmarish black-rock terrain of the surrounds. The carvings run for around 12km, although only a small section, which is fortunately the best, is open to the public. Like any wadi, and as unlikely as it may seem, Wadi Methkandoush is subject to flash-flooding; if you don't believe us, look for the watermark above head high on the northern wall of the wadi, which dates from 2006.

Dozens of other wadis lead into the Msak. Most are lined with rock carvings and are home to gazelle that have retreated into the valleys to escape hunters and tourists alike. The most accessible wadis for carvings lie just to the west of Wadi Methkandoush. These include **Wadi In Ghanjuwan**, which has good elephant engravings, and **Wadi Wan Habeter** where you'll find some excellent giraffe engravings. Further west again is **Wadi Tiksateen**, where the woman milking a cow is extraordinarily realistic.

PROTECTING SAHARAN ROCK ART

As remarkable as it seems, tourists pose the greatest threat to the survival of the rock art of Wadi Methkandoush, the Jebel Acacus and Jebel al-Uweinat. Although it happens rarely, enough tourists have decided that the region's famous rock art would make a wonderful souvenir of their time in Libya – actions which were largely responsible for Libya ushering in the current era of escorted group tourism. To acquire their piece of priceless Libyan heritage, tourists have chipped away sections of the rock walls, thrown water on the paintings to enhance the light for taking photographs or used complex silicon processes designed to copy the paintings. It seems incredible that we should have to make such an obvious point, but whatever you do, please leave the paintings and carvings as you find them.

If you want to learn more about Saharan rock art or about efforts being undertaken to preserve rock art across Africa, contact the **Trust for African Rock Art** (TARA; ☎ 254-20-884467; www.africanrockart.org; PO Box 24122, Nairobi, Kenya).

It may just be us, but the black stones that surround these wadis are not our favourite spot for camping. Apart from the gloom that seems to envelope the landscape, known by the Tuareg as the Ocean of Stone and which looks like a post-apocalyptic vision of the end of the earth, snakes abound in the rocky clefts when the weather's warm. If you're continuing west towards the Jebel Acacus, we much prefer the sand dunes of the Idehan Murzuq (p203), which are an hour's drive away. Alternatively, many travellers visit on a day trip from Germa, 150km away.

MURZUQ مرزق

pop 44,909

Murzuq was one of the most important Saharan towns of history, but it has never been the most beautiful place to live. The capital of the chiefs of Awlad Muhammad tribe who ruled Fezzan from the late 15th century until 1813, Murzuq was one of the desert's true centres of power. When the German explorer Frederick Hornemann visited her in 1798, he found a prosperous town through whose gates passed countless traders. Their merchandise included slaves, gold, tiger skins, ostrich feathers, copper and silk. Goods came from all four corners of the Sahara, and Cairo, Tripoli, Ghadames, Tuat (in Algeria), Agadez (Niger), Bornu (Chad), Turkey and India.

That said, few ancient travellers have ever had too many kind words to say about Murzuq, in part because of the historical dangers of desert travel around its perimeter and also because of its unhealthy and once-malarial climate. Frederick Hornemann was one of many European explorers to fall ill; he was stuck here for seven months. After 1813, Murzuq quickly lost its wealth and stature, a process accelerated by the shift from trans-Saharan to ocean-borne trade. Its time had passed and that's how it feels to this day.

The modern town (170km south of Sebha) is downright ugly, but it does house a petrol station (which often runs out of supplies), a grocery store, whose stocks are similarly limited, and a post office.

The highlight of the town remains the shady, open-air **market** which seems to belong more to African village life than to the clamour of a large Libyan town. The **castle** (admission 3LD) is still intact and open to the public as a museum; it might take a while to track down the caretaker who has the key. It was home to the Sultan of Fezzan and his considerable household and later to a Turkish garrison of 500 men. Next to the castle is one of the most charming **vernacular-style mosques** in Libya. The prayer hall is vividly painted in Fezzan colours and the mud-brick minaret curves unusually. The town is notable for being one of the few cities in Libya to have a largely Toubou population (for more information see p49).

Unless the *buyut ash-shabaab* (youth hostel) has reopened, there's nowhere to stay and camping is the only option. Nor are there any restaurants to speak of, although the occasional café serves chicken and couscous.

AL-QATRUN القطرون

This remote settlement, 310km south of Sebha, is little more than a few shacks, houses and a checkpoint. Located on Wadi Ekema, it was historically Fezzan's most southerly town on the trade route to the kingdom of Bornu at Lake Chad. It's now the last town of any size en route to the Niger border and the end of the tarmac road. The authorities at the checkpoint will be keen to scrutinise your papers before allowing you to pass – it's here that you'll find out whether the advice you received in Tripoli about the logistics of crossing the border into Niger was correct; we hope for your sake it was. If the border has reopened, the Libyan authorities may require that you complete exit formalities here unless the border post at Tumu is staffed.

THE EASTERN SAHARA

Libya's far southeast has a number of standout highlights, most notably Waw al-Namus and Jebel al-Uweinat, and by the time you venture beyond Waw al-Namus you've well and truly left the beaten track. To travel in this region, you'll need plenty of time, because it can be a long road to anywhere, but the empty Saharan landscapes are more than adequate compensation.

ZUEILA زويلة

Zueila is another former home of the Fezzan sultans (the town used to be called Balad ash-Shareef or Town of the Chiefs) and a rendezvous point for caravans, although it never rivalled Murzuq as a centre of trade. When the Arab traveller Al-Bakri visited in the 11th century, he described seeing a cathedral, mosque, bath and markets, while Frederick Hornemann in 1798 found it one of the most hospitable towns on his travels across the Sahara.

There is a handy petrol station at the eastern entrance to town although, as always in this part of the country, supplies can be unpredictable.

The **fort** overlooking the old town is quite impressive, but the town's main attraction – a set of **seven tombs** (known as As-Sahaba) – is around 7km east of town. Architecturally the two-storeyed tombs are distinctive, made of sun-dried bricks and stone and each topped with a dome; six of the seven have been restored to something resembling their original appearance. But it's the fact that the tombs date to AH 27 and belong to seven Companions of the Prophet Mohammed who died here in a battle to defend the town in the 7th century that gives the site its real significance. If you're asking for directions, ask for *'maqbara Sahaba'*.

There is nowhere to stay in town and as for food, take what you can find in Zueila, which will hopefully be better than that Frederick Hornemann found in the 18th century when the food was 'apt to produce flatulencies and diarrhoea'.

Zueila is 130km east of Murzuq or 200km southeast of Sebha.

WAW AL-NAMUS واو الناموس

The Libyan Sahara has everything you longed for in a desert landscape: from soaring sand dunes to palm-fringed pools, from remote desert massifs to oasis towns of antiquity. And yet, even amid such splendour, Waw al-Namus feels like an unimaginable bonus, for it's the sort of place that you never dreamed existed. This extraordinary extinct and steep-sided volcanic crater is a weird-and-wonderful place, one of the most remote destinations in the world and arguably the most captivating in the Libyan Sahara. The black volcanic sand is stunning both from afar and when examined in miniature; look closely at some of the lava fragments and you may find green crystals from beneath the earth encased in the black crust. The three palm-fringed lakes arrayed around the crater are as surprising as they are beautiful, with each one a different colour – red, green and blue. Even here, so far from the nearest stand of trees, small but plentiful animal footprints leading towards the lakes tell of a micro ecosystem all its own. The crater is 7km in circumference and the summit of the rocky mountain in the centre affords stunning views. The sense of being somewhere *really* remote – Waw al-Namus is around 300km from the nearest towns – is another highlight of coming here.

You could easily spend half a day exploring the crater, but don't for a minute consider sleeping here – not for nothing is Waw al-Namus known as the Crater of the Mosquitoes. One other important point: it is preferable to leave your 4WD at the crater's rim and descend into the crater on foot using existing tracks in order to avoid scarring the landscape for others.

Visiting here is a major undertaking and involves a two-day round trip in reliable, well-equipped vehicles. The road east from Zueila goes as far as the tiny town of Tmissah (76km). Thereafter, it's unsurfaced for about another 100km to Waw al-Kabir, an army camp where you'll find showers and basic meals. Beyond Waw al-Kabir are two army checkpoints, including one just before you arrive at Waw al-Namus; dropping off cigarettes and reading matter is much appreciated by the bored conscripts staffing them. A permit is officially needed to visit Waw al-Namus, but this should be handled by your tour company and the price included in the overall cost of your tour.

You may be thinking that this is a lot of trouble and expense just to see a crater. But this is not a place you'll easily forget.

TIBESTI جبال تيبيستي

Libyan guides to whom we spoke claim this breathtaking chain of extinct volcanic mountains (which are also known as Jebel Nuqay on the Libyan side) has Libya's most superb desert scenery: dramatic cliffs, curious rock formations and deep ravines. It is also home to more fine examples of prehistoric rock art. Most of the range lies across the border in Chad, including the highest peak in the Sahara, Emi Koussi (3415m).

Sadly, the area is presently closed to tourists. The main reason is the presence of thousands of unexploded mines left over from Libya's border conflict with Chad in the 1980s, as well as continuing unrest across the border in Chad. For more information, see p218.

TAZERBO تازربو

Most people turn back from Waw al-Namus, but a hardy few continue eastwards towards Tazerbo, skirting the northern reaches of the **Ramlat Rabyaneh**, home to some splendid sand dunes of fine sand – the *ramlat* (sand sea) involves some of the most difficult desert driving in Libya.

Tazerbo is a small place, but it can seem like a metropolis if you're arriving from the empty desert wastes. Tazerbo has taken on national significance as a source of water for the Great Man-Made River project; the well fields are south of town. In the town itself, the remains of an old **Toubou fort** are all that catch the eye. There's nowhere to stay and only a few grocery stores.

If you found that your experience of the Ubari Lakes (p187) was somewhat spoiled by the convoys of 4WDs in the vicinity, consider taking the desert route to Al-Kufra (the paved road is appalling for the last 200km into Al-Kufra in any event; see p132) because it passes through the oasis of **Buzeima**. Although not a match for the dramatic surrounds of the Ubari Lakes, Buzeima is beautiful (and deserted) nonetheless, with plenty of dunes nearby. This would-be spa town and lake has very hot spring water that is supposedly good for rheumatism. Once famous for its dates, Buzeima was long ago abandoned.

AL-KUFRA الكفرة

☎ 0652 / pop 47,919

Al-Kufra is one of the most remote towns in the world – if you discount tiny Tazerbo off on a minor side road on the road to Benghazi, the nearest town is Jalu, an epic 625km away to the north. Although it is possible to fly here from Benghazi, Al-Kufra's sense of isolation is enhanced by the fact that the only paved road linking the town to the outside world is the worst in Libya; for more information, see p132. The state of the road may be why the cluster of oases that make up Al-Kufra are such a welcoming sight as you approach the town. In truth, however, Al-Kufra is a place to transact essential business (obtain travel permits, sleep in your last bed for a while) before continuing southeast to Jebel Arkno and Jebel al-Uweinat.

Al-Kufra was once an important staging post for trans-Saharan trade and, from the 19th century, it was an important centre of the Sanusi Movement in their resistance against Italian rule. It was finally occupied by the Italians in the 1930s. During WWII the oasis became a base for the Long Range Desert Group under the British.

Orientation & Information

The main road in from the north passes a petrol station, with another on the second road leading left (east). This latter road leads into the city centre (around 2km from the turn-off), passing the town's hotel, grocery stores, a number of restaurants and police station where travel permits are issued en route; **travel permits** (free) are required to visit Jebel Arkno and Jebel al-Uweinat, and although you won't need to visit the police station in person, you will need to bring two passport-sized photos so that your tour company can obtain the permit. The town centre contains the post office, a number of private telephone offices and cheap eateries.

Sights

The only sight worthy of note is the massive **camel market** 10km south of town alongside the road to Jebel Arkno. Many of the camels you see in Libya have, at some time, passed through this market after the arduous 40-day forced march from Sudan and Chad.

Where the road peters out into the sand, impossibly overladen **trucks** bound for Chad or, if the border is open, Sudan, gather to load their human and other cargo ready for the seven-day journey across the border. Always ask before taking photos.

Sleeping & Eating

Al-Waha Hotel (☎ 7502701; tw with shared/private bathroom 15/22LD) If you encounter the same receptionist we did, you most definitely may *not* see the room until you've paid for it. Given that you're not exactly spoiled for choice in Al-Kufra (what are you going to do, drive back to Benghazi on principle?), fork out the cash and climb the stairs to large, generally clean rooms illuminated by a bare light bulb. Some have balconies, some toilet seats are missing and don't even think of asking reception for towels. (They're actually quite friendly once you get to know them.)

Friends Restaurant (meals from 6LD) Along the main road into town, this is hugely popular for its 'Kentucky Chicken' and salads; it may take a while to arrive but servings are enormous. It also does hamburgers and other hearty dishes.

In the centre of town, cheap restaurants serving kebabs and Egyptian-style felafel abound.

Getting There & Away

It's not often that we feel inclined to say this, but thank God for Libyan Arab Airlines. Twice-weekly flights (one-way/return 37/74LD) from Benghazi save you a two-day return journey, not to mention allow you to avoid the thoroughly uninteresting and almost as often arduous road journey; for information on the road from Ajdabiya to Al-Kufra see (see p132). The airport is 8km west of town.

If you belong to the school of thought that air travel to the Sahara is somehow cheating, two far more interesting desert routes from Tazerbo (p207) and Al-Jaghbub (p155) lead to Al-Kufra.

THE ROAD TO JEBEL ARKNO

The trails leading southeast from Al-Kufra to Jebel Arkno (around 325km) are marked only by tyre tracks and by the desiccated carcasses of camels that didn't quite make it on the 40-day journey from Sudan.

Coming from Al-Kufra, the first landmark of note is the rock monolith of **Gara Khamsin** (50km) followed by the sight of the low sand dunes of **Seif Saba'een** (70km) away to the east. After 140km of unrelenting sand sheets, you enter the soft sand hills of **Gur Zwaya** where the low rock formations resemble nothing so much as the fossilised skeletons of long-extinct animals. There's a Libyan army checkpoint close to here. By the time you reach the small chain of dunes known as **Seif al-Matar**, you've broken the back of the journey.

Just beyond the dunes is an abandoned restaurant; hard as it is to believe, this place was not so long ago a buzzing meeting place of traders and travellers, smugglers and long-haul truck drivers where you could order a cold soft-drink and a meal then pay in Sudanese pounds, Chadian francs or Libyan dinars. As the western Sudanese region of Darfur descended into violence, borders were closed, trade dried up to a trickle and the restaurant closed its doors.

Soon, the **Gar'at el-Rih** (Mountain of the Wind) should come into view to the west, while Jebel Arkno itself should also be visible on the horizon to the southeast. Don't mistake the rocky pyramids of **Ashreef** for Jebel Arkno. Instead follow them south, skirt **Jebel Arkno** on its western side until you reach the tree marking the only entrance into the jebel.

JEBEL ARKNO جبل اركنو

You wouldn't come all this way just to see Jebel Arkno – a series of barren rocky outcrops encircling a central wadi – but you should definitely stop here as you make your way to Jebel al-Uweinat.

Jebel Arkno has three main attractions. The first – a well-preserved **armoured car** – greets you soon after entering the wadi. It belonged to the Libyan-backed Chadian forces of Goukouni Oueddei, who were based here during Libya's long war with Chad in the 1980s. Libya's protégé served as Chadian president from November 1979 until 1981 and would fight against Hissene Habré until 1987, when Libya officially ended its armed campaign to win control of the uranium-rich Aouzou Strip in northern Chad. Oueddei was so close to his Libyan sponsors that in 1981 he announced plans to unify the two countries. Hard to imagine, however, that a would-be president would have felt too at home in this arid corner of the desert. For more information on the war with Chad, see p41.

There is also the shell of an abandoned jeep from the same era, 3km into the wadi.

Also concealed within Jebel Arkno are some clear **giraffe and ostrich engravings** on a rock face of the western wall of the wadi, 5km after the tank (2km after passing the jeep). The carvings are thought to date back 12,000 years.

The meagre grasses and bushes of Jebel Arkno somehow support desert creatures of more recent vintage with the notoriously shy gazelle, waddan and fennec fox all reasonably prevalent. With the nearest Libyan army post some 40km away and tourists making only rare appearances here, this is

STUCK IN THE SAND *Anthony Ham*

There's something gloriously remote about Libya's extreme southeast, but I quickly lost my enthusiasm for it when we awoke one morning in the sands between Jebel Arkno and Jebel al-Uweinat to find the car's battery was a complete nonstarter.

I'm accustomed to my Libyan guides and drivers being able to fix anything – a legacy of the embargo years when spare parts were scarce: Libyans had to make do with what they had and went on to become some of the most skilled mechanics (and improvisers) in the world. I have watched, somewhere between Waw al-Namus and Al-Haruj al-Aswad, as my driver dismantled a Landrover's suspension and then rebuilt it in just over two hours. I have marvelled in the Idehan Ubari (Ubari Sand Sea) as my guide and driver changed the entire gear system of a Toyota Landcruiser. Most of my five years of desert travel in Libya has also been in the west of the country, where passing travellers who can send for help or share supplies or parts are a regular occurrence. So I wasn't worried at first.

We dug the wheels from the sand and pushed. When that failed, they jacked the car and tried to spin the wheels, hoping they would coax the engine to life. They dismantled the fanbelt and tried to charge the battery by hand. Then, at a particular moment, my two guides and driver stopped peering into the engine and, as one, looked hopefully out to the horizon. That's when I knew we had problems and began to wonder just how much trouble we were in.

And so it was that one guide and one driver set out to walk 25km across the sand to the police post just beyond Jebel al-Uweinat, leaving us to contemplate what it truly meant to be stuck in the sand with no prospect of passing traffic. As the hours passed, with the sun overhead, we crawled under the car for shade. What if they got lost and never returned? What if the police vehicle was under repair or away on patrol? We knew we had enough food and water for at least a week, but the sense of helplessness soon morphed into morbid thoughts.

Although I often break my own rule and venture into the Sahara in just one 4WD, I do so only with experienced drivers who know their car. Where possible, I also always travel off the beaten track with a satellite phone. In this case, in part because the east simply doesn't have the tourist infrastructure or experience that southwestern Libya has mastered, I had neither.

After six hours, a machine-gun-mounted patrol car of the Libyan police appeared over the horizon, bearing our guide and driver (who were originally mistaken by the police for illegal immigrants from Egypt) and the means to restart our car.

A happy reunion. Relief that you could almost taste. And one of the most important lessons of Saharan travel learned – always know your vehicle before taking it into the desert.

one of the best places to see some of the Libyan Sahara's most iconic species (for more information see p63).

JEBEL AL-UWEINAT جبل الوينات

Rising from the sands where the borders of Libya, Sudan and Egypt converge, Jebel al-Uweinat (two-thirds of which lie in Libya with the rest shared between Sudan and Egypt) is worth every kilometre of the long journey to get here. That's partly because there are some outstanding rock-art sites hidden in the rocky clefts, and also because the scenery is exceptional. But perhaps above all else, it's because this is like the rest of the Libyan Sahara used to be before the tourists arrived; you'll find yourself revelling in the idea of just how deep in the Sahara you are and just how quiet it all is.

There are two main wadis that run into the heart of the Libyan section of Jebel al-Uweinat. Although you could easily follow these routes in reverse, we suggest that if you're coming from Jebel Arkno (38km away), you enter the massif via the northernmost wadi, **Kerkur Bou Hlega**, which follows a southeasterly path into the jebel for around 7km.

Kerkur Bou Hlega is reminiscent of Jebel Arkno, with very little vegetation and a sun-seared hue to the boulder-strewn mountains. On the western side of the wadi, hidden in caves, are two **rock art sites**. One has fine representations of cows and a goat (or perhaps a waddan), but the second one you come to after entering the wadi is quite possibly the most extensive single gallery of rock paintings in Libya. There are clearer and arguably more beautiful scenes in the Jebel Acacus (p198) in Libya's far southwest, but the array of human figures here is astonishing. If it brings to mind the scenes of the Cave of the Swimmers from *The English Patient*, that could be because the inspiration for the movie came from rock-art sites a few short kilometres from here on the Egyptian side of the border. Sadly, crossing the border here is not permitted. One Libyan guide with whom we spoke did try and was promptly dispatched with a military escort to Cairo. So near…

Near the southeastern end of the wadi, a narrow thoroughfare between the rocks allows you to cross into the other main wadi, **Kerkur Ibrahim**. Almost without warning, you've entered another world where vegetation carpets the valley floor and catching sight of the relatively abundant **desert wildlife** of Jebel al-Uweinat suddenly seems possible; it was here that we saw our first fennec fox, when rival armies of them fought over our dinner scraps at night.

In addition to watching for wildlife, keep an eye out for the macabre camel carcass beneath a tree – the glue-like liquid secreted by the tree has preserved the upper side of the body, which has solidified even as the underside has been eaten away.

One local guide told us that around halfway through the roughly 10km-long wadi, a steep valley climbs away to the south until it reaches an elevated spring surrounded by palm trees; *'ain'* is the Arabic word for spring and their prevalence in the massif give it its name. Having lost so much time with car problems earlier in the day (see Stuck in the Sand, p209), we weren't able to investigate, but it's highly recommend that you do.

As the wadi continues its northwestern path, and you approach the point where the wadi leaves the mountains, you'll find some of the jebel's most dramatic and unusual rock formations. We can think of no better way to describe some of them than by evoking a Flake chocolate bar. Magnificent stuff! Also in the vicinity here are three rock-art sites – one in a cave in the southern rock wall of the wadi and the others in the folds of a rocky island surrounded by sand, close to the wadi's north side. Look particularly for the **ochre giraffe paintings**, as well as more representations of **cattle**.

There are some fine places to camp around here.

To get an evocative sense of the lie of the land at Jebel al-Uweinat, track it down on Google Maps (http://maps.google.es/). Saul Kelly's *The Hunt for Zerzura: The Lost Oasis and the Desert War* is one of few works of history to describe Jebel al-Uweinat in detail, all the while evocatively capturing its remote, end-of-the-earth feel.

Directory

CONTENTS

ACCOMMODATION

Gone are the days when hotels in Libya were restricted to a small handful of rundown government establishments where there was always the danger of sudden eviction when a government delegation arrived in town. A new breed of international-standard private hotels has swept through northern Libya and, although top-end hotels are nowhere to be found outside Tripoli and Benghazi and budget hotels remain conspicuous by their absence, midrange hotels are very comfortable and well-maintained. In the south of Libya, Sebha (p181) is the only place with a good range of accommodation, although the combination of camps and hotels in Germa (p190), Ubari (p192) and Ghat (p197) are also reasonable. Otherwise, people tend to sleep in the desert under a canopy of stars (see below).

In addition to hotels and hostels, there are also well-run camps in the Saharan oasis towns and, found along Libya's coastline, *qaryat as-siyahe* (tourist villages) are aimed at a Libyan clientele and offer proximity to the beach and a break from hotel ambience.

In this era of escorted tours to Libya, your choice of hotel will depend on the company through whom you organise your visit. Larger groups are likely to have little choice and the information on individual hotels throughout this book is designed to give you some idea of what to expect. Smaller groups may be able to lobby for the hotel of their choice based on the information provided in this guide, although you'll need to give the tour company plenty of notice.

Throughout this book, budget hotels and hostels refer to places where dorm beds cost 5LD and a single/double in a hotel costs up to 25/35LD. Midrange hotels and tourist villages range from 35/40LD up to 75/90LD, while top-end choices start from 90/100LD and can go much higher.

Note that your passport will be held by the hotel for the duration of your stay – don't forget to collect it when you leave.

Throughout this book, all quoted prices for hotels and tourist villages are for rooms with private bathroom and breakfast unless otherwise stated. A full list of abbreviations and icons used when giving prices and hotel facilities can be found inside the front cover of this book.

Camping

There are two kinds of camping possibilities while in Libya. The first is to sleep in the Sahara wherever your guide finds a secluded spot. Sleeping under the stars in this way is one of Libya's great travel experiences and you should do this at least once on your tour. Remember, however, that desert nights can drop below freezing from late November until February (see p19). Tour

PRACTICALITIES

- The *International Herald Tribune, Financial Times, Newsweek* and *Corriere Della Sera* are only available in Tripoli (see Bookshops, p73). The *Tripoli Post* (www.tripolipost.com) is Libya's government-run English-language newspaper and a good place to read the official take on world and local news; it's widely available in Tripoli.
- Radio coverage in Libya includes the BBC World Service (15.070MHz and 12.095MHz) and other European radio on short-wave. International satellite TV channels (available in many hotels) include CNN, BBC World and a small range of Italian, French and German channels.
- Libya uses the Secam video system that is commonly used in France and Greece and some Eastern European countries. Libyan DVDs belong to DVD region 5 (also used in Russia, India and elsewhere in Africa) and so may not work back home.
- Libya's electricity system caters for 220V to 240V AC, 50Hz; plugs are mostly of the European continental-style two-pin type, although the three-pin UK plugs are also common.
- Libya uses the metric system for weights and measures.

companies provide tents, sleeping bags and mattresses, and most expeditions are fully equipped when it comes to food with a cook, kitchen car and even fold-out tables.

The other option is to sleep in one of the permanent camps in the desert oases of Ghat (p197), Al-Aweinat (Serdeles; p193), Ubari (p192), Germa (p190), Tekerkiba (p186) and Sebha (p181). These usually consist of basic thatched-huts with shared bathroom and shower facilities, a kitchen and simple restaurant. Unless you have some reason for not wanting to sleep in the open desert (eg campervans for whom a dune is a road too far), we recommend that you use these camps for showering, using the toilet and not much more. Many of them are well-run, but also overrun by mosquitos in the evenings.

Some companies have also set up camps in the Awiss region in the north of the Jebel Acacus, but they're a scar on the landscape and a considerable drain on local water resources just so that you can have a shower.

The thatched huts in camps usually cost 10LD per person, while setting up tents costs 5LD and parking your campervan and connecting it to the electricity source costs 10LD. Parking your 4WD at the camp sometimes costs an additional 5LD to 10LD.

Some hotels and youth hostels will allow you to set up tents in their compound for 5LD or 10LD and are usually happy for you to use their shower and toilet facilities. It's also possible to set up your tent in car park No 1 (see p118) at the entrance to Leptis Magna.

Sleeping amid the spectacular sand dunes is, of course, free.

Hostels

Libya has an extensive network of *buyut ash-shabaab* (youth hostels), which can be pretty basic but dirt-cheap and fine for a night; a bed in a dormitory with shared bathroom costs 5LD. There are also some hotels for under 20/30LD for a single/double. Many youth hostels have areas set aside for women. Some also have very cheap meals available and can arrange breakfasts for larger groups.

At the time of writing, there were youth hostels in Tripoli, Sabratha, Al-Khoms, Zuara, Misrata, Sirt, Benghazi, Shahat, Yefren, Zintan, Nalut, Ghadames, Sebha, Houn and Fjeaj.

The headquarters for youth hostels in Libya is the **Libyan Youth Hostel Association** (Map p75; ☎ /fax 021-3330118; 69 Sharia Amr ibn al-Ass, Tripoli). The office is in Tripoli's central youth hostel (see Buyut ash-Shabaab; p92).

Hotels

Libya's new crop of private hotels are outstanding with high-quality rooms, friendly service and high standards of cleanliness and maintenance. Almost all have private bathrooms, air-con, minibars, satellite TV, and prices include a reasonable breakfast buffet. Although very few of these new hotels are budget-oriented, the prices (an average of around 40/50LD per single/double) are eminently reasonable. In contrast, the government-run hotels may occupy the best patches of real estate (at least in Tripoli), but service ranges from uninterested and painfully slow to downright dysfunctional, and prices can be excessive.

If we had one complaint about the new private hotels – and it's a minor one – it would be that most are international clones and few bear any traces of Libyan character. The only two significant exceptions where traditional architecture has been beautifully incorporated into the rooms and public areas are in the top-end category – in the Zumit Hotel (p90) in Tripoli and the Dar Ghadames Hotel (p174) in Ghadames.

Otherwise, you'll find excellent, recently opened hotels in Tripoli, Benghazi, Al-Bayda, Cyrene, Susa, Tobruk, Yefren, Ghadames, Sebha and Ghat, with other good choices of longer-standing in Zliten, Misrata, Derna, Sirt, Nalut, Germa and Ubari.

Libya's only international standard five-star hotel is the Corinthia Bab Africa Hotel (p91) in Tripoli.

Although the situation is changing, many hotels are still signed only in Arabic. For this reason, in most cases we have used the Arabic names ('funduq' means hotel).

Tourist Villages

Libya's tourist villages *(qaryat as-siyahe)* are not really set up for foreign tourists, but rather for locals who flock to the coast in summer, and they're often packed out by Libyan families for months on end. As such, facilities get a thorough working over and maintenance levels don't always keep pace. Outside the peak period (mid-May to mid-September) getting a room is usually no problem, although many tourist villages close down at this time for repairs and maintenance. In the warmer months you'd need to book months in advance as Libyan families frequently block-book the rooms or villas for up to four months. Accommodation is usually right on the beachfront in self-contained, air-conditioned rooms or villas (with a kitchen, including fridge) and there's usually a restaurant, teahouse and children's play area. Some villages also have an on-site bakery, swimming pool, tennis courts, laundry and grocery store.

Although these villages offer some variety from the hotel experience, remember that these places can be impossibly crowded with large groups making noise throughout the night. Lone female travellers have also sometimes felt a little uncomfortable as some rooms are booked out by groups of young males. That said, most travellers who stay here enjoy the chance to mix with Libyan families and learn more about

RESPONSIBLE DESERT TRAVEL

When exploring the desert, there are some general rules to keep in mind in order to minimise your impact upon what is a surprisingly fragile environment.

- Carry out all your rubbish. If you've carried it in, you can carry it out. Most Libyan tour companies are sensitive to these concerns and leave behind little rubbish from camp sites, but you can play your part by making sure they do.
- Minimise the waste you must carry out by taking minimal packaging and instead take reusable containers or stuff sacks.
- Never bury your rubbish. Digging disturbs soil and ground cover, and encourages erosion. Buried rubbish will more than likely be dug up by animals, who may be injured or poisoned by it. It may also take decades to decompose in the dry desert air.
- Don't rely on bought water in plastic bottles. Disposal of these bottles is creating a major problem.
- Sanitary napkins, tampons and condoms should also be carried out despite the inconvenience. They burn and decompose poorly.
- Where there's no toilet, bury your waste. Dig a small hole 15cm (6in) deep. Cover the waste with soil and a rock. Use toilet paper sparingly and bury it with the waste, or burn it.
- If you light a fire don't surround it with rocks, as this creates a visual scar.
- When collecting firewood, only use dead wood and never take from a living tree.

(and from) the locals than you ever could in a hotel.

Chalets or villas usually range from 25LD to 75LD per night.

The best tourist village in Libya is undoubtedly Zuara's Farah Resort (p106), which is open year-round and has excellent facilities, while Benghazi's Qaryat Qar Yunis as-Siyahe (p129) is also good.

ACTIVITIES

As Libya's tourism industry begins to diversify, an increasing range of activities is becoming possible. The Jebel Nafusa (Western Mountains; p157) of northwestern Libya and the Jebel al-Akhdar (Green Mountains; p124) in the northeast are enticing worlds of as-yet-unexplored trekking opportunities.

Snorkelling is also yet to take off although long stretches of Libya's Mediterranean Coast could be a snorkellers' paradise, especially the sunken ruins off the ancient city of Apollonia (p147) were it not for the fact that, given Libya's history of plunder by explorers, colonial officers and tourists, the local authorities are understandably reluctant to let people venture underwater, especially close to ancient sites. Before you pack your mask and flippers, remember also that such activities may also require Libyan government permission elsewhere; ask your tour company what's possible.

Camel Safaris & 4WD Expeditions

An increasing number of travellers are choosing to explore the Libyan Sahara by camel. Most tour companies can arrange camel expeditions to the Jebel Acacus or Wadi Meggedet.

The main advantage of seeing the desert in this way is that it slows you down to the pace of a loping desert rhythm, allowing you to truly experience the solitude of the desert without engine noise.

Camel safaris are also the most environmentally friendly way to see the Sahara; for more information on the environmental impacts, see Environmentally Piste-off, below.

The major disadvantage of travelling by camel is that you will be restricted to seeing just a small corner of the desert – so vast are the distances of the Libyan Sahara that exploring other regions astride a camel would involve more time than you probably have.

There's almost nowhere that you can't reach in the Libyan Sahara in a 4WD and that's certainly how most travellers travel while in the desert. For the best places to visit in the Libyan Sahara see Top Picks, p21.

ENVIRONMENTALLY PISTE-OFF

Before you decide to travel by 4WD it is worth considering the environmental cost of what is known as the 'Toyotarisation' of the Sahara. With their large wheels, 4WDs break up the surface of the desert, which is then scattered into the air by strong winds. By one estimate, the annual generation of dust has increased by 1000% in North Africa in the last 50 years. And in case you thought that your 4WD tracks across the sands would soon be erased by the winds, remember that tracks from WWII vehicles are still visible in the Libyan desert five decades after the cessation of hostilities.

Airborne dust is a primary cause of drought far more than it is a consequence of it, as it shields the earth's surface from sunlight and hinders cloud formation.

The consequences of our impatience in the desert extend far beyond Libya and its desert communities. The stirred-up sand threatens to envelop the world in dust with serious consequences for human health, coral reefs and climate change. Plankton on the surface of the world's oceans is also being smothered by sand with devastating implications for marine life. Dust storms are increasingly common in cities such as Madrid and the dust-laden winds threaten to transform 90% of Spain's Mediterranean regions into deserts. Once these deserts gain a European foothold, the process of desertification is extremely difficult and costly to reverse. Sand from the Sahara has even reached as far away as Greenland, settling on icebergs and causing them to melt faster.

Travelling by camel may be more restricting, but it's the best way to ensure that you leave behind nothing but easily erasable footprints in the sand.

TOP PLACES FOR A SWIM

You may not have thought about bringing your swimming costume, but with 1770km of Mediterranean coastline, Libya has some fine beaches with white sand and a wonderful absence of Tunisian-style tourist resorts dominating the coastline. Further south, swimming in one of the Saharan lakes is the stuff of legend.

Gebraoun (p188) Swimming in a lake in the middle of the Sahara and surrounded by sand dunes and palm trees – what more could you want?

Leptis Magna (p110) A picnic on the beach and a dip in full view of ancient Leptis – priceless.

Neqezzah (p107) One of the prettiest beaches along the Libyan coast and an ideal way to cool off after exploring Leptis Magna.

Ras al-Hammamah (p140) The beaches around here are some of the loveliest in Cyrenaica.

Ras al-Hillal (p149) Set against the backdrop of Libya's most picturesque coastal scenery.

Sabratha (p100) Bobbing in the Mediterranean alongside the astonishing ruins is one of the world's great swimming experiences.

Zuara to Ras al-Jedir (p106) Long miles of deserted shoreline, pristine white sand and crystal-clear water make for delightful and secluded swimming.

If travelling by 4WD, make sure that your vehicle is in excellent condition and that you're carrying sufficient water, petrol and spare parts.

Dune Skiing

Many Libyan sand dunes are so high as to resemble mountains and a novel way to experience this is to hire a set of skis or a snowboard available from the shore of Gebraoun (p188), one of the Ubari Lakes in the Idehan Ubari. The descents are exhilarating, but as dangerous as any ski-slope, so please take care.

Swimming

Taking a dip at one of the beaches along Libya's coast or in the salt lakes of the Sahara is a wonderful experience. For a list of our favourite places for a swim while in Libya, see above. Although Libyans are fast-becoming accustomed to the idiosyncrasies of foreign tourists, you should always be discreet and dress modestly.

BUSINESS HOURS

Friday is considered a holiday and most official businesses and shops are closed. Standard hours for banks are 9am to 1pm Sunday to Tuesday and Thursday; they open from 8am to 12.30pm and then again later in the day at 3.30pm to 4.30pm (sometimes 5.30pm) on Wednesday and Saturday.

Government offices, plus post offices, are usually open 7am to 2pm Saturday to Thursday April to September, and 8am to 3pm Saturday to Thursday October to March.

Most internet cafés operate 9am to 1am from Saturday to Thursday, but also open from 5pm until midnight on Friday.

Restaurants generally open 12.30pm to 3pm (for lunch) and 6.30pm to 10pm Saturday to Thursday. Most eateries may also open 6.30pm to 10pm Friday.

Shops generally open their doors from 10am to 2pm then again from 5pm to 8pm Saturday to Thursday; some also open Friday evening.

Reviews in this book won't list business hours unless they differ substantially from these standards.

CHILDREN

Many Libyans live with or have close ties to their extended families and you'll find that most are terrific in dealing with children.

The difficulty you're most likely to encounter is keeping your children entertained during long journeys. Also, most sites in Libya (admission 1LD for children under 12) are more 'adult' in their appeal, although some can be fun if you think creatively – see Top Sights & Activities for Children, p216. Travelling with children also increases your chances of meeting and spending time with Libyan families, especially if you're travelling in a small group – it's a great way for your kids to make new friends and for you to learn a lot about Libyan families and about your kids' interaction with other cultures.

TOP SIGHTS & ACTIVITIES FOR CHILDREN

With a little imagination (and your kids will probably have it in bucketloads) some of Libya's best-loved sights can become playgrounds of the mind.

- Berber *qasrs* (fortified granary stores) at **Qasr al-Haj** (p160) and **Nalut** (p162) are like a *Star Wars* set come to life.
- Underground Berber homes at **Gharyan** (p158) – the mere idea of living underground brings a smile to the face of a child.
- The old city of **Ghadames** (p164) offers the sort of labyrinth of which dreams are made.
- **Leptis Magna** (p110) – no-one will be better able to hear the ghosts of the Romans or bring Leptis to life than your children.
- A **camel safari** (p214) is so much better than a ride in a fun-fair back home.
- Take to a desert lake for a **swim** (p215); they'll never forget this.
- The sand seas of **Idehan Ubari** (p186) or **Idehan Murzuq** (p203) provide mountain ranges built entirely of sand that is ripe for sandcastles.
- Rock art of the **Jebel Acacus** (p198) or **Wadi Methkandoush** (p204) – yes, the Sahara really once was green and let's see if you can draw any better.
- **Waw al-Namus** (p206) has multicoloured lakes, black sand and the wonder of a volcano.

For more information and hints on travelling with children, Lonely Planet's *Travel with Children* by Cathy Lanigan is highly recommended.

Practicalities

Nappies (diapers), powders and most simple medications are available at pharmacies and grocery stores in most cities (especially Tripoli and Benghazi), although you should bring any special foods required and high-factor sunscreen. Disposable nappies are a practical solution when travelling despite the environmental drawbacks (and as long as they are disposed of responsibly).

Most hotels and many tour companies will not charge children under two years of age. For those between two and 12 years sharing the same room as their parents, it's usually 50% of the adult rate.

To avoid stomach upsets, stick to purified or bottled water. UHT, pasteurised and powdered milk are also widely available. You should also avoid travelling during summer when temperatures regularly exceed 50°C. Beware of dehydration and sunburn, even on cloudy days. For more health information, see p244.

CLIMATE CHARTS

Summer is generally very hot, with average temperatures on the coast approaching 30°C often accompanied by high humidity. In the south temperatures can reach a sweltering 50°C.

The historian Herodotus claimed that 'in the upper parts of Libya, it is always summer'. And yet, in winter the weather can be cool and rainy on the coast between October and March, even snowing occasionally in the mountains. Most rain falls in the Jebel al-Akhdar in the northeast and, to a lesser extent, the Jebel Nafusa. Desert temperatures can drop to subfreezing at night and, in a good year, Libya's desert regions receive less than 100mm of rain for the whole year.

During the spring (March to May) in northern Libya, you may encounter the *ghibli*, a hot, dry, sand-laden wind, which can raise the temperature in a matter of hours to between 40°C and 50°C. The *ghibli* can last from just a few hours to several days. For advice on the best time to visit Libya, see p19.

CUSTOMS

Libyan customs checks on arrival at airports are pretty cursory with the quick passage of tourists seen as a priority. Bags are, however, X-rayed before you're allowed to enter the country with customs officials keeping an eagle eye out for alcohol, which is forbidden. Private cars entering Libya are searched more rigorously; expect up to

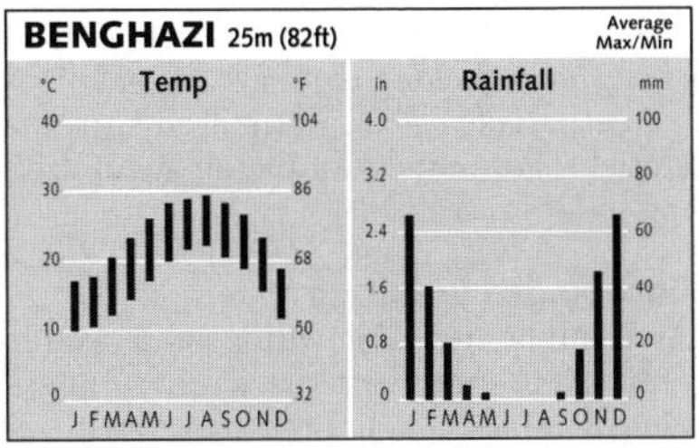

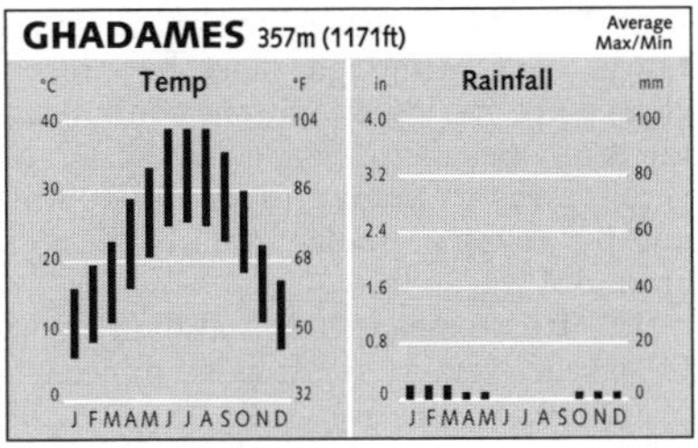

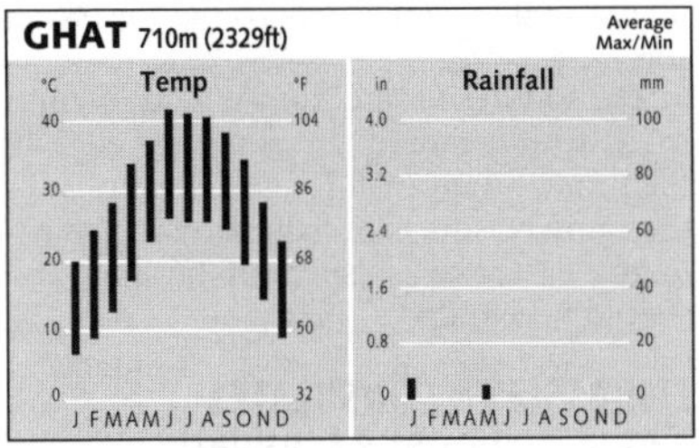

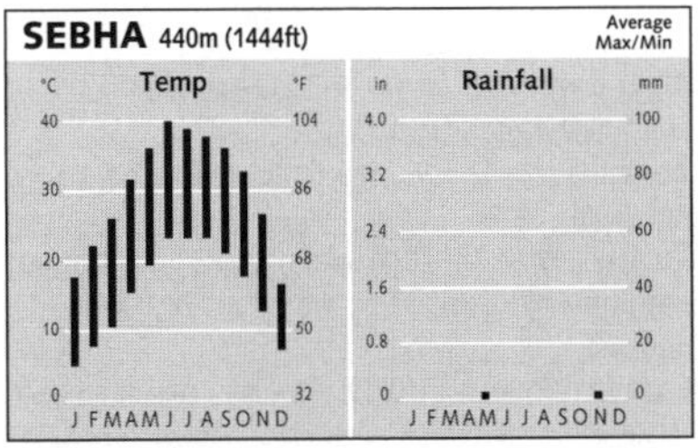

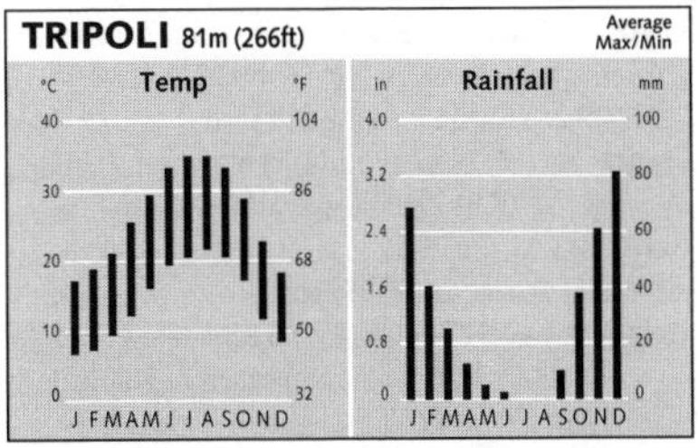

an hour of inspections. If alcohol is discovered in your car or baggage, it will be confiscated, although it may be returned to you if you later depart from the same land border.

For details on minimum currency requirements when entering Libya, see p231.

Upon departure, your bags are also likely to be X-rayed or searched, although this time they are looking for antiquities or fragments of Saharan rock art; to find out why see The Day the Vandals Came to Libya, p229.

DANGERS & ANNOYANCES

Libya is an extremely safe country in which to travel. Hostility of any kind towards foreigners is practically nonexistent, theft is extremely rare and Libyans will go out of their way to make you feel welcome. Unlike elsewhere in North Africa, Libyans will rarely hassle you for information about getting a visa to your country. Overcharging of foreign visitors is also very rare.

Security

You're unlikely to come into contact with Libyan police or soldiers unless you point your camera at a restricted site (see p223) and even then you're likely to be warned off than in serious trouble. The only other time you'll encounter them at close quarters are at the ubiquitous checkpoints along Libya's major roads (see p239); they're little more than a minor inconvenience and corruption is unheard of.

The only time when you may want to be particularly careful is when world events impact upon Libya, even indirectly, although even then the Libyan authorities are likely to make protecting tourists a top priority. One of very few examples was in February 2006 when an Italian government minister publicly wore a T-shirt which showed the cartoons of the Prophet Mohammed whose publication in a Danish newspaper had sparked worldwide protests in late 2005. Demonstrations in Benghazi turned violent with the Italian consulate set on fire and nine protesters killed. Although no tourists were directly targeted that's partly because the Libyan police were quick to shepherd tour groups away from potential flashpoints, especially in Cyrenaica. Any risk quickly subsided

THE LATEST TRAVEL ADVICE

Lonely Planet's website (www.lonelyplanet.com) contains information on what's new etc, and any new safety reports, as well as reports from other travellers recounting their experiences while on the road. The following government websites offer travel advisories and information on current hot spots.

Australian Department of Foreign Affairs and Trade (☎ 1300 139 281; www.smarttraveller.gov.au)

British Foreign Office (☎ 0845-850-2829; www.fco.gov.uk)

Canadian Department of Foreign Affairs & International Trade (☎ 800-267 6788; www.dfait-maeci.gc.ca)

Italian Ministero degli Affari Esteri (☎ 06491115; www.viaggiaresicuri.mae.aci.it in Italian)

Japan Ministry of Foreign Affairs (www.anzen.mofa.go.jp in Japanese)

US State Department (☎ 888-407 4747; http://travel.state.gov)

and within days it was business as usual for most travellers.

The major lesson from episodes such as these should be clear – keep an eye on world events, remember that situations like this are extremely rare and avoid demonstrations wherever possible.

Theft

Petty crime does occasionally occur in larger cities, but it's exceptionally rare. In fact, we've heard of only one example of a minor theft involving a traveller in the past six years. That said, be careful with your belongings on beaches while you're out in the water. If you're on a group tour, it is usually safe to leave your bags in the company's vehicle provided someone (preferably a direct employee of the company) will be keeping a watch over them. Valuables should either be carried with you in a money belt under your clothing or locked in the hotel safe.

Traffic

Driving in Libya can be hazardous with people driving at high speed the major danger, and police enforcement of road rules is marked by a decided lack of enthusiasm. The danger is particularly acute in Tripoli (see p76) and along the main coastal highway, especially between Tripoli and Misrata at night. For more information about driving in Libya, see p238.

Unexploded Ordnance

As you'll be travelling with a guide, you're unlikely to stray into areas where unexploded mines still lie, but it is worth remembering that at the end of WWII there were 11 million such mines on or under Libyan soil. Although most have been cleared up, every year, Libyans continue to die from ones that haven't. The most dangerous areas are in the area around Tobruk and the Egyptian border south to the area around Al-Jaghbub.

The Tibesti area (p206) is also off-limits to travellers due to unexploded mines left over from Libya's war with Chad in the 1980s. In the late 1990s, a 4WD vehicle set off one of these mines, whereafter the region was closed.

The southern route from Waw al-Namus to Al-Kufra around the southern edge of the Ramlat Rabyaneh is also dangerous for the same reason, especially around the Kilingue Pass, and is especially perilous and should be avoided.

EMBASSIES & CONSULATES

Libyan Embassies & Consulates

Libyan embassies are known as Libyan People's Bureaus.

Algeria (☎ 92 15 02; 15 Chemin Cheikh Bachir el-Ibrahimi, El-Biar, Algiers)

Australia (☎ 02-6290 7900; 50 Culgoa Circuit, O'Malley, ACT 2606)

Austria (☎ 01-367 7639; Balaasstrasse 33, 1190 Vienna)

Belgium (☎ 02-649 37 37; Ave Victoria 28, B-1050 Brussels)

Canada (☎ 0613-230 0919; www.libya-canada.org/consulate-eng; Suite 1000, 81 Metcalfe St, Ottawa K1P 6K7)

Chad (☎ 519289; Rue de Mazieras, N'Djaména)

Egypt Cairo (☎ 02-735 1269; fax 735 0072; 7 Sharia el-Saleh Ayoub); Alexandria (☎ 03-494 0877; fax 494 0297; 4 Sharia Batris Lumomba, Bab Shark)

France Paris (☎ 01 47 20 19 70; 18 rue Kepler, 75116); Marseilles (☎ 04 91 29 03 80; 6 blvd Rivet, 13008)

Germany (☎ 030-20 05 96 0; info@libysche-botschaft.de; Podbielskiallee 42, 14195 Berlin)

Italy Milan (☎ 02-86 46 42 85; Via Barrachini 7, 20123); Rome (☎ 06-86 32 09 51; Via Nomentana 365, 00162); Palermo (☎ 091-34 39 30, Via Libertà 171, 90143)

Netherlands (☎ 031 70 35 588 86; Parkweg 15, 1285 GH, The Hague)
Spain (☎ 91 563 57 53; Calle Pisuerga 12, 28071 Madrid)
Sudan (☎ 011 83222085; Mashtel St, Khartoum)
Switzerland (☎ 031-351 3076; Travelweg 2 CH-3006, Bern)
Tunisia (☎ 01-780 866; 48 Bis Rue due 1er Juin, Tunis 01)
Turkey İstanbul (☎ 212 25 18100; Miralay Sefik Bey Sok No 5, Gümüssuyu, Taksim); Ankara (☎ 312 43 81110; Cinnah cd 60, Cankaya)
UK (☎ 020-7589 6120; libya.embassyhomepage.com; 61-62 Ennismore Gardens, London SW7 1NH)
USA (Liaison office ☎ 202-944-9601; 2600 Virginia Ave NW, Suite 705, Washington DC 20037)

Embassies & Consulates in Libya

Algeria Embassy (Map p72; ☎ 021-4440025; 12 Sharia Kairaoun); Consulate-General (Map p75; ☎ 021-3610877; off Sharia Jama'a as-Saqa'a, Tripoli)
Australia (Map p72; ☎ 021-3351468; Office 203, Level 20, Tower 1, Burj al-Fateh, Tripoli)
Belgium (☎ 021-4782044; www.diplomatie.be/tripoli; Jasmin St, Hay Andalus, Area 2, Tripoli)
Chad (☎ 021-4443955; 25 Sharia Mohammed Mossadeq, Tripoli)
Egypt Tripoli (Map p75; ☎ 021-4448909; egyemblib@hotmail.com; Sharia al-Fat'h, Tripoli); Benghazi (Map p128; ☎ 061-2223099, Sharia el-Awarsi)
France (Map p72; ☎ 021-4774891; www.ambafrance-ly.org in French; Sharia Beni al-Amar, Hay Andalus, Tripoli)
Germany (Map p72; ☎ 021-4448552; www.tripolis.diplo.de; Sharia Hassan al-Mashai, Tripoli)
Italy (Map p75; ☎ 021-3334131; www.ambtripoli.esteri.it; 1 Sharia Uaharan, Tripoli)
Japan (Map p72; ☎ 021-4781041; Jamal al-Din al-Waeli St, Hay al-Andalus, Area 1, Tripoli)
Netherlands (Map p75; ☎ 021-4440216; tri@minbuza.nl; 20 Sharia Galal Bayar, Tripoli)
Niger (☎ 021-4834700)
Spain (☎ 021-3620051; Sharia al-Hawana, Al-Menshia, Tripoli)
Sudan (☎ 021-4778052; www.sudtripoli.net in Arabic; Sharia Mohammed Mossadeq, Tripoli)
Tunisia (Map p72; ☎ 021-3607181; off Sharia al-Jrabah, Bin Ashour, Tripoli)
UK (Map p72; ☎ 021-3351416; tripoliconsular@fco.gov.uk; 24th fl, Burj al-Fateh, Tripoli)
USA (Map p75; ☎ 021-3351848; libya.usembassy.gov; Corinthia Bab Africa Hotel; Souq al-Thalatha, Tripoli)

YOUR OWN EMBASSY

It's important to realise what your own embassy can and can't do to help you if you get into trouble.

Generally speaking, it won't be much help in emergencies if the trouble you're in is remotely your own fault. Remember that you are bound by the laws of Libya. Your embassy will not be sympathetic if you end up in jail after committing a crime locally, even if such actions are legal in your own country.

In genuine emergencies you might get some assistance, but only if other channels have been exhausted. If you need to get home urgently, a free ticket home is exceedingly unlikely – the embassy would expect you to have insurance.

If you have all your money and documents stolen, it might assist with getting a new passport, but a loan for onward travel is out of the question.

FESTIVALS & EVENTS

Although there are festivals in Germa (p190) and Kabaw (p162), they don't happen every year. The festivals that have become an annual feature of the Libyan year are listed here. Check with your tour company for exact dates.

Ghadames (October/November; p173) This festival centres on a celebration of traditional culture and is held in October most years, but will most likely be in November in 2007 to avoid Ramadan.
Ghat (late December; p197) The Acacus Festival celebrates the town's Tuareg heritage.
Houn (March; p185) The coming of spring in the Fezzan is welcomed by a decadent round of sweet-making in keeping with the oasis' reliance upon the seasons.
Zuara (August; p106) The Awussu Festival takes place on the beach or in the water.

FOOD

Prices given for restaurant meals throughout this book include soup, salad, main course, dessert and one drink unless otherwise stated. Most towns and cities in Libya don't have a sufficient number of restaurants to warrant separation into price categories in this guide and the cost of your meals should, in any event, be covered in the cost of your tour. For the record, a budget meal in Libya should cost up to 10LD, a midrange restaurant will cost you from 10LD to 15LD and top-end prices generally don't go much higher than 25LD.

For detailed information on Libyan food, see p66.

GAY & LESBIAN TRAVELLERS

Homosexuality is illegal in Libya, but it's an issue that rarely makes it into the public domain. Occasionally, you may see groups of Libyan men holding hands, but this is invariably an indication of friendship rather than homosexuality. Gay and lesbian travellers should experience no difficulties in Libya and most tour companies are discreet in handling such matters should it come to their attention. That said, it's unlikely to be an issue as the only questions Libyans will ask, and which are easily enough deflected, is whether you are married. If you're travelling with a partner, the rules are the same as for heterosexual couples: discretion is the key and public displays of affection are almost never appropriate.

HOLIDAYS

There are both religious and national holidays that are worth remembering as most businesses will be closed on these days. The major secular holiday to be wary of is 26 October (Day of Mourning, see right), when international phone lines are cut off between 6am and 6pm and all flights into and out of the country are cancelled.

National Holidays

Declaration of the People's Authority Day (2 March) Commemorates the founding of the Jamahiriya in 1977 with speeches and rallies.

Evacuation Day (28 March) Celebrates the evacuation of British forces from Libyan soil.

Evacuation Day (11 June) Celebrates the evacuation of other (non-British) foreign military bases with anti-imperialist speeches.

Revolution Day (1 September) The biggest nonreligious holiday in the Libyan calendar is a bonanza of speeches, rallies and even a military parade.

Day of Mourning (26 October) Pays tribute to Libyans killed during the Italian occupation with, yes, more speeches, closed borders, closed airports and phone communications cut off from the outside world.

Islamic Holidays

Islamic holidays vary in date according to the lunar calendar. For the dates of Islamic holidays in forthcoming years, see below. The significance of Ramadan is covered in detail in The Five Pillars of Islam, p53; for advice on travelling in Libya during the holy month of Ramadan, see p19.

INSURANCE

A travel insurance policy to cover theft, loss and medical treatment is a good idea. There is a wide variety of policies available, so check the small print. Some policies specifically exclude 'dangerous activities', which may include scuba diving, motorcycling, 4WD expeditions and even trekking. In Libya, you'll have to pay for medical care on the spot and claim later so make sure you keep all documentation. Some insurance companies will ask you to call back (reverse charges) to a centre in your home country where an immediate assessment of your problem is made. Check that the policy covers ambulances or an emergency flight home (for more details on medical insurance see p244).

Also check that your policy covers travel to Libya as some insurers still consider the region a 'danger zone' and either exclude it altogether from the policy or demand you pay premiums.

For advice on insurance for your car while in Libya, see p240.

ISLAMIC HOLIDAYS

Holiday	2007	2008	2009	2010
Ramadan begins	13 Sep	2 Sep	22 Aug	11 Aug
Eid al-Fitr (end of Ramadan)	14 Oct	3 Oct	20 Sep	9 Sep
Tabaski	19 Dec	8 Dec	28 Nov	17 Nov
Moulid an-Nabi (feast celebrating Mohammed's birthday)	31 Mar	20 Mar	9 Mar	27 Feb
New Year begins	21 Jan (1428)	10 Jan (1429)	31 Dec (1430)	20 Dec (1431)
Eid al-Adha (Feast of Sacrifice)	21 Dec	10 Dec	30 Nov	19 Nov

INTERNET ACCESS

Just about any small town in Libya has an internet café, although connections can be slow beyond Tripoli or Benghazi. One hour's surfing costs a uniform 1LD.

If you intend to rely on cybercafés and you don't have a web-based email address (eg Hotmail, Yahoo! or Gmail), you'll need to carry three pieces of information with you to enable you to access your internet mail account: your incoming (POP or IMAP) mail server name, your account name and your password. Your internet service provider or network supervisor will be able to give you these. Armed with this information, you should be able to access your internet mail account from any internet-connected machine in Libya, provided it runs some kind of email software (which most do). It pays to become familiar with the process for doing this before you leave home.

Unless you are travelling in Libya for a prolonged period or there on business, taking a portable computer is not worth the hassle. Most international servers don't have reciprocal arrangements with servers in Libya, even those with global roaming facilities and wireless access is extremely rare. A handful of Libyan hotels do, however, have in-room internet access, such as Corinthia Bab Africa Hotel (p91), while Funduq Winzrik (p92) has computers in every room; both hotels are in Tripoli.

If you plan to carry your notebook or palmtop computer with you, remember that the power supply voltage in Libya may vary from that at home, risking damage to your equipment. The best investment is a universal AC adaptor for your appliance, which will enable you to plug it in anywhere without frying the innards. You'll also need a plug adaptor for Libya – buy it before you leave home.

See also Internet Resources (p21) for other information.

LEGAL MATTERS

Since the days of the revolution, Libya's judicial system has been heavily influenced by Islamic precepts, although modern laws are a mixture of religious and secular tenets. There are both civil and religious courts, but foreign visitors are highly unlikely to have need of the latter. Judges are appointed by the General People's Congress, and judicial independence and due process are largely observed. All proceedings are conducted in Arabic with interpreters usually provided for non-Arabic aliens.

Libya's judicial system has come under the microscope in recent years as a result of the trial of five Bulgarian nurses and a Palestinian doctor charged with deliberately infecting over 400 Libyan children with HIV in a Benghazi hospital. A sensitive issue in Libya, the trial has drawn international criticism from Western governments and human rights organisations, although the first death sentence was overturned on appeal. A second death sentence was handed down in the retrial and a further appeal was pending at the time of writing.

The best piece of advice we can give you is to stay within the law because Libyan prisons are no place for the faint-hearted. Generally, the same activities that are illegal in your own country are illegal in Libya. Foreigners will simply be deported for committing most minor crimes. Remember that alcohol is forbidden in Libya and drug offences carry stiff penalties. And if you try to smuggle antiquities out of the country you will be imprisoned, possibly for weeks while they decide what to do with you. If you flout these laws, don't expect your embassy to get you out, although it should be your first port of call in arranging legal representation.

In the extremely unlikely event that you're the victim of a crime, you're likely to find the police are very much on your side and vigorous (perhaps excessively so when it comes to dealing with Libyan suspects) in bringing the perpetrator to justice. The epic paperwork and time involved will, however, soon have you wondering whether it's all worth it.

MAPS

Many of the maps throughout this book have been drawn using satellite technology and should be enough to satisfy most travellers, although more-detailed maps would be necessary for desert expeditions in remote areas. For detailed advice on the best maps for expeditions in the Libyan Sahara, see p179. Among the maps covered is the best map on the market for the Sahara, the outstanding *Jebel Acacus – Tourist Map & Guide* (1:100,000).

The most reliable country map would be *953 –Africa North and West* by Michelin

(1:4,000,000). Other decent maps are Cartographia's *Libya* (1:2,000,000) and *Libya* (1:1,650,000) by Cartes de Voyage Internationale. The best map available inside Libya is published by Malt International and entitled *Map of the Socialist People's Libyan Arab Jamahiriya* (1:3,500,000), although its southern borders are not to be trusted as they're unjustifiably generous in Libya's favour. Also available inside Libya is the *Map of Libya & Ancient Cities,* which is of no use for navigation other than for the fact that it has the names of many towns written in Arabic alongside the English version.

Most of the maps mentioned in this book are available from **Stanfords** (☎ 0044 20 7836 1321; www.stanfords.co.uk), which is the world's largest map shop. You could also try www.sahara-overland.com.

MONEY

The official unit of currency is the Libyan dinar. Notes include 0.25LD, 0.5LD, 1LD, 5LD, 10LD and, although we've seen very few, 20LD. The dinar is divided into 100 piastres, or 1000 dirhams (also known as *mileem*), although the latter is less used these days. There are coins for 10 piastres, 25 piastres, 50 piastres and 1LD.

The ideal approach to bringing your money to Libya is to bring cash euros, US dollars or British pounds and carry a Visa card for emergency cash advances.

For details on minimum currency requirements when entering Libya, see p231.

ATMs

They've taken their time arriving, but ATMs are finally becoming commonplace in Libya, at least in Tripoli and Benghazi. However, maintenance levels are not always as they could be, so it would be a risk to rely on these as your primary source of funds. Most ATMs have a daily 200LD withdrawal limit.

The Masraf al-Tijara Watanmiya (Bank of Commerce & Development), which has branches throughout the country (including in Tripoli, Benghazi, Al-Bayda and Tobruk and possibly elsewhere by the time you read this), is the place to go for Visa or Visa Electron cash advances; some of its branches have ATMs.

MasterCard holders will need to rely on far less frequent branches of the Aman Bank for Commerce & Investment. The only two branches we found were in the arrivals hall of Tripoli International Airport and on Sharia Mizran in downtown Tripoli (see p76).

Black Market

A small black market in foreign exchange exists in Libya, although rates are generally the same as in banks and it's more to serve the purposes of Libyans in need of foreign currency than tourists. Its only advantage is when you're in need of cash outside banking hours (eg Friday). You should always go with your guide and always check the prevailing bank exchange rate as rates can be subject to negotiation. Souq al-Mushir and Souq al-Turk (p76) in Tripoli's medina or the southern entrance to Souq al-Jreed (p126) in Benghazi are the main places to try. Otherwise, the gold shops of souqs (markets) are good places to start.

Cash

Cash is king in Libya and euros have become the currency of choice, although US dollars and British pounds are also easy to change. You should bring mostly large denomination notes as these sometimes attract slightly higher rates on the street (although rates are the same in banks) with a few smaller notes for changing as you near the end of your trip. Some shopkeepers, especially in Tripoli, will sometimes accept payment in foreign currency, and Libyan tour companies prefer foreign currency when you pay for your tour.

In case you're worried about bringing so much cash with you, remember that theft in Libya is extremely rare (see p218) and you should have no problems if you carry your money in a money belt.

Officially, any bank is able to change money, although some are surprisingly reluctant to do so. To change money at a bank ask your hotel for your passport in case the bank asks for identification, although this is becoming increasingly rare.

Before crossing into Libya, you can change money on the Egyptian or Tunisian side of the land borders, although if you don't manage to do it, your tour company representative should be waiting for you on the Libyan side and can explain the easiest way to get your hands on some dinars. If you're arriving by air, the airports in Tripoli and Benghazi have foreign-exchange counters and ATMs, although the latter don't always work.

The Libyan dinar is not a hard currency, but if you find yourself stuck with dinars at the end of your trip, it's sometimes possible to change them at the airport exchange counters or across the land borders. That said, try not to get stuck with too many dinars in case currency regulations change. As a last resort, ask your tour company for advice.

Credit Cards

Paying with credit card is becoming increasingly widespread in Libyan hotels, restaurants, airlines and shops, but it remains the exception rather than the rule. As your single greatest expense is likely to be the cost of your tour and most tour companies still don't accept payment by credit card (some accept international bank transfers in advance of your visit), carrying a credit card will be of limited use. This is reinforced by the fact that the cost of most hotels and restaurants are most likely included in the cost of your tour, rather than requiring you to pay them directly. If you do pay by credit card, ask for the price to be credited in euros or US dollars to ensure the most favourable bank rates.

Cash advances against credit cards are, however, possible – for details see ATMs opposite.

Tipping

As more tourists visit the country, tipping is becoming more common in Libya, but there's rarely any pressure to do so. In restaurants, for helpful hotel staff or mosque caretakers, a dinar or two is suitable although up to 5LD may be appropriate depending on the circumstances.

The only time when larger tips are appropriate are for guides (eg in the desert or your escort around the country). In this case, it's entirely up to you, but any amount will generally be appreciated. A good starting point is 15LD per person for a few days, up to 50LD if the help has been exceptional over a couple of weeks.

Travellers Cheques

Don't bring travellers cheques as we're yet to find a Libyan bank that's willing to exchange them.

PHOTOGRAPHY & VIDEO

Film & Equipment

Digital photography is catching on fast in Libya, although you should arrive in the country self-sufficient in equipment and flash cards. If you want to burn photos to CDs, it's possible at some internet cafés in Tripoli and Benghazi. However, this applies only to dedicated internet cafés and not to the ubiquitous phone centres that have a few computers out the back. If you're having trouble finding a place that can help, ask your tour company for advice.

Although print film is widely available in larger cities, you should bring all the film with you; you're unlikely to have any choice and many films on sale in Libyan shops are approaching their use-by dates if they haven't expired already. The most commonly available print film is Konica – a roll of 36 costs from 3LD to 5LD. Slide film is difficult to track down, even in Tripoli, and more expensive; expect to pay 10LD for a roll of 36-exposure Konica slide film or 12LD for Kodak if you're lucky enough to find it.

If you have a video camera, you should also bring your own video film. You may get lucky at one of the better photo studios or find an electronics store in one of Tripoli's more upmarket shopping centres that may stock film, but don't count on finding what you need.

Photographing People

Most Libyan men seem perfectly happy to have their photo taken, although you should still ask permission, especially in rural areas.

Male travellers should never take photos of local women without first being granted express permission; this may be refused even for women photographers. Some Tuareg in the Jebel Acacus have taken to asking for money (a negotiable 5LD seems to be the going rate) in return for having their photo taken.

Restrictions

Never point your camera at military installations of any description, or at any border posts, checkpoints, ports, police stations or at uniformed police or soldiers. Most of these are easy to avoid, although police stations are often poorly signposted – always ask if you're not sure. As one traveller reported:

> Towards the end of the trip I realised that I had very few photos of the giant posters of the 'great leader' (Colonel Gaddafi), which are all over the coast regions. At a roadblock I chanced my luck by getting my guide to ask if I could photograph a good one depicting the 'hero' of the Great Man-Made-River Project. The officer in charge said (as I well knew) that photography was forbidden near roadblocks, but then went back into his office, ripped off the wall a large cardboard-backed picture of Gaddafi addressing the masses and presented it to me as a consolation prize!
>
> *David Boyall, Australia*

Still and video photography are permitted in all museums, archaeological sites and the medinas of the Saharan oases (eg Ghadames and Ghat), but you must buy a ticket for 5LD for still cameras and 10LD for a video camera.

Technical Tips

Lonely Planet publishes *Travel Photography – A Guide to Taking Better Pictures* by renowned travel photographer Richard I'Anson; it's filled with useful tips. In the same series, *People Photography* (by Michael Coyne) and *Landscape Photography* (by Peter Eastway) are great primers to carry in your suitcase.

POST

Libya's postal system is slow but reliable and almost every Libyan town has a post and telephone office, always easily recognisable by the tall telecommunications tower rising above the building.

Postal Rates

It costs 30 piastres (0.3LD, or 300 dirhams) to send a postcard to most places, including Europe and Australia. Sending letters is similarly cheap, generally between 50 piastres and 1LD. A 1kg parcel to Europe costs 15LD, while the same weight to Australia is 45LD. The best strategy is to travel as lightly as you can to allow for any souvenirs you buy.

Receiving Mail

Unless you're in the country for an extended period, you'd be unwise to get mail sent to you in Libya as in-bound deliveries can take an age. If you simply can't wait until you get home, there are generally reliable poste-restante services (letters only) at the central post offices in Tripoli (p76) and Benghazi (p126). Address mail to:

Your Name
Poste Restante
Main Post Office
Tripoli (or Benghazi)
Libya (GSPLAJ)

Libya doesn't have a system of postal deliveries to street addresses, only post-office boxes. If you're sending a letter or package to someone in Libya, make sure that you write the post-office-box number and city on the envelope. In the Fezzan, many addressees use the French equivalent, BP, followed by the number of the box and the town.

Sending Mail

Postcards and letters sent from the central post offices in Tripoli or Benghazi usually reach their destination within a week to ten days for the UK and Continental Europe or two weeks for Australia and the USA. Sending from a post office in a small town could take a lot longer. Always hand your mail to a post-office worker (never leave it in a post box), and write the address details as clearly as possible; if you can, write the name of the country in Arabic.

SHOPPING

Libya may not have the selection of handicrafts to rival Morocco or Egypt, but shopping in Libya is wonderfully hassle-free, prices are low and the quality is generally high. The best place in Libya to do your shopping is in the souqs of Tripoli's medina (p96). Many Tuareg in the Fezzan spread out their items for sale on a rug alongside the lakes and a few camping grounds.

For the most eye-catching souvenirs that you'll find while in Libya, see p226, while for Tuareg handicrafts see opposite.

The better Libyan (primarily Berber) rugs consist of high-quality, flat-weave kilim cushions and larger rugs, although in most places you'll mostly come across

TUAREG HANDICRAFTS

Tuareg jewellery and leatherwork are very distinctive and make wonderful gifts or souvenirs of your time in the Libyan Sahara.

The most unusual item is the *croix d'Agadez* (Tuareg cross of stylised silver with filigree designs) named after Agadez in Niger. Every town and region with a significant Tuareg population has its own unique version of the cross. Although European explorers saw the design as evidence of prior Christianity, traditional Tuareg see them as powerful talismans designed to protect against ill fortune and the evil eye. Some also serve as fertility symbols. The crosses are still used by Tuareg men as currency (eg for buying camels), although these days this is rare in Libya. At times, the crosses are worn by their wives as a sign of wealth.

Other silver items include a wide range of silver necklaces (those containing amber are generally from across the border in Niger); striking square, silver amulets that are worn around the neck by elders as a symbol of status (some are also used in weddings by women); and ornamental daggers made of silver with leather hilts.

Leather items include tasselled pouches worn around the neck by men for carrying tobacco or money when out on the desert trails (some contain a surprising number of pockets), and saddlebags or cushions. The strong odour of camel comes at no extra cost.

The best places in the Fezzan to find these items include many of the tourist camps across the Fezzan and around the lakes – the itinerant sellers at Umm al-Maa (p188) had the best selection when we visited.

heavy woven Berber rugs with simple, almost childlike animal motifs. The rugs on offer in the Misrata souq (p119) are noted for their bright colours.

Gharyan is the undisputed pottery capital of Libya (see p159). The road into town from Tripoli is lined with stalls offering colourful bowls decorated with swirling designs in different sizes. The quality is high and surprisingly reasonable in price.

Palm-woven products such as mats, baskets and bowls are the speciality of the coastal Tripolitanian towns of Tauorga (p120) and Ghadames (p175). The products are lightweight but bulky.

Bargaining

Don't come to Libya all primed to hone your bargaining skills; this is definitely not Egypt. For most purchases prices are fixed, any reductions are likely to be negligible and the process is never adversarial. There are always exceptions (some shops in the souqs of Tripoli's medina and the Tuareg jewellery sellers of the south). You're more likely to get a discount if you develop a friendly rapport with the vendor and if you go on your own, rather than as part of a group.

SOLO TRAVELLERS

Travelling to Libya on your own has a number of advantages, not least among them a greater likelihood of flexibility in choosing your itinerary, being able to meet locals more readily than if you were in a group, and forming a closer bond with your Libyan guide who may soon become a friend.

There are, however, a number of disadvantages. For a start, it can be prohibitively expensive as you must shoulder the full cost of transport. A private car costs at least 35LD per day while a 4WD in the desert starts from 80LD and could go as high as 120LD; if you're required to take two 4WDs into the desert as you should, costs really begin to escalate. Guiding fees (50LD) in Libya's ancient cities will also make a dent in your wallet that you wouldn't otherwise notice if travelling with other people.

Another disadvantage is that many tour companies will simply not be interested in arranging your visit (and may not even answer your initial query; see No Answer, Try Again, p228) because it's simply not worth their while financially. Libyan visa regulations also sometimes require a minimum of four travellers although most companies easily circumvent this requirement (see p228). To find a Libyan tour company willing to take you – international tour companies usually have set departure dates and require a minimum number of travellers for the tour to go ahead – requires persistence

TOP LIBYAN SOUVENIRS & WHERE TO FIND THEM

- Embroidered Ghadames slippers from the Bin Yeddar family workshop (p175)
- Colonel Muammar Qaddafi's masterpiece, *The Green Book,* in a range of languages from Fergiani's Bookshop (p74) in Tripoli
- A Colonel Qaddafi watch from the watch shops in Tripoli medina or Sharia al-Rashid (p96)
- Tuareg jewellery from the Tuareg salesmen next to Umm al-Maa (p188) in the Idehan Ubari
- Colourful Gharyan pottery (p159) from the roadside stalls as you enter Gharyan from Tripoli
- Berber flat-weave rugs from Carpet Bazaar – Ben Zeglam Shop (p96) in Tripoli's medina
- Tuareg turbans and baggy camel-riding pants from the clothes market in Ghat (p197)

and you should start contacting companies at least two months in advance of your visit.

TELEPHONE & FAX

The cheapest way to make international phone calls is via an internet-connected line in an internet café. Most cafés in Tripoli, and some in Benghazi and elsewhere, sell phone cards with come with a pin number. One of the better networks is Net2Phone with whom a 3.75/5.75/11LD card gets you 165/275/550 minutes to the UK, slightly less to other European countries and Australia. Another option is PC2Call, where cards cost 5.50/10LD for similar results. The quality of the lines is generally good, although it depends on the internet connection.

If there's no internet café nearby or you can't buy a card, Libya's landline phone system is excellent and connections are usually instant for domestic and international calls. All such calls, whether international or domestic, are best made at the government telephone offices attached to any post office. To make an international call, go to the counter, write out the number in full for the clerk who will make the connection, and then take the call in the allocated private booth. After completing the call, you pay at the counter. There are also private telephone offices around most towns – they're ever so slightly more expensive than the post offices but they're open longer hours. Avoid making international phone calls from hotels, where the rates can be ridiculous.

Calls within Libya invariably receive instant connections and are quite cheap (around 0.25LD, or 25 piastres).

Fax

The best places from which to send faxes are also the government telephone offices. For international faxes, the cost depends on how long the fax takes to go through. An international fax will rarely cost more than 2LD and a fax within Libya around 0.5LD.

The main post office in Tripoli (p76) provides a very handy **fax-restante service** (fax 021-3331199). For a small fee (no more than 1LD), staff will hold faxes for up to one month.

Mobile Phones

GSM Mobile networks now cover most Libyan towns and their hinterlands, although you'll obviously be out of range while in the Sahara or anywhere too far off-the-beaten track. There are two mobile-phone operators in Libya. **Libyana** (www.libyana.ly in Arabic) has the most extensive network, although **Al-Madar** (www.almadar.ly in Arabic) is fast catching up although still restricted to the northwest. There is a fair chance that your mobile will work in Libya, although using it for anything more than sending and receiving SMS can be prohibitively expensive; check with your carrier for their global roaming rates for Libya before setting out. To get the lowdown on Libyana and Al-Madar (including their international roaming partners and a map of their coverage inside Libya), click on to the following website at www.gsmworld.com/roaming/gsminfo/cou_ly.shtml.

If your mobile carrier doesn't have a Libyan affiliate, you can easily buy a 5LD or 10LD SIM card from Libyana and put it in your phone. International calls are surprisingly cheap when calling from a Libyan mobile and are often even cheaper than landlines. If you need to buy a SIM card, ask your tour company (Libyans are very mobile savvy) for the nearest store.

Satellite Phones

Whenever venturing off-road into the Libyan Sahara, you should always consider taking a satellite phone with you – this recommendation becomes a necessity if you're travelling in just a single vehicle. Most experienced Libyan drivers of 4WDs in southwestern Libya have a phone or know where you can find one. It is also possible in some places (your driver or guide should know where to ask) such as Sebha to rent (usually Thuraya) satellite phones. Expect to pay a minimum of 5LD per day plus pre-paid phone cards. Such phones should be used only for emergency purposes and not to call home as costs start from at least €3 per minute to Europe.

TIME

Despite its size, Libya has only one time zone – it's two hours ahead of Greenwich Mean Time (GMT) – which means that the sun sets at least half an hour earlier in the east so take that into account, especially if you're travelling in the desert. There is no changing of the clock for summer, and offices and their employees simply adjust their attendance times to suit climatic conditions instead.

For a comprehensive guide to world time zones, see p270.

TOILETS

Public toilets are something that other countries have so if you're out and feel the urge, ask at a restaurant, teahouse, mosque or hotel if you can use their toilet; you'll rarely be refused. Ask for *'al-hammam'* or *'mirhad'*.

It's rare to come across a squat toilet in a hotel as most hotel rooms have sit-down flush toilets and a rare few even present you with a choice between a toilet and a bidet. Squat toilets are, however, found in most mosques and cheap restaurants. In all but the cheapest hotels or in desert camps, toilet paper is provided. Remember that some toilets are not designed for paper; if you're not sure, use the rubbish bin.

TOURIST INFORMATION

Libya has no tourist offices in Libya or elsewhere, and the country's tourism authorities operate as overseers of the tourism industry and tour companies rather than sources of practical information. Their only visible tourist services are the excellent series of tourist posters on Libya that you'll see around the country.

The best sources of information about Libya (apart from this guidebook, of course) are the internet (see p21), books about Libya (p20) or Libyan tour companies.

TRAVELLERS WITH DISABILITIES

As long as you're healthy, there's no reason why people with a disability shouldn't enjoy travelling in Libya. If you're going as part of a group, notify your tour company well in advance of any special requirements you may have. Most of the better hotels have entrances at ground level and functioning lifts. Most group tours involve transport to all sites, which relieves the process (for all travellers) of negotiating public transport. Even in the desert, transport is usually by 4WD, rather than camel. Depending on your disability, you may find it difficult exploring some of the archaeological sites where paths are uneven and access for wheelchairs can be difficult. However, Ghadames, Tobruk and the major cities are generally no problem. Discuss the possibilities with your tour company before travelling. As one wheelchair traveller from the UK found, 'whilst there is very little access to anywhere for wheelchair users, there never seems to be a shortage of people who are more than eager and willing to lend a hand.'

You should also bring your own medications and prescriptions with you.

VISAS

Nationals of most African and Arab countries don't require visas to enter Libya. Everyone else does.

Registration

All holders of tourist visas must register with the Libyan authorities at any *jawazat* (passport office) within seven days of arrival in the country. Those who don't do this by the end of the seventh day face a minimum fine of 50LD. In this era of organised tourism, the process will invariably be completed by the tour company responsible for you during your stay. If you must complete the process yourself, it's better if you can find an Arabic speaker to go with you as few officers speak English and the forms are in Arabic.

Tourist Visas

Entire books could be written about the Libyan tourist visa dance, but the process is actually quite simple.

First you need an invitation from an accredited Libyan tour company (see p243). Unless you're travelling with an international company (see right), obtaining this invitation involves writing to the company in question around six weeks or one month (a minimum) in advance, outlining your travel dates and your desired itinerary. If the company answers and agrees to arrange your visa and visit, you will need to send your passport details (they sometimes ask for a faxed copy of the front page of your passport) and sometimes your flight details. Once the invitation has been approved by the Libyan authorities, you can either pick up your visa at the Libyan People's Bureau in your country (see Embassies & Consulates; p218) or, more conveniently, on arrival in Libya. If picking up your visa on arrival, before leaving home you should make sure that your tour company sends you a scanned or faxed copy of the Arabic visa approval and, if you're arriving by air, a copy of the letter they should have sent to your airline confirming that your visa has been approved.

> **NO ANSWER, TRY AGAIN**
>
> Libya has numerous professionally run tour companies, although almost all of them suffer from an occasional inability to answer emails promptly. In fact, many of them don't answer emails at all. The actual visa process takes only a couple of weeks, but you're advised to start contacting tour companies long before that to take into account the incomprehensible periods of silence from the Libyan capital. This is a problem that particularly afflicts lone travellers (see p225) but it's something of an established Libyan business practice in all fields. Be persistent, try following up with phone calls and, as a last resort, threaten to write to us at Lonely Planet if visa deadlines are approaching.

If you are arranging your visa through a non-Libyan company (see p236), they should handle the process of dealing with the Libyan affiliates and the Libyan authorities and all you should need to provide to them are your passport details.

Choosing which company to travel with is one of the most important choices you'll make when visiting Libya and is about far more than arranging your visa to enter the country. The company which arranges your visa is also responsible for you during your time in Libya and will arrange all transport, accommodation, meals and a guide or escort in your language for the duration of your stay. We suggest that you contact a number of companies (both Libyan and international) to see which one best suits your needs.

When dealing with your tour company prior to the issuing of a visa, make sure you specify the point where you plan to enter Libya. At least one reader was turned away from the Egyptian border because his visa stated his entry point as Tripoli International Airport. If you have picked up your visa from a Libyan People's Bureau prior to departure, always check any conditions to make sure this doesn't happen to you.

Visas cost 15LD (the cost will most likely be included in the cost of your tour), are valid for 30 days from the date of entry and you must usually enter Libya within 30 days of the visa being issued. Although some Libyan government departments follow the lunar calendar, all visas and visa extensions are calculated using the Western calendar.

A couple of restrictions to bear in mind. Israeli citizens will not be issued with a visa under any circumstances, nor will those with Israeli stamps in their passport. The situation with regard to US nationals depends on the prevailing political winds – at the time of writing, no tourist visas were being issued to US citizens in retaliation for US restrictions on Libyan visitors, although the situation has probably changed by the time you read this.

Libyan visa regulations do change from time to time and even from embassy to embassy. Very occasionally, travellers have been issued with a tourist visa from an out-of-the-way Libyan embassy and found themselves free to explore the country without a guide. Things have tightened up since then and the rules restricting travellers to escorted visits

THE DAY THE VANDALS CAME TO LIBYA

The restrictive change in visa regulations at the end of 2000 is largely the fault of a small minority of tourists who took advantage of their freedom in Libya.

The story goes that a group of freewheeling European visitors visiting the Jebel Acacus (p198) of southwestern Libya decided that the region's famous rock art would make a wonderful souvenir of their time in Libya. Using silicone gel to take copies from the rock located in the Awiss region of the Acacus, they vandalised priceless art that had survived untouched for thousands of years. The thieves were caught with their shameful booty by government officials in Tripoli, detained for a couple of weeks, fined and then deported.

This incident was not the first, but it confirmed to the government that tourists were responsible for the increasing damage to ancient sites, and it shut down the independent travel option. Ever since, the Libyan government has insisted that you be accompanied by a Libyan escort from a tour company.

For details on protecting Saharan rock art, see p204.

remain firmly in place and are likely to remain so for the foreseeable future.

The rules also officially require that you travel in a group comprised of a minimum of four people, although such rules are easily circumvented by most Libyan tour companies with the full knowledge of the Libyan authorities. If you are planning to travel in a group of less than four people, arrange to pick your visa up on arrival in Libya, so as to avoid dealing directly with an embassy.

For details on minimum currency requirements when entering Libya, see p231.

OTHER VISAS

Unless you're visiting Libya on business, the only other way to get a Libyan visa is if a private Libyan citizen invites you to visit him or her in Libya. While that sounds simple enough, it can be a long and drawn-out process that takes even longer than obtaining a tourist visa. Your Libyan friend will need to get the process started, be pretty savvy on the Byzantine workings of the Libyan bureaucracy and all you can really do is sit back and wait for the wheels to grind.

Travel Permits

Travel permits are required for some remote desert areas of Libya, including the Jebel Acacus, Waw al-Namus and Jebel al-Uweinat. You're unlikely to have any inkling, however, that you even have a permit as obtaining it is the responsibility of your tour company. For more information on permits for the Jebel Acacus, see p199.

Visa Extensions

If you wish to stay in Libya longer than one month, extensions (15LD; no photo) are possible, although rare. Applications are handled by the *jawazzat,* of which there is usually one in most towns. Extensions are usually no problem, but you're much more likely to be granted an extension if you allow your local tour operator to make the application on your behalf.

Visas for Onward Travel

At the time of writing, it was not possible to obtain visas in Libya for Algeria, Chad, Niger or Sudan. Check with the embassies in question (p219) to see whether the situation has changed.

Although visas can be obtained at their respective consulates or embassies in Tripoli, both Egypt and Tunisia grant tourist visas on arrival to nationals of most (and perhaps all) Western countries. An Egyptian border visa costs around €15, while its Tunisian equivalent should cost no more than 5TD.

WOMEN TRAVELLERS

Balancing the liberal and the conservative strands of Libyan society is an inexact science, but it's one that causes few difficulties for the overwhelming number of female visitors to Libya.

In general, Libya is one of the easiest countries in the region for women to travel in. This is partly because the overwhelming majority of people working in Libya's tourist industry are accustomed to negotiating potentially awkward cross-cultural misunderstandings. It is also true that most

Libyans are paragons of discretion and even if you have offended local sensibilities you're unlikely to know about it. But the policies of the Libyan government in relation to women (see p55) also deserve their fair share of credit as, since the 1969 revolution, government laws favouring gender equality have contributed to a less-misunderstood view of Western women than can be found elsewhere in the Middle East or North Africa. As a result, most female travellers have reported being treated with respect, with few incidents of unpleasant behaviour. When foreign visitors are introduced to Libyan men, men will in most circumstances shake hands with Western women.

Most Libyan restaurants do not have a segregated family area where women are expected to eat. Unlike many countries in the region, there's no need for single women to wear a wedding ring or carry a photo of 'their' children – most Libyans understand that Western societies have different rules – although travelling with a male friend can reduce further the small risk of problems. We haven't heard of unmarried couples encountering difficulties in getting accommodation or in other situations, although you should always be discreet.

The risk of serious assault in Libya is virtually nonexistent. Nonetheless, women should take the precautions of always locking their hotel room and never attempting to hitchhike on their own. Attracting looks from Libyan men can also be uncomfortable and it's worth remembering that most sectors of Libyan society remain deeply traditional in both a religious and cultural sense. As one traveller reported:

> The Libyan people are very curious and friendly, but as a woman I find Tripoli a little bit difficult, as the Libyan men can be a little too curious sometimes.
>
> *Anna Norman, Sweden*

If you are harassed, tell your unwanted friend firmly, but politely, to desist and try to enlist the support of other Libyans, most of whom will be appalled enough to shame the man responsible. If you scream blue murder, the situation could get out of hand. If he persists, mentioning the police will most likely have the desired effect.

Given that Libya is a conservative society, choosing what to wear can be important. Trousers are perfectly OK as long as they're loose-fitting. The same applies to T-shirts and other tops, although these should have sleeves to cover the upper arm. There's no need to cover your head, except when entering a mosque (although even in mosques it's not always required), and you and your hosts may feel more comfortable wearing a headscarf if you visit a family home or small village, although no-one will expect you to. Swimsuits (not bikinis) should definitely be worn only on the beach, preferably with a T-shirt and shorts. Shorts (again, nothing too skimpy) are fine for desert expeditions when the only people around are other members of your party, but elsewhere even men in shorts will attract curious looks.

Transport

CONTENTS

GETTING THERE & AWAY

There are three main ways to enter Libya: by air (to Tripoli, Benghazi or, less often, Sebha), by public transport to Libya's border with Egypt or Tunisia, or in your own vehicle, most often by boat to Tunisia and then driving into Libya. Many travellers also arrive and leave by cruise ship, although there are no ferry services. Land borders with other countries – Algeria, Niger, Sudan or Chad – are rarely open to travellers and were closed at the time of research.

ENTERING LIBYA

Entering Libya is generally a trouble-free process, provided you have an invitation from an accredited Libyan tour company (see p243 for details). Customs formalities are usually pretty cursory, especially if you're polite, but remember that your bags are likely to be X-rayed. The main item that officials will be looking for is alcohol, which is forbidden in Libya. On the way out, searches are sometimes stricter, with rock-art souvenirs the main target.

If you're collecting your visa on arrival in Libya, try to ensure that your tour company has a representative waiting for you inside the immigration area to smooth the process of obtaining your visa. It's also a good idea to carry with you contact details (ie a mobile phone number) of the tour company in question in case they don't turn up on time. Before leaving home, you should also ask for a copy of the letter confirming details of your visa approval that Libyan tour companies routinely send to airlines to ensure that you're allowed to board the plane, as well as a copy of the Arabic visa approval from the Libyan authorities.

A 2005 Libyan government regulation requires that anyone entering Libya should be carrying with them a foreign-currency equivalent of a minimum of 500LD (for exchange rates see inside the front cover of this book). Although this is rarely enforced and seems to be aimed at deterring immigrants from sub-Saharan Africa, you should make sure that you're carrying at least this amount of money just in case. The only exceptions are those visiting Libya on government business and those who have already paid for their Libyan tour in full before arriving.

Passport

To enter Libya, your passport must be valid for six months from the date of entry. If you need to renew your passport, allow plenty of time, as it can take up to several months.

Travellers with passports bearing Israeli stamps are not allowed to enter Libya. For more detailed visa information see p227.

THINGS CHANGE...

The information in this chapter is particularly vulnerable to change. Check directly with the airline or a travel agent to make sure you understand how a fare (and ticket you may buy) works and be aware of the security requirements for international travel. Shop carefully. The details given in this chapter should be regarded as pointers and are not a substitute for your own careful, up-to-date research.

CLIMATE CHANGE & TRAVEL

Climate change is a serious threat to the ecosystems that humans rely upon, and air travel is the fastest-growing contributor to the problem. Lonely Planet regards travel, overall, as a global benefit, but believes we all have a responsibility to limit our personal impact on global warming.

Flying and climate change

Pretty much every form of motorised travel generates CO_2 (the main cause of human-induced climate change) but planes are far and away the worst offenders, not just because of the sheer distances they allow us to travel, but because they release greenhouse gases high into the atmosphere. The statistics are frightening: two people taking a return flight between Europe and the US will contribute as much to climate change as an average household's gas and electricity consumption over a whole year.

Carbon offset schemes

Climatecare.org and other websites use 'carbon calculators' that allow travellers to offset the level of greenhouse gases they are responsible for with financial contributions to sustainable travel schemes that reduce global warming – including projects in India, Honduras, Kazakhstan and Uganda.

Lonely Planet, together with Rough Guides and other concerned partners in the travel industry, support the carbon offset scheme run by climatecare.org. Lonely Planet offsets all of its staff and author travel.

For more information check out our website: www.lonelyplanet.com.

AIR

Airports & Airlines

Libya's two main international airports are Tripoli International Airport and Benghazi's Benina International Airport. Metiga Airport, 10km east of Tripoli, also handles international flights for Al-Buraq Air (right), although these services may soon be moved to Tripoli International Airport. Libya's other international airport is Sebha International Airport which handles flights for Point Afrique (opposite).

Libyan Arab Airlines is the national carrier and, although its safety record and service are patchy, many of these problems date back to the embargo years and things are improving all the time. It flies throughout Europe, Africa and the Middle East.

Of the two other Libyan-based airlines, Afriqiyah Airways services Europe and sub-Saharan Africa and the private Al-Buraq Air has been subjected to operational restrictions in the EU, although only for its cargo services.

AIRLINES FLYING TO/FROM LIBYA

All of the phone numbers for the following airlines are Tripoli numbers unless stated otherwise.

Afriqiyah Airways (8U; Map p75; ☎ 021-4449734; www.afriqiyah.aero; Sharia Omar al-Mukhtar)

Air Algerie (AH; Map p72; ☎ 021-4444016; www.airalgerie.dz; Burj al-Fateh, Sharia al-Corniche)

Air Malta (KM; Map p72; ☎ 021-3350579; www.airmalta.com; ground level, Dhat al-Ahmat Tower 5, Sharia al-Corniche)

Al-Buraq Air (UZ; Map p75; ☎ 021-4444811; www.buraqair.com; Sharia Mohammed Megharief)

Alitalia (AZ; Map p72; ☎ 021-3350298; www.alitalia.com; Dhat al-Ahmat Tower 3, Sharia al-Corniche)

Austrian Airlines (OS; Map p72; ☎ 021-3350242; www.aua.com; Dhat al-Ahmat Tower 3, Sharia al-Corniche)

Blue Panorama Airlines (BP; ☎ in Italy 06 602 14 577; www.blue-panorama.com, www.blu-express.com)

British Airways (BA; Map p72; ☎ 021-3351278; www.britishairways.com; Burj al-Fateh, Flat 191, Sharia al-Corniche)

EgyptAir (MS; Map p72; ☎ 021-3335781; www.egyptair.com; Burj al-Fateh, Sharia al-Corniche)

Emirates (EK; Map p72; ☎ 021-3350597; www.emirates.com; Burj al-Fateh Tower 1, 10th fl, fl No 103)

Hemus Air (DU; Map p75; ☎ 021-4445560; www.hemusair.bg; 11 Sharia al-Baladiya)

JAT Yugoslav Airlines (JU; Map p72; ☎ 021-3351299; www.jat.com; Burj al-Fateh, Sharia al-Corniche)

KLM Royal Dutch Airlines (KL; Map p72; ☎ 021-3350018; www.klm.com; Office 91, Level 1, Burj al-Fateh, Sharia al-Corniche)

Libyan Arab Airlines (LN; Map p75; ☎ 021-3616738)
Lufthansa (LH; Map p72; ☎ 021-3350375; www.lufthansa.com; 12th fl, Dhat al-Ahmat Tower 4)
Point Afrique (☎ in Paris 04 75 97 20 40; www.point-afrique.com in French)
Qatar Airways (QR; Map p72; ☎ 021-3351818; www.qatarairways.com; 18th fl, Office 181-182, Burj al-Fateh, Sharia al-Corniche)
Royal Air Maroc (AT; Map p72; ☎ 021-3350111; www.royalairmaroc.com; Burj al-Fateh, Sharia al-Corniche)
Royal Jordanian (RJ; Map p75; ☎ 021-4442453; www.rja.com.jo; Sharia Mohammed Megharief)
Saudi Arabian Airlines (SV; Map p75; ☎ 021-4446468; www.saudiairlines.com; Sharia Mohammed Megharief)
Sudan Airways (SD; Map p72; ☎ 021-3351330; www.sudanair.com; Office 123, 12th fl, Burj al-Fateh, Sharia al-Corniche)
Swiss International Airlines (LX; Map p72; ☎ 021-3350052; www.swiss.com; Dhat al-Ahmat Tower 3, Sharia al-Corniche)
Syrianair (RB; Map p75; ☎ 021-4446716; www.syriaair.com; Sharia al-Baladiya)
Tunis Air (TU; Map p75; ☎ 021-3336303; www.tunisair.com in French; 3rd fl, 59 Sharia 1st September)
Turkish Airlines (TK; Map p72; ☎ 021-3351252; www.turkishairlines.com; Office 161, 16th fl, Burj al-Fateh, Sharia al-Corniche)

Tickets

Very few budget airlines fly to Libya and very little discounting takes place, but prices are falling all the time so it's worth shopping around. Booking your ticket well in advance also helps lower prices.

Reputable online agencies for scheduled carriers:

Cheap Tickets (www.cheaptickets.com)
ebookers (www.ebookers.com)
Expedia.com (www.expedia.com)
Lowestfare.com (www.lowestfare.com)
Orbitz (www.orbitz.com)
STA Travel (www.sta.com)
Travelocity (www.travelocity.com)
Travel.com.au (www.travel.com.au)

Africa

Given that heads of African governments were the ones who flew to Libya in defiance of the international air embargo in the late 1990s, it's surprising how few African airlines fly to Tripoli. That's probably because Afriqiyah Airways (www.afriqiyah.aero) does such a fine job, connecting Tripoli to Abidjan (Côte d'Ivoire), Accra (Ghana), Bamako (Mali), Bangui (Central African Republic), Cairo (Egypt), Cotonou (Benin), Douala (Cameroon), Kano (Nigeria), Khartoum (Sudan), Lagos (Nigeria), Lomé (Togo), N'Djaména (Chad), Niamey (Niger) and Ouagadougou (Burkina Faso). Some flights also fly via Benghazi. The Afriqiyah Airways website has a list of ticket offices around Africa and elsewhere.

Other airlines which fly to/from African capitals include Air Algerie (Algiers), Sudan Airways (Khartoum), EgyptAir (Cairo and Alexandria), Libyan Arab Airlines (Casablanca, Cairo and Tunis), Tunis Air (Tunis) and Royal Air Maroc (Casablanca).

Asia & Australia

There are no direct flights to Libya from Asian cities, so travellers from Asia will need to fly to Europe and catch a connecting flight.

Similarly, if you're coming from Australia you'll need to pick up a connection elsewhere, preferably the Middle East. Emirates in particular has direct services from a number of Australian cities direct to Dubai with onward connections to Tripoli. EgyptAir also flies regularly to Tripoli via Southeast Asia and Cairo, although Emirates is usually a better choice. Qatar Airways from Doha is another possibility. Otherwise you'll need to pick up a connection in Europe.

Try the following agencies:

Flight Centre Australia (☎ 133 133; www.flightcentre.com.au); New Zealand (☎ 0800 243 544; www.flightcentre.co.nz) Has branches throughout Australia and New Zealand.
STA Travel Australia (☎ 1300 733 035; www.statravel.com.au); New Zealand (☎ 0508 782 872; www.statravel.co.nz) Has offices throughout Australia and New Zealand.
www.travel.com.au Online booking agency.

Continental Europe

Europe has the widest selection of direct flights to Libya. The national airlines of various European countries (see opposite) fly direct to Tripoli or Benghazi from their capitals although they're rarely cheap. Other airlines to consider include Blue Panorama Airlines (opposite; which offers return tickets for Rome–Tripoli for as low as €198), Point Afrique (left; which flies from Paris and Marseilles to Sebha), Afriqiyah Airways (opposite) and Libyan Arab Airlines (left). A return ticket for under €300 is generally an extremely good deal.

Eastern European travellers may want to consider flying from Sofia (Hemus Air; p232) or Belgrade (JAT Yugoslav Airlines; p232).

FRANCE

Lastminute (www.fr.lastminute.com in French) Online agency.
Nouvelles Frontières (☎ 08 25 00 07 47; www.nouvelles-frontieres.fr in French)
OTU Voyages (☎ 01 55 82 32 32; www.otu.fr in French) Student travel agency with 29 offices around the country; specialises in student and youth travellers.
Travelprice (http://voyages.travelprice.com in French) Online agency.
Voyageurs du Monde (☎ 01 73 00 81 88; www.vdm.com in French)

GERMANY

Darr Travel Shop (☎ 089-28 20 32; Theresienstrasse 66, Munich) A great source of travel information and equipment.
Expedia (www.expedia.de in German) Online agency.
Lastminute (☎ 01805 284 366; www.lastminute.de in German) Online agency.
STA Travel (☎ 1805-45 64 22; www.statravel.de) An ever-reliable agency, with offices across Germany.

ITALY & SPAIN

Atrapalo (www.atrapalo.com) Good online Spanish booking agency.
Barcelo Viajes (☎ 902 116 226; www.barceloviajes.com in Spanish) Spaniards should consider this agency.
CTS Viaggi (☎ 06 462 0431; www.cts.it in Italian) Travellers from Italy will want to check out this operator.
Despegar (www.despegar.es) Another good online Spanish booking agency.

NETHERLANDS

Airfair (☎ 020-620 5121; www.airfair.nl in Dutch) This agency is recommended.
Kilroy Travel Group (☎ 020-524 5100; www.kilroygroups.com) This excellent group offers discounted travel to people aged 16 to 33; it also has offices in Denmark, Sweden, Norway and Finland.
My Travel (☎ 020-638 1736; www.mytravel.nl in Dutch) Dutch travellers will also find this to be a reliable source of discounted tickets, with 42 branches across the country.

Middle East

Libya is well-connected to Amman, Beirut, Damascus, Doha, Dubai, İstanbul, Jeddah and Riyadh with Libyan Arab Airlines or the national airlines of the country concerned. One alternative, however, is to fly with Al-Buraq from Tripoli to Aleppo via Benghazi.

Sample one-way fares which we found within Libya include İstanbul (180LD) and Cairo (144LD).

The best place to pick up cheap tickets is in Turkey, especially from the travel agencies in Divan Yolu in Sultanahmet (İstanbul), which specialise in cheap airfares. Egypt is best avoided as hefty government taxes can make prices prohibitive.

UK

British Airways (London–Heathrow) and Afriqiyah Airways (London–Gatwick) both fly direct to Tripoli; Afriqiyah is generally much cheaper with fares from UK£230.

Discount air travel has always been big business in London; good places to try include the following (all have offices throughout the UK):

Flight Centre (☎ 0870 499 0040; www.flightcentre.co.uk)
STA (☎ 0870-160 0599; www.statravel.co.uk)
Trailfinders (☎ 0845 050 5891; www.trailfinders.com)

Advertisements for many further agencies appear in the travel pages of the weekend newspapers, such as the *Independent* and the *Guardian* on Saturday and the *Sunday Times*, as well as in publications such as *Time Out*.

USA & Canada

There are no direct flights to Tripoli from the US or Canada – you'll need to fly to Europe and hook up with an onward connection there.

Council Travel (☎ 800-226 8624; www.ciee.org; 205 E 42 St, New York, NY 10017) America's largest student travel organisation has around 60 offices in the USA. Call the head office for the office nearest you or visit its website.
STA Travel (☎ 800-777 0112; www.statravel.com) Has offices in many major US cities; call the toll-free ☎ 800 number for office locations or visit its website.
Travel CUTS (☎ 800-667 2887; www.travelcuts.com) Canada's national student travel agency; has offices in all major cities.

LAND

The most commonly used land borders for travellers are the coastal frontiers with Tunisia (Ras al-Jedir) and Egypt (Amsaad). At the time of writing, Libya's borders with Algeria, Niger, Chad and Sudan were closed to Western travellers, although these borders open and close often, depending on the prevailing political winds. In all cases, check the latest situation with the relevant embassy or the Libyan authorities in Tripoli and, if the borders are open, make sure you have the necessary visas firmly ensconced in your passport before setting out – it's a long way to back track if there's some kind of problem.

Border Crossings

Libya's land borders with Tunisia (Ras al-Jedir; see p236) and Egypt (Amsaad; see right) are relatively hassle-free although customs searches of those travelling in their own vehicles are more rigorous; they're looking for alcohol above all else.

A representative from your Libyan tour company should be waiting for you at the immigration section on the Libyan side of the border. Their presence will ensure a smooth passage into Libya, unless of course your papers are not in order (see Visas, p227) or you're found to be carrying alcohol, in which case things will take longer. Again, carry the mobile-phone number of your guide or tour company representative in case they're not there waiting for you.

Car & Motorcycle

Drivers of 4WDs and campervans and riders of motorcycles will need the vehicle's registration papers, liability insurance, an international drivers' permit in addition to their domestic licence and a *carnet de passage en douane*. For more information on what you'll need to get across the border, see p239.

Algeria

Due to a dispute over the Libya–Algeria border close to Ghat (for more information see p195) in Libya's extreme southwest, the border was closed to travellers at the time of writing. If it reopens, roads lead from Ghat to Djanet and the Tassili-n-Ajjer. There's always talk of opening the crossing between Ghadames and Burj Messouda in the northwest of Libya, but for now it remains just talk.

Chad

The main Libyan–Chadian border post is close to the historically contested town of Aouzou in Chad, but it's years since this border has been open to foreign travellers because of mines in the area and ongoing rebel activity on the Chadian side of the border.

Egypt

The Libyan–Egyptian border, 139km east of Tobruk and 12km west of Sallum in Egypt is Amsaad. This remote and, in summer, perishingly hot frontier is another busy crossing point, which one traveller described as having a 'Wild West atmosphere… dirty, chaotic and very busy'; bring your own water. Embarrassingly, however, foreign travellers are usually shepherded to the front of the considerable queue. We've never heard of anyone turning down such an offer as a matter of principle.

As your tour company will arrange all of your transport inside Libya, you don't need to worry about public transport on the Libyan side of the border. For the record, however, there are long-distance buses from Benghazi to Alexandria (50LD) and Cairo (60LD).

On the Egyptian side of the border, shared taxis shuttle between the frontier and Sallum (E£3 to E£4) where you can get buses (E£12) or service taxis (E£15) to Marsa Matruh.

Niger

The Libya–Niger border was closed to Western travellers at the time of research; it does open from time to time so check the situation in Tripoli before setting out. The border post is at the incredibly remote shacks of Tumu, 310km south of Al-Qatrun, although you may have to complete Libyan exit formalities in Al-Qatrun.

The route between Niger and Libya is only for serious desert travellers and for the thousands of immigrants from sub-Saharan Africa making the dangerous journey north in search of work. The sandy journey would be madness in summer and at all times you'll need to be fully self-sufficient and aware of the risks involved.

Sudan

The Libyan–Sudanese land border was closed at the time of research due to the ongoing conflict across the border in the Darfur region of Sudan. Given that this conflict seems to be a long way from resolution, the frontier is unlikely to open any time soon. For the record, the border post is in the remote southeast of the country, close to Jebel al-Uweinat, 325km southeast of Al-Kufra.

Tunisia

The Tunisian border crossing at Ras al-Jedir, 169km west of Tripoli, is the Libyan land border most frequented by Western travellers. Accustomed as they are to travellers, border officials on either side are generally quite friendly (although little English is spoken) and eager to get you on your way in the shortest time possible.

As with Egypt, because your tour company is responsible for arranging your transport inside Libya, you won't need to worry about public transport in Libya as they should be waiting for you on the Libyan side of the border. Buses run daily between Tripoli and Tunis (50LD from the Libyan side).

From the Tunisian side, you will need to take a shared taxi (known as a *louage* in Tunisia) or bus as far as Ben Guerdane which has a hotel and is 33km short of the border. From Ben Guerdane, a seat in a *louage* should cost no more than 12TD.

SEA

There are no scheduled ferry services connecting Libya with the outside world and the only way to enter and leave Libya by sea is aboard a cruise ship.

Travellers who want to bring their own vehicle to Libya usually do so by loading it (and themselves) aboard a ferry bound for Tunis (Tunisia) from France or Italy. If that's your plan, the following companies are good places to start:

Compagnie Tunisienne de Navigation (www.ctn.com.tn) Services from Marseilles or Nice to a number of Libyan ports, including Tunis, Sousse and Sfax.

SNCM (www.sncm.fr) French and Italian departures to Tunis.

Viamare (www.viamare.com) Departures from Civitavecchia, Genoa, Livorno, Naples, Palermo and Salerno to Tunis.

TOURS

European tour companies run professional tours of Libya and, in conjunction with their Libyan partners can arrange visas (see p227). These operators do, however, have set departure dates and less flexibility than their Libyan counterparts in allowing you to custom-design your itinerary.

Australia

Few Australian companies offer tours to Libya, but it's easy enough to hook up with a UK agency. Companies offering tours:

Adventure Associates (☎ 02-8916 3000; www.adventureassociates.com; Level 7, 12-14 O'Connell St, Sydney NSW 2000)

Intrepid (☎ 03-8602 0500; www.intrepidtravel.com; 360 Bourke St, Melbourne, Victoria 3004)

Middle East Tours (☎ 02-9605 3981; www.middleeasttours.com.au)

Passport Travel (☎ 03-9867 3888; www.travelcentre.com.au; Suite 11, 401 St Kilda Rd, Melbourne, Victoria, 3004)

Continental Europe

FRANCE

For advice from other travellers on making the choice on a tour company to Libya, see www.voyageforum.com. Some agencies recommended by travellers:

Ailleurs.com (☎ 0892 161 192; www.ailleurs.com in French)

Atalante (☎ 04 72 53 24 80; www.atalante.fr in French; 36 Quai Arloing, 69256 Lyon)

Couleurs Sables (☎ 06 13 61 55 32; www.couleurs-sables.com in French; Place Mailly, 66600 Rivesaltes)

Hommes et Montagnes (☎ 0438 86 69 19; www.hommes-et-montagnes.fr in French; 10 Blvd Gambetta, BP 122, 38001, Grenoble)

Point Afrique (☎ 01 44 88 58 39; www.point-afrique.com in French; 26 rue de la Grande Truanderie, 75001 Paris)

Voyailes (☎ 01 34 70 40 89; www.voyailes.fr in French; 69 rue Aurélien Cronnier, 60230, Chambly)

Zig-Zag Randonnées (☎ 01 42 85 13 93; www.zigzag-randonnees.com; 54 rue de Dunkerque, 75009 Paris)

GERMANY

Blue Planet Reisen (☎ 040-386 123 11; www.blue-planet-reisen.de in German)

Dabuka Expeditions (☎ 0605-987 98 96; www.dabuka.de; Feldwiesenstrasse 1, D-35647, Waldsolms)

Djoser (☎ 0221-920 15 80; www.djoser.de in German; Kaiser Wilhelm Ring 20, 50672 Köln)

ITALY

Antichi Splendori Viaggi (☎ 011-8126715; www.antichisplendori.it in Italian; Via Vanchliga 22a, 10124 Torino)

Best Tours (☎ 02-336331; www.besttours.it in Italian; Corso Sempione 36, 20154 Milano)

Exodus (☎ 072-130318; www.exodusviaggi.it in Italian; Corso XI Settembre 200, 61100 Pesaro)
Harmattan Tours (☎ 041-5420654; www.harmattan-tours.com in Italian; Via Orlanda 217-219, Tessera, Venezia)
Meta Mondo (☎ 041-8899211; www.metamondo.it in Italian; via Ca' Rossa 21A, 30174 Mestre)
NBTS Viaggi (☎ 011-0519575; www.nbts.it; Via Massena 48, 10128 Torino)
Osservando il Mondo (☎ /fax 030-3534778; www.osservandoilmondo.com in Italian; Via Boves 5, 25124 Brescia)
Shiraz Travel Tours (☎ 065-115708; www.shiraztravel.com in Italian; Via Tito Omboni 9, Roma)
Viaggi Dell'Elefante (☎ 06-6784541; www.viaggidellelefante.it in Italian; Via dei Condotti 61A, 00187 Roma)

ELSEWHERE

Afrika Tour (☎ 234 704 711; www.afrika-tour.cz in Czech; Voroněžská 20, 101 00 Prague, Czech Republic)
Anders Reizen (☎ 013-33 40 40; www.andersreizen.be in Flemish; Refugiestraat 15, 3290 Diest, Belgium)
Indigo Reisen (☎ 31 951 29 30; www.indigoreisen.ch in German; Dorfstrasse 84, Postfach 167, CH–3073 Gümligen, Switzerland)
SRC Cultuurvakanties (☎ 050-3 123 123; www.src-cultuurvakanties.nl in Dutch; Oude Boteringestraat 37-39, 9701 BR Groningen, The Netherlands)
Viajes Tuareg (☎ 932 652 391; www.viajestuareg.com in Spanish; Calle Consell de Cent 378, Barcelona, Spain)

UK

Ancient World Tours (☎ 020 7917 9494; www.ancient.co.uk; PO Box 838 Guildford GU3 3ZR)
Andante Travels (☎ 01722 713800; www.andantetravels.co.uk; The Old Barn, Old Rd, Alderbury, Salisbury SP5 3AR)
Caravanserai Tours (☎ 020 8855 6373; www.caravanserai-tours.com; 1-3 Love Lane, Woolwich, London SE18 6QT)
Cox & Kings (☎ 020 7873 5000; www.coxandkings.co.uk; Gordon House, 10 Greencoat Pl, London SW1P 1PH)
Dragoman (☎ 01728 861133; www.dragoman.com; Camp Green, Debenham, Stowmarket, Suffolk IP14 6LA)
Exodus (☎ 0870 950 0039; www.exodus.co.uk; Grange Mills, Weir Rd, London SW12 0NE)
Prospect Cultural Tours (☎ 01227 773 545; www.prospecttours.com; 94-104 John Wilson Park, Whitstable, Kent CT5 3QZ)
Responsibletravel.com (☎ 01273 600030; www.responsibletravel.com)
Silk Road and Beyond (☎ 020 7371 3131; www.silkroadandbeyond.co.uk; 371 Kensington High St, London W14 8QZ)
Simoon Travel (☎ 020 7622 6263; www.simoontravel.com)

USA & Canada

Bestway Tours & Safaris (☎ 1 800 663 0844; www.bestway.com; Suite 206, 8678 Greenall Ave, Burnaby, British Columbia V5J 3M6 Canada)
Mountain Travel Sobek (☎ 1-510-594-6000; www.mtsobek.com; Suite 4, 1266 66th St, Emeryville, CA 94608, USA)

GETTING AROUND

In this era of organised tours, if you're not driving your own vehicle, getting around Libya couldn't be easier because all transport within the country will be organised by your tour company. Most travellers to Libya get around by a combination of domestic flights, chartered buses and 4WDs. As you're extremely unlikely to be travelling by public transport while in Libya, our coverage of buses, minibuses and shared taxis in this chapter and throughout this book is restricted to general information only.

If you're bringing your own vehicle to Libya, you and/or your group must be at all times accompanied by a local representative or guide from the tour company that arranged your visa. In practical terms that means not much more than an extra body on board, although a good guide will greatly enhance your trip without interfering too much in it. Road conditions are generally good, although the incessant checkpoints, while painless and fewer in number than they used to be, can slow your journey.

AIR

Libya's domestic airline network seems to ebb and flow. Just when it looks like there are scheduled services to Ghadames and

LIBYA'S TRANSPORT NETWORK AT A GLANCE

- Domestic airports: Tripoli, Benghazi, Sebha, Lebreq and Al-Kufra
- Airports closed at time of writing: Ghadames, Ghat, Houn and Tobruk
- Railways: 0km
- Paved roads: 47,590km
- Unpaved roads: 35,610km
- Unmarked desert trails: endless

TRANSPORT

Ghat, the routes are closed without explanation. Tobruk's airport, meanwhile, was undergoing major renovations when we were there although it should reopen during the life of this book. As the closed airports represent some of the most far-flung Libyan destinations, this means that you'll spend a lot of time on often monotonous roads (the exception is the Benghazi–Al-Kufra service, which is a godsend).

Cancellations are more common from April through summer as the fiercely hot *ghibli* wind (for information see p216) can make flying hazardous. And if you're flying between Tripoli and Benghazi, keep an eye out the window for the ruins of Leptis Magna, which the planes sometimes fly over.

Airlines in Libya

At the time of writing, there were services from Tripoli (see p97) to Benghazi, Sebha and Lebreq (near Al-Bayda), with further services from Benghazi (see p131) to Sebha and Al-Kufra.

There are two airlines that fly domestically in Libya:

Al-Buraq Air (www.buraqair.com) Tripoli (☎ 021-4444811); Benghazi (☎ 061-2234469) Operates a Tripoli-Benghazi service that's more expensive but more reliable and comfortable than Libyan Arab Airlines. In Tripoli, its domestic services operate from Tripoli International Airport.

Libyan Arab Airlines Tripoli (☎ 021-3331143); Benghazi (☎ 061-9092064) The ageing workhorse of the Libyan skies, it's plagued by delays and even cancellations, but it's your only choice for Sebha and Al-Kufra.

If you're part of a large enough group with limited time and money to burn, you can reach Ghadames or Ghat by chartering a plane. An-Nakhl al-Khafeef, a subsidiary of Libyan Arab Airlines, runs a small number of 15-seater aircraft. A one-way flight from Tripoli to Ghadames costs 3500LD. Trying to book this through Libyan Arab Airlines is like the search for the Holy Grail so make the arrangements through your tour company.

BICYCLE

In this era of group tourism in Libya, it's rare to find cyclists traversing the roads, and indeed cycling is not a passion to which Libyans are generally predisposed. Although the roads are often well-surfaced and flat (apart from in the Jebel Nafusa in the northwest and Jebel al-Akhdar in the northeast), the speed at which most Libyan traffic moves would make it an adventurous undertaking. Cycling lanes are also unheard of and even on some highways there is little additional space on the road outside the motor-vehicle lanes. Overtaking is also sometimes done on the inside with little forethought for two-wheelers that may be trying to stay out of trouble. If you do decide to cycle, you'll also need to be self-sufficient in spare parts, which, along with replacement bikes, can be hard to come by in Libya. *Always* wear a helmet.

BUS

Libya doesn't have the largest fleet of buses, but there are daily connections between the major cities and services along the coast are quite frequent. Beyond that, you'd be fortunate to find one travelling further south than Sebha. Most are air-conditioned, although the quality is variable, ranging from cramped buses well past their use-by date to those of more recent vintage and very comfortable. The two major companies are the government-owned An-Nakhl as-Seria (Fast Transport Company), and Al-Itihad al-Afriqi (the United Africa Company), which tends to have a slightly newer fleet. In Tripoli and Benghazi, these companies have depots close to the centre of town. Elsewhere, there are an insufficient number of departures to merit a dedicated bus station so bus-company offices are usually a stone's throw from the shared-taxi station.

CAR & MOTORCYCLE

The advantage of having your own vehicle, especially a 4WD, is that there are few limits on where you can go (one exception is the Tibesti region; see p206 for details). Until the Libyan Government decides to relax its visa regulations, you will need to be accompanied by at least one representative of the Libyan tour company who arranged your visa and who remains responsible for you for the duration of your stay, although this is unlikely to limit your freedom.

Indeed, if you're travelling in the desert, there's no substitute for an experienced local guide who knows the terrain. A Global Positioning System (GPS) can also be useful for pinpointing locations, but it can't

QADDAFI'S ROCKET CAR

In September 1999 at the Organisation of African Unity summit, Colonel Muammar Qaddafi unveiled his (or rather his scientists') latest invention – a prototype of the safest car on earth. The Saroukh al-Jamahiriya (Libyan rocket) is, dare we say it, surprisingly stylish and a far cry from the days when the coup leader got around in an old VW Beetle. The sporty lines (the front and rear are shaped like a rocket) and tinted windows are enhanced by a metallic shade of Libyan revolutionary green. Safety features included air bags, an in-built electronic defence system and specially designed collapsible bumper.

Libyan press reports, true to form, described the car as a 'revolutionary' moment in automotive history. A Libyan spokesman assured the sceptics that 'The invention of the safest car in the world is proof that the Libyan revolution is built on the happiness of man' and evidence that despite sanctions, Colonel G has been 'thinking of ways to preserve human life all over the world'. In a none-too-subtle play on words, the car's name was seen as proof that while other countries made rockets designed to kill, Libya designed them 'for humane and peaceful purposes'.

For all the fanfare, we're yet to see a single rocket car on Libya's roads.

tell you which route to take. Libyan guides weary of recounting stories of the know-more-than-the-local European drivers who think that with a GPS they can go anywhere only to lose half a day stuck in the sand. A good guide will know that not all sand dunes are the same: some areas in the Libyan Sahara, especially in the east in the Ramlat Rabyaneh (p207) or the Great Sand Sea (p155) but also elsewhere, consist of extremely fine, soft sand which makes for slow going and dramatically increases your fuel consumption.

Automobile Associations

You're unlikely to need to contact the **Automobile & Touring Club of Libya** (☎ 3605986; fax 3605866; Sharia Sayedy, Tripoli), unless bringing your own vehicle, but it is responsible for your local insurance while in the country and may be able to help out with any questions regarding vehicle documentation.

Bringing Your Own Vehicle

To enter Libya in your own vehicle, you'll need a number of documents:

- *Carnet de passage en douane* – a passport for your car; see p240 for details.
- International Driving Permit (IDP) – although most foreign licences are accepted in Libya, an IDP issued by your local automobile association is highly recommended.
- Vehicle registration documents – in addition to carrying all ownership papers, check with your insurer whether you're covered for Libya.

Upon entering Libya in your own vehicle, you'll also need to pay temporary membership of the Automobile & Touring Club of Libya (4WD/motorbike/campervan US$50/50/100), local insurance (10LD per week for all kinds of vehicles) and local license or number plates for your vehicle which cost 110.50LD; upon returning the plates when you leave Libya, you'll receive a refund of 50LD.

Checkpoints

Checkpoints are a wearying feature of driving in Libya and while they are generally restricted to the roads into each town and major road junctions, their prevalence can considerably slow travel times.

It is rare that a checkpoint will, for foreign travellers, be anything more than a formality. On most occasions you may be asked for your carnet, passport or, if you're travelling as a part of a group, a copy of your itinerary. No matter how many times you have been waved through a checkpoint, never assume that you will be. Always slow down or stop until you get the wave from your friendly machine-gun-toting soldier.

There are two types of checkpoints. Those manned by the army (green uniforms) are on the lookout for people who haven't completed their military service, while the police (blue uniforms) are more concerned with flushing out illegal immigrants and drivers who have been involved in accidents or stolen cars. Tourists are rarely the target and there seems to have been a government directive to allow visitors to progress without delay.

CARNETS

A *carnet de passage en douane* is like a passport for your car, a booklet that is stamped on arrival and at departure from a country to ensure that you export the vehicle again after you've imported it. It's usually issued by an automobile association in the country where the vehicle is registered.

Should the worst occur and your vehicle is irretrievably damaged in an accident or catastrophic breakdown, you'll have to argue it out with customs officials. Having a vehicle stolen can be even worse, as you may be suspected of having sold it.

The carnet may also need to specify any expensive spare parts that you're planning to carry with you (such as a gearbox), which is designed to prevent any spare part importation rackets. Contact your local automobile association for details about all necessary documentation at least three months in advance.

Driving Licence

An international driving licence is required for any foreign visitor who intends to drive a car in Libya, although it's rarely checked other than perhaps at the border upon entry.

Fuel & Spare Parts

Petrol is ridiculously cheap, a fact that has encouraged a high rate of ownership in Libya (close to one car for every seven Libyans). 'Normal' petrol costs 0.15LD per litre, with diesel 0.14LD. Where else in the world can you fill your car for around €3? When asking for directions to the nearest petrol station, you'll need to ask *'wayn Shell?'* Leadfree petrol is not available in Libya.

Libyans became masters of improvising without spare parts during the years of the embargo and as mechanics they have few rivals in the world. Spare parts for 4WDs are reasonably widely available for older-model vehicles, especially Toyota and Land Rover, but you should be self-sufficient in parts for newer or more-obscure model vehicles.

Hire

You're unlikely to need to rent a car while in Libya as all transport should be arranged by your tour company and most cars come with a local driver attached. Renting from a local company without a driver usually costs 40LD per day.

Very few of the major international car-rental agencies operate in Libya. One exception is **Europcar** (Map p75; ☎ 021-4780906; www.europcar-libya.com; Corinthia Bab Africa Hotel, Souq al-Thalatha, Tripoli).

Insurance

For details on obtaining liability insurance upon your arrival in Libya, see p239.

Road Conditions

Libyan roads are generally good, although heavy truck traffic can lead to rapid deterioration on more frequented routes. This is particularly the case along the busy coastal highway. In particular, watch out for occasional potholes and cracks and always be careful when approaching bridges as many

LIBYAN ROADS – OUR WORST FIVE

While Libya's roads generally present few problems, there are a few that we'll be happy never to travel again.

- Ajdabiya to Al-Kufra (p132) – for the first 700km there's nothing to see, while the last 200km into Al-Kufra is the worst road in Libya with crevasse-like potholes that make driving all but impossible. They're fixing the road but it'll take a while.
- Sebha to Houn – further advanced than the Al-Kufra repairs but still a bone-jarring, axle-threatening experience in the first third of the journey.
- Tobruk to Ajdabiya – a leading candidate for the most boring road in the world.
- Derj to Al-Qaryat – would probably win second prize in the same competition.
- Tripoli to Misrata – the road itself isn't bad but the traffic is heavy, some lanes have deteriorated and so trucks use the only good lane. You should definitely avoid driving this road after dark.

ROAD DISTANCES (KM)

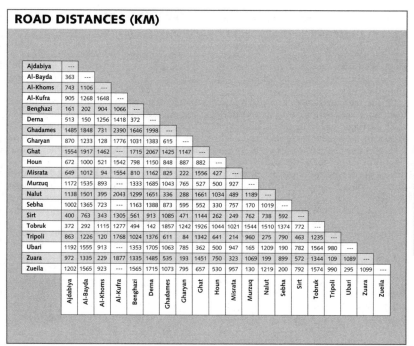

	Ajdabiya	Al-Bayda	Al-Khoms	Al-Kufra	Benghazi	Derna	Ghadames	Gharyan	Ghat	Houn	Misrata	Murzuq	Nalut	Sebha	Sirt	Tobruk	Tripoli	Ubari	Zuara	Zueila
Ajdabiya	---																			
Al-Bayda	363	---																		
Al-Khoms	743	1106	---																	
Al-Kufra	905	1268	1648	---																
Benghazi	161	202	904	1066	---															
Derna	513	150	1256	1418	372	---														
Ghadames	1485	1848	731	2390	1646	1998	---													
Gharyan	870	1233	128	1776	1031	1383	615	---												
Ghat	1554	1917	1462	---	1715	2067	1425	1147	---											
Houn	672	1000	521	1542	798	1150	848	887	882	---										
Misrata	649	1012	94	1554	810	1162	825	222	1556	427	---									
Murzuq	1172	1535	893	---	1333	1685	1043	765	527	500	927	---								
Nalut	1138	1501	395	2043	1299	1651	336	288	1661	1034	489	1189	---							
Sebha	1002	1365	723	---	1163	1388	873	595	552	330	757	170	1019	---						
Sirt	400	763	343	1305	561	913	1085	471	1144	262	249	762	738	592	---					
Tobruk	372	292	1115	1277	494	142	1857	1242	1926	1044	1021	1544	1510	1374	772	---				
Tripoli	863	1226	120	1768	1024	1376	611	84	1342	641	214	960	275	790	463	1235	---			
Ubari	1192	1555	913	---	1353	1705	1063	785	362	500	947	165	1209	190	782	1564	980	---		
Zuara	972	1335	229	1877	1335	1485	535	193	1451	750	323	1069	199	899	572	1344	109	1089	---	
Zueila	1202	1565	923	---	1565	1715	1073	795	657	530	957	130	1219	200	792	1574	990	295	1099	---

entry/exit points have deteriorated to quite a bump on either side of the bridge.

Road Hazards

All road signs are in Arabic so it's a good idea to familiarise yourself with the written Arabic for your destination and other towns en route – these are provided throughout the book alongside the name of each town.

If someone flashes their lights at you, it's usually a warning of some impending danger up ahead, such as an accident or sheep or camels grazing by the roadside. Camels can be a particular problem and they're at their most dangerous when on both sides of the road – slow to a crawl until you're well past. Camels are also a big danger if you're travelling desert roads at night.

Everywhere throughout the country, cars with a single (or no) headlight are a common hazard after dark. Sunset can also be a problem as farmers returning from the fields often amble onto major roads at a snail's pace. Overtaking on blind corners is also more common than you'd like.

Sand blown across the road in southern and western Libya is also a problem.

Motorcyclists should be especially careful as Libyan drivers are not on the lookout for two-wheeled transport and rarely take such possibilities into account when overtaking.

Road Rules

Believe it or not, Libya does have road rules.

Driving is on the right-hand side of the road, and speed limits, which are rarely enforced, follow a set pattern with gradations depending on the type of road and car.

For the record, cars (including 4WDs) must stay on or below the following limits:

- 100km/h on highways
- 85km/h on main roads outside towns
- 70km/h on small roads outside towns
- 50km/h inside towns

The corresponding figures for larger vehicles (trucks, campervans and buses) must adhere to limits of 65/60/50/30km/h.

In reality, Libyan drivers generally drive along as fast as they think they can get away with. Fines are indeed the official punishment for speeding, but no Libyans we spoke to had heard of anyone getting one, nor did they know how much they amounted to.

Of far more credence than the official road rules are the unwritten ones. Many dual carriageways are punctuated with breaks in the roads where drivers undertake perilous U-turn manoeuvres. If you slow down too much, these drivers take that as permission to cross, but if you approach with a succession of short, quickly consecutive toots, they'll generally wait until you pass. The same applies to traffic entering from a side road – these drivers will generally expect you to watch out for them.

Parking restrictions also apply in most cities of any size and these are often enforced to the tune of a 30LD fine. The 'No Parking' areas are indicated by signs sporting a black circle with a white cross or red diagonal line. Be especially careful around Green Sq in Tripoli as the whole area can be cleared for public events and your car towed away.

HITCHING

Hitching is never entirely safe in any country, and we don't recommend it. Travellers who decide to hitch should understand that they are taking a small but potentially serious risk. In Libya, given that you will be travelling around the country in the company of a guide and in transport organised by your tour company, it is extremely unlikely that you will have reason to hitch. People who do choose to hitch will be safer if they travel in pairs and let someone know where they are planning to go. Women travellers in Libya should never hitch without a male companion.

Hitching among Libyans is relatively common along roads with little or no public transport, especially in the remote towns of the Fezzan and the quiet back roads of the Jebel Nafusa or Jebel al-Akhdar. If someone wants a lift, they'll stand by the side of the road with their arm extended and their open palm facing down. It would be unusual in Libya for owners of private vehicles to ask hitchers to pay.

LOCAL TRANSPORT

Micro

There are no bus services within Libyan towns, but white-and-yellow micros (minibuses) crisscross most towns, usually for half the price of a shared taxi on the same route. They usually congregate at the main shared-taxi station and follow roughly set routes, although they sometimes make small detours as demand requires. There are no timetables and micros usually don't leave the station until full. If the stations aren't convenient, stand on a main street en route to your general direction, hail down a micro and call out your destination as it slows.

Shared & Private Taxi

Libyan cities generally have plenty of shared taxis and they operate under the same system as the micros. While more expensive, shared taxis fill more quickly and can therefore be better if you're in a hurry and don't want to pay for a private taxi.

Private taxis are reasonably priced and journeys within towns, other than those to outlying airports, are unlikely to cost more than 2LD.

TAXI & SHARED TAXI

The yellow-and-white shared taxis are alternately called *siara al-arma*, *taksi moshtarak* or *saba'a taksi* (seven seater). This workhorse of the Libyan public transport system can be found anywhere where there's a paved road. They, and micros that operate on the same principle but take longer to fill, leave from designated areas that are often indistinguishable from parking lots and drivers shout out their destination to passers-by. Most leave not to a set timetable but when full.

Like shared taxis throughout the Arab world and Africa, Libyan shared taxis make no concessions to comfort and, although they don't cram you in quite as tight as in the African countries south of the Sahara, the absence of leg and shoulder room can still make for an uncomfortable journey.

As a general rule of thumb, shared-taxi fares cost 2.5LD per 100km or 0.5LD per 20km. Overcharging of foreigners is rare and any problems are more likely to arise from misunderstandings over language; few drivers speak anything other than Arabic.

Private taxis (black-and-white) are not really an economical way of getting around (eg a taxi from Tripoli to Nalut can cost 60LD), but they do enable you to dictate the journey.

TOURS

Organising your visa (see p227) and tour of Libya through a Libyan-based company has a number of advantages. For a start, most are more flexible in allowing you to tailor your itinerary and some operators (but not all) will happily organise tours for individual travellers or groups as small as two. Libyan companies also tend to be cheaper than international companies – remember international companies cannot travel to or within Libya without a local affiliate (ie a Libyan tour company) and so going with an international company usually means using two sets of bills. You can't cut out the middle man, so why not make him your sole guide?

If you go with a good company, everything is organised for you – hotel bookings, airport transfers, transport, visa applications and passport registration, guides for major sites – and included in the price, which can be calculated on a full- or half-board basis. Clearly, economies of scale demand that members of smaller groups will pay more per person.

We recommend that you contact a number of Libyan companies to see first of all which one answers (see No Answer, Try again, p228). All can arrange guides in most languages, especially English, Italian, French and, increasingly, Spanish.

The following companies are excellent places to start.

Aania Tours (☎ in Zuara 025-20436; www.aania.com)

Al-Muheet Tours (Ocean Tours; ☎ in Benghazi 061-9082084; info@almuheettours.net) The owner, Sami el-Gaibany has a reputation for running an efficient and flexible company.

Arkno Tours (☎ 021-4441452; www.arkno.com) Patchy record with lone travellers but long-standing company that works with Caravanserai Tours in the UK.

Bright Focus (☎ in Benghazi 061-9096608; www.brightfocus.com.ly)

Destination Libye (☎ in Tripoli 021-4779854; www.dlibye.com) Specialises in French-language tours.

Medusa Travel & Tourism Services (☎ mobile 0913158229; www.medusatours.com) Specialises in German-language tours.

Oea Net (☎ mobile 0913221338; www.oeanet.net) Works almost exclusively with Japanese groups.

Robban Tourism Services (☎ in Tripoli 021-4441530; www.robban-tourism.com) Outstanding and professional small company with flexible itineraries and good guides. Hussein Founi should be your first port of call.

Sabri Tours & Travel (☎ in Tripoli 021-4775095; www.sabritours.com)

Sahara Friends Tours (☎ in Sebha 071-633354; www.saharafriendstours.com)

Sahara Link Travel (☎ in Tripoli 021-3343209; saharalink@hotmail.com)

Sari Tours (☎ in Tripoli 021-4873017; www.sarilibyatravel.com)

Sea & Desert Tours (☎ in Tripoli 021-4447864; www.sea-desert.net)

Shati Zuara Travel & Tourism (☎ mobile 0913222418; info@shati-zuara.de; www.shati-zuara.de) Very good Libyan company with its main base in Germany.

Sukra Travel & Tourism (☎ in Tripoli 021-3340604; www.sukra-travel.com)

Taknes Co (in Tripoli ☎ 021-3350526; fax 3350525) The owner is the helpful Ali Shebli.

Tilwan Tourism Services (in Tripoli ☎ 021-4836243; www.tilwan.com) Good for small-group Italian- or English-language tours.

Wings Travel & Tours (☎ in Tripoli 021-3331855; www.wingstours.com)

Winzrik Tourism Services (☎ in Tripoli 021-3611123; www.winzrik.com)

TRAIN

At the time of writing there were no rail services in Libya and the long-planned rail lines along the Libyan coast from Ras al-Jedir (Tunisia) to Amsaad (Egypt) and from Sirt to Sebha and beyond remain little more than barely discernible bumps in the landscape. Don't expect that to change in the foreseeable future.

TRANSPORT

Health

CONTENTS

Prevention is the key to staying healthy while travelling in Libya, although given that most travellers spend no more than two weeks in the country, you'd be pretty unlucky to have any problems. The most common reason for travellers needing medical help is as a result of accidents – cars are not always well maintained and poorly lit roads are littered with potholes and other potential hazards. Medical facilities can be good in large cities, but in remoter areas may be more basic.

BEFORE YOU GO

A little planning before departure, particularly for pre-existing illnesses, will save you a lot of trouble later. See your dentist before a long trip; carry a spare pair of contact lenses and glasses (and take your optical prescription with you); and carry a first-aid kit.

Travellers can register with the International Association for Medical Advice to Travellers (IMAT; www.iamat.org). Its website can help travellers to find a doctor with recognised training. Those heading off to very remote areas may like to do a first-aid course (Red Cross and St John Ambulance can help), or attend a remote medicine first-aid course such as those offered by the Royal Geographical Society (www.rgs.org).

Bring medications in their original, clearly labelled containers. A signed and dated letter from your physician describing your medical conditions and medications, including generic names, is a good idea.

If carrying syringes or needles, also carry a physician's letter documenting their medical necessity.

INSURANCE

Find out in advance if your insurance plan will make payments directly to providers or reimburse you later for overseas health expenditures (in Libya doctors usually expect payment in cash); it's also worth ensuring your travel insurance will cover repatriation home or to better medical facilities elsewhere. Your insurance company may be able to locate the nearest source of medical help, or ask at your hotel. In an emergency contact your embassy or consulate. Your travel insurance will not usually cover you for anything other than emergency dental treatment. Not all insurance covers emergency aeromedical evacuation home or to a hospital in a major city, which may be the only way to get medical attention for a serious emergency.

RECOMMENDED VACCINATIONS

The World Health Organization (www.who.int/) recommends that all travellers regardless of the region they are travelling in should be covered for diphtheria, tetanus, measles, mumps, rubella and polio, as well as hepatitis B. While making preparations to travel, take the opportunity to ensure that all of your routine vaccination cover is complete. The consequences of these diseases can be severe and outbreaks do occasionally occur in Libya.

MEDICAL CHECKLIST

Following is a list of other items you should consider packing in your medical kit.

- Antibiotics (if travelling off the beaten track)
- Antidiarrhoeal drugs (eg loperamide)
- Acetaminophen/paracetamol (Tylenol) or aspirin
- Anti-inflammatory drugs (eg ibuprofen)
- Antihistamines (for hay fever and allergic reactions)
- Antibacterial ointment (eg Bactroban) for cuts and abrasions
- Steroid cream or cortisone (allergic rashes)
- Bandages, gauze, gauze rolls
- Adhesive or paper tape
- Scissors, safety pins, tweezers
- Thermometer
- Pocket knife
- DEET – containing insect repellent for the skin
- Permethrin – containing insect spray for clothing, tents, and bed nets
- Sun block
- Oral rehydration salts
- Iodine tablets (for water purification)
- Syringes and sterile needles (if travelling to remote areas)

INTERNET RESOURCES

There is a wealth of travel health advice on the internet. For further information, the Lonely Planet website (www.lonelyplanet.com) is a good place to start. The World Health Organization (www.who.int) publishes a superb book, *International Travel and Health*, which is revised annually and is available online at no cost. Another website of general interest is MD Travel Health (www.mdtravelhealth.com), which provides complete travel health recommendations for every country, updated daily, also at no cost. The Centers for Disease Control and Prevention website (www.cdc.gov) is a very useful source of traveller's health information.

TRAVEL HEALTH WEBSITES

It's usually a good idea to consult your government's travel health website before departure, if one is available.

Australia (www.dfat.gov.au/travel/)
Canada (www.hc-sc.gc.ca/english/index.html)
UK (www.dh.gov.uk)
USA (www.cdc.gov/travel/)

FURTHER READING

Recommended references include *Traveller's Health* by Dr Richard Dawood (Oxford University Press), *International Travel Health Guide* by Stuart R Rose, MD (Travel Medicine Inc) and *The Travellers' Good Health Guide* by Ted Lankester (Sheldon Press), an especially useful health guide for volunteers and long-term expatriates working in the Middle East.

IN TRANSIT

DEEP VEIN THROMBOSIS (DVT)

Deep vein thrombosis occurs when blood clots form in the legs during plane flights, chiefly because of prolonged immobility. The longer the flight, the greater the risk. Though most blood clots are reabsorbed uneventfully, some may break off and travel through the blood vessels to the lungs, where they may cause life-threatening complications.

The chief symptom of deep vein thrombosis is swelling or pain of the foot, ankle, or calf, usually but not always on just one side. When a blood clot travels to the lungs, it may cause chest pain and you may have difficulty breathing. Travellers with any of these symptoms should immediately seek medical attention.

To prevent the development of deep vein thrombosis on long flights you should walk about the cabin, perform isometric compressions of the leg muscles (ie contract the leg muscles while sitting), drink plenty of fluids, and avoid alcohol and tobacco.

JET LAG & MOTION SICKNESS

Jet lag is common when crossing more than five time zones; it results in insomnia, fatigue, malaise or nausea. To avoid jet lag try drinking plenty of fluids (nonalcoholic) and eating light meals. Upon arrival, seek exposure to natural sunlight and re-adjust your schedule (for meals, sleep etc) as soon as possible.

Antihistamines such as dimenhydrinate (Dramamine) and meclizine (Antivert, Bonine) are usually the first choice for treating motion sickness. Their main side-effect is drowsiness. A herbal alternative is ginger, which works like a charm for some people.

IN LIBYA

AVAILABILITY & COST OF HEALTH CARE

Libya's health-care system is patchy. It can be excellent in Tripoli and other large cities and there are hospitals throughout the country, even in many small towns, although conditions can be pretty basic once you venture beyond the major cities. Many Libyan doctors did their training in the West. Reciprocal arrangements with Libya rarely exist and you should be prepared to pay for all medical and dental treatment, although medical care is cheap – expect to pay no more than 5LD to 10LD for a standard consultation.

In remote areas, medicine, and even sterile dressings or intravenous fluids, may need to be bought from a local pharmacy. Nursing care may be limited or rudimentary as this may be something families and friends are expected to provide. The travel assistance provided by your insurance may be able to locate the nearest source of medical help; otherwise ask your tour company. In an emergency contact your embassy or consulate.

Standards of dental care are variable and there is a risk of hepatitis B and HIV transmission via poorly sterilised equipment. And keep in mind that your travel insurance will not usually cover you for anything other than emergency dental treatment.

For minor illnesses such as diarrhoea, pharmacists can often provide valuable advice and sell over-the-counter medication. They can also advise when more specialised help is needed.

INFECTIOUS DISEASES

The following infectious diseases are extremely rare in Libya.

Diphtheria

Diphtheria is spread through close respiratory contact. It causes a high temperature and severe sore throat. Sometimes a membrane forms across the throat requiring a tracheostomy to prevent suffocation. Vaccination is recommended for those likely to be in close contact with the local population in infected areas. The vaccine is given as an injection alone, or with tetanus, and lasts 10 years.

Hepatitis A

Hepatitis A is spread through contaminated food (particularly shellfish) and water. It causes jaundice, and although it is rarely fatal, can cause prolonged lethargy and delayed recovery. Symptoms include dark urine, a yellow colour to the whites of the eyes, fever and abdominal pain. Hepatitis A vaccine (Avaxim, Vaqta, Havrix) is given as an injection: a single dose will give protection for up to a year while a booster 12 months later will provide a subsequent ten years of protection. Hepatitis A and typhoid vaccines can also be given as a single dose vaccine (Hepatyrix or Viatim).

Hepatitis B

Infected blood, contaminated needles and sexual intercourse can all transmit hepatitis B. It can cause jaundice, and affects the liver, occasionally causing liver failure. All travellers should make this a routine vaccination. (Many countries now give hepatitis B vaccination as part of routine childhood vaccination.) The vaccine is given singly, or at the same time as the hepatitis A vaccine (Hepatyrix). A course will give protection for at least five years. It can be given over four weeks, or six months.

HIV

Although official figures suggest that Libya's HIV prevalence rate is just 0.3% of the population, a risk (albeit small) remains of contracting HIV from poorly sterilised equipment or inadequately screened blood.

Leptospirosis

Leptospirosis is spread through the excreta of infected rodents, especially rats. It can cause hepatitis and renal failure that may be fatal. It is unusual for travellers to be affected unless they are living in poor sanitary conditions.

Malaria

While we've never heard of travellers contracting malaria, mosquitos carrying the disease are found in some oases of the Sahara; for example, occasional cases have been reported in the Egyptian oasis of Siwa, close to the Libyan border. We're yet to meet a traveller whose doctor has advised antimalarial medication when travelling to

Libya, but for up-to-date information about the risk of contracting malaria in Libya, contact your local travel health clinic.

Anyone who has travelled in a country where malaria is present should be aware of the symptoms of malaria. It is possible to contract malaria from a single bite from an infected mosquito. Malaria almost always starts with marked shivering, fever and sweating. Muscle pains, headache and vomiting are common. Symptoms may occur anywhere from few days to three weeks after the infected mosquito bite. The illness can start while you are taking preventative tablets if they are not fully effective, and may also occur after you have finished taking your tablets.

Poliomyelitis

Libya is officially free of polio, which is generally spread through contaminated food and water, although check with your doctor for the latest situation. Polio is present, though rare, throughout the Middle East. It is one of the vaccines given in childhood and should be boosted every 10 years, either orally (a drop on the tongue), or as an injection. Polio may be carried asymptomatically, although it can cause a transient fever and, in rare cases, potentially permanent muscle weakness or paralysis.

Rabies

Spread through bites or licks on broken skin from an infected animal, rabies (present in Libya) is fatal. Animal handlers should be vaccinated, as should those travelling to remote areas where a reliable source of post-bite vaccine is not available within 24 hours. Three injections are needed over a month. If you have not been vaccinated you will need a course of five injections starting within 24 hours or as soon as possible after the injury. Vaccination does not provide you with immunity, it merely buys you more time to seek appropriate medical help.

Schistosomiasis

Otherwise known as bilharzia, this is spread through the freshwater snail. It causes infection of the bowel and bladder, often with bleeding. It is caused by a fluke and is contracted through the skin from water contaminated with human urine or faeces. Paddling or swimming in suspect freshwater lakes or slow running rivers should be avoided, which shouldn't be too difficult to do as Libya has very little freshwater of any kind (the Saharan lakes are almost invariably salty). There may be no symptoms. Possible symptoms include a transient fever and rash, and advanced cases of bilharzia may cause blood in the stool or in the urine. A blood test can detect antibodies if you have been exposed and treatment is then possible in specialist travel or infectious disease clinics.

Tuberculosis

Tuberculosis (TB) is spread through close respiratory contact and occasionally through infected milk or milk products. BCG vaccine is recommended for those likely to be mixing closely with the local population. It is more important for those visiting family or planning on a long stay, and those employed as teachers and healthcare workers. TB can be asymptomatic, although symptoms can include cough, weight loss or fever months or even years after exposure. An X-ray is the best way to confirm if you have TB. BCG gives a moderate degree of protection against TB. It causes a small permanent scar at the site of injection, and is usually only given in specialised chest clinics. As it's a live vaccine it should not be given to pregnant women or immunocompromised individuals. The BCG vaccine is not available in all countries.

Typhoid

This is spread through food or water that has been contaminated by infected human faeces. The first symptom is usually fever or a pink rash on the abdomen. Septicaemia (blood poisoning) may also occur. Typhoid vaccine (Typhim Vi, Typherix) will give protection for three years. In some countries, the oral vaccine Vivotif is also available.

Yellow Fever

Yellow fever vaccination is not required for Libya. However, the mosquito that spreads yellow fever has been known to be present in some parts of North Africa. It is important to consult your local travel health clinic as part of your predeparture plans for the latest details. For this reason, any travellers from a yellow fever endemic area may need to show proof of vaccination against yellow fever before entry. This normally means if arriving directly from an infected country or if the traveller been in an infected country during the last 10 days. We would recommend however that travellers carry a certificate if they have been in an infected country during the previous month to avoid any possible difficulties with immigration. There is always the small possibility that a traveller without an up-to-date certificate will be vaccinated and detained in isolation at the port of arrival for up to 10 days, or even repatriated. The yellow fever vaccination must be given at a designated clinic, and is valid for 10 years. It is a live vaccine and must not be given to immunocompromised or pregnant travellers.

TRAVELLER'S DIARRHOEA

If you develop diarrhoea, be sure to drink plenty of fluids, preferably an oral rehydration solution containing salt and sugar. A few loose stools don't require treatment but, if you start having more than four or five stools a day, you should start taking an antibiotic (usually a quinolone drug) and an antidiarrhoeal agent (such as Loperamide). If diarrhoea is bloody, persists for more than 72 hours, is accompanied by fever, shaking chills or severe abdominal pain, you should seek medical attention.

ENVIRONMENTAL HAZARDS

Heat Illness

Heat exhaustion is a particular risk in Libya and occurs following heavy sweating and excessive fluid loss with inadequate replacement of fluids and salt. This is particularly common in hot climates when taking unaccustomed exercise before full acclimatisation. Symptoms include headache, dizziness and tiredness. Dehydration is already happening by the time you feel thirsty – aim to drink sufficient water such that you produce pale, diluted urine. The treatment of heat exhaustion consists of fluid replacement with water or fruit juice or both, and cooling by cold water and fans. The treatment of the salt loss component consists of salty fluids as in soup or broth, and adding a little more table salt to foods than usual.

Heatstroke is much more serious. This occurs when the body's heat-regulating mechanism breaks down. Excessive rise in body temperature leads to sweating ceasing, irrational and hyperactive behaviour and eventually loss of consciousness and death. Rapid cooling by spraying the body with water and fanning is an ideal treatment. Emergency fluid and electrolyte replacement by intravenous drip is usually also required.

Insect Bites & Stings

Mosquitoes may not carry malaria but can cause irritation and infected bites. In Libya, mosquito bites can occur just about anywhere around sunset and at night, but are especially prevalent in Saharan oasis towns (especially camps) and even in the Jebel Acacus. Using DEET-based insect repellents will prevent bites.

Bees and wasps only cause real problems to those with a severe allergy (anaphylaxis). If you have a severe allergy to bee or wasp stings you should carry an adrenaline injection or similar.

Sand flies are located around the Mediterranean beaches. They usually only cause a nasty itchy bite. Bites may be prevented by using DEET-based repellents.

Scorpions are frequently found in arid or dry climates – anywhere in the Sahara or Jebel Nafusa, especially when the weather's warm. They can cause a painful bite which is rarely life threatening.

Bed bugs and scabies are extremely rare in Libyan hotels. They lead to very itchy lumpy bites. Spraying the mattress with an appropriate insect killer will do a good job of getting rid of them. Scabies are also frequently found in cheap accommodation. These tiny mites live in the skin, particularly between the fingers. They cause an intensely itchy rash. Scabies is easily treated with lotion available from pharmacies; people who you come into contact with also need treating to avoid spreading scabies between asymptomatic carriers.

Snake Bites

Do not walk barefoot or stick your hand into holes or cracks. Half of those bitten by venomous snakes are not actually injected with poison (envenomed). If bitten by a snake, do not panic. Immobilise the bitten limb with a splint (eg a stick) and apply a bandage over the site, apply firm pressure, similar to a bandage over a sprain. Do not apply a tourniquet, or cut or suck the bite. Get the victim to medical help as soon as possible so that antivenin can be given if necessary.

Water

Tap water in Libya is technically safe to drink, but we recommend that you stick to bottled water for the duration of your visit to prevent diarrhoea and avoid tap water unless it has been boiled, filtered or chemically disinfected (iodine tablets). Also avoid dairy products that might contain unpasteurised milk. Do not drink water from rivers or lakes, this may contain bacteria or viruses that can cause diarrhoea or vomiting.

TRAVELLING WITH CHILDREN

All travellers with children should know how to treat minor ailments and when to seek medical treatment. Make sure the children are up to date with routine vaccinations, and discuss possible travel vaccines well before departure as some vaccines are not suitable for children aged under one year.

In hot, moist climates any wound or break in the skin may lead to infection. The area should be cleaned and then kept dry and clean. Remember to avoid contaminated food and water. If your child is vomiting or experiencing diarrhoea, lost fluid and salts must be replaced. It may be helpful to take rehydration powders for reconstituting with boiled water. Ask your doctor about this.

Children should be encouraged to avoid dogs or other mammals because of the risk of rabies and other diseases. Any bite, scratch or lick from a warm blooded, furry animal should immediately be thoroughly cleaned. If there is any possibility that the animal is infected with rabies, immediate medical assistance should be sought.

WOMEN'S HEALTH

Emotional stress, exhaustion and travelling through different time zones can all contribute to an upset in the menstrual pattern. If using oral contraceptives, remember some antibiotics, diarrhoea and vomiting can stop the pill from working and lead to the risk of pregnancy – remember to take condoms with you just in case. Condoms should be kept in a cool dry place or they may crack and perish.

Emergency contraception is most effective if taken within 24 hours after unprotected sex. The International Planned Parent Federation (www.ippf.org) can advise about the availability of contraception in different countries. Tampons and sanitary towels are not always available outside of major cities in the Middle East.

Travelling during pregnancy is usually possible but there are important things to consider. Have a medical check-up before embarking on your trip. The most risky times for travel are during the first 12 weeks of pregnancy, when miscarriage is most likely, and after 30 weeks, when complications such as high blood pressure and premature delivery can occur. Most airlines will not accept a traveller after 28 to 32 weeks of pregnancy, and long-haul flights in the later stages can be very uncomfortable. Antenatal facilities in Libya are reasonable but you should always think carefully about whether you want to negotiate the major cultural and language differences from home. Taking written records of the pregnancy, including details of your blood group are likely to be helpful if you need medical attention while away. Ensure your insurance policy covers pregnancy delivery and postnatal care, but remember insurance policies are only as good as the facilities available.

Language

CONTENTS

Arabic is the official language of Libya and the government has decreed that all street and business signs and radio programmes must be in Arabic. Generally, the Arabic spoken in the east of the country leans more towards that spoken in Egypt, while to the west it's closer to the Tunisian variety. All publications and signs are written in Modern Standard Arabic (MSA), which is the common written form in all Arabic-speaking countries. Unusually, however, both Western and Arabic numbers are used almost universally in Libya (for example for road distances).

Although Libya has its own distinct culture, hundreds of thousands of Egyptians and Tunisians live and work there, and their presence has served to lessen the differences between the dialects. The dominance of the Egyptian film and music industries as the entertainment of choice among many Libyans has also worked to minimise the differences. There are nonetheless some subtle differences in pronunciation that are worth noting, though they're unlikely to impact upon beginners. These include a tendency towards more guttural pronunciations, especially in Cyrenaica, and some of the long vowel sounds are discernibly shorter than in other dialects. The content we provide here has been specifially tailored to suit the Libyan dialect, so you should encounter few problems – and with the popularity of group tourism, an interpreter is never likely to be too far away if you do get stuck.

If you take the time to learn even a little of the language, you'll discover and experience much more while travelling through the country. For a more comprehensive guide to the major regional varieties of Arabic, get hold of Lonely Planet's *Middle East Phrasebook*.

TRANSLITERATION

Converting what for most outsiders is just a bunch of squiggles into meaningful words (ie those written using the Roman alphabet) is a tricky business – in fact, no really satisfactory system of transliteration has been established, and probably never will be. For this book, an attempt has been made to standardise some spellings of place names and the like.

There is only one article in Arabic: *al* (the). It's also sometimes written as 'il' or 'el', occasionally contracted to 'l' and sometimes modifies to reflect the first consonant of the following noun, eg in Saladin's name, Salah ad-Din (righteousness of the faith), the 'al' has been modified to 'ad' before the 'd' of 'Din'.

The whole business of transliteration is fraught with pitfalls, and the reality is that it simply isn't possible to devise a truly 'correct' system. The locals themselves can only guess at how to make the conversion – and the result is often amusing. Don't be taken aback if you start noticing half a dozen different spellings for the same thing.

For some reason, the letters **q** and **k** have caused major problems, and have been interchanged willy-nilly in transliteration. For a long time, Iraq (which in Arabic is spelled with what can only be described in English using its nearest-sounding equivalent: 'q') was written, even by scholars, as 'Irak'. Other examples of an Arabic **q** receiving such treatment are *souq* (market), often written 'souk', and *qasr* (literally castle, but actually fortified granaries), sometimes written 'kasr'. It's a bit

THE STANDARD ARABIC ALPHABET

Final	Medial	Initial	Alone	Transliteration	Pronunciation
ـا			ا	**aa**	as in 'father'/as the long 'a' sound in 'air'
ـب	ـبـ	بـ	ب	**b**	as in 'bet'
ـت	ـتـ	تـ	ت	**t**	as in 'ten'
ـث	ـثـ	ثـ	ث	**th**	as in 'thin'
ـج	ـجـ	جـ	ج	**j**	as in 'jet'
ـح	ـحـ	حـ	ح	**H**	a strongly whispered 'h', like a sigh of relief
ـخ	ـخـ	خـ	خ	**kh**	as the 'ch' in Scottish *loch*
ـد			د	**d**	as in 'dim'
ـذ			ذ	**dh**	as the 'th' in 'this'; also as **d** or **z**
ـر			ر	**r**	a rolled 'r', as in the Spanish word *caro*
ـز			ز	**z**	as in 'zip'
ـس	ـسـ	سـ	س	**s**	as in 'so', never as in 'wisdom'
ـش	ـشـ	شـ	ش	**sh**	as in 'ship'
ـص	ـصـ	صـ	ص		emphatic 's' (see below)
ـض	ـضـ	ضـ	ض		emphatic 'd' (see below)
ـط	ـطـ	طـ	ط		emphatic 't' (see below)
ـظ	ـظـ	ظـ	ظ		emphatic 'dh' (see below)
ـع	ـعـ	عـ	ع	**’**	the Arabic letter *'ayn*; pronounce as a glottal stop – like the closing of the throat before saying 'Oh-oh!' (see Other Sounds on p252)
ـغ	ـغـ	غـ	غ	**gh**	a guttural sound like Parisian 'r'
ـف	ـفـ	فـ	ف	**f**	as in 'far'
ـق	ـقـ	قـ	ق	**q**	a strongly guttural 'k' sound; also often pronounced as a glottal stop
ـك	ـكـ	كـ	ك	**k**	as in 'king'
ـل	ـلـ	لـ	ل	**l**	as in 'lamb'
ـم	ـمـ	مـ	م	**m**	as in 'me'
ـن	ـنـ	نـ	ن	**n**	as in 'name'
ـه	ـهـ	هـ	ه	**h**	as in 'ham'
ـو			و	**w**	as in 'wet'; or
				oo	long, as in 'food'; or
				ow	as in 'how'
ـي	ـيـ	يـ	ي	**y**	as in 'yes'; or
				ee	as in 'beer', only softer; or
				ai/ay	as in 'aisle'/as the 'ay' in 'day'

Vowels Not all Arabic vowel sounds are represented in the alphabet. For more information on the vowel sounds used in this language guide, see Pronunciation on p252.

Emphatic Consonants To simplify the transliteration system used in this book, the emphatic consonants have not been differentiated from their non-emphatic counterparts.

like spelling English 'as she is spoke'; imagine the results if Australians, Americans, Scots and Londoners were all given free rein to write English the way they pronounce it!

PRONUNCIATION

Vowels

a	as in 'had' (sometimes very short)
aa	like the 'a' in 'father'
e	as in 'bet' (sometimes very short)
ee	as in 'beer', only softer
i	as in 'hit'
o	as in 'hot'
oo	as in 'food'
u	as in 'put'

Diphthongs

ow	as in 'how'
ai	as in 'aisle'
ay	as in 'day'

Consonants

Pronunciation of Arabic consonants is covered in the alphabet table (p251). Note that when double consonants occur in transliterations, each consonant is pronounced. For example, *il-Hammaam*, (bathroom), is pronounced 'il-ham-maam'.

Other Sounds

Arabic has two sounds that are very tricky for non-Arabs to produce, the *'ayn* and the glottal stop. The letter 'ayn represents a sound with no English equivalent that comes even close - it is similar to the glottal stop (which is not actually represented in the alphabet) but the muscles at the back of the throat are gagged more forcefully and air is allowed to escape, creating a sound that has been described as reminiscent of someone being strangled! In many transliteration systems 'ayn is represented by an opening quotation mark, and the glottal stop by a closing quotation mark. To make the transliterations in this language guide (and throughout the rest of the book) easier to use, we have not distinguished between the glottal stop and the 'ayn, using the closing quotation mark to represent both sounds. You'll find that Arab speakers will still understand you.

ACCOMMODATION

I'm looking for a ...	*inlowij 'ala ...*
hotel	*fundug*
youth hostel	*daar ash-shabaab*
Where can I find a cheap hotel?	*wayn fundug rakhees?*
What is the address?	*shinnee l-'unwaan?*
Could you write the address, please?	*mumkin tiktib lee l-'unwaan*
Do you have rooms available?	*'andkum ghiraaf faarigha?*
I'd like (a) ...	*inHebb ...*
I'd like to book (a) ...	*inHebb naHjiz ...*
bed	*sareer*
single room	*ghurfa li waaHid*
double room	*ghurfa li shakhsayn*
room with two beds	*ghurfa ma' sareerayn*
room with a bathroom	*ghurfa ma' ham-maam*
room with a fan	*ghurfa ma' mirwaha*
in the name of ...	*bi 'ism ...*
date	*taareekh*
from (date) **to** (date)	*min yowm (...) li yowm (...)*
credit card ...	*karta ...*
number	*ragum*
expiry date	*taareekh al-'intihaa*
How much is it ...?	*bi-gaddaash ...?*
per night	*bi gaddaash kul layla*
per person	*lil waaHid*
Do you have any cheaper rooms?	*'andkum ghiraaf arkhas?*
May I see it?	*mumkin inshoofoo?*
Where is the bathroom?	*wayn il-ham-maam?*
I'm/We're leaving today.	*(ana nimshi/aHna nimsheeoo)l nimsheeyowm.*

CONVERSATION & ESSENTIALS

Hello.	*ahlan*
(response)	*ahlan beek*
Hello/Welcome.	*marHaba beek* (to one person) *marHaba beekum* (to a group)
(response)	*oo beek/beekum*
Good morning.	*sbaaH al-kheer*
(response)	*sbaaH an-noor*
Good evening.	*masa' l-khayr*
(response)	*masa' an-noor*
Good night.	*tisbaH 'ala khayr*
(response)	*tisbaH 'ala khayr*
Goodbye.	*ma' salaama*
Yes.	*ayy* (or *na'am* - more formal)
No.	*la*
Excuse me.	*saamaHnee* (to one person) *saamHoonee* (to group)

Please.
birabbi (used when asking for something in a shop)
tfaddel/tfaddloo (to man/group; used when offering something or inviting someone)
itfaddel//itfaddloo (to man/group; similar, or can mean 'Please, go ahead and do something)

Thank you.	*barkalla oo feek*
(response)	*min ghayr muziyya*
That's fine/You're welcome.	*min ghayr muziyya*
Sorry. (ie forgive me)	*mitaasif/a* (m/f)
What's your name?	*shismek?*
My name is ...	*ismee ...*
Pleased to meet you.	*nitsharrafoo* (pol)
How are you?	*shinnee Haalek?* (to one person) *shinnee Haalkum?* (to a group)
I'm fine.	*ilHamdu lillah*
Where are you from?	*minayn inti?*
I'm from ...	*ana min ...*
I like/don't like ...	*ana inHebb/manHebbish*
Just a minute.	*dageega waaHida*

DIRECTIONS

Where is ...?	*wayn ...?*
Go straight ahead.	*tool*
Turn left.	*door al-lisaar*
Turn right.	*door al- limeen*
at the (next) corner	*fi iz-zaaweeya (il-gaadima)*
at the traffic lights	*fi simafaaroo*
behind	*wara*
in front of	*guddaam*
far (from)	*ba'eed ('ala)*
near (to)	*greeb (min)*
opposite	*moogaabil*
here	*hinaa*
there	*ghaadee*
this address	*haadha l-'unwaan*
north	*shamaal*
south	*janoob*
east	*sharg*
west	*gharb*
beach	*il-bHar*
bridge	*il-gantara*
castle	*il-gala'*
main square	*is-saaHa l-kabeera*
mosque	*il-jaami'*
museum	*il-matHaf*
old city	*il-madeena*
palace	*il-gasr*
ruins	*il-athaar*
sea	*il-baHr*
square	*is-saaHa*
street	*ish-shaara'*
village	*al-qarya*

EMERGENCIES

Help!	*saa'adnee!*
There's been an accident.	*kaan haaditha*
I'm lost.	*ana dhaayi'/dhaay'a*
Go away!	*khalleenee raayidh/a!*
Call a doctor!	*jeeboolee it-tabeeb!*
Call the police!	*jeeboolee ish-shurta!*
I've been robbed.	*sargoolee*
Where are the toilets?	*wayn il-mirhaad?*

HEALTH

I'm ill.	*ana mreedh/a* (m/f)
My friend is ill.	*sadeegee mreedh/sadeegatee mreedha* (m/f)
It hurts here.	*yuwja'ni hinaa*
I'm ...	*ana mreedh/a bi ...* (m/f)
asthmatic	*ir-raboo*
diabetic	*is-sukkar*
epileptic	*l-epilepsee*
I'm allergic ...	*'andee Hasaseeya ...*
to antibiotics	*min antbiotik*
to aspirin	*min asbireen*
to bees	*min naHl*
to nuts	*min looz*
to peanuts	*min fool soodaanee*
to penicillin	*min penisileen*
I have ...	*'andee ...*
diarrhoea	*ishaal*
fever	*humaa*
headache	*wjee'it ir-raas*
antiseptic	*kreem mootahhar*
aspirin	*asbireen*
condoms	*preservateef*
contraceptive	*wasaa'il mana' il Haml*
hospital	*mustashfa*
medicine	*dwaa*
pharmacy	*saydaliyya*
pregnant	*Haamila*
prescription	*wargit at-tabeeb*
sanitary napkins	*foota saHeeya*
stomachache	*wjee'it il-maada*
sunblock cream	*kreema did ish-shams*
tampons	*tamponay*

LANGUAGE DIFFICULTIES

Do you speak English?	*titkallim ingleeziyya?*
Does anyone here speak English?	*skhoon yitkallim bi l-ingleeziyya?*

How do you say ... in Libyan Arabic?	*kifaash tagool ... bi lahja leebeeya?*
What does ... mean?	*aash ta'nee ...*
I understand.	*nifhim*
I don't understand.	*ma nifhimsh*
Please write it down.	*mumkin tiktibhaalee*
Can you show me (on the map)?	*mumkin twarreenee (fi l- khareeta)?*

NUMBERS

Arabic numerals are simple to learn and, unlike the written language, run from left to right. Pay attention to the order of the words in numbers from 21 to 99. When followed by a noun, the pronunciation of *meeya* changes to *meet* for the numbers 100 and 300–900, and the noun is always used in its singular form.

0	*sifr*	٠
1	*waaHid*	١
2	*ithneen*	٢
3	*thalaatha*	٣
4	*arb'a*	٤
5	*khamsa*	٥
6	*sitta*	٦
7	*sab'a*	٧
8	*thamaanya*	٨
9	*tis'a*	٩
10	*'ashra*	١٠
11	*Hadaasher*	١١
12	*ithnaasher*	١٢
13	*thlattaasher*	١٣
14	*arba'taasher*	١٤
15	*khamastaasher*	١٥
16	*sittaasher*	١٦
17	*saba'taasher*	١٧
18	*thamantāsh*	١٨
19	*tisa'tāsh*	١٩
20	*'ashreen*	٢٠
21	*waaHid oo 'ashreen*	٢١
22	*ithnayn oo 'ashreen*	٢٢
30	*thalatheen*	٣٠
40	*arba'een*	٤٠
50	*khamseen*	٥٠
60	*sitteen*	٦٠
70	*sab'een*	٧٠
80	*thamaneen*	٨٠
90	*tis'een*	٩٠
100	*meeya* (*meet* before a noun)	١٠٠
200	*meeyatayn*	٢٠٠
1000	*alf*	١٠٠٠
2000	*alfayn*	٢٠٠٠

PAPERWORK

name	*ism*
nationality	*jinsiyya*
date/place of birth	*tareekh/maHal il-milâd*
sex (gender)	*jins*
passport	*jawaaz is-safar*
visa	*tasheera*

QUESTION WORDS

Who?	*shkoon?*
What?	*shinnee/aash?*
When?	*wagtaash?*
Where?	*wayn?*
How?	*keefaash?*
Which?	*aama?*
How many?	*gaddaash min?*

SHOPPING & SERVICES

I'd like to buy ...	*inHebb nishree ...*
How much is it?	*bi-gaddaash haadha?*
I don't like it.	*ma y'ajibneesh*
May I look at it?	*mumkin inshoofu?*
I'm just looking.	*qa'ad inshoof bass*
It's cheap.	*hiyya rakheesa*
It's too expensive.	*ghaalee shwayya*
No more than ...	*mush akthaar min ...*
I'll take it.	*nishreeha*

Can you give me ...?	*tagder t'amelee ...?*
a discount	*takhfeedh*
a good price	*soom behee*

Do you accept ...?	*taakhudh ...?*
credit cards	*karta*
traveller cheques	*sheekaat siyaHiyya*

more	*akthir*
less	*agall*
smaller	*asghar*
bigger	*akbar*

I'm looking for ...	*inlowij 'ala ...*
a bank	*bank*
the bazaar/market	*is-soog*
the city centre	*wist il-blaad*
the (...) embassy	*as-sifaara (...)*
an internet café	*internet* café (as in English)
the post office	*il-maktab bareed*
the telephone centre	*telfoon 'umoomee*
the tourist office	*maktab is-siyaaHa*

I want to change ...	*inHebb nijbid ...*
money	*floos*
travellers cheques	*sheekaat siyaHiyya*

TIME & DATES

What time is it?	*gaddaash il-wagt?*
It's (8 o'clock).	*tawwa (ith-thamaanya)*
in the morning	*fi s-sbaaH*
in the afternoon	*fi l-'ashaya*
in the evening	*fi l-layl*
today	*il-yowm*
tomorrow	*ghudwa*
yesterday	*ilbaaraH*
day	*yowm*
month	*sh-har*
week	*jim'a*
year	*snaa*
early	*bikree*
late	*makhkhir*
daily	*kull yowm*

Monday	*yowm il-ithnayn*
Tuesday	*yowm ith-thalaatha*
Wednesday	*yowm il-arba'*
Thursday	*yowm il-khamees*
Friday	*yowm ij-juma'*
Saturday	*yowm is-sibt*
Sunday	*yowm al-aHadd*

January	*yanaayer*
February	*febraayer*
March	*mars*
April	*abreel*
May	*maayoo*
June	*yooneeyoo*
July	*yooleeyoo*
August	*aghustus*
September	*sebtember*
October	*uktoober*
November	*noofember*
December	*deesamber*

TRANSPORT

Public Transport

When does the ... leave/arrive?	*wagtaash timshee/tuwsil ...?*
boat	*il-flooka*
bus	*il-baas*
ferry	*il-ferry*
plane	*it-tayyaara*
train	*il-gitaar*

I'd like a ... ticket.	*inHebb tidhkira ...*
one-way	*maashee bass*
return	*maashi oo jayy*
1st-class	*daarija oola*
2nd-class	*daarija thaaneeya*

I want to go to ...	*inHebb nimshee ...*
What is the fare to ...?	*gaddaash it-tidhkira li ...?*
The train has been delayed.	*il-gitaar wakher*
The train has been cancelled.	*naHaaoo il-gitaar*
Which bus goes to ...?	*enayhee il-baas yimshee li ...?*
Does this bus go to ...?	*il-baas haadhee yimshee li ...?*
Please tell me when we arrive in ...	*birabbi gullee imta nuwsiloo fi ...*
Stop here, please.	*birabbi wagif hinaa*
Wait!	*istanna!*

the first	*il-awwil/oola* (m/f)
the last	*il-aakhir*
the next	*il-gaadim*
airport	*il-mataar*
bus station	*mHattat il-baas*
bus stop	*mHatta*
city	*il-madeena*
platform number	*ragum ir-raseef*
station	*il-maHatta*
ticket office	*il-geeshay*
timetable	*jadwal awgaat*
train station	*maHattat il-gitaar*

Private Transport

I'd like to hire a/an ...	*inHebb nikree ...*
car	*sayaara*
4WD	*sayaara feeha dabal*
motorbike	*mutoor*
bicycle	*bisklaat*
camel	*jimal*
donkey	*himmaar*
guide	*geed*
horse	*Hsaan*

Is this the road to ...?	*it-treeg haadha eehizz li ...?*
(How long) Can I park here?	*mumkin inwaggif sayaartee hinaa (Hatta wagtaash)?*
Where do I pay?	*wayn inkhallis?*
I need a mechanic.	*Haajti bi mekanisyan*
The car/motorbike has broken down (at ...)	*is-sayaara maksoora (fee...)*
The car/motorbike won't start.	*is-sayaara/mutoor matikhdimsh*
I have a flat tyre.	*'andee 'ajla mafshoosha*
I've run out of petrol.	*oofaalee il-benzeena*
I've had an accident.	*'amelt haadith*
Where's a service station?	*wayn il-kiyosk?*

Please fill it up.	*birabbi 'abbeehaalee*
I'd like (30) litres.	*inHebb thalaatheen eetra*
diesel	*diyaysel*
leaded petrol	*benzeena normaal (regular)*
benzeena	*sooper (super)*
unleaded petrol	*benzeena senza ploma*

TRAVEL WITH CHILDREN

Is there a/an ...?
fee ...?
I need a/an ...
Haajti bi ...

car baby seat
kursi mtaa' baybiyaat li sayaara
child-minding service
kresh
children's menu
menyu mtaa' awlaad
(disposable) nappies/diapers
koosh
infant milk formula
Haleeb baybiyaat
(English-speaking) babysitter
babysitter (illi titkallim bi l-ingleeziyya)
highchair
kursi baybiyaat
potty
kasreeya
stroller
karoosa

Are children allowed? *tigbloo awlaad?*

Glossary

For culinary terms see p66.

acanthus – stylised leaf used in Greek and Roman decoration
agora – main public square or marketplace of ancient Greek cities
ain – well or spring
akerbai – loose-fitting Tuareg pants
akhle – haphazard network of sand dunes without discernible pattern
'alaam – traditional musical form
Al-Qubba – canopy for women in some Ghadames houses
An-Nahr Sinai – Great Man-Made River
apodyteria – changing rooms in Roman baths complex
aquifer – layers of rock holding underground water
ashaersh – Tuareg turban

bab – gate or door
baladiya – municipal or town hall
barchan – crescent-shaped sand dune
basilica – court or assembly building (Roman) or church (Byzantine)
bey – provincial governor or leader in the Ottoman Empire
buyut ash-shabaab – youth hostel

calidarium – hot room in Roman baths complex
caliph – Islamic ruler
Camel Period – period of Saharan rock art from 200 BC to the present
capital – decorated top part of a column
cardo – main road running north-south through a Roman city
cavea – seating area in a Roman theatre
cipolin – white marble with veins of green or grey
croix d'Agadez – Tuareg cross of stylised silver with filigree designs
cryptae – Roman promenade corridors
curia – senate house or municipal assembly in ancient Rome
cuzca – Tripolitanian dance

dammous – underground, troglodyte (Berber) houses
decumanus – main road running east-west through a Roman city
divan – court or council of senior officers who advised the *pasha* in Ottoman times
djinn – a genie in Muslim belief; a being that can assume human or animal form

emir – Islamic ruler, military commander or governor
exedra – semicircular recess, frequently used for games in Roman times

fakhar – pottery, also *gilal*
foggara – underground channels leading to water
forica – latrines in ancient Rome
frigidarium – cold room in Roman baths complex
funduq – hotel

galabiyya – full-length loose-fitting robe worn by men
gheeta – clarinet-like musical instrument from north-western and southern Libya
ghibli – hot, dry wind of northern Libya
ghurfas – Berber fortified granaries, see also *qasr*
gilal – pottery, also *fakhar*
ghelta – natural spring

haj – pilgrimage to Mecca; one of the five pillars of Islam
hamada – plateaus of rock scoured by wind erosion
hammam – bathhouse
haram – prayer hall in a mosque
harathin – ploughers and cultivators
Horse Period – period of Saharan rock art from 1000 BC to AD 1

idehan – vast area of shifting sand dunes known as sand seas; see also *ramlat*
ijtihad – individual interpretation of sacred texts and traditions
ikhwan – followers of the Grand Sanusi
imam – man schooled in Islamic law; religious leader of Muslim community

jamahiriya – 'state of the masses' in post-revolutionary Libya
jammour – crescent atop a minaret
janissaries – professional soldiers committed to life of military service who became rulers of Ottoman Libya
jawazzat – passport office
jebel – mountain range

al-kadus – literally, bottle; system of water regulation in Ghadames
khutba – sermon delivered by imam, especially at Friday noon prayers
kishk – dance from eastern Libya

laconica – sweat baths in a Roman baths complex
Lebdah – Arabic name for Leptis Magna

madrassa – school where the Quran and Islamic law are taught
maidan – square or large intersection
majruda – dance from eastern Libya
malouf – musical form that originated in Andalusia and now played in Tripolitania
maqbara – cemetery
ma'sered zeytoun – olive press
masraf – bank
mat'am – restaurant
mathaf – museum
miftah – key
mihrab – vaulted niche in wall of mosque indicating direction of Mecca
minbar – pulpit that stands beside the mihrab in a mosque
mriskaawi – musical form that's the basis for the lyrics of many Libyan songs
msak – Tuareg for mountain
muezzin – man who calls the faithful to prayer from the minaret

nay – flute-like musical instrument
nargileh – water pipe or sheesha for smoking

natatio – entrance hall to Roman baths complex
nymphaeum – building with fountains; dedicated to nymphs

osban – dish of sheep's internal organs

palaestra – exercise area or sporting ground in Roman times
pasha – Ottoman governor appointed by the sultan in Constantinople
Pastoral Period – period of Saharan rock art from 5500 BC to 2000 BC, also known as the Bovidian Period
Pentapolis – ancient federation of five cities (Tolmeita, Cyrene, Eusperides, Tocra and Apollonia) in Greek Libya
peristyle – colonnade or portico of columns surrounding building or courtyard
Punic – ancient Phoenician people in North Africa

qaryat as-siyahe – tourist village
qasr – literally, castle, palace; Berber fortified granary stores; see also *ghurfas*

Ramadan – ninth month of lunar Islamic calendar during which Muslims fast from sunrise to sunset
ramlat – sand sea; see also *idehan*
ras – headland
Riconquista – 1922 policy of reconquest of Libya by the Italians under Mussolini
Ar-Ridda – Islamic principle of confinement for women after husband's death
Round Head Period – period of Saharan rock art from 8000 BC to 6000 BC

saadi – dominant tribes with lineage from Bani Salim and living in Cyrenaica
sabkha – low-lying area of marshland or salt pans
sahn – courtyard of mosque
Sanusi Movement – organised Islamic opposition to Ottoman and Italian occupation
seif – Arabic for sword; also the name for sand dunes with long, sweeping ridges
sharia – street or road
sheikh – tribal chief; religious leader
souq – market or bazaar
Sufi – follower of Islamic mystical orders that emphasise dancing, chanting and trances in order to attain unity with God
suras – verses or chapters in the Quran

tagelmoust – Tuareg turban
Tamashek – Tuareg language
Tamazight– Berber language
tawle – backgammon
tende – a drum made of skin stretched over a mortar
tepidarium – warm room in a Roman baths complex
Tfinagh – letters of the Tuareg alphabet
Tripolis – literally Three Cities; referring to Leptis Magna, Oea and Sabratha in Roman Libya

wadi – a dry watercourse (except after rains)
Wild Fauna Period – period of Saharan rock art from 10,000 BC to 6000 BC

zawiya – religious college or monastery especially under the *Sanusi Movement*
Az-Zlabin – Tripolitanian dance performed at weddings
zukra – bagpipe-like musical instrument

Behind the Scenes

THIS BOOK

Both the first edition and this second edition of *Libya* were researched and written by Anthony Ham. The Health chapter in this edition is based on information supplied by Dr Caroline Evans. This guidebook was commissioned in Lonely Planet's Melbourne office, and produced by the following:

Commissioning Editor Kerryn Burgess
Coordinating Editor Gina Tsarouhas
Coordinating Cartographer Joshua Geoghegan
Coordinating Layout Designer Jacqueline McLeod
Managing Editor Suzannah Shwer
Managing Cartographers Shahara Ahmed; Amanda Sierp
Assisting Editors Elisa Arduca; Michael Day; Evan Jones; Anne Mulvaney
Assisting Cartographer Owen Eszeki
Cover Designer Brendan Dempsey
Project Manager Eoin Dunlevy
Language Content Coordinator Quentin Frayne

Thanks to Sin Choo, Sally Darmody, Ryan Evans, Aaron Miller, Raphael Richards, Averil Robertson, Kathryn Stapley and Gerard Walker.

THANKS

ANTHONY HAM

The biggest possible *bari kelorfik* to Hakim Saleh Ashour who has been my companion and close friend on so many Libyan trails – there's no better nor wiser guide in Libya. It was my supreme good fortune to be driven around the Sahara by Brahim Massoud bin Bayed az-Zintani, one of the wise men of Saharan driving. Najib al-Mehdi al-Garbasi was also outstanding. Among my Libyan friends who have taught me so much and in many cases welcomed me into their homes, special thanks to Dr Mustafa Turjman who carefully read through the first edition and made some important corrections, Muawia Wanis, Hussein Founi, Dr Basset Nejaha, Moussa Massoud bin Bayed az-Zintani, Fathi and Salem al-Bourfely, Ahmed Saad, Othman el-Hashhashie, At-Tayeb Mohamed Hiba, Miftah Mansour, Ali Hamed, Mustapha and Musab Gaim, Dr Ali Skaki in Sebha. Thanks also to Paul Grech and to Asalheen and El-Mehdi who walked across the sand to find help (and the boys from the police post at Jebel al-Uweinat), Abd al-Salam and all my friends in Zuara, Zintan and Al-Bayda. A huge *shukran* to Kerryn Burgess who is a good writer's dream, and to Amanda Sierp. Thanks also to Joshua Geoghegan who made the maps a reality and to Michael Day, Anne Mulvaney and Gina Tsarouhas whose editorial touch was light but always wise. Back home in Spain and Australia, words cannot say how much I miss my family and friends while away. And to Marina: *te quiero cada día más.*

OUR READERS

Many thanks to the travellers who used the last edition and wrote to us with helpful hints, useful advice and interesting anecdotes:

Helene Aoki, George Assouad, Craig Baguley, Jan Beukema, Willem & Tiny Beekenkamp, Jonathan Bird, Rowland Burley, Jenny Carter-Manning, Kenneth Colin, Janet Collier, Robert Crothers, Brigitte

THE LONELY PLANET STORY

The story begins with a classic travel adventure: Tony and Maureen Wheeler's 1972 journey across Europe and Asia to Australia. There was no useful information about the overland trail then, so Tony and Maureen published the first Lonely Planet guidebook to meet a growing need.

From a kitchen table, Lonely Planet has grown to become the largest independent travel publisher in the world, with offices in Melbourne (Australia), Oakland (USA) and London (UK). Today Lonely Planet guidebooks cover the globe. There is an ever-growing list of books and information in a variety of media. Some things haven't changed. The main aim is still to make it possible for adventurous travellers to get out there – to explore and better understand the world.

At Lonely Planet we believe travellers can make a positive contribution to the countries they visit – if they respect their host communities and spend their money wisely. Every year 5% of company profit is donated to charities around the world.

Daenens, Naser Edeeb, Limido Elisabetta, Gustav Ellingsen, Jamal Fteis, David C Gasda, Kuno Gross Alan Hakim, Leen B Hanenberg, Kate Harding, Jan F Huson, Cathie Hutchison, Malgorzata Januszko, Matthias Junken, Ralph Lawson, Carmne C Lee, Chris Little, Colin Lovell, David Mackertich, Cedric McCallum, Jacopo Mascheroni, Phyllis Mifsud, Birgit & Dietrich Nelle, Sarah Ohring, Arie van Oosterwijk, Sara Partington, Caroline Priestley, Torben Retboll, Edu Romero, Nahla Saleh, Christopher Sap, Adrienne Simpson, Hilary Smith, Tania Swift, Steve Tober, Bill Torbitt, Iva, Andjela & Momir Turudic, Paul Ullmann, Eddy & Angeline Veraghtert, Christine Wagner, Paul Walstra, Rosanne Zammit

SEND US YOUR FEEDBACK

We love to hear from travellers – your comments keep us on our toes and help make our books better. Our well-travelled team reads every word on what you loved or loathed about this book. Although we cannot reply individually to postal submissions, we always guarantee that your feedback goes straight to the appropriate authors, in time for the next edition. Each person who sends us information is thanked in the next edition – and the most useful submissions are rewarded with a free book.

To send us your updates – and find out about Lonely Planet events, newsletters and travel news – visit our award-winning website: **www.lonelyplanet.com/contact**.

Note: we may edit, reproduce and incorporate your comments in Lonely Planet products such as guidebooks, websites and digital products, so let us know if you don't want your comments reproduced or your name acknowledged. For a copy of our privacy policy visit www.lonelyplanet.com/privacy.

Index

INDEX

000 Map pages
000 Photograph pages

INDEX

INDEX

INDEX

000 Map pages
000 Photograph pages

INDEX

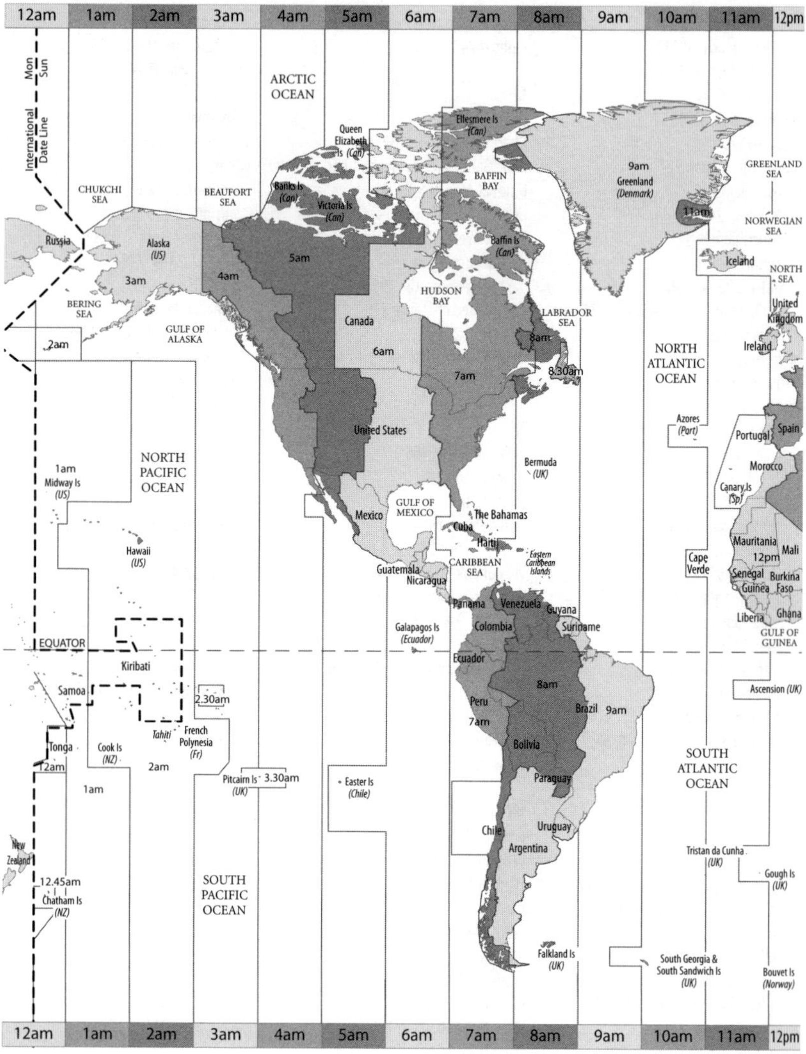
12am
1am
2am
3am
4am
5am
6am
7am
8am
9am
10am
11am
12pm
Mon
Sun
International Date Line
ARCTIC OCEAN
Queen Elizabeth Is (Can)
Ellesmere Is (Can)
Greenland (Denmark)
GREENLAND SEA
NORWEGIAN SEA
Iceland
NORTH SEA
United Kingdom
Ireland
CHUKCHI SEA
BEAUFORT SEA
Banks Is (Can)
Victoria Is (Can)
BAFFIN BAY
Baffin Is (Can)
Russia
Alaska (US)
BERING SEA
GULF OF ALASKA
HUDSON BAY
Canada
LABRADOR SEA
8.30am
NORTH ATLANTIC OCEAN
United States
Azores (Port)
Portugal
Spain
Bermuda (UK)
Morocco
Canary Is (Sp)
NORTH PACIFIC OCEAN
Midway Is (US)
GULF OF MEXICO
Mexico
The Bahamas
Cuba
Haiti
Hawaii (US)
CARIBBEAN SEA
Eastern Caribbean Islands
Guatemala
Nicaragua
Cape Verde
Mauritania
Mali
Senegal
Burkina Faso
Guinea
Panama
Venezuela
Guyana
Suriname
Colombia
Liberia
Ghana
Galapagos Is (Ecuador)
EQUATOR
GULF OF GUINEA
Ecuador
Kiribati
Samoa
2.30am
Peru
Brazil
Ascension (UK)
Tahiti
French Polynesia (Fr)
Tonga
Cook Is (NZ)
Bolivia
SOUTH ATLANTIC OCEAN
Pitcairn Is (UK)
3.30am
Easter Is (Chile)
Paraguay
Chile
Uruguay
Argentina
New Zealand
Tristan da Cunha (UK)
Gough Is (UK)
12.45am
Chatham Is (NZ)
SOUTH PACIFIC OCEAN
Falkland Is (UK)
South Georgia & South Sandwich Is (UK)
Bouvet Is (Norway)